Portsmouth Record Series
Borough Sessions Papers 1653-1688

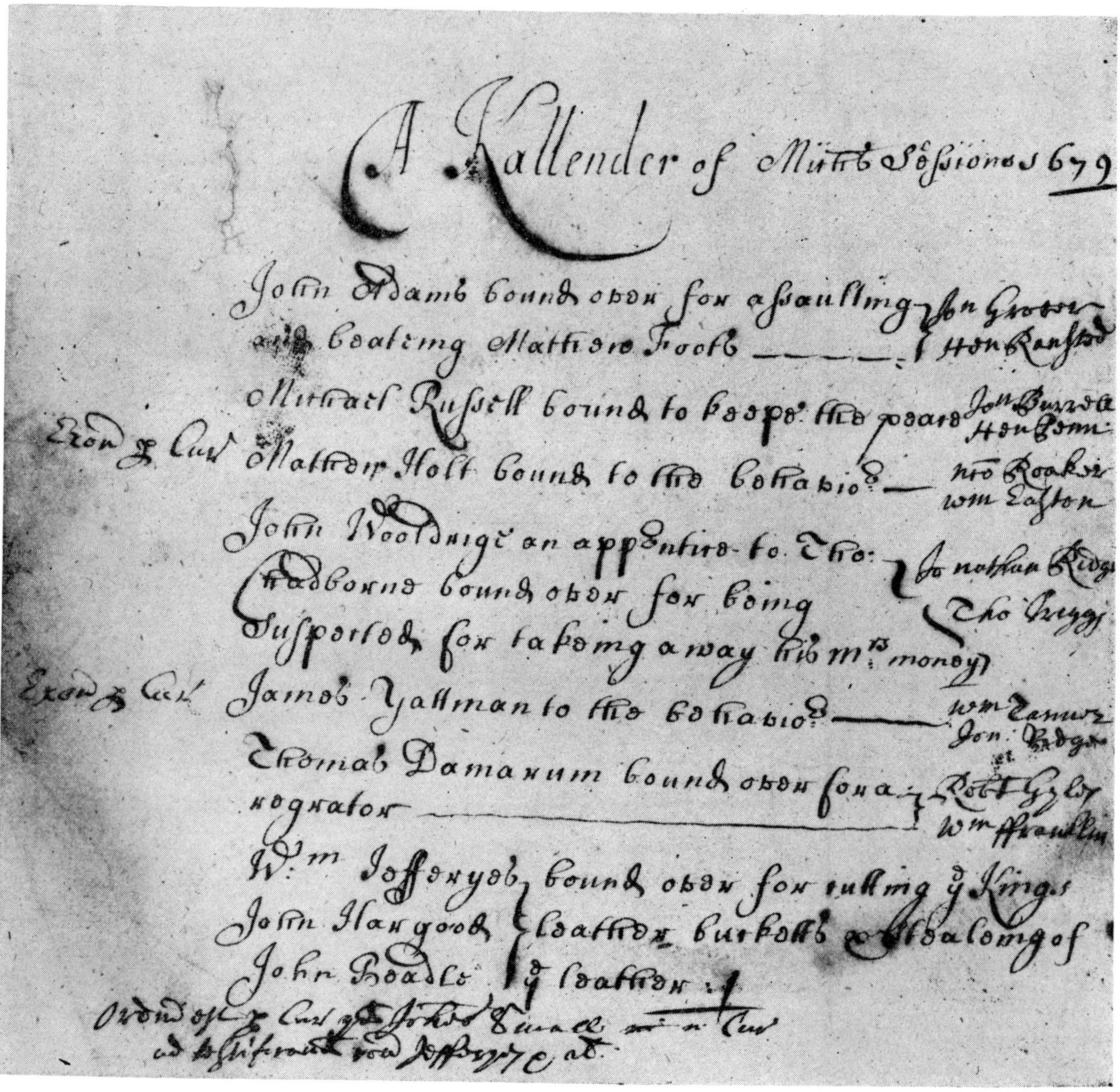

Fig. I CALENDAR FOR MICHAELMAS SESSIONS, 1679 (no. 232). S3/6/15

Portsmouth Record Series
Borough Sessions Papers 1653-1688

A Calendar compiled by Arthur J. Willis, FRICS, FSG
and edited by Margaret J. Hoad, MA
with an Introduction by
Margaret J. Hoad and Robert P. Grime, BA, BCL

Published with and for the City of Portsmouth by
Phillimore, London and Chichester

P. D. A. HARVEY, MA, D.PHIL, FSA, FR.HIST.S, *General Editor*
S. G. KERRY, MSIA, MSTD, *Technical Adviser and Art Editor*

Published by Phillimore & Co. Ltd. Shopwyke Hall, Chichester, Sussex,
SBN 85033 011 4
Bound in Black Reliance Cloth No. 73   Text set in 'Monotype' Baskerville
and printed letterpress on Abbey Mills Smooth Process Cartridge 107 g/m², by
Eyre & Spottiswoode (Portsmouth) Ltd., Grosvenor Press

General Editor's Preface

This is the first volume to be published in the Portsmouth Record Series. Its appearance is due to the enthusiasm of many people in Portsmouth and elsewhere, but special tribute should be paid to Miss D. Dymond, CBE, Chairman of the Editorial Board of the Series, to Alderman F. A. J. Emery-Wallis, in whose term of office as Lord Mayor the scheme was inaugurated, and to Mr M. J. W. Willis-Fear, who as City Archivist has been responsible for much of the administrative work involved.

The purpose of the Series is twofold. Primarily it is intended to make the written sources for Portsmouth's history widely available. The style and arrangement of the volumes will be as uniform as their varied subjects will allow, and it is hoped that their form will commend them to the general reader as well as to the specialised scholar. Many aspects of the history of Portsmouth are of far more than local interest and significance, a fact that by itself amply justifies the production of the Series. But beyond this it is hoped that the Series may help to set a new pattern for the publication of local records in Great Britain. For well over a hundred years record societies and other bodies in all parts of the country have been publishing documents that are the sources of local history. In this they have done great service: they have made available a vast range of texts, often from private archives that would otherwise be inaccessible, and by drawing attention to the importance of this type of material they have done much to preserve it for posterity. Historical scholarship is greatly in their debt. But during the last twenty-five years the situation has changed. The establishment of local record offices in cities and counties has made the majority of manuscripts easily available to research, while cheap photographic methods enable the searcher to use records from scattered repositories without recourse to printed texts. What is needed now is not the complete texts of a necessarily limited number of documents, but guides that will direct the reader in using a wide range of sources. It is with this in mind that the Portsmouth Record Series has been planned. It is proposed to print complete texts only of three types of record: first, a very few documents that are of basic importance to the history of the City; second, any records of Portsmouth that are sufficiently unusual to give their publication more than purely local interest; and, third, records of types found elsewhere but hitherto unpublished. For the rest the Series will consist of calendars, catalogues, indexes and bibliographies as seems most appropriate for the particular class of material. The volumes will deal with records in repositories outside Portsmouth as well as with those preserved in the City itself.

When the detailed plans for the Series were finally worked out it was found that there was just nearing completion a calendar of Portsmouth's earliest Borough Sessions Papers that fitted admirably into the proposed pattern. Combining historical value with lively human interest it seemed the ideal text to inaugurate the new Series. I am most grateful to Mrs Hoad and Mr Willis for so patiently accepting the revision of their calendar to meet the needs of a Series that had not been conceived when they began their work. For the compilation of the index I am myself responsible.

P. D. A. HARVEY
University of Southampton

Contents

List of Illustrations

Introduction

1 The Manuscripts

SOURCES OF SESSIONS PAPERS

The Sessions papers as they survive at the present day in the Portsmouth City Record Office have been found scattered in a number of places. Although these loose paper and parchment documents were originally strung on files, over the centuries many of the files, especially the early ones, have got broken up, the contents dispersed and many lost so that today, while what remain have mostly been kept in the possession of the Corporation, a good many have been gathered together from private collections and even from St Thomas' Church, now the Cathedral. On one in particular there is a note in a nineteenth-century hand saying it was 'found in an old book of records of Penny Street Chapel by one of the foremen of the Brewery of Pike, Spicer & Co.'.[1] Thus it is perhaps fortunate that the earliest Sessions papers do in fact go back in date as far as 1653.

The main groups of these papers which form the text are:

1. S3A. This forms the earliest collection of Sessions Papers, dating from 1653–1666. It comprises odd papers from many files which have been brought together in one bundle and flattened. This group, with the next two, has always remained in the hands of the Corporation.

2. S3. This series, which starts in 1669, is arranged on the whole Sessions by Sessions, but even here some papers have been misplaced and there are many gaps. On the other hand, at times it seems reasonably possible that all the papers have survived for a Sessions, though one could never say this with absolute certainty.

3. S3B. This group is made up entirely of strays which probably were accidentally detached from their files and were much later collected up again and flattened. Some have a note attached in a nineteenth-century hand describing briefly what the case is about.[2] Some have been clearly cut from their original file and many others have been roughly repaired in the past.[3]

4. D11A/16. These papers are strays and were for many years in the hands of the Portsmouth City Librarian. They were probably brought together by Mr James Hutt, the City Librarian in the 1920's, who acquired what Corporation documents he could from shops and private sources whenever they became available. They have now been returned to the Record Office. Most of the Sessions papers among them give the impression they were abstracted for some special reason. Those appearing in this volume deal mainly with immorality in various forms and dissenters' meetings.

---

[1] D3A/1/2 (no. 209).
[2] S3B/5, 9 (nos 48, 156).
[3] E.g. S3B/19, 20, 21 (nos 258, 263, 266).

5 D22A/1/7-9. This small group of Sessions papers was found among the records of Portsmouth Parish Church. There is no obvious reason why they should be found there.

6 D3A/1/2-3. These papers came from a private collector.

In addition, because the Election and Sessions Books until 1660 contain the enrolments of so many recognisances which no longer survive as papers on the files, these have been calendared in Appendix II with all the other spasmodic references in these books to Sessions business.

It has also been found that the State Papers (Domestic) of the Commonwealth and the reign of Charles II, especially when the country was at war with Holland and Spain, contain some examinations and informations taken in Portsmouth concerning such things as thefts from ships or the dockyard and the disposal of goods from prize ships. Many of these were taken before the representatives of the Navy Commissioners and sent by them direct to London but a few were taken before the Portsmouth Justices. As these few could truly be considered Sessions papers, they have been calendared for this text and placed in Appendix III. Those which completely by-passed the local magistrates have not been mentioned.

Although efforts have been made to trace any other material that may have strayed, only one other document has been found and that is in the Madden Collection in the British Museum. A calendar of this document has been made for Appendix IV.

ARRANGEMENT OF THE TEXT

Because the surviving material is so scattered it was decided in this text to attempt to assemble together again the papers relating to each Sessions and not to keep them in the groups in which they are now kept in the Record Office. It was felt that this re-assembly would give a clearer idea not only of what does survive for each Sessions but also of what business was done. In the text an over-all number has been given to all the papers in any one case but, if one paper refers to several totally unrelated cases, then separate text numbers have been given to each one. A concordance (Appendix VII) has been compiled to show the position of each document in the text.

It will also be noticed that headings, giving the nature of the case, have been placed by each item but these are not in the originals. They are in broad terms and are not intended to be the exact wording of the charge. Theft, for instance, would include the present-day classification of larceny, housebreaking and burglary. The various offences of traders, where not specifically named as 'regrating the market', 'forestalling', etc., are described as 'trading irregularly'. Various charges of defying or disobeying authority are classed as 'abusing authority' or 'contempt', though it would not be contempt of court in the strict legal sense. The greater on occasion includes the less; for example, riot may include assault and assault may include abuse. Sexual offences are classified as bastardy when an illegitimate child is born or conceived; otherwise they appear as adultery, fornication or immorality.

Cases on the whole have been arranged in strictly chronological order and where there are several papers concerning one matter the latest date has been used to decide the position of the group. Sometimes it will be found that a document has been placed with those of a later Sessions than that to which it belongs.[4] This is because it was not dealt with till the later date. The only slight exception to this chronological rule is where a Sessions Calendar survives and it reveals that the cases were not always dealt with strictly in the order in which they arose, though this was usually the rule. On two occasions even, at the Easter Sessions 1672 and at the Easter Sessions 1681, the cases were heard in reverse order and those which arose last were dealt with first, but in these instances the papers have been arranged chronologically to avoid muddle.[5]

Throughout the whole period covered by this volume there are only three documents which cannot be dated with any close accuracy.[6] They have therefore been placed in close association with the other documents with which they have been found. Of these three it is possible that no. 222 may not be a Sessions or Court Leet paper at all but a document relating to the Court of Record, which was a court for civil cases.

Indeed, although this volume is entitled a calendar, it will be found to be a good deal more detailed than many calendars, each document being given a précis or abstract rather than the few lines that would be allotted to it in a normal calendar. In fact, all the material points in the documents should be found here so that they can, for the most part, be fully studied without reference to the originals.

THE SESSIONS FILES AND THEIR CONTENTS

Owing to the method of filing, it is perhaps not surprising that many Sessions papers got detached and lost from the early files. Those on which these papers were originally placed were made by piercing a hole, which can still be seen, in each document and then passing through a parchment thong. The file when complete was made into a roll and the long thong would be wrapped round to secure it. Only at the very end of the seventeenth century was a shoe-lace type thread used for threading and an old deed made into a cover to protect the whole file, but in the period covered by this volume the file had no protection other than a parchment or paper stub placed at the base of the file.[7]

As regards the contents of a file, it is probable that Edward Archer, the Clerk of the Peace from 1666, first began to make calendars of the cases to be heard at the Sessions Court. When it is first found in Easter 1672 it was simply called a 'list of recognizances',[8] but all that survive after this date are called calendars.[9] In many, though not all of these calendars, the cases were numbered by the original compiler and it has been found that this number was also put on the papers relating to that case. Where this occurs, this has been noted in the text. Thus it is possible to tell in Sessions where no calendar survives which cases were taken to the Court and in what order they were heard.[10]

Apart from the calendars, the Sessions files contained examinations of accused persons, informations given by complainants and witnesses, recognisances and presentments. All documents were headed 'Borough of Portsmouth', except in the years 1682–3 when a number of documents were headed 'Borough of Portsmouth and Vill of Gosport'. This

---

[4] Nos 166 (S3/2/13), 265 (S3/7/11), 266 (S3B/17).
[5] Nos 156–169, 271–282.
[6] Nos 83, 222, 323.
[7] A parchment stub and thong survive for the Michaelmas Sessions 1673, paper stubs for the Sessions of Easter 1682 and Easter 1685 and a parchment stub for the Michaelmas Sessions 1688.
[8] No. 169.
[9] Nos 204, 232, 256, 270, 282, 326, 345, 388, 408.
[10] E.g. Michaelmas 1670, Michaelmas 1672, Michaelmas 1682, Easter 1685.

was at the start of the period when Charles II's Charter was in force.[11] This heading was, in the majority of cases, followed by a statement giving the date and saying before which Justices the evidence was taken. Very often this statement was written in Latin and in a very abbreviated form,[12] but the evidence in examinations and informations was always written in English and then was signed by the individual concerned either by name or by mark. This evidence could and did on a number of occasions, and particularly in cases of abuse, include the exact words spoken, however obscene they were. When quotation best illustrated these in the present text, they have been repeated if possible.

Most of the cases that were brought before the Sessions were those which normally caused trouble in everyday life. At times the political upheavals in the country are reflected, especially in the years 1660, 1685 and 1688, and there are a few references to the Great Plague of 1665.[13] It will be noticed too that a Royal Proclamation can produce a sudden spate of a certain type of case as in 1662-3, when there are at least four instances of theft of Crown property, all brought probably as a result of such a Royal Proclamation.[14] This is also true when it is desired to enforce an Act of Parliament. In 1677, after the passing of the Act for the better observation of the Lord's Day, a number of cases are found brought under the Act to suppress seditious conventicles.[15]

By the 1680's it becomes clearer that some of the cases that arose in the course of the year were dealt with by the Mayor alone, as Justice of the Peace, but throughout the period some matters were brought up directly before the Sessions itself, informations and examinations were taken and recognisances made. Often in such a case, the matter would not be settled till the following Sessions but the positioning in this text of the papers concerned depends largely on where they have been found filed. Another tendency by the 1680's, too, was for use to be made of the fictional John Doe as a second surety in a recognisance.[16] Two sureties were the general rule but where a second one was not insisted upon, the legal requirements were observed by naming a fictional person, John Doe being one of the commonest names used for this purpose.

During the Commonwealth Latin is found only by chance in official documents but its general use returned with the Restoration in 1660. Thus after 1660 recognisances were made in Latin though the conditions attached to them were written in English. Presentments were always in Latin and they never give an exact date, only the date when the offence was said to have been committed and then the year is that of the regnal year of the King and not the year A.D.[17]

These formal presentments written on parchment only begin to occur with any regularity on the Sessions files after 1670. Prior to this date only one has been found and it concerns a riot in 1660.[18] As the Court Leet and Sessions Court were held at the same time in Portsmouth and the Jury was common to both, it would seem that this Jury was uncertain how far its presentments should be considered Court Leet affairs and how far they should be matters for the Sessions Court. Many presentments to the Court Leet survive in separate books. Generally, as might be expected, they deal with encroachments, nuisances and the maintenance of Corporation property but even after the grant of a Sessions Court to Portsmouth the Court Leet presentments also regularly

---

[11] See below, p. xxviii.
[12] No. 85 is an example where there is a full heading. Translated from the Latin it reads 'Before . . . Justices of the Lord King assigned to keep the peace within the Borough aforesaid'.
[13] Nos 125, 142, 143; see below, p. xxv.
[14] Nos 86, 87, 90, 92.
[15] Nos 205, 206, 208-10. See Appendix VI for the full titles and citations of Acts of Parliament mentioned in the Introduction.
[16] Instances are to be found in nos 290, 345, 417, 422.
[17] See Appendix I for examples in full of the various types of document found.
[18] No. 56.

dealt with faulty weights and measures, the licensing of beer-sellers, the assize of bread and forestalling the market, matters which later were considered to be more the concern of the Justices of the Peace. In addition until 1670 there are also a number of cases in these Court Leet books concerning illegal gaming and trading without serving an apprenticeship, even an odd case of assault in 1661 and of riot in 1668, but after this date it becomes clear that the Jury increasingly decided to present these cases in formal fashion direct to the Justices at the Sessions.

With the exception of the presentments, which were written fair and were signed by the Clerk of the Peace, the handwriting on all documents was obviously done at speed, though with few exceptions it was always remarkably legible. As this handwriting differs inevitably from other records, such as the Election and Sessions Books where speed in their compilation was not necessary, it is not possible to tell with any certainty who wrote these Sessions papers. It is probable that the Clerk of the Peace wrote many himself throughout this period, though at times it is clear that his assistant clerk acted for him.

Original signatures of the Mayor or Clerk of the Peace do sometimes occur but only infrequently. However, it is curious to find in these papers that one Mayor, Thomas Hancocke, made use of a hand-stamp engraved with his name in place of a personal signature in the years 1682-3. In the first instance it is on a document bearing his seal,[19] but in the second he used it to sign an information he gave.[20] In searching the Election and Sessions Books two other people have been found to have used a hand-stamp in place of a signature, Thomas Clemence in August 1676 and December 1686 and William Stockman in April 1683. On all occasions they were used to sign oaths taken. It is possible that all three hand-stamps were engraved by the same person and it is thought the matrix was a metal one, possibly bronze, and was used with a pad soaked in printer's ink. Although office stamps in place of a seal are known to date from the last third of the seventeenth century, it is not known when ordinary people first used these possibly expensive hand-stamps engraved with their names to sign documents, as had English kings from time to time from the reign of Henry VI.

Another point that will be noticed is that on a good number of the recognisances, presentments and calendars legal comments have been written either in the margin or at the bottom generally stating what happened in the case. Most of these were written in Latin but they have all been translated for this text except where the Latin has some legal meaning.[21] Of the two Clerks of the Peace who were in office for most of the period covered by this volume, Thomas Mullins made much briefer notes and often used a mixture of English and Latin.[22] Edward Archer, his successor, used on the whole quite different phrases and though there might be much similarity between the wording of some of them and obviously legal jargon was being used, there is clearly no hard-and-fast rule as to the phrase which must be written in a certain set of circumstances.

The general impression gained from the phrases used is that, in most of the cases, the judgment given is vague or even non-existent. In addition, in the entries of recognisances, where there is more than one surety, it is sometimes doubtful to which individual a marginal note refers.[23] In fact these legal notes are the only indication as to what action was taken. Only for the Michaelmas Sessions 1687 are a few court orders to be found. For the vast

---

[19] No. 297.
[20] No. 309.
[21] See Glossary.
[22] E.g. 'bound de novo': bound anew; 'vide the examination': see the examination.
[23] An example of this is no. 62.

majority the note 'exoneratur', i.e. discharged, is written on one of the relative papers, though the accused may have had to face court expenses whatever the result. What these were is not known but no. 222 probably gives some indication. Only on some of the presentments is there a note of what fine was levied.

Part of the explanation for this absence of information about the outcome of cases may be found in the entry dated 5 September 1682 in the Book of Constitutions which laid down that in addition to an annual allowance of £20 the Mayor had the right to receive a number of other specified dues and fees including 'Court Fees, and Fynes at the Sessions'.[24] This had probably been the custom for long before it was put in writing and one cannot help but think that it left the way wide open for corruption.[25]

These papers therefore, the recognisances, examinations, presentments and informations, form in fact all the preliminary paper-work for the business the Sessions Court was to transact. In this sense the collection is something of a legal rag-bag and they are not complete records of cases before the court. Thus all we have usually is a preliminary enquiry into an alleged crime.

2 The Justices of the Peace and their work

THE EARLY HISTORY OF THE JUSTICES OF THE PEACE

The Justice of the Peace is an ancient institution with a very long history. Throughout that history, his purpose and functions have changed many times. The Justices began as Keepers of the Peace, amateur policemen of a sort, became local administrators and, slightly later, judges as well. The full flowering of their usefulness occurred in the eighteenth century, and in the period covered by these papers they are just achieving their maximum load of responsibilities. These papers show the Portsmouth bench spending most of its time dealing with fairly petty crime, much of it with a substantial public-order element. In addition, they see to questions arising under the poor-law and seek out the facts about bastard children. They dispose of difficult matters under the Statutes of Labourers and Apprentices and enforce the economic laws by punishing forestallers, regraters, engrossers and other irregular traders. And much else.

At this time, the Justices are still partly policemen, partly local administrators and partly judges of criminal courts. But it would be a mistake to approach their activities with any one of those functions too firmly in the mind. Perhaps the easiest way to understand their peculiar position is to trace, in very brief outline, the main stages in their development up to the dates that concern us.

The idea of a Keeper of the Peace, a local man of substance called upon to help enforce the law, is probably as old as the twelfth century. Certainly by the thirteenth century the existing methods of peace-keeping were becoming inadequate. They were based upon the frankpledge system of corporate local responsibility which is traceable in some form to Saxon times, but with the addition of the Norman Sheriff and the Angevin General Eyre, a general inspection carried out by royal judges from the central government. The Statute of Winchester, 1285, sought to provide some sort of general answer to the problems of law and order, but it contained more good intentions than efficient organisation for it provided

---

[24] A full transcript of this is to be found in R. East, *Extracts from the records of the Corporation of Portsmouth* (1891), p. 11. Compare this allowance with the total income of the Corporation which in 1693 was only £123 (ibid., p. 443).
[25] There is some evidence of this in CE1/9, f. 29 (App. II, no. 85).

no method for its own enforcement. So the practice grew of issuing Royal Commissions to men of substance, 'Keepers of the Peace', to enforce the Statute.

Gradually, these Commissioners of the Peace began to take a greater part in law enforcement. They began to take over the Sheriff's work of apprehending offenders and imprisoning them until the royal judges should appear in the county. More than this, they were given some power to act as judges themselves. By a Statute of 1344, 'two or three of the best of reputation in the counties shall be assigned Keepers of the Peace . . . with others wise and learned in the law . . . to hear and determine felonies and trespasses done against the peace . . . and to inflict punishment reasonably according to law and reason and the manner of the deed'.

The requirement that the Justices should be assisted by those 'wise and learned in the law' was not persisted with. Gradually, successive statutes altered existing powers and conferred new ones upon the Justices. A Statute of 1360 set out the following list of powers exercisable by the Justices of the Peace:

1 'To restrain the offenders, rioters and all other barraters and to pursue, arrest, take and chastise them according to their trespass or offence'.

2 To cause such offenders 'to be imprisoned and duly punished according to the laws and customs of the Realm' and according to the discretion of the Justices.

3 To 'inquire' of those who have been robbers and are now vagrants who will not work.

4 To 'take and arrest all those they may find by indictment or suspicion' and imprison them.

5 To take all those 'not of good fame' and to bind them over to keep the peace 'towards the King and his people'.

6 To hear and determine 'all manner of felonies and trespasses'.

But statutes were not the only source of power for the Justices. They were still essentially royal agents, particularly commissioned by Royal Commission. That annual Commission itself laid down what the Justices were to do. And it did not always agree with the general empowering statutes. In 1368 and 1376, for example, the Commission did not contain the power of the Justices to hear and determine felonies and trespasses. The Commission was eventually standardised and, according to Lambarde's *Eirenarcha* (the classic Justices' manual), in 1590 a 'new model' was worked out in consultation with the judges. One important power included in that Commission is the power to take surety from (that is, to bind over) all those who threaten to break the peace. Such persons could either be bound over to be of good behaviour generally or, more specifically, to come before a court at a date in the future, to answer a charge.

It is clear, then, that even the most general of the powers of the Justices were at once wide and vague and hard to classify. They seek out, they inquire and, above all, they take surety, or bind over. Some further details of this process will be given later. In addition to the general powers, from the fourteenth century onwards, successive statutes gave further special work to the Justices. A great deal of this work had a substantial administrative as well as a judicial element.

From 1351 a complex code of legislation was built up to regulate the labour market. At the dates to which these papers refer, the governing statutes were the Statute of Artificers and Apprentices of 1563 and the Statute of Labourers of 1602. Under these statutes, the Justices were empowered to fix wages and work-prices and to regulate apprenticeships. This enabled them to control both the supply and price of labour in any given area. But it incidentally gave them the duty of hearing and determining all sorts of disputes that might arise between master and servant or apprentice.

Then there was the poor-law. The great Elizabethan Poor-Relief Act was passed in 1601. Its scheme was, essentially, to provide relief for paupers from a fund set up with the proceeds of a poor-rate levied on the inhabitants of every parish. The fund was not administered by the Justices, but by the Overseers of the Poor who worked in close association with the Churchwardens of the parish in question. Nevertheless, there was much work for the Justices to do in their own capacity. Disputes as to liability to pay poor-rate as they arose (and they often did) were referred in the first instance to the Justices.

The poor were relieved largely by (theoretically) providing them with work to do in return for subsistence. But the Overseers could take other action. They could build houses for paupers on convenient waste ground. They could bind pauper children apprentices to some trade. They could even, in some circumstances, have able-bodied paupers transported to the plantations. It should not be forgotten that the poor-law was intimately connected with an equally complex code of law dealing with 'sturdy rogues and vagabonds'. Powers to 'move people on' fit more happily into this context. But whatever their origin, or justification, such powers need sanctions. And the sanction was the common gaol. At this point too, therefore, the Justices had a part to play in the administration of the poor-law.

Again, the paupers that each parish was obliged to relieve were those settled there. At first very little attention was given to this potentially difficult idea, but attention soon had to be given, for settlement was the centre of an obvious type of dispute. Quite simply, the number of paupers chargeable to the parish fund determined the level of the local poor-rate. Inevitably there was keen local interest in reducing the number of persons chargeable and in disputing their right to relief. Indeed, it was not unknown for paupers to be shipped, more or less clandestinely, to another parish. In 1662 an Act was passed which made some attempt to deal with this problem. This Act laid down that if a pauper attempted to settle in another, presumably richer or kinder, parish, he could be removed to the parish where he was last legally settled. This clearly raised the question of how a pauper obtained a legal settlement. Several methods were recognised: birth in a parish, being a householder in a parish, serving for a year under a yearly hiring, or being apprenticed in a parish. The complexities grew with the years. At our period the point was, if not simple, at least relatively free from the metaphysical encrustations of the eighteenth century.

The last important group of burdens cast upon the Justices was those involved in the general regulation of the economy. The most ancient part of this was the Assize of Bread and the Assize of Ale. Under these (which date back at least to Henry II's reign), the Justices laid down the maximum price for given qualities of bread and ale. The penalties for 'breaking the Assize', either as to quality or as to price, were originally severe and picturesque. Bakers had to stand in the pillory, and brewers in the dung-cart or tumbrel. All this was laid down in what became known as the Statute of Pillory and Tumbrel ascribed to 1266. Article III of that same Statute deals with forestallers and regraters. These were two species of a genus of criminals (which later included the third species of engrossers), whose offence was essentially that they had acted in a way regarded as distortive of the market. At the time of these papers, the relevant Statute was an Act of 1552 as amended by a Statute of 1623. These matters will be described in more detail later.[26]

---

[26] See below, pp. xxiv–xxv.

The Justices exercised their various powers in a number of ways, but their most important occasion was when they sat in General Session. In the counties General Sessions were held, by virtue of a Statute of 1414, four times a year, Michaelmas, Epiphany, Easter and 14 July (the week after the translation of St Thomas the Martyr). They were thus called Quarter Sessions. Quarter Sessions did not have to be held in the boroughs, but the boroughs generally held General Sessions which operated in the same way as county Quarter Sessions. In Portsmouth, Borough Sessions were at this period held twice a year, at Michaelmas and Easter.

General Sessions were primarily a court of law – in fact one of the most important criminal courts. As we have seen, the Justices had jurisdiction to try all criminal cases, both felony and trespass, or misdemeanour. In practice cases of especial difficulty and cases of murder and manslaughter were invariably referred to the Assizes where they were tried by the professional lawyer judges of the Court of King's Bench, but thefts and assaults were generally dealt with at Sessions.

Trial was by jury in the normal way and the procedure was by indictment, that is, a formal accusation at the suit of the Crown. Indictments were drawn up after a presentment had been made. A presentment was an accusation coming from an appropriate source, upon which the officer of the court in question was obliged to draw up an indictment. Strictly speaking, therefore, the term presentment covers a fairly wide range of different occasions.

The Attorney-General, and certain other royal officers and officials were empowered to make presentments to courts for trials on indictment. So too were Coroner's Courts, which investigated the circumstances of sudden deaths, deaths in prison and a variety of occasions such as the discovery of buried treasure, or the taking of royal fish, such as the whale or the sturgeon, which might involve the royal interest. Clearly the first two of the above items were very likely to produce an accusation of crime. But the most important source of presentments was the Grand Jury. The Grand Jury originally represented all the men of the area, brought together and charged to disclose from their own knowledge what crimes had been committed there. Very quickly the institution became more formal. By the time of these papers Grand Juries, though still theoretically able to present suspects from their own knowledge, invariably only presented those who had been put before them.

At the start of every Assize and of every Sessions, a Grand Jury of at least twelve was chosen from a panel of 24 jurors. This jury was offered the prosecution's case against an accused person. The defence might, but rarely did, question the evidence at this stage. The case – or the prosecution half of it – was considered with a view to deciding whether or not there was a basis upon which a trial might be held. In modern parlance, whether there was a case to answer. If it did, it found 'billa vera' or 'a true bill' and the indictment was duly drawn up. If it did not, it reported 'ignoramus' or 'not found'. The prisoner would then be discharged.

Of course, the natural practice grew up of providing the Grand Jury with a relatively formal accusation, or presentment, often written in Latin, before they came to their decision. This document could then be endorsed 'billa vera' or 'ignoramus' as the case might be. Several of these documents appear in the papers; they were inserted with greater regularity after Edward Archer becomes Clerk. They are called presentments. Strictly, as we have shown, this is inaccurate. They are specific charges to the jury; they may become presentments if a true bill is found.

Whether or not such a document was drawn up beforehand (and whether or not it survived), the Grand Jury would also be offered evidence. And the responsibility for getting that evidence lay with the Justices. They did two things. Firstly, they examined those who had been arrested, or otherwise brought before them on suspicion of some crime. This examination was taken down in writing. Many of the papers in this volume are examinations. Secondly, they took voluntary statements, or depositions, from accusers and potential witnesses. When the statement came from an accuser, it was generally described as an information, a usage which still persists in this area of the law. We still 'lay an information before' a Justice of the Peace in order to start criminal proceedings. Of course, in the seventeenth century too the information of some accuser might in fact be the first item on the dossier to be made up for the Grand Jury. This would be supplemented later by the results of the examination of the apprehended prisoner and the voluntary depositions of witnesses.

All this taking of depositions and examinations of prisoners did not, of course, take place at General Sessions. These jobs were done between Sessions by one or two Justices sitting either in private or in open Court. Such sittings became known as Petty Sessions. But this was not the whole of the business of Petty Sessions. From time to time, and increasingly in the fifteenth, sixteenth and seventeenth centuries, various offences could be tried by the Justices summarily, that is not on indictment and without a jury. The punishments meted out in such cases were usually fines, corporal punishments and short periods of incarceration in the house of correction or the common gaol. In addition, especially in boroughs, the Justices tended to take over the summary criminal jurisdiction anciently exercised by the Court Leet and the Sheriff's Tourn, both of which were greatly decayed by the seventeenth century. The position was never clear. The standard books on the subject, such as Lambarde's *Eirenarcha*, tended simply to list vague powers the Justices exercised without any close attempt to analyse their origin. The only real distinction that could be drawn was between the specific statutory and the vague common-law summary jurisdiction.

These affairs were all minor and were speedily dealt with. The Justice would hear the information, examine witnesses and the accused, if he were present, and either issue a warrant for his arrest or, again if he were present, proceed to exact the penalty, by ordering execution on his property in order to raise a fine, by committing him to prison or by ordering the appropriate corporal punishment.

THE TAKING OF RECOGNISANCES

The activity which is perhaps best represented in these papers is the taking of recognisances, or sureties. In modern terms, binding over. The principle is simple. One or more persons (usually three) is required to enter into a bond, or legally enforceable promise, that he will pay a sum of money if he, or another, does not appear in court on a certain day, or if he does not keep the peace, etc.

A recognisance continues until it is either performed by the principal carrying out his obligation, discharged by the court releasing the parties from their obligation, or estreated, that is, the sum in question forfeited. A recognisance is a useful legal tool. It is widely used to secure performance of obligations even today. It is the basis of bail. It can be used in much more complex legal situations. It formed the basis of a sophisticated system for the enforcement of obligations for services at a time when there was no useful direct legal remedy available. The services would be put into a 'bond with a conditional defeasance'.

But in court procedure, especially at the lower end of the hierarchy, the recognisance is the true maid-of-all-work. There are several sorts of such recognisances.

Justices were anciently the Keepers of the Peace. It was always claimed, therefore, that they had an innate power to bind over to keep the peace all those likely to break it. This indeed was recognised by the Commission, as we have seen. It was clear that this power extended beyond the binding over of those that had in fact actually committed a breach of the peace. The Justice could also restrain those suspected of having done such a thing, even those suspected of being likely to do such a thing in the future. Further, the Statute of 1360 had given him power to restrain 'rioters and barraters', which came to mean persons known to him to have a rowdy disposition.

A further aspect of this particular type of recognisance was the peculiar phenomenon of 'swearing the peace'. For if a member of the public came before a Justice and swore that he was in reasonable apprehension of suffering bodily harm at the hands of X, then the Justice might on that account bind X over to keep the peace. Such a jurisdiction brought a substantial number of neighbours' and family quarrels into the Petty Sessions, as the following pages will show.

The second type of recognisance has a much clearer historical basis. By virtue of the Statute of 1360 that has already been mentioned, as well as of other statutes, the Justices were empowered to bind over those 'not of good fame' to be of good behaviour towards King and people. This was a very flexible and useful weapon. 'Good fame' imports moral considerations. The power could be used to restrain roisterers, bawdy-house keepers, persons who abused authority, local or national, drunkards, cheats, vagabonds, libertines or even, as Blackstone put it a century later, 'such as sleep in the day and wake in the night'. All depended upon the discretion of the Justice and the temper of the times. The number of cases in this volume of 'scandalous words' and 'abuse of authority' would argue that the age was not one where violently held opinion was tolerated. A power such as this was invaluable in combating it.

Thirdly, recognisances were used as a part of the legal process, to ensure the attendance at court of accused, witnesses and prosecutor. This, perhaps, is their most common use in the present volume. The power to take this sort of recognisance was not as old-established as the others we have mentioned. By a Statute of 1487, the bench of Justices, or any two of them, sitting in open court, were permitted to bail prisoners accused of felony to their next General or Quarter Sessions. The alternative was to keep them in prison. The common gaol was a scandal at that time and for several centuries thereafter.

In 1554 this power was reformed. It had, the preamble of the new Statute recited, been much abused, in that Justices of the Peace 'hath oftentimes by sinister labour and means set at large the greatest and notablest offenders . . . to the high displeasure of almighty God, the great peril of the King and Queen's true subjects, and encouragement of all thieves and evil-doers'. Among the reforms enacted was the new requirement that, when a prisoner was brought before the Justices accused of felony, they should 'take the examination of the said prisoner, and information of them that bring him, of the fact and circumstances thereof, and the same, or as much thereof as shall be material to prove the felony, shall put in writing . . .'. The Justices were given a further power to take recognisances. They could 'bind all such . . . as do declare any thing material to prove such murder or manslaughter, offences or felonies, or to be accessory or accessories to the same as aforesaid, to appear . . . to give evidence . . .'. The new system, with its somewhat greater formality and substantially wider powers, had clear advantages. In the following year (1555) the new powers were extended to cases where no bail was sought. Here too witnesses, accessories and prosecutors could be bound by recognisance to appear at the trial.

These statutes formed the basis of a general practice of Justices. They would examine any accused person, take down information and depositions, and take recognisances from the accused and all material witnesses as a matter of course. All this would be reduced to writing. It is these documents that provide the subject-matter of much of this volume.

However, the power to take recognisances was so wide, the grounds so various, and the number taken so great that it is not always easy to discover what sort of recognisance has been taken and for what purpose. Indeed, many of the recognisances recorded in these papers are recorded barely, simply by names and amount of money at stake. There is no indication of the circumstances of the recognisance. This above all shows how important a device this was.

FELONIES AND MISDEMEANOURS

A little perhaps might be said about felonies and misdemeanours, or, to use the term more common at this period, trespasses. Felony has always eluded precise definition. There are two main approaches to the problem. One can either attempt to describe it in terms of the types of offences comprised within it or one can define it in terms of the special consequences attendant upon felonies. The first approach was only useful in the days when the royal criminal law was sparse in extent; then felony could be defined in terms of murder, mayhem, rape, robbery, etc. But this simple picture had long gone by the time under review. New crimes had been created, many of them as felonies. Old crimes had been broken up into different sub-species. All that could be produced was a long list of the more serious offences, with no obvious unifying factor.

The second approach always produced a formula that was easy to state. Felonies were offences which involved forfeiture of lands or goods to the crown and, usually, the penalty of death. Forfeiture had most significance in the unusual case of an offender who had goods or lands worth having: it was much more common for there to be no lands or chattels known to the jury. And therefore no exercise of the royal power.

As has been indicated, the death penalty, although the usual punishment for felony, was not the only one. Nor was it strictly true to say that the punishment of death was never inflicted on persons guilty of offences short of felony. The glaring exception was heresy, which was accounted only a misdemeanour at common law, yet which involved the death penalty. Perhaps the most important felonies not punishable by death were simple mayhem, or wounding, and petty larceny. The difference between grand larceny, punishable by death, and petty larceny, not so punishable, lay only in the value of the goods stolen. Grand larceny was the theft of goods over the value of twelvepence, petty larceny the theft of goods below that value. There was from time to time some rather unseemly wrangling as to whether the theft of goods of the value of exactly twelvepence was grand or petty larceny. By this time it was settled that thieves of twelvepence were not hanged. The level of twelvepence was fixed in the reign of Henry I, which made Sir Henry Spelman comment drily in his *Glossaries* that while all other commodities had risen in price over the years, the life of man alone had grown cheaper.

The loophole in this harsh law was found in the presentment made by the Grand Jury. It was there that the value had to be set to the goods stolen. And even at this period goods are valued so often at elevenpence that one cannot but suspect the operation of that 'pious perjury' which at a later date was to value a stolen half-sovereign at sixpence.[27]

---

[27] An example of undervaluation of this sort can be seen in no. 353.

Some felonies involving the death penalty were clergyable, or subject to the benefit of clergy. This institution is probably well known. At this time, it was just reaching its final period. In the reigns of William and Mary and of Anne successive statutes took away from it many of its previous advantages. The origin of the plea of clergy lies in the Angevin disputes between Church and State. The compromise achieved in the question of criminous clerks was that the secular courts should try them, but on proof of their clergy they should be passed to the Church courts, the bishop's Ordinary, for punishment. Punishment there could be a very mild affair. Canonical purgation became the rule, that is, the accused took a solemn oath as to his innocence, which oath was 'helped' by similar oaths taken by several others to the effect that the accused had sworn truly. Certainly by the sixteenth century this procedure had lost its acceptability. From the time of Henry VII, therefore, reforms were enacted which had a far-reaching effect. They changed the very nature and purpose of the plea of benefit of clergy.

Proof of clergy was originally a very strict affair. The accused's dress and habits of life were examined, and his head examined to see whether he was tonsured or not. But by the end of the fifteenth century the test had become much simplified. The only question asked was whether the accused could read. And this was tested by handing to the prisoner the 'neck verse', the first verse of the 51st Psalm. If he could read it, he obtained the benefit. It was, of course, not impossible for an unlettered man, for a fee, to be tutored in the 'neck verse'. In 1490 some attempt was made to avoid that particular problem by distinguishing between 'mere lay scholars' and clerks that really were in holy orders. The former class – by far the larger – were only to claim their clergy once and to prevent evasion, they were to be branded on the hand. (Hence the practice of requiring an accused to hold up his hand when he pleaded guilty or not guilty.)

Perhaps oddly, at the Reformation no attempt was made to do away with benefit of clergy. Indeed it was somewhat extended, to bigamists and peers of the realm in 1547 and to women in 1624. These persons had for different reasons been deprived of the plea in the past mainly because of their incapacity as true clerks in holy orders. At the same time, the jurisdiction of the Ordinary to punish was abolished. In 1576 it was enacted that instead of punishment at the hands of the Ordinary, a prisoner who had successfully pleaded his clergy should be imprisoned for up to a year instead. Benefit of clergy became a way of reducing sentences from death to a term of imprisonment and it was only available, in practice, to first offenders.

After the Reformation, too, many felonies were made unclergyable. At the time of these papers, many of the more serious felonies were unclergyable – for example, murder, piracy, highway robbery, aggravated larceny, rape, burglary, were unclergyable. Thus, to return to our first point, if one was to define the difference between felony and misdemeanour in terms of the punishments appropriate, in our period we would have to distinguish carefully between non-clergyable felony punishable by death, clergyable felony punishable by death, felony not punishable by death at all, and a mere trespass. All these distinctions are in fact found in theft, one of the most common of offences. Aggravated grand larceny (for example, theft of more than twelvepence worth of goods from the person of the victim) was non-clergyable and punishable by death. Simple grand larceny was punishable by death, but clergyable. Petty larceny was not punishable by death. Embezzlement, or diverting to one's own use property or money handed to one by another, which was not technically larceny since there was no *taking* of the property out of the possession of another, was not felony at all – except in the case, of considerable importance in Portsmouth, of embezzlement of the royal stores and munitions of war.

To this already confused picture should be added one further complication. Transportation, as we have already seen, had been known as a punishment even in the time of Elizabeth. The Poor Relief Act ordained that certain healthy paupers could in certain circumstances be transported to the plantations. In the late seventeenth century the practice was certainly growing of giving pardons to felons on condition that they be transported to the colonies. The system did not really begin to operate until certain technical obstacles to the granting of pardons had been removed. The whole thing was reformed and put on a sounder footing in the reign of George III.

In conclusion, one point must be made. Difficult as the distinction between felony and misdemeanour was, it was in the end precise. Although it broadly represented a difference between serious and less serious crime, there are certain dangers in thinking of it only in those terms. Other legal distinctions had been made on that same difference. For example, the important distinction between offences triable on indictment and offences triable summarily – this also reflects a difference in the seriousness of the offence. But the two distinctions are themselves quite distinct. Many misdemeanours were triable on indictment.

SOME ACTIVITIES OF THE JUSTICES RECORDED IN THE SESSIONS PAPERS

Something has already been said of the economic laws which the Justices had to administer. There are several such cases in these papers, and their frequency is not uniform. It would seem at least possible that the enforcement of these difficult laws was only undertaken in times of economic scarcity.

The governing Statute at the time in question was the Act of 1552 described as 'an Act against regraters, forestallers and engrossers'. The first two types of offenders were already well known to the law. Forestalling was essentially interposing oneself between the producer and the market. In 1552 it was expressed to include not only buying or agreeing to buy goods that had not yet reached the market, but also attempting to persuade any seller to enhance the price at which he was to sell in a market, by any means, and dissuading sellers from going to the market at all. This was relatively clear. So was regrating. That was the purchase of 'dead victuals', that is meat, corn, butter, cheese, etc., in a market and reselling them in that market or within four miles thereof. The preamble to the Statute of 1552 recited that although there were many good statutes against forestallers and regraters, engrossers were not properly dealt with. Engrossers were those who bought goods lawfully – for example at a lawful market, or before the goods began their journey to a market – and stored them while the prices rose in order to resell them later. And the Act of 1552 sought to deal with them by making it an offence to buy corn while it was growing or to buy any dead victuals for resale. But this was far too wide, as it included perfectly legitimate retail trading. In 1623, therefore, a Statute saw to it that retailers were not to be included in the category of engrossers.

Even so, the possible area of liability was extremely wide. There were, therefore, many exceptions. The Justices were empowered to issue licences to permit, for example, the transport of corn from one port to another. The system became complex as well as vague. In these papers we find persons being prosecuted for selling goods and food in an irregular way. Sometimes it is called forestalling, sometimes regrating, often nothing at all. Certainly the law was wide enough to catch such activities.

Moreover, there were other laws to regulate trading. Under the Statutes of Artificers and Apprentices that have already been mentioned, no one was permitted to exercise any trade or calling anywhere in the Realm unless he had been properly apprenticed to that trade for a period of seven years. So, in one case in 1679 'John Garrett of Portsmouth, mariner, and Elizabeth his wife' were presented for 'carrying on the business of a mercer in Portsmouth on 10 October 30 Cha. II by selling mercer's wares and continuing for twelve months to the date of this inquiry, neither having been instructed in the art by practice or apprenticeship for seven years contrary to the Statute'.[28] A true bill was found. In addition, we find the Justices prosecuting, and dealing summarily with, itinerant traders and shopkeepers who ply their trade in Portsmouth without leave or licence. In this they no doubt act in execution of their ancient common-law powers to suppress nuisances and prevent breaches of the peace as well as of the Act of 1554. Still, one has some sympathy for Henry Alford of Gosport who, at the height of one of the periodic enforcements of this sort of law, was bound over to appear at the next Sessions 'for selling hats on the Point'.[29] He was fined four shillings.

A very large number of cases concern disloyalty, abuse of the government or of authority. It is a large category and it includes many things. People regularly abuse the Mayor – sometimes with considerable sophistication. At the appropriate times of political upheaval they make much more dangerous statements. One cannot help but admire the ingenuity of Daniel Winston, a soldier, who was heard to say in January 1661 'when the King was in Portsmouth' that 'he had served the King and Parliament and that he hoped that it would come round that he would serve the King and Parliament again'[30]. When examined about these very foolish words, his somewhat naive defence was that 'then he served the King, but if the King did call Parliament, he would serve the King and Parliament again'. He was bound over and released by proclamation the following April.

An interesting small group of cases occurs in 1665 and 1666. On 10 August 1665 Richard Symms was bound over for entertaining one Prangnell from Southampton, 'a place infected with the plague, contrary to the orders of the King, the Mayor and the Justices'[31]. On 17 January 1666 Robert Hawks was similarly bound over for a similar offence and on 3 February William White was bound over for 'entertaining one from London without leave, against the order of the Justices, who died at his house'[32]. 1665 was, of course, the year of the Great Plague, though it affected Portsmouth more the following year, and such precautions were sensible.

Finally it might be in order to say a short word on the subject of bastardy, which was a matter that occupied quite a considerable amount of the time of the Justices. There were basically two issues to be settled.

Firstly, the mother of a bastard child, like its father, was an immoral person and in some cases immorality was punishable as a crime. We have already mentioned the general power of binding over those not of good fame. There was also power to punish such people at common law, and Justices not infrequently ordered the mothers and putative fathers of bastard children to be whipped.

Secondly, bastards were usually a charge to the parish, being almost by definition paupers in need of relief. Under the Poor Relief Act of 1575, 'as well as for the punishment of the mother and reputed father of such bastard child, as also for the better relief of every such parish', the Justices were empowered to make orders that the mother or the

---

[28] No. 233.
[29] No. 237.
[30] No. 70.
[31] No. 125.
[32] Nos 142, 143.

reputed father should pay towards the upkeep of the child. Such persons could be imprisoned in default of payment and released from prison only on condition that they entered into a recognisance that the sums owing should be paid.

This system was somewhat reinforced by the Statute of 1609 which empowered the Justices to incarcerate any 'lewd' woman who had had a bastard child for up to one year in the house of correction, where she would be set to work. The same Statute made it an offence to run away from a parish leaving one's children, bastard or legitimate, as a charge to the parish.

A lot depended upon where bastards were born. They were the charge of the parish in which they were born. So there was some concern to ensure that 'foreign' women did not come into the parish to have their bastards there. In 1671 Mary Phillips, a single-woman, being with child, was closely examined as to her recent movements so as to see where she had a lawful settlement.[33] The matter was ultimately resolved by the putative father, Richard Westbrooke of Fareham, giving security 'for ye discharging of ye parish'.

The Poor-Law Amendment Act of 1662 made some changes to this system by prohibiting the sending of women out of one parish to another, even to the parish whence they had come, so as to avoid their bastards being a charge on the parish. It also contained procedures for the taking of recognisances from mothers and putative fathers for the upkeep of the child. Throughout the approach was twofold, to punish the wrong-doing of the parents and to see to the relief of the child.

These are but some of the problems which came before the Justices and the laws which were made to guide them in dealing with them. The cases reflect some aspects of the everyday life and behaviour of the times. Much of it is perhaps humdrum but there are highlights on occasion.

3 The Portsmouth Borough Sessions

EARLY HISTORY OF THE COURT, 1600–1653

While parts, if not the whole, of the files of Portsmouth Sessions papers survive from 1653 onwards, the records of the first fifty years of holding Sessions Courts in this borough are much more meagre, but such as they are, they throw some light on the methods of holding these courts.

On 15 February 1600, in the Charter of Incorporation granted by Queen Elizabeth I, Portsmouth obtained for the first time the right to have its own independent Justices of the Peace. These were to be the Mayor and three burgesses, who were to be elected as Justices annually, and they were to carry out all the duties relating to that office without any interference whatsoever from the Justices of the County of Hampshire. Three Justices only, not four, were mentioned by name in Queen Elizabeth's Charter and no reference was made in it to any Recorder to give them legal advice. Whether any of these three had previous experience as Justices of the Peace for Hampshire to guide them in their new posts cannot be discovered, as Commissions of the Peace were only spasmodically enrolled in her reign on the Patent Rolls and none of those named in the Charter are referred to in the surviving commissions.

Prior to 1600 Portsmouth had held Courts Leet and Views of Frankpledge twice a year, once in early December and again at the end of June. Much of the business dealt

---

[33] No. 164.

with at these courts, such as that concerning the Assize of Bread and Ale, overlapped with many of the recognised duties of the Justices of the Peace. Therefore it is perhaps not surprising that the new Sessions Court was held from the start at the same time as the Courts Leet and Views of Frankpledge. In fact these courts continued to be held together throughout the seventeenth century, though, as has been said, the presentments made by the Court Leet jury were always kept as a separate record.

The only source of information about the Portsmouth Sessions Courts in the earliest years of their existence is therefore the series of Election and Sessions Books. In the seventeenth century these volumes were used to record primarily two things: first, the annual elections at which the Mayor and other Corporation officers were appointed, and second, the attendance at the twice yearly Sessions Courts and Views of Frankpledge. Thus only from these volumes can be ascertained the date when these Sessions Courts were held and the dates to which they were on occasion adjourned, generally a week or a fortnight later and usually in order to give the Court Leet jury time to make its presentments. All those individuals who were entitled or in duty bound to attend these Courts were listed and there is often a faint dash or dot by a name which suggests that this symbol was used to indicate whether that official did in fact attend. Apart from this, little is recorded in these books of the business carried on in the first combined Sessions Courts and Views of Frankpledge except for the admission of burgesses and the admission of tenants to Corporation property. Until 1627, only very occasionally is obvious Sessions business mentioned and this is confined to recording the release of someone from his recognisance to appear.

It was the Charter of Charles I dated 17 November 1627 which brought about considerable changes in the conduct of the Sessions Courts. The number of Justices of the Peace was increased to include the immediate past Mayor, while the three others, apart from the Mayor, were to be Aldermen. Their duties were more precisely described as to 'cause to be observed corrected and kept the Statutes of Artificers and Labourers and of Weights and Measures within the Borough aforesaid the liberties and precincts thereof' and 'to enquire hear and determine . . . all manner of felonies and imprisonments riots routs oppressions extortions forestallings regratings trespasses misdeeds and offences'. For the first time the Corporation is authorised to appoint a Recorder to give legal advice to the Mayor and Aldermen in all the Borough courts, and it is stated that the Town Clerk should also be Clerk of the Peace. Special stress was laid on the fact that the Town Clerk was to enrol the recognisances of all debtors. Although this applied primarily to the Court of Record where cases of debt were heard, it seems to have had the effect that all recognisances to appear at the Sessions were also enrolled, in this case in the Election and Sessions Books, for there they are found in considerable numbers starting in 1628 and continuing until 1660, by which time the existence of the copy of the recognisance on the Sessions file appears to have been considered sufficient. Finally the 1627 Charter, in authorising the holding of the Court Leet and View of Frankpledge, said it was to be held twice a year 'once on Monday next after the feast of St Andrew the Apostle [30 November] and again on Thursday in the week of Easter or at other convenient days within one month of the feast of Easter and the feast of St Michael the Archangel [29 September] in every year'. As the Sessions met at the same time as these other courts, this led in 1629 to a permanent change in the dates when they were regularly held from June and December to April and October.

From the evidence that survives it would seem that the Sessions Courts were first really activated by this Charles I Charter and it is quite possible that the Sessions files were only begun around this time. This Charter in fact was to remain the governing charter of Portsmouth down to 1835, with the exception of the period 1682–8 when Charles II's Charter briefly superseded it. This Charter of Charles II brought the Vill of Gosport within the Borough of Portsmouth, which will explain the number of cases dealt with in that time relating to that township, which was part of the parish of Alverstoke. No boundaries for this extension of Portsmouth's rule have ever been specified, but it is feasible that Sir Bernard de Gomme's defence fortifications for Portsmouth and Gosport started in 1668 both prompted this extension and set a limit to it on the Gosport side.

JUSTICES OF THE PEACE IN PORTSMOUTH

In considering the duties of the Justices of the Peace in Portsmouth, it should be remembered that the boundaries of the Borough, and hence their authority, extended not just over the fortified town of Portsmouth but over much of the western half of Portsea Island where its common lands and town fields were, as far north as Tipner. Thus it included a fair portion, though not the whole, of the parish of Portsea.

From surviving evidence it appears that right from the start all those elected as Justices of the Peace in Portsmouth had previously served the office of Mayor. The Mayor himself was the only new Justice each year and again, right from 1600, it had become the custom for him to serve a second year as Justice immediately following his term as Mayor, a custom recognised in the Charter of 1627. The other Justices of the Peace quite often were elected to hold office for a number of years in succession, the average being between four and six years, but some held office for considerably longer and in the period covered by this volume Hugh Salesbury was a Justice for eighteen years, St John Steventon for fourteen years and Samuel Williams for fifteen years.[34] In fact the three of them were Justices over much the same period of years.

It would seem from these Sessions papers that the Mayor was the Justice generally sought out to attend to matters, though on a considerable number of occasions he was assisted by one or even more of the other Justices, usually those who had several years' experience behind them. If by any chance the Mayor was ill or had to go away from the borough for a time he could and did appoint a deputy, just for the period of his absence. This is made clear in the following extract from a letter by Benjamin Johnson, who, when he was Mayor, was ordered to stay in the Dockyard because of the plague in Portsmouth: 'the deputy[35] who was sworne before I came to London continues actually soe stil, appeares for me in al places, hath possession of the mace seales etc & in effect (with the rest of the Justices) does al my part of the business'.[36] The Charter of 1627 which permitted this said that the deputy was to be one of the Aldermen, though when one was appointed, which might not happen every year, he was always one of the other Justices and frequently not the immediate past Mayor.[37] In fact in 1659–60, in the mayoralty of John Tippetts, three different Justices were at various times appointed his deputy.

The duties of the Justices were laid down in the charters but the Election and Sessions Books reveal that they were also always appointed Auditors and Keepers of the Keys of the town chest. In addition they performed the extra duties laid on them by Acts of Parliament. The poor-law acts thus led to the examinations for bastardy and settlement found in these papers, but it is noteworthy that the Corporation left the practical main-

---

[34] See Appendix V.
[35] I.e. Anthony Haberley.
[36] Public Record Office, S.P.29/152/14: 25 Mar. 1666.
[37] The existence and names of Deputy Mayors are often to be obtained only from the Sessions Papers.

tenance of the poor entirely to the parish officers of Portsmouth and Portsea. Occasionally it will be noticed that the Justices took examinations at the request of the Navy Commissioners or in a case which occurred outside the borough boundaries.[38] In these instances, if the case were made out against the accused, it was referred either to the Navy Board in London or to the General Sessions for Hampshire for sentence.[39]

Although the trade or profession of many mayors cannot be discovered, over the years it has been found that a number of senior Dockyard officers became Mayor and were for a long time Justices of the Peace. Among the most notable of these were Hugh Salesbury, Clerk of the Survey, St John Steventon, Clerk of the Check, and Benjamin Johnson, Storekeeper. In 1666 when all three were Justices together, concern was expressed by the Navy Board in London that their Dockyard officers were using their position as Justices to prevent action being taken against other Dockyard workmen accused of theft of the King's goods. In the end, it led to an order forbidding any of the King's servants in Portsmouth to act as magistrates there. This order caused some confusion as to whether it applied to existing Justices or only to those who might be appointed in the future. The Mayor, Benjamin Johnson, thought he could only be removed from his office by the King and Council[40] and in a letter he himself wrote explaining what had happened he said 'my title of mayor hath not bene nor shal be any hindrance to my duety of the storekeeper's charge'.[41]

However, the resident Navy Commissioner in Portsmouth, Thomas Middleton, had other thoughts for he says: 'I take notice what you say in order to ye Kings officers being Maiestrats of ye towne, I was in hoape the order had extended to thayre present dismission from towne service, had it been soe, I should not have iudged it any prejudice to ye Kinge. I have discorsed ye busnes with them, thay are now under an oath for this yeare, that is untell Michhillmas & then Mr. Steventon doeth promys me to leave all towne service & I hoape ye rest wilbe soe wise as to doe ye same'.[42]

As to the administration of justice, Middleton says: 'How ye corse of iustice is ordered heare I am a stranger to, & hoape allways to continue in ye sam condition. . . . It seems it is a priviledge of this playce to live by playinge ye (*blank*) . . . two or 3 words to Mr Maiour from your Board or from Sir William Coventry myght helpe one ye busnes as to [the] poynt of iustice which I bege of you to mynd & let it be efechtuall'.[43] 'The corse usuall in this playce is & hath beenn when an offender hath been taken . . . and [I] have delivered them up to iustice, they have beenn put in prison, next busnes is yt bayll is offerred by som of his consorts, its taken, ye busnes noe more mynded & soe falls. . . . I could say much mor to this busnes if it weare convenyent, for its moer easyer to speake trewth then to prove trewth to be trewth by law, neither am I willinge to be spatter ye governor of such a thinge as a corporation, yet I am apt to beleve . . . that weare this corporation as it ought to be ye Kings sufferinge need not nor would not be soe great as it is.'[44]

Four months later when this matter had died down Middleton, who was himself a burgess, was able to write more calmly: 'As long as the storekeeper[45] or any other officer is Maior of Portsmouth it cannot be imagined but thay must be in towne mor then in

---

[38] On three occasions Navy Commissioners actually assisted the Justices to take the examinations (nos 112, 203, App. III 6).

[39] Nos 292, App. II 45, App. III 1–11.

[40] *Calendar of State Papers Domestic*, 1665–6, p. 308 (Public Record Office, S.P.29/151/74): letter of Commissioner Thomas Middleton to Samuel Pepys, 20 Mar. 1666.

[41] Public Record Office, S.P.29/152/14: 25 Mar. 1666.

[42] Public Record Office, S.P.29/152/15: letter to Samuel Pepys, 25 Mar. 1666.

[43] Public Record Office, S.P.29/151/54: letter to Samuel Pepys, 18 Mar. 1666.

[44] Public Record Office, S.P.29/151/3: letter to Samuel Pepys, 13 Mar. 1666.

[45] I.e. Benjamin Johnson.

ye Yard and wheare you are pleased to say you have put a fynall purge to ye Kings officers from beinge concerned in ye towns affayrs, I assur you Sir wee are not willinge to believe any such thinge, but [that] ye purge you have mayd is that the officer that is not concerned in ye towns affayrs shall not be admitted to it, but praye doe you believe Sir that we that are concerned in ye towne affayrs doe intend to continue ourselves in it . . . our choys of Maior wil be next month, you need not feare that the towne will make choyse of me for is not my turne yet, but if I mistake not our turn will come about apayce, & I heard a wise man say that ye Kinge had as good take away ye charter from ye towne as to prohibit his officers at ye Yard to be maiestrats.'[46]

In the event it proved impossible to exclude Dockyard officers from being re-elected Justices that year as Hugh Salesbury explained to the Navy Board in asking for their permission for him to serve as a Justice. He said that as 'non can be chosen a Justice till he had served ye office of Mayor & since ye last regulacon there was but three left besides myself that had been Mayor', he had therefore been chosen 'against my will or consent'.[47] Indeed the following year Salesbury was elected Mayor for the second time.

RECORDERS AND TOWN CLERKS

It is much to be regretted that there are so few contemporary records concerning Portsmouth in the seventeenth century. At every turn there is lack of information to confirm or expand facts learned elsewhere. This seems particularly so in trying to discover some details about the Recorders and Clerks of the Peace who probably exercised considerable influence over the Sessions Courts.

Before 1600 the Mayor had the assistance of John Moore as Steward to the Court Leet and View of Frankpledge. When the Sessions Court came to be held at the same time as these other courts, Moore would appear to have assumed the title of Recorder, though he is not called such in the Election and Sessions Books until just before his death in 1615. His successor, Thomas Whatman, was called Recorder at the time of his appointment and his status is confirmed in the Charter of Charles I in 1627. He seems to have effected some changes in the way the court was held at the start of his tenure by making the junior officers concerned in enforcing law and order in various capacities attend the Sessions Courts, but soon after this, there is some doubt as to whether the Recorder himself always attended, though he always drew his allowance. This was £2 a year plus hospitality in the 1620's,[48] but by the 1680's his successors are found receiving the increased sum of £10 a year.[49] It is probable that these figures reflect the change in importance of the Sessions Courts as much as a rise in prices.

From the attendance marks in the Election and Sessions Books, it appears that many Recorders were frequently absent from the Court but, whenever this was the case, the Clerk of the Peace was always there. Sir John Biggs of Petersfield, Recorder of Portsmouth from 1673 till 1685, seems to have been most regular in his attendance, but in 1685 he resigned. He is said to have done so 'voluntarily' but what was the real reason is unknown. The post was first offered to the loyal supporter of James II, Lord Dartmouth, Governor of Portsmouth 1673–82, or his nominee,[50] but in fact it was Sir George Jeffreys, Lord Chief Justice, and soon to be Lord Chancellor, who took the place of Sir John. Judge

---

[46] Public Record Office, S.P.29/163/69: letter to Samuel Pepys, 17 July 1666.
[47] Public Record Office, S.P.29/172/18: letter to Sir William Batten, Surveyor of H.M. Navy, 18 Sept. 1666.
[48] See Chamberlain's Accounts for 1622 in R. East, *Extracts from the records of the Corporation of Portsmouth* (1891), p. 438. Only three Chamberlain's Accounts for the 17th century now survive and all date to the 1620's.
[49] See Book of Constitutions in East, op. cit., p. 12.
[50] Historical MSS. Commission, *MSS. of the Earl of Dartmouth* (3v., 1887–96), i, p. 123.

Jeffreys as far as can be seen never came himself to Portsmouth but always acted through his deputy, William Westbrooke.

It is perhaps natural to find that the Clerks of the Peace had more obvious influence on the Sessions Courts as it was they who kept the records. In Portsmouth the Town Clerk was generally in addition Clerk of the Peace and Coroner. His office was not a full-time position as all these duties were performed by an attorney in the town. His fees in the 1620's were £6 13s. 4d. a year plus 5s. 10d. for ink, paper and parchment,[51] a sum which by the 1680's had increased to £10 13s. 4d. a year, the 13s. 4d. being for pen, ink and paper.[52]

In the period covered by this volume there were, with the exception of the last few months, only two Town Clerks. Thomas Mullins was appointed Town Clerk, Clerk of the Peace and Coroner in 1645 during the Civil Wars and he remained in office, even after the Restoration, until his sudden death in 1666. However, prior to 1660 he ceased to be Coroner and from 1659 others were appointed in his place to this office.

The other Town Clerk was Edward Archer, who was probably responsible for bringing to an end the enrolment of recognisances in the Election and Sessions Books and for keeping the files in a more systematic manner. He first appears as clerk to Mullins in April 1656,[53] and in October 1659 he is appointed Coroner 'for the time being', but in the next few months he is accused of 'using threatening language to the Mayor, Mr Child, and the Justices'.[54] Precisely what happened is not known, but the trouble arose during the uncertain time immediately before the Restoration of Charles II in May 1660. Archer was a Royalist and Josiah Child was a Parliamentarian, who was to be removed with others from the office of Alderman in 1662 as a result of the Corporations Act.[55] For a time Thomas Seymour served as Coroner but by 1661 Archer was back in favour, for in October of that year he was re-appointed Coroner and in December he was admitted a Burgess.

On Archer's abilities, some enlightening comments are to be found in the correspondence from Commissioner Thomas Middleton to Samuel Pepys in the few months before Archer was appointed Town Clerk and Clerk of the Peace in October 1666. In March of that year Middleton says of finding an attorney to attend to the matter of goods embezzled from the Dockyard: 'I confes you have put me to a hard taske to get an honest attorney; [it] is a busnes beyond my capassytye, for if I knew wheare such a one weare to be found I should deify him. However I shall doe my indevour & when I shall have found such a one, as I can meett with, I shall present him to yow & his terms'.[56]

A week later Middleton reports: 'I . . . have found out one, which albeit a stranger to me yet the repute is of him that he knoweth how to be boath honest & knavish, for its sayd he is an able man, he is very willinge to accept of the imployment & trewth is if it weare noe mor then that it weare knowne that such a man weare apoynted to mynd ye Kings busnes, albeit for present he did little in it, yet it would be som awe uppon ye offenders. . . . The man I have pitched uppon is an attorney which liveth in this towne, his name is Edward Archer. He hath promysed dilligence & faythfillnes & I am apt to beleve he wilbe soe'.[57]

[51] See Chamberlain's Accounts for 1622 in East, op. cit., pp. 437–9.
[52] See Book of Constitutions in East, op. cit., p. 12.
[53] App. II, no. 47.
[54] App. II, no. 73.
[55] East, op. cit., pp. 168–9.
[56] Public Record Office, S.P.29/150/49: 6 Mar. 1666.
[57] Public Record Office, S.P.29/151/3: 13 Mar. 1666.

Archer was therefore empowered to act and prosecute but in August Middleton was forced to say: 'I did when first advised you of him tell you that he was a man knew sufficiently well how to do your busnes & his o[w]ne to, how his fees com to be soe great I know not but if I mistake not ye examynation was taken by Capt. Johnson that is Mayor in ye payhouse & written by the town clerke,[58] I confes I am not soe good a lawyer as to know ye fees in things of this natuer but . . . I bege of you that you . . . for this tyme give him content because I am very zelus to have this busnes prosecuted to ye full. . . . [It] is better for ye Kinge to loos £500 then that theas roages should escape full punishment'.[59]

Nevertheless Archer's involvement in the affairs of Portsmouth Corporation continued to increase, for in 1671 he was elected an Alderman and in the year 1674-5 he even became Mayor, though for his year of office and the following year he did temporarily hand over his duties as Town Clerk to Robert Holloway, because he himself was acting as a Justice of the Peace by virtue of his being Mayor. In 1676 he once more resumed his duties as Town Clerk, Clerk of the Peace and Coroner and continued to perform them till his death in the early months of 1688.

In that year on 8 March Charles Bissell 'late clerke to Mr Edward Archer was admitted and sworne Clerke of ye Peace & Towne Clerke of this Burrough'. From his distinctive handwriting he would seem to have been assisting Archer since 1683 but the above entry in the Election and Sessions Books was followed immediately by this statement in a quite different hand: 'but this was for the time being viz: during the good will of the Mayor and the major part of the Aldermen'. However on 24 April 1688 Bissell was admitted a Burgess and at the opening of the Easter Sessions on 26 April he was named as Clerk of the Peace. At this point unusual things begin to happen. For the first time the court was adjourned for as long as a month till 29 May and then again for a further fortnight till 13 June. On the day before this eventual meeting, on 12 June, a Samuel Ely was made a Burgess. That this Ely supplanted Bissell becomes clear in two presentments, one dated about 4 May and a later one dated 28 September, for they are both signed 'Bissell for Ely'.[60] On the earlier one it can be seen that an original signature has been scratched out and changed. It thus seems fairly certain that someone must have taken strong objection to the appointment of Bissell as Clerk of the Peace and had ordered the appointment of his own nominee, Samuel Ely, in Bissell's place. As Bissell signed the presentments for Ely there is reason to suppose that Ely did not live in Portsmouth and that in fact Ely only came to the town to attend the Sessions Courts.

On 2 October at the opening of the Michaelmas Sessions, Samuel Ely was named as Clerk of the Peace with as usual George, Lord Jeffreys, as Recorder and William Westbrooke as his deputy. Also at this Sessions is the last record of the attendance of the Constable for Gosport, for already the national opposition to the policies of James II was making itself felt. This Sessions Court of 2 October seems to have been adjourned without a date for its re-assembly being named, for it was about this time that the Charter of Charles II of 1682 was revoked along with the many others granted at that period to many other boroughs. This naturally caused a hiatus in the Corporation's status, but upon enquiry it was found that the surrender of the 1627 Charter had not been enrolled and that the Charter itself was in the possession of Francis Gwyn at Whitehall. He told the Corporation that before he could return it, they must get the authority of

[58] I.e. Thomas Mullins.
[59] Public Record Office, S.P.29/168/48: 19 Aug. 1666.
[60] Nos 416, 423.

the former Governor of Portsmouth, Lord Dartmouth.[61] This they obtained possibly with the help of their prospective Member of Parliament, Henry Slingsby.[62] Meanwhile the adjourned Sessions Court met again on 6 November and, as it was in effect convened afresh, a complete attendance list was given. No Recorder at all was named though William Westbrooke did become Recorder in his own right by the next spring. Charles Bissell was put once more as Clerk of the Peace and from then on remained in office till 1711.

Of Samuel Ely no further trace is to be found. If he had been a nominee of Lord Dartmouth it is doubtful whether he could have been removed from office so easily owing to the Corporation's need to regain its old Charter, nor would it have been possible so readily to cancel his admission as Burgess, for it is now found thoroughly crossed out. Although no definite proof has been found of the interference of Judge Jeffreys, the other possible patron of Ely, in his appointment as Portsmouth's Town Clerk in 1688, all the evidence points to it, for he disappears from the scene just prior to the time when William of Orange landed in the West Country on 5 November. Judge Jeffreys himself attempted to flee the country at the same time as James II early in December, only to be foiled and imprisoned in the Tower of London, but Lord Dartmouth who had been leading the fleet against William of Orange decided to acknowledge the new king.

---

[61] Historical MSS. Commission, *MSS. of the Earl of Dartmouth* (3v., 1887–96), i, pp. 202, 223: letters from Francis Gwyn to Lord Dartmouth, 14 Nov. and 4 Dec. 1688.
[62] Election and Sessions Book: copy of letter from Slingsby, 1 Dec. 1688.

Notes on the form of the calendar

1 All documents calendared are in English unless otherwise stated.

2 Editorial additions and explanations are given in square brackets or italics ; for the rest the calendar is a straightforward paraphrase of the documents.

3 The spelling of all surnames has been copied as it has been found in the original document. It will be noticed that on occasion the spelling of the surname of the same individual can vary even in the same document.

4 The more common male forenames of more than five letters have been abbreviated as follows:

Alex.	=	Alexander	Humf.	=	Humfrey
And.	=	Andrew	Jos.	=	Joseph
Ant.	=	Antony	Mar.	=	Martin
Art.	=	Arthur	Mat.	=	Matthew
Bart.	=	Bartholomew	Mic.	=	Michael
Ben.	=	Benjamin	Nat.	=	Nathaniel
Bern.	=	Bernard	Nic.	=	Nicholas
Cha.	=	Charles	Phil.	=	Philip
Chr.	=	Christopher	Ric.	=	Richard
Dan.	=	Daniel	Rob.	=	Robert
Edm.	=	Edmund	Sam.	=	Samuel
Edw.	=	Edward	Step.	=	Stephen
Fra.	=	Francis	Tho.	=	Thomas
Geo.	=	George	Walt.	=	Walter
Godf.	=	Godfrey	Wil.	=	William
Hub.	=	Hubert			

The forenames of women have not been abbreviated.

5 The place of origin of an individual has sometimes been found to be 'of P.'. This has not been extended as it could refer to either Portsmouth or Portsea.

Calendar of Portsmouth Borough Sessions Papers 1653-1688

EASTER SESSIONS 18 April 1653

For further recognisances in Sessions Books see Appendix II nos 1–3.

1
TRADING IRREGULARLY

S3A/2 (entry i)
25 January 1652/3. No name of Justice.
Information
John Eastman said that Wil. Bryant bought of him 2½ cwt of cheese last Saturday morning. He sells it in his shop and was to pay 38s. per cwt.

2
Subject unknown

S3A/2 (entry ii)
8 February 1652/3. No name of Justice.
Information
Tho. Beeston. *No entry against the name.*

3
TRADING IRREGULARLY

S3A/2 (entry iii)[1]
22 February 1652/3. Before the Mayor and Aldermen.
Sentence
Roger Baker of Petersfield fined £10 for setting up shop without leave of the Town, unless he be gone by Tuesday next.

4
FORNICATION

S3A/3
26 March 1653. Before Ant. Belbin, esq., Mayor, John Holt, esq., and Edw. Deane, gent.
Examinations
(a) Margaret Collens of Portsmouth, spinster, said that on Monday night, 14th of this month, Step. Eddin and Lydia Jackman were together in a low room in the house of Rob. East in Portsmouth. Eddin had Lydia on his lap and asked her to come into the bakehouse, but she refused because the baker's boy was there. He thereupon lay with her there on the floor and used her body. *Signed by mark.*
(b) Elizabeth, wife of Rob. East of Portsmouth, said she heard Lydia confess to the above and say that she was so hurt that she was sore for three days after. *Signed by mark.*
The said Lydia was present at the examinations and confessed.
Sentence
To be whipped at the cart's tail out of Town and sent to Whiteparish, [Wilts.], where she says she was born.
Footnote: 'She broke prizon'.

5
THEFT

S3A/4
8 April 1653. Before Ant. Bellbin, gent., Mayor, Wil. Stephens, esq., Recorder, and John Holt, esq.
Examinations
(a) Jane Martin, aged about 16, servant to Mr James Austen of Portsmouth, said that on this very day she went into the storehouse of Mr Ant. Bellbin and Mr Hugh Salisburie in Portsmouth, adjoining the house of Mr James Austen, to collect some wheat which had fallen through some boards in the floor of the room over, which was in the possession of Mr Austen. She found a fellow-servant, an apprentice boy John Smyth, had taken white sugar from a chest. She put in her hand to take some but could not reach it. *Signed by mark.*

---

[1] Memorandum added to S3A/2:
6 September 1653. John Patten admitted Guardian etc. John Meader admitted etc. Quit rent [received by] J. Monsey.

(b) Phil. Mansbridge of Portsmouth, labourer, aged about 35, said he saw Jane Martin put her hand in the chest; he did not see her take any away but saw sugar on the tips of her fingers. He saw John Smyth, but did not see him take anything.
Signed by mark.

(c) Godf. Lloyd of Portsmouth, servant to Mr Hugh Salesbury, aged about 21, said that Phil. Mansbridge told him that Jane Martin was on the sugar chest, so he went in and found her there. About a third part of the sugar from two chests was gone. *Signed.*

MICHAELMAS SESSIONS 10 October 1653
For further recognisances in Sessions Books see Appendix II, nos 4–5.

6
BASTARDY

S3A/5
25 July 1653. Before Ant. Belbin, esq., Mayor.
Examinations

(a) Christian Lawrence, wife of Rolvo (?) Lawrence of Portsmouth, said that about five weeks ago Elizabeth Lawrence, servant of Wil. Card of Portsmouth, told her that she was with child having lain with a man who lodged at the house of Ric. Sweete and who wore clothes trimmed with green ribbons. His name she understood was John Bromley and he had promised to marry her next day. *Signed by mark.*

(b) Edw. Ansell of Portsmouth, carpenter, told of what Ric. Sweete of Portsmouth, mason, told him last Friday. Elizabeth Lawrence about three weeks ago came to the house of Widow Buckle where Sweete was working and asked him if she might stay at his house a week or two till she found service. Sweete said that if she did she might fall in love with John Bromley who was lodging with him. She did not think he would look at her, but Sweete offered to arrange a match. Later Elizabeth sent for Bromley to come to the house of Wil. Hawley of Portsmouth where she claimed marriage, but Bromley said he had never promised marriage and could find it in his heart to kick her. *Signed by mark.*

(c) Tho. Heyham (*signs* Hamie) of Portsmouth said that about noon yesterday he went to the house of Ric. Sweete where John Bromley lay sick and heard from Sweete that Wil. Card sent to one of Sweete's servants to know if he would marry Elizabeth Lawrence, late servant of Card. He did not know what the answer was. *Signed.*

(d) Ric. Sweete of Portsmouth, mason, said that Wil. Card sent for John Knight, carpenter, late one of Sweete's servants, to know if he would marry Elizabeth Lawrence. He did not know what answer was given, but believed that Card was guilty of getting Elizabeth with child because he has taken so much trouble in the matter. Card also told him that he would not be in Bromley's coat for £40 if he did not marry her, as Bromley had known Lawrence twelve months. Sweete then told Card that Bromley had not been out of Ireland above six weeks. *Signed by mark.*

(e) John Knight of Portsmouth, mason. *No further entry.*

(f) Elizabeth Lawrence of Portsmouth, singlewoman, said she had been a servant for over a year to Wil. Card who had put away his wife while she was with him. She was in that time begotten with child of Tho. Hill of Portsmouth, carpenter, and had lain with him three times at Card's house and again five weeks ago when Hill promised her marriage. *Signed by mark.*
See also App. II, no. 4.

7
FORNICATION AND ABUSING AUTHORITY

S3A/6
8 August 1653. Before Ant. Belbin, esq., Mayor, and John Holt, esq.
Information
Mary Greene last Saturday evening heard James Wexford and Jane Arthur together in the house of Eleanor Hewes, widow, in the sink between that house and the house of the informant. She opened her door and looked out and saw Jane half naked and Wexford having carnal knowledge of her body. Eleanor keeps a common bawdy-house and Mary cannot sleep for what goes on. About three weeks ago she heard Eleanor call Mr Belbin, the Mayor, 'old grisle bearded rogue', because he had committed her to prison before for her misdemeanours. *Signed by mark.*

Examinations

(a) Jane Arthur of Portsmouth, spinster, said that she was with James Wexford in the sink belonging to the house of Eleanor Hewes last Saturday afternoon. He kissed her; that was all. *Signed by mark.*

(b) James Wexford of Braintree, Essex, weaver, confirmed that on Saturday evening last he kissed Jane Arthur, servant of Alex. Carter, baker, at the house of Eleanor Hughes and that was all. *Signed by mark.*

(c) Eleanor Hewes of Portsmouth, widow, said that James 'catched' the said Jane and kissed her, but she saw no harm. *Signed by mark.*

EASTER SESSIONS 3 April 1654

For further recognisances, etc., in Sessions Books see Appendix II, nos 6–9, and see also Appendix III, no. 1.

8
THEFT

S3A/7

17 January 1653/4. Before Roger Grainger, esq., and John Holt.
Recognisances
Tho. Chilton of Portsmouth, mariner, and Wil. Worthen took from John Voaks half a hogshead of brandy by confession and a parcel of wax from Henry Woods by confession.

Tho. Chilton and Wil. Worthen in £10 each.
Nic. Peirson and Tho. Rowter in £5 each.

For appearance of Chilton and Worthen at the next Sessions.
See also App. II, no. 6.

9
TRADING
IRREGULARLY

S3A/8

20 January 1653/4. Before Roger Grainger, esq., Mayor, and Edw. Deane.
Examination
Lettice ('Letuce') Buck of Portsmouth, widow, said that on Tuesday 3 Jan. last she bought from Ann, wife of Tho. Woodyer, and paid for, a blue petticoat (20s), a handkerchief and a pair of linen sleeves (3s 6d), a white waistcoat (3s) and a green apron (3s). She believed they were taken out of a chest of Woodyer's, which she had seen Ann try to open with a hatchet the day before. *Signed by mark.*
Recognisances
Lettice ('Letuce') Buck in £20.
Ric. Thomas of Portsmouth, tailor, in £10.
Wil. Erle of Salisbury, fishmonger, in £10.

For appearance of Lettice at the next Sessions.
See also App. II, no. 7.

MICHAELMAS SESSIONS 9 October 1654

For further recognisances, etc., in Sessions Books see Appendix II, nos 10–22, and see also Appendix III, no. 2.

10
ABUSING
AUTHORITY

S3A/9

6 June 1654. Before Roger Granger, esq., Mayor.
Examination
Wil. Ransted of Portsmouth, labourer, said that about a month ago he was appointed special Surveyor of the Highways by Nic. Peirson and authorised for mending and paving the streets and levying forfeitures for nuisances. He went with Peirson and John Collins, one of the constables, to distrain for such offences. While they were doing this Wil. Saynt of Portsmouth openly declared that if anyone should come to distrain his goods or horses they were no more than thieves and highway robbers and he was prepared for them. *Signed.*

Footnote: 14 June 1654. A warrant of good behaviour to be issued against Saynt and order for committal till good sureties are given for bail till the next Sessions.
Initialled by W[il]. St[ephens, Recorder].

See also App. II, no. 15.

| **11** | S3A/10 |
| **BRIBERY** | **5 September 1654.** Before Roger Granger, esq., Mayor, and Ric. Lardner. |

Examination

James Austin of Portsmouth, baker, said that Wil. Taylor told him that Mr Belbin and Mr Holt had offered Taylor £5 to take an oath that Austin had broken into a storehouse amongst the sugars.

| **12** | S3A/11 |
| **TESTAMENTARY** | **19 September 1654.** No name of Justice. |

Examination

Ric. Merrit of Southsea Castle said that John Scrace on his deathbed declared that he gave £10 to the poor of Portsmouth and £10 more to the poor of the Garrison, with £10 more to each if his son did not return, and this was in his written will. When his son came home, he promised to perform his father's will.

EASTER SESSIONS 23 April 1655

For further recognisances in Sessions Books see Appendix II, nos 23–31.

| **13** | D11A/16/1 |
| **FORNICATION** | **20 October 1654.** Before Fra. Holt, esq., Mayor. |

Examinations

(a) Dorothy Hayter of Portsmouth, singlewoman, said that last Monday about 8 p.m. she was sent for by John Sanders and she went to him at the house of Mrs Marshawe called the Queen's Head in Portsmouth. With one Sachell they drank six pints of sack there. After about two hours Sanders took her to the house of office in the backside of the house and threw her down but did not meddle with her body. Then he took her to Godshouse Yard where he lay on her for about three hours and had carnal knowledge of her body. Then they went to the back gate of Mr Granger in Portsmouth but whether he lay with her there she did not know as she had drunk too much wine, otherwise she would not have yielded. She asked Sanders if he would father the child if she was with child and he said he would and would marry her. If he had kept his promise she would not have complained.   *Signed by mark.*

(b) John Sanders of Portsmouth, butcher, confirmed her evidence and his promise.
          Signed by mark.

Footnote: Both were committed to prison the same day by the Mayor.
See also App. II, no. 26.

| **14** | S3B/1 |
| **ASSAULT** | **23 October 1654.** Before Fra. Holt, esq., Mayor, and Ric. Lardner, gent. |

Information

Wil. Andrewes of Portsea, yeoman, said that last Friday about 6 p.m. he was near Newgate in the liberties of Portsmouth going home to Portsea when Tho. Coleman came and walked with him for about half a mile and then threw him down and demanded his money or he would pistol him. Seeing two horsemen a little way off, Coleman went off and said he would see him hanged before he would take anything from him.   *Signed.*
See also App. II, no. 24.

| **15** | S3A/12 |
| **ABUSING AUTHORITY** | **2 January 1654/5.** No name of Justice. |

Examination

John Patten, Chamberlain, said that on demand of town rent James Mills made answer that the Corporation were cheating knaves and that Patten was the same.
          Signed.

12 January 1654/5.

The above confirmed before Fra. Holt, esq., Mayor, John Holt, Roger Granger and Ric. Lardner.
See also App. II no. 27.

16
WRONGFUL
ARREST

S3B/2

10 January 1654/5. Before Fra. Holt, esq., Mayor.
Examinations

(a) Wil. Naxton, mariner, said that Henry Johnson living in Portsmouth sells beer retail. Within the last six or seven weeks he spent 37s at Johnson's house for beer and some victuals. Others had called for beer and paid for it at the rate of 2d per flagon. He believes 20s of the 37s was for beer.   *Initialled by* T[ho.] M[ullins].

Later the same day Naxton further said that Johnson and Wil. Cromwell went to Havant and pretended they had a warrant from Commissioner Willoughby to carry him to his ship Little Charity and brought him to Portsmouth. Yesterday Johnson took 14s and Cromwell 8s from Naxton to clear him, though they had neither warrant to apprehend him nor power to discharge him.

(b) John Penford, Constable of Havant, said Johnson and Cromwell had another seaman in custody, but he did not know what became of him. Johnson confessed in the presence of Ric. Gillingham and Bart. Harris, both of Havant, that he brought the other seaman to Portsmouth. Cromwell carried the other seaman, being a young lad with a new suit of clothes costing £5 and a scarf costing 15s, behind him from Havant, but it is not known what became of them. Cromwell charged Naxton with felony or he would not have seized him without a warrant.

17
ABUSE

S3A/13

5 February 1654/5. No name of Justice.
Information

Informant (*not named*) said that John Sheppard's wife 'grossly abused his wife calling her copper-nosed jade' and 'copper-nosed whore' and that she 'would never leave her old whores tricks'. His wife answered not a word.

Marginal note: Proved by the oaths of Mary Swetland and John Damarec.
See also App. II, no. 31.

18
ABUSE

S3B/3

26 February 1654/5. Before Fra. Holt, esq., Mayor, and Ric. Lardner, gent.
Examinations

(a) Tho. Follard, soldier under the command of Capt. Carter, said that last Saturday night at the house of Widow Gunter in Portsmouth one Joan Jones, a pedlar woman, was there somewhat overtaken in drink. She said that he and the rest of the soldiers there were a company of Roundhead dogs and said 'Ile see you hanged before Ile drinke with such rogues, I hope to see the wrath of God poured on you within these two yeares'.   *Signed.*

(b) John Dunton, a soldier under the command of Capt. Runnell, confirmed the above evidence.   *Signed by mark.*
See also App. II, no. 28.

MICHAELMAS SESSIONS 8 and 19 October 1655

For further recognisances, etc., in Sessions Books see Appendix II, nos 32–37, and see also Appendix III, nos 3–5.

19
ILLEGAL
MARRIAGE

S3A/14

9 May 1655. Before Fra. Holt, esq., Mayor, and Ric. Lardner, gent.
Examinations

(a) James Beale of Portsmouth, tailor, said that on Easter Tuesday last, 17 Apr., at the church of Hound he married Grace Whitman, being then about 17½ years old. No notice of his intended marriage was published in church or market. He paid the minister 10s. He never had carnal knowledge of her body.   *Signed.*

(b) Grace Whitman of Portsmouth *confirmed the above.*   *Signed by mark.*

20

SETTLEMENT AND ABUSING AUTHORITY

S3A/15

16 May 1655. No name of Justice.
Note of evidence
Tho. Knolles of Shipley, near Horsham, Suss., threatened to leave his children, Elizabeth and Thomas, to the parish.

17 May 1655.
Sentence
Ordered by Fra. Holt, esq., Mayor, to be whipped. He was drunk and swore and cursed the Mayor, Constables and all who came near him.
   Footnote: He was accordingly whipped and a pass made for him and his children to Shipley.

21

KEEPING A BAWDY HOUSE

D11A/16/2

12 September 1655.
Certificate
Certifies that Joan wife of Tho. Wilks, seaman, lives in a house on the Point generally accounted a bawdy-house and that she is reputed a notorious whore, an uncivil and ungodly woman, who curses and swears and is a great disturber to her neighbours.
Signed by:

Jo[hn] Collens, Constable	Rob. Hawkes (*by mark*)
James Barton	Ric. Deaniye
Rob. Uphman	Tho. Seymor, Constable
John Okeshott	John Beell
Fra. Gardner	Peter Gooustree
Henry Lyme	Geo. Garnham
Sebastian ('Sebasten') Watts	Edm. Whittingtonn
Henry Scott (*by mark*)	Wil. Chubb (*by mark*)
Mic. Ford	Ric. Skarvill (*by mark*)
Fra. Gardner (*by mark*)	Phil. Mansbridge
John Goly	Tho. Mills, Constable
	David Lucas

See also App. II, no. 43.

22

DISLOYALTY

S3A/16

17 September 1655. Before Fra. Holt, esq., Mayor, Wil. Stephens, esq., Recorder, and Wil. Michell, gent.
Informations
   (a) Margaret Pope of Portsea, widow, aged 47, said that about six months ago Jos. Rickman, who lodged with her, had said that no honest man took up arms against the King and that her husband (who had been in Parliament service) did not go to Heaven. He also said that all the women in Portsmouth were whores, and when the fleet was gone there was no woman in Portsmouth 'but would play ye whore for an egg'.   *Signed by mark.*
   (b) Ellen Pope, daughter of the said Margaret, said that when she was servant to John Rives she heard Jos. Rickman, within the last twelve months, call Rives a cheating rogue.   *Signed by mark.*
See also App. II, no. 37.

EASTER SESSIONS 14 and 21 April 1656

For further recognisances in Sessions Books see Appendix II, nos 38–45.

23

ABUSING AUTHORITY

S3A/17

19 February 1655/6. Before John Tawke, esq., Mayor, John Holt, esq., and Ric. Lardner, gent.
Information
Tho. Butteres (*also* Butteresse) said that on 1 Feb. last Henry Jenner said that Mr Lardner was one of the 'Justasses' and he was a burgasse. Mr Lardner had

sent for Henry Jenner for selling brooms and he used many scandalous words against Mr Lardner saying that if he went to the Court, took off his hat and said he was sorry he should be cleared.

See also App. II, no. 39.

24
THEFT

S3A/18

10 March 1655/6. Before John Tawke, esq., Mayor.

Information
Peter Francis said that on Saturday last, the 8th, Ric. Ascue came ashore at the Point at Portsmouth about 11 p.m., came to the yard of Nic. Peirson and took away three billet sticks, value 4d. *Signed by mark.*

Recognisances
> Ric. Ascue in £10.
> Tho. Jones and Henry Cornish in £5 each.
For appearance of Ascue at the next Sessions.

See also App. II, no. 41.

MICHAELMAS SESSIONS 13 October 1656

For further recognisances in Sessions Books see Appendix II, nos 46–60, and see also Appendix III, no. 6.

25
TRADING
IRREGULARLY

S3A/19

No date [circa 24 April 1656]. No name of Justice.

Examination
Sam. Southam, aged 28, said that Capt. Taylor and Capt. Short at the Point came to the boatswain's boy of the Wildman, whose name was Wil. Norman, for a coil of rope which weighed about ¾ cwt. It was delivered to Taylor and was sold the same night being 12 April for 15s or 17s. At the same time Taylor also bought some spikes, some half round nails and other nails for which he paid Norman 4s 6d and sold them the same night to Beswell's (?) wife for 22s. Also old iron hoops which he bought for 6d and sold for 4s and two sticks of 'lignam euphratiscome'[2] which he paid 6d for and which weigh 42 lb. (The boy told him that the boatswain sold two coils of rope to one in Portsmouth, *scored through*.) *Signed.*

> *Marginal notes:*
> (a) 'Truth upon oath'.
> (b) 'Confession of the partie'.

24 April 1656. Before the Mayor.

Examination
Wil. Norman, aged 16, said that his master, boatswain of the Wildman, Ant. Atkinson, sold at the beginning of the month to Henry Woods, who lived next door to the sign of the London on the Point, two coils of new rope, one of 4 in. the other about 3 in. *Signed.*

See also App. II, nos 46, 50.

26
THEFT

S3A/20

10 May 1656. Before John Tawke, esq., Mayor, and Ric. Lardner, gent.

Examinations
(a) John Smith, butcher, said that on Thursday last he sold the loin of veal produced to Mrs Jelloffe.

(b) Margaret Jelloffe said she found the said loin of veal in Edith Carter's hands, she being sent with it from Mr Wormewell's.

Sentence
Edith was ordered to be whipped and was whipped the same day.

---

[2] 'lignam euphratiscome' – this item of boatswain's stores could be 'lignum nephriticum' spelled wrongly. It seems to be a heavy wood like lignum vitae and, like lignum vitae, it comes from central America and was also used as a medicine (A. Rees, *Cyclopaedia* (1819)).

27

HOUSEBREAKING

S3A/21

12 May 1656. No name of Justice.

Examinations

(a) John Coulever said that about 1 o'clock he was at the Three Mariners in Gosport from which he went to the waterside and met the carpenter and John Gray. About 2 o'clock they went across the fields intending to go to church, but when they came to Forton ('Fortine') they saw a woman and asked the way to the church. She said it was 1½ miles away, so the two of them parted with the carpenter and coming by the waterside lay down and 1½ hours afterwards the carpenter came and woke them and all three remained together till night. *Signed.*

(b) John Gray *confirmed the above evidence.* *Signed by mark.*

12 May 1656. Before J. Tawke, Mayor, and Ric. Lardner, gent.

Endorsement of discharge

Chr. Mijer, seaman of the frigate Wexford, suspected of housebreaking at Tho. Stare's house at Forton ('Fortine') yesterday was committed, but as the said Stare could not lay any suggestion of felony he was discharged.

S3A/22

12 May 1656. Before John Tawke, esq., Mayor, and Ric. Lardner, gent.

Examination

Chr. Mijer, seaman of the frigate Wexford, said he was at Gosport yesterday but otherwise said nothing else about the breaking of Tho. Staires' house at Forton ('Fortune').

EASTER SESSIONS 6 April 1657

For further recognisance in Sessions Book see Appendix II, no. 61.

28

ABUSE AND THREATENED RIOT

S3A/23

25 March 1657. Before John Comfort, esq., Mayor, and Roger Granger, gent.

Examinations

(a) Wil. Gomm said that on Friday last he heard John Kent's wife say that she would turn Kingston (meaning the place or street within the liberties of Portsmouth) upside down. At the time Kent's wife and Joan Mosier, her sister, were scolding and brawling at Mrs Ayliffe, whom Joan called old bawd, jade and old whore.

Signed by mark.

(b) Edw. Ridge *confirmed Kent's wife's statement.* *Signed by mark.*

(c) Ric. Crocker *confirmed the evidence of Wil. Gomm.*

(d) Mrs Ayliffe said that on the same day Joan Mosier called Katherine, wife of Edw. Ellis, bitch and other foul names.

S3A/26

25 March 1657. No name of Justice.

Examination

Nic. Foster said that Joan Mosier or John Kent's wife said she would turn 'Kingston upside down within a month'. *Signed.*

29

ILLICIT GAMING

S3A/24

25 March 1657.

Certificate

By Fra. Percivall that he saw card playing at the house of John Kent, the Anchor ('Ancker'), on Friday week last, the 13th, at 9 o'clock at night. 1s in money which was lost in play was paid in drinks. Rob. Smart can prove the same. *Signed.*

Footnote: John Kent acknowledged this, and said that he took away the cards from them and that Wil. Batten and John Bettesworth were at play and stayed at his house till 11 o'clock.

30
SABBATH
BREAKING

S3A/25

25 March 1657. No name of Justice.
Information
Rob. Smart said that Nic. Foster of Kingston sold beer on the Lord's Day, both at morning and evening service time. *Signed by mark.*
    Footnote: For his offence Foster paid 10s.

31
Subject unknown

S3A/27

6 April 1657. By John Comfort, Mayor, to Mr Mollomes.[3]
Court order
Take Henry Woods and Rob. Shafte security for the appearance of Ann Woodyier alias Prescott before me on 13 Apr. *Signed.*
    Footnotes:
    (a) That recognisance is taken. *Signed by* Th[o]. Mullinns.
    (b) 'Chr. Peck pray return me this note.' *Initialled by* Th[o]. M[ullinns].
    See also App. II, no. 61.

MICHAELMAS SESSIONS 12 October 1657

For further entries in Sessions Books see Appendix II, nos 62, 63.

32
FORNICATION (?)

D11A/16/3

2 May 1657. No name of Justice.
Recognisances
        Averne Stubber of Portsea, widow, in £10.
        Tho. Jellett in £5.
        James Mills in £5.
For appearance of Averne at the next Quarter Sessions in the Guildhall, Portsmouth, and to keep the peace, especially towards John Bateman and Hester Goodeeve.
    Marginal note: 'Forfeited'.
    See also no. 35.

33
ABUSING
AUTHORITY

S3A/28

6 June 1657. Before John Comfort, esq., Mayor, and John Tawke, gent.
Recognisances
        Cha. Bentham in £20.
        Nic. Hedger in £10.
        Wil. White in £10.
For appearance of Bentham at the next Sessions.
Bound over for scandalous words spoken against Col. Clarke and the soldiery. Examination taken before the Mayor.
    Marginal note: Discharged at the Sessions, 12 Oct. 1657.

34
ASSAULT (?)

S3A/29

22 July 1657. Before John Comfort, esq., Mayor.
Recognisances
    (a) Rob. Hawkes of Portsmouth in £10.
        Wil. Haberley of the same in £5.
        James Mills of the same in £5.
For appearance of Hawkes at the next Sessions and to keep the peace, especially towards Wil. Gregory.
    Marginal note: Discharged by the Court, 12 Oct. 1657.
    (b) Mic. Morfell of Portsmouth, mariner, in £10.
        Henry Elzey of Portsmouth in £5.
        Sebastian Watts in £5.
Morfell to keep the peace towards Wil. Gregory.
    Marginal note as for (a).

---

[3] Mollomes is here wrongly spelt for Mullinns.

EASTER SESSIONS 19 April 1658

For further recognisances in Sessions Books see Appendix II, nos 64, 65.

35
FORNICATION

S3A/30

13 October 1657. Before Hugh Salesbury, esq., Mayor, and John Comfort, gent.
Recognisances
> John Farley jun. of Portsea, yeoman, in £40.
> Wil. Portbury of Portsea, yeoman, in £20.
> Rob. Shafte of Portsmouth, yeoman, in £20.

For appearance of Farley at the next Assizes or Gaol Delivery for Hampshire charged with 'carnall and unlawful knowledge of the body of one Averne Stubber widdow' and that he was not to depart [the jurisdiction of] the Court without licence.

15 October 1657. Before Hugh Salesbury, esq., Mayor, and Roger Granger, gent.
Recognisances
> (a) Averne Stubber of Portsea, widow, in £40.
> Henry Crowcher of Portsea, yeoman, in £20.
> John Rockwell of Portsea, blacksmith, in £20.

For appearance of Averne Stubber at the next Assizes or Gaol Delivery *as for Farley.*
> (b) John Batman in £10.
> Hester Goodeve in £10.

To prosecute and give evidence against Farley and Averne.
See also no. 32.

MICHAELMAS SESSIONS 11 and 25 October 1658

For further recognisances in Sessions Books see Appendix II, nos 66–68.

36
THREATENED
ASSAULT

S3A/31

No date [April 1658].
Petition against committal
By John Gollop to the Mayor against his committal to prison. One of his two adversaries had affirmed that Gollop said he would stab him and the other that he said they were Cavaliers. His committal was on slender account and in an unchristian spirit, because he would not get Capt. Hopegood to be bail and the Mayor had refused to let him appear in public before him owing to Mr Bragg's denial. *Signed.*

Footnote: Cha. Chapman swore the peace against Gollop 27 Apr. 1658 before Hugh Salesbury, esq., Mayor, John Comfort, gent., Roger Granger, gent., and Ric. Lardner, gent. Then Henry Perryn, gent., took oath that yesterday Gollopp said he could willingly stab Chapman.

EASTER SESSIONS 15 and 22 April 1659

For further entry in Sessions Books see Appendix II, no. 69.

37
REFUSING TO
ASSIST
CONSTABLE

S3A/32

9 February 1658/9. Before H. Salesbury, esq., [Deputy] Mayor, and R. Grainger.
Recognisances
> Ric. Apleford of Portchester, shipwright, in £20.
> Ric. White 'of P.', shipwright, in £10.
> Ric. Apleford jun. in £10.

For appearance [of Ric. Apleford sen.] at the next Sessions.
Bound over for refusing to assist Mr Hedger, the Constable, in the execution of his office.
Marginal note: Discharged by the Court, 15 Apr. 1659.

38
REFUSING TO
ASSIST
CONSTABLE
	S3A/33
	11 February 1658/9. Before H. S[alesbury], Deputy Mayor, and R. Granger.
	Recognisances
	      Wil. George '[of] P.', labourer, in £20.
	      Rob. Smith '[of] P.', shoem[aker], in £10.
	      Wil. Waterman, husb[andman], in £10.
	For appearance [of George] at the next Sessions.
	Footnote: Bound over for not assisting the Constable.

39
THEFT

S3B/4

1 March 1658/9. Before Hugh Salesbury, esq., [Deputy] Mayor, and John Comfort, gent.

Information

Margery, wife of John Eastman of Portsmouth, cheesemonger, said that on Thursday night 17 Feb. she had three gold rings in her purse hanging on her girdle, and when she went to bed put them under the bolster. The next night she missed her purse and rings when she was going to bed. When she put off her purse with the rings there was nobody in the bedroom, except her two small children and Mary Gold, her servant. She asked Mary several times if she knew anything of the rings. Each time she said she did not, with a smile. On the day she missed the rings she had a great company of soldiers in the house.   *Signed by mark.*

Examination

Mary Gold of Portsmouth, spinster, said she knew Margery Eastman her dame had three gold rings, but she does not know when or how she lost them.   *Signed by mark.*

S3A/34 (entry i)

1 March 1658/9. Before H. S[alesbury], Deputy Mayor, and Ric. Lardner.

Recognisances
      Mary Gold in £20.
      Rob. Kippyn of Freshwater in £10.
      Wil. Taylor in £10.
For appearance [of Mary] at the next Sessions.
Marginal note: Discharged ('dd').

40
Subject unknown

S3A/34 (entry ii)

1 March 1658/9. Before H. S[alesbury], Deputy Mayor, and Ric. Lardner.

Recognisances
      Wil. Thatcher in £20.
      Dan. Massingham in £10.
      Ric. Clare in £10.
For appearance [of Thatcher] at the next Sessions.
Marginal note: Discharged 15 Apr. 1659.

MICHAELMAS SESSIONS 10 October 1659

41
Subject unknown

S3A/35

28 June 1659. Before Josiah Child, Mayor, and Hugh Salisbury.

Recognisances[4]
      Margaret Clarke, James Austin and Ric. Coggs in £100.
For appearance of Margaret at the next Sessions and to keep the peace, especially towards James Beale.
Footnotes:
(a) 'Appeared'.
(b) Discharged by the Court, 10 Oct. 1659.

---

[4] For a reproduction of this recognisance see fig. 3, and for a transcript see App. I, no. 2(1).

42
Subject unknown

S3A/37

11 July 1659. Before H. Salesbury, esq., Deputy Mayor, and John Comfort.
Recognisances
      Tho. Richards of Soberton, maltster, in £20.
      Solomon Richards of Soberton, butcher, in £10.
      Nic. Lee 'of P.', husbandman, in £10.
  For appearance of Tho. Richards at the next Sessions. The peace was sworn against him by John Cozens 7 July 1659.
  Footnote : Discharged by the Court, 10 Oct. 1659.

43
THEFT

S3A/36 (entry i)

28 July 1659. Before Josiah Child, esq., Mayor.
Examination
Walt. Evans of Portsmouth, labourer, said that last evening he went with Edm. Austen into the orchard of Fra. Willoughby, esq., and gathered some apples but took nothing else.

S3A/39

No date. Before Peter Murford, esq., and Hugh Salesbury, esq.
Examination
Edm. Austin of Portsmouth, aged 27, confessed that on 27 July 1659 he got over the wall of the house belonging to the Commissioner for the Navy in Portsmouth and went into the orchard and beat down some apples. He was taken with Walt. Evans, an inhabitant of the Town, who went with him purposely for the apples. Neither he nor Evans saw or touched any iron hoops there which were lost about the same time.
                        Signed. Countersigned by both Justices.

[. . .] July 1659.
Recognisances
      Edm. Austin in £10.
      Tho. Parkes in £5.
      Ric. Parkes in £5.
  For appearance of Austin at the next Sessions.

10 October 1659.
Appearances
  At Sessions Edm. Austen, Tho. Parks and Edm. Austen, sen.
  Walt. Evans, Tho. Parkes and Edm. Austen bound over to reappear at the next Sessions.
  Marginal note : Discharged by the Court, 27 Apr. 1660.

44
THEFT

S3A/36 (entry ii)

28 July 1659. Before Josiah Child, esq., Mayor.
Examination
Ric. Jones, aged about 14, said that last Tuesday at Portsbridge seeing a pear-tree he went into the orchard (he knew not whose) and took some of the pears.
  Footnote : Not bound over, but discharged by the Mayor.

45
ASSAULT

S3A/40

3 September 1659. Before Jos[iah] Child, esq., Mayor.
Recognisances
      Rob. Hawks, in £20.
      Tho. Parks, in £10.
      'Jo.' Pope, in £10.
  For appearance of Hawks at the next Sessions for beating soldiers.
  Footnote : Discharged by the Court, 10 Oct. 1659.

S3A/38

3 October 1659. Before Jo[hn] Tippetts, esq., Mayor, Ro[ger] Granger, gent., and Ric. Lardner, gent.

Examinations

(a) Dan. Davis committed to prison for bringing a torn pass from the Mayor of Exeter and saying three others were on the pass when only he was. He said he was the son of Tho. ('John' *erased*)[5] Davis living in Southwark, [Surr.], sometime a linen-draper and now a kind of merchant 'and doeth adventure for France'. The man with him, Hannibal Hoskins, had served his father as a servant for $1\frac{1}{2}$ years. They have two other companions John Feld and Tho. Browne.

(b) Hannibal Hoskins said he was taken coming from Ireland and not having employment put himself to be a servant to John Davys of Southwark, merchant, and had been only one voyage to France. His companions John Browne and John Feild both live in London and were taken coming out of Bruges (? 'Burges') in the ship John of London, 200 tons with twelve guns. He was taken at sea and came from Exeter: they were robbed about 12 miles off. He had no pass, but his name was on the other pass.

(c) Dan. Davis further said that he met this Hannibal Hoskins near Andover and, as he was poor and pretended he came from Ireland, he brought him along on his pass; they were not robbed of any money.

(d) Hannibal Hoskins further said that he had been in the State's service but out of it for $1\frac{1}{2}$ years. He had not dwelt anywhere nor paid rent. Since he had lived in London he had had harvest work. He had been with Davis about a week. They were at Weyhill last Thursday.

Footnote: Committed 1 Oct. 1659 by the Mayor.

EASTER SESSIONS 27 April and 7 May 1660

For further recognisances, etc., in Sessions Books see Appendix II, nos 70–74.

S3A/41

26 November 1659. Before Ric. Lardiner, gent.

Recognisances

> Tho. Smith of Kingston upon Hull, mariner, in £20.
> John Clansy of London, mariner, in £10.
> Farrall Greene of Bristol, mariner, in £10.

For appearance of Smith at the next Sessions and to keep the peace, especially towards Rob. Long.

Tho. Long, master of the Gloucester, swore the peace against Smith 15 Nov. 1659 before John Tippetts, esq., Mayor, and Josiah Child.

Marginal note (Latin): He forfeited.

S3B/5

6 April 1660. Before John Tippetts, esq., Mayor, and Ric. Lardner, gent.

Examinations

(a) Mary, wife of John Poore of Portsmouth, tailor, said that last Wednesday about 11 p.m. John Poore, her husband, brought home two dead lambs, one black and one white. Soon after, two women came who had a quarter of a lamb. She said she did not know where her husband had got the lambs. He told her in Portsea Island but he did not know whose they were. He told her that these two women Dowsabel Wolven and Elizabeth Laster had been with him when he took the lambs.   *Signed by mark.*

(b) Dowsabel Wolven of Portsmouth, widow, said she was with John Poore and Elizabeth Laster in Portsea Island when he took the lambs. She and Elizabeth had only one quarter of the lamb, which they had eaten.   *Signed by mark.*

(c) Elizabeth Laster, wife of Tho. Laster, seaman, said she was with John Poore and Dowsabel Wolven in Portsea Island when he took the lambs in a green lane. She helped carry the lambs to Poore's house. She and Dowsabel had a quarter which they had eaten.   *Signed by mark.*

---

[5] The confusion over the forenames of Davis and Browne is found in the original documents.

Information

Tho. Steane, one of the Constables of Portsmouth, said that on that present day he went to the house of John Poore to search for some lambs that were stolen on Portsea Island. He found John Poore's wife with five quarters she was carrying out by the back way of her house in a linen cloth.   *Signed.*

Footnote: Dowsabel Wolven and Elizabeth Laster ordered to be whipped.

MICHAELMAS SESSIONS 12 October 1660

**49
ASSAULT**

S3A/42

7 May 1660. Before John Tippetts, esq., Mayor, Jo[siah] Child and Ric. Lardner.
Recognisances

  James Hateley 'of P.', seaman, in £40.
  Ric. Joyce 'of P.', butcher, in £20.
  Edw. Avery 'of P.', mariner, in £20.

For appearance of James Heatly (*sic*) at the next Assizes or General Gaol Delivery for Hampshire to answer for beating and wounding Jane, wife of Rob. Parker.

 Footnote (English and Latin): Discharged by consent of Rob. Parker and his wife.

**50
DISLOYALTY**

S3A/49

10 May 1660. Before Josiah Child.
Examinations

 (a) Alex. Paice, being at John Tarrant's house, spoke opprobrious words against the King, saying that he kept lewd company and was a bastard. Testified by Henry Hill, a soldier in Capt. Bull's Company.

 (b) John Gates about three weeks ago in the same house spoke similarly. Testified by John Hurrall, a soldier in Capt. Bull's Company, also by Tho. Alcocke, a soldier in the Deputy Governor's Company.

11 May 1660. Before Josiah Child.
Recognisances

  Alex. Payce of North Warnborough, tanner, in £40.
  Alex. Eastwoort 'of P.', yeoman, in £20.
  Chr. Wilmot 'of P.', yeoman, in £20.

For appearance [of Payce] at the next Sessions.

14 May 1660. Before John Timbrell, gent.
Recognisances

  John Gates of Alton, cordwainer, in £40.
  Chr. Wilmott 'of P.', yeoman, in £20.
  John Allum 'of P.', carrier, in £20.

For appearance [of Gates] at the next Sessions.

 Endorsement: Note from Jos[iah] Child to Mr Mullins, 12 May 1660, asking to be given notice when recognisances for the soldiers had been taken.

**51
TRADING
IRREGULARLY**

S3A/43 (attached sheet)

18 May 1660. Before John Tippetts, Mayor, and Ric. Lardner.
Examinations

 (a) Elizabeth Byssell said that she bought of Ric. Rutter at three several times within a fortnight six bundles of lambheads and 'hafting joynts' containing (?'cont.') three dozen pieces (?'pc'), for which she paid Rutter 2s a dozen.   *Signed by mark.*

 (b) Elias Fisher, servant to Elizabeth Bissell, said that about a month ago he weighed a piece of iron crow which weighed 24 lb, which he supposed was brought into the yard where he worked by Fra. Clement and Ric. Rutter.   *Signed.*

 (c) Fra. Clement said that in Easter week he was called out of the house of Ric. Sparcks by Ric. Rutter, who told him he had bought a parcel of iron of a young man, and if Clement would go with him he would give him 9d. He went with Rutter who went to the stable of Tho. Parcks and brought out a piece of iron crow for Clement to sell, but he refused, though he lent Rutter a coat to cover it with. They went to Elizabeth Bissell's, where the iron was weighed and Rutter received 2s from her for it.

Signed by mark.

31 May 1660. Before Roger Grainger, esq., Deputy Mayor.
Recognisances
    (a) Ric. Rutter 'of P.', nailer, in £20.
        Wil. Pritchet 'of P.', worsted comber, in £10.
        Wil. Dymock 'of P.', gunsmith, in £10.
For appearance [of Rutter] at the next Sessions.
Note (Latin): He forfeited, because he did not appear.
    (b) Fra. Clement 'of P.', blacksmith, in £20.
        Wil. Pritchet of the same in £10.
        Wil. Dymock of the same, gunsmith, in £10.
On condition as above.
Footnotes:
    (a) See the examination taken by Mr Tippetts, Mayor.
    (b) Clement discharged by the Court, 12 Oct. 1660, by virtue of the Act of Oblivion.
    (c) Tho. Parks in £10 to prosecute at the next Sessions.

52
DISLOYALTY

D22A/1/7

30 May 1660. Before John Tippetts, Mayor.
Examination
John Shore, seaman of H.M.S. Tiger, said that two or three days after Sir Art. Hazelrig and the other gentlemen came to Portsmouth in December last, he was at the house of Wil. White of Portsmouth, victualler, and heard White say that rather than a King should come in he would fight up to the knees in blood.   *Signed by mark.*

    John Shore further said that when the above words were spoken Peter Hayward of the Tiger and Gilbert West of the Phoenix, seamen, were there.   *Signed by mark.*
Marginal note (Latin and English): See other examination.
Recognisances
    (a) John Shore of London, in £20.
For appearance at the next Sessions to prosecute and give evidence against Wil. White.
    (b) Wil. White in £40.
        John Lewin, baker, in £20.
        Edw. Heberden in £20.
For appearance of White at the next Sessions to answer such trespasses and offences as shall be objected against him for speaking scandalous words concerning His Majesty.

53
THREATENED ARSON

S3A/43 (entry i)

31 May 1660. Before Roger Grainger, esq., Deputy Mayor.
Recognisances[6]
        John Voake in £20.
        Ric. Goldfinch in £10.
        Peter Jackman in £10.
For appearance of Voake at the next Sessions.
    Bound over for saying he would set his house on fire by testimony of John Moone and Abraham Parbus (*also* Porbus) to Mr Timbrell and by him committed.
See also nos 69, 75.

54
ADULTERY

S3A/44

21 July 1660. Before John Timbrell, gent.
Recognisances
        Nic. Lee 'of P.', yeoman, in £20.
        Henry Atkins 'of P.', labourer, in £20.

---

[6] Extra marginal note: 'Chr. Peck promised payment'. Peck was Sergeant-at-Mace.

For appearance of Elizabeth, wife of Ric. Harris 'of P.', clothier, at the next Sessions.

Footnotes:

(a) Committed by Mr Lardner for being taken a-bed with a man.

(b) Released by the Court.

55
BASTARDY

S3A/45

24 July 1660. Before Ric. Lardner, Deputy Mayor ('D.M.').

Recognisances

      Mat. Gellet in £20.

      Griffith Roades in £10.

      Wil. White in £10.

For appearance of Gellet at the next Sessions.

Footnotes:

(a) Bound over by reason Dorothy Hayter is with child and lays the child to him.

(b) Discharged by the Court, 12 Oct. 1660.

56
RIOT

S3A/1

[August 1660].

Presentment (Latin; damaged)

Presents John La[mbert], Tho. Pay, lately of Portsmouth, shipwright, Nat. [Strong], Tho. Langford and [Tho.] Eastwood, shipwright, as malefactors and disturbers of the King's peace, holding illicit assemblies to the serious injury of John Osmont contrary to the Statute.[7]

    Note over each surname: By confession.

    Endorsement: True bill.

S3A/46

7 August 1660. Before Roger Granger, Deputy Mayor.

Recognisances

      John Lambert in £20.

      John White in £10.

      Sam. Taylor in £10.

For appearance of Lambert at the next Sessions.

14 August 1660. Before Ric. Lardner, gent.

Recognisances

      Tho. Pay in £20.

      Israel Pownall in £10.

      Wil. Cooper in £10.

For appearance of Pay at the next Sessions.

15 August 1660. Before Roger Granger, gent.

Recognisances

(a) Nat. Stronge in £20.

      Tho. Hatch in £10.

      Hezekiah Parnell in £10.

For appearance of Strong at the next Sessions.

(b) Tho. Eastwood in £20.

      Theophilus Sacheverell in £10.

      Hezekiah Parnell in £10.

For appearance of Eastwood at the next Sessions.

S3A/48 (entry i)

15 August 1660. Before Roger Granger.

Recognisances

      Tho. Langford in £20.

      Hezekiah Purnell in £10.

      Tho. Hatch in £10.

For appearance of Langford at the next Sessions.

---

[7] The reference to a Statute here is probably a mistake; no Statute relating to riot or unlawful assembly was in force between 1603 and 1714 and such cases were normally dealt with under common law (W. S. Holdsworth, *History of English law*, viii (2nd edn, 1937), pp. 324–331).

57
Subject unknown

S3A/48 (entry ii)

14 August 1660. Before John Tippetts, esq., Mayor.

Recognisances

Paul Hatton in £20.
Sebastian Watts in £10.
Tho. Tomes in £10.

For appearance of Hatton at the next Sessions.

Marginal note (Latin): He forfeited because he did not appear.

58
Subject unknown

S3A/47

15 August 1660. Before Roger Granger, gent.

Recognisances

Ann, wife of Thomas Jones (*no sum stated*).
Dan. Baker 'of P.', cook, in £20.
Tho. Cooke 'of P.', glover, in £20.

For appearance of Ann at the next Sessions and to keep the peace, especially towards Elizabeth Harris.

Footnote: Released by the Court.

59
THEFT

S3A/50

16 August 1660. Before John Tippetts, esq., Mayor, Roger Granger, gent., and Ric. Lardner, gent.

Examination

Anne Okeford, servant-maid to Edith Fowler of Portsmouth, said that last night she took out of her dame's chamber three linen changes, some head clothes, a waistcoat and a woollen petticoat and took them to one Goody Davis' house.

Sentence

To be whipped till her body be bloody.

Information

Given by Edith Fowler, that the clothes taken are worth about 10½d.

60
DISLOYALTY

D22A/1/8a

24 August 1660. Before John Timbrell, gent.

Information

Sarah, wife of Rob. Pitter of Portsmouth, said that three weeks ago last Monday she was in the fields of Tho. Ray of Fratton, reaping wheat, when it came on to rain. She, with Rob. Annett and his wife, John Cleverley, John Wheatland, Tho. Ray and one Goody Phillipps, went and sat down for shelter under a hedge. Cleverley said 'I heare that there are seaven mens heads to be cut off this weeke, wee cutt off their heads and they cutt off our heads of this side, and ere long they'l cutt off of their side againe and soe wee shall have cutting off of heads againe as long as I live'. About a fortnight ago there was a man at her house (she had forgotten his name) who told her that Cleverley had been in the time of the wars an informer about the country and had undone many a gentleman and went under the name of an Anabaptist or Quaker.

Signed by mark; countersigned by the Justice.

D22A/1/8b

24 August 1660. Before John Tippetts, esq., Mayor.

Informations

(a) Dinah, wife of Rob. Phillipps of Portsmouth, seaman, said that about three weeks ago she was leazing in the field of Tho. Ray and heard him say that there were seven heads to be cut off. Another man there (she did not know his name) said the King went or was to go to Oxford whilst it was done. John Cleverley was there and said that there would be cutting off of heads so long as he lived, and afterwards too when he was dead. *Signed by mark.*

(b) Margaret, wife of Rob. Annet of Portsmouth, *confirmed the words that John Cleverley said.* *Signed by mark.*

No date. Before John Tippetts, esq., Mayor and John Timbrell, gent.

Examination

John Cleverley of Portsmouth said that about three weeks ago he was reaping in a field of Tho. Ray at Milton, in the parish of Portsea, where he heard Ray say that there were seven men to suffer. Afterwards Cleverley said to Sarah Pitter *what she reported.*

Signed by mark.

D22A/1/8c

[24 August 1660]. Before the Justice aforesaid (*i.e. John Tippetts*), the day and year aforesaid.

Information

John Wheatland of Portsmouth said he was with the others above when he heard Rob. Annett's wife say that the King was gone to Oxford. *He too confirmed what John Cleverley said.*

Signed.

No date. Before John Tippetts, esq., Mayor, and John Timbrell, gent.

Information

Rob. Annett (*signs* Annott) of Portsmouth *confirmed what his wife, Tho. Ray and John Cleverley said. The field is said to be* in Milton ('Fratton' *scored through*).

Signed.

[. . .] August 1660. Before John Tippetts, esq., Mayor.

Recognisances

> John Cleverley, box-maker, in £20.
> John Barfoote in £10.
> David Baker in £10.

For appearance of Cleverley at the next Sessions to answer such trespasses and offences as shall be objected against him.

Footnote (English and Latin): Released by the Court; see the examinations.

61

ABUSING THE MAYOR

S3A/51

11 September 1660. Before John Tippetts, Mayor, and Roger Granger, gent.

Recognisances

> James Yeatman in £20.
> John Farrant in £10.
> Rob. Grigg in £10.

For appearance of Yeatman at the next Sessions.

Bound over for abusing the Mayor at weighing of his bread on 6 Sept. 1660, when it was found to be light. He refused to have it weighed or taken from him. He accused the Mayor of robbing him and threatened that he would question the Mayor, when he was out of his time.

EASTER SESSIONS 25(?) April 1661

62

APPRENTICESHIP

S3A/52

16 October 1660. Before Ric. Lardner, esq., Mayor, and Josiah Child, esq.

Order of Justices

Wil. Sweete, son of Ric. Sweete deceased, was placed as apprentice to Edw. Wigmore. For this Wigmore received certain goods to the value of £5. For unreasonably correcting the child, as proved by his body in Court, it is ordered that the child be discharged.

The master is to return the deed of apprenticeship and the goods to the Overseers of the Poor by tomorrow night. He is meanwhile to find sureties for his appearance to answer for the beating of the child.

Signed by Tho. Mullinns, clerk.

20 October 1660. Before John Timbrell, esq., Deputy Mayor.

Recognisances

> Edw. Wigmore in £20.
> Rob. Levesley 'of P.', mariner, in £10.
> Wil. Sheppard in £10.

For appearance of Wigmore at the next Sessions.

Marginal notes (English and Latin):

(a) Released by the Court at the Sessions, 25 Apr. 1661.

(b) He owes 8*d.*

63
THEFT

S3A/53

10 November 1660. No name of Justice.

Examinations

(a) Fra. Tither, aged about 14, confessed that on 9 Oct. he took two spikes from the yard of Mr David Lucas and today took four ringbolts out of his outhouse. He sold the two spikes to Justinian Wyat, a smith, for 1*d*. Wil. Little, a servant of Lucas, took the ringbolts from him. *Signed by mark.*

(b) Wil. Little, aged about 25, said that on this day 10 Nov. he caught Fra. Tither taking the ringbolts and took them from him, knowing that they belonged to his master. *Signed by mark.*

Sentence

Ordered by the Mayor and Mr Timbrell to be whipped.

64
THEFT

S3A/54

7 December 1660. Before Ric. Lardner, esq., Mayor.

Information

Sebastian Watts of Portsmouth, turner, said that on this day he met Tho. Limeburner at Watts' back-gate. Limeburner opened the gate with a key to it. In the last half year he had lost cabbages and herbs out of his garden; they must have been taken by Limeburner, because he knew of no one else with a key. *Signed.*

Recognisances

Tho. Limeburner in £20.
Ric. Joyce in £10.
Christian Cray, widow, in £10.

For the appearance of Limeburner at the next Sessions.

Marginal note: Released by the Court, 20 Apr. 1661.

65
THEFT

S3A/55

11 December 1660. Before Ric. Lardner, esq., Mayor.

Recognisances

Henry Acton 'of P.' in £20.
Wil. Cozens in £10.
Derek ('Derricke') Curtis in £10.

For appearance of Ann, wife of Henry Acton, at the next Sessions to answer such trespasses and offences as shall be objected against her.

Bound over as Ann Acton was charged with feloniously taking a kever found in her house from Wil. Ransteed, by information of the said Ransteed and his wife. She said she took it out of the street.

Footnote: Released 25 Apr. 1661.

66
TREASON

S3A/56

3 January 1660/1. No name of Justice.

Informations

(a) Tho. Harris, soldier under Maj. Fincher, said that on this day in the house of John White he heard White say in dispute with his wife, Mary, that she had intent to kill the King. *Signed.*

(b) John Knight, labourer, *confirmed this evidence.* *Signed by mark.*

S3A/57

14 January 1660/1. Before Ric. Lardner, esq., Mayor.

Recognisances

Tho. Tomes (*also* Tommes) in £20.
John Merricke in £20.

For appearance of Mary, wife of John White of Portsmouth, block maker, at the next Sessions to answer such trespasses and offences as shall be objected against her.

Marginal note: Released by proclamation at the Court, 25 Apr. 1661.

67
THEFT

S3A/58

9 January 1660/1. Before Ric. Lardner, esq., Mayor.
Recognisances
        Edw. Newe of Portsmouth, blacksmith, in £20.
        John Rockwell of the same, blacksmith, in £10.
        Phil. Elmes of the same, cutler, in £10.
For appearance of Newe at the next Sessions to answer such trespasses and offences as shall be objected against him.
Bound over for being taken with a parcel of lead which he said he bought of a seaman.
Footnote: 25 Apr. 1661. Released by the Court by proclamation.

68
THEFT

S3A/59

25 January 1660/1. Before Ric. Lardner, esq., Mayor.
Examinations
(a) John Sampson of Portsmouth, soldier, said that last Wednesday night he and his wife took from the house of John Buttcher where they lodged a pair of sheets, a pillow, a pillow-tie, a towel, a curtain, a small pewter dish and a small skillet, carrying them on board the ship Henrietta Maria, intending to go in the ship to Guinea ('Guiennea'). *Signed by mark.*
(b) Rebecca, wife of John Sampson of Portsmouth, *confirmed the above evidence.*
Signed by mark.

Information
Frances, wife of John Buttcher of Portsmouth, bricklayer, said that John Sampson and Rebecca his wife lodged with her since last Michaelmas and last Thursday morning she found them gone. She missed the articles (*as listed above*) and got a letter from the Mayor of Portsmouth to send Sampson ashore.
Marginal note: Sampson being a soldier was punished by the Governor and turned out of the Garrison.
Sentence
The Mayor and Justices ordered that his wife be publicly whipped, which was done accordingly.

69
DRUNKEN BEHAVIOUR

S3A/60

1 February 1660/1. Before Ric. Lardner, esq., Mayor.
Informations
(a) Ric. Penticost said that on Wednesday night last he was at the house of John Voake and saw him drunk and swearing.
(b) John Howell said that last night he (*i.e. John Voake?*) broke open his door, broke the looking-glass, nailed up his door and called his wife bitch and whore. He was very drunk and swore.

7 February 1660/1. Before Ric. Lardner, esq., Mayor, and John Timbrell.
Recognisances
        John Voake in £20.
        Phil. Elmes in £10.
        Ralph Fry 'of P.', tailor, in £10.
For appearance of Voake at the next Sessions to answer such trespasses and offences as shall be objected against him.
Marginal note: Released by the Court, 25 Apr. 1661.
See also nos 53, 75.

70
DISLOYALTY

S3A/61

8 February 1660/1. Before Ric. Lardner, esq., Mayor.
Information
James Supple of Portsmouth, soldier, said that at the beginning of January last, when the King was in Portsmouth, he was with two of His Majesty's servants in the house of Mat. Symonds in Portsmouth. One Dan. Winston, who drew the beer there, said that he had served the King and Parliament and that he hoped it would come round that he would serve the King and Parliament again. *Signed.*

Examination

Dan. Winston of Portsmouth, soldier, said that then he served the King, but if the King did call a Parliament he would serve the King and Parliament again.

Signed.

18 February 1660/1.

Recognisances

>Dan. Winston in £20.
>
>Wil. Reeve 'of P.', rope maker, in £10.
>
>John Knight 'of P.', victualler, in £10.

For appearance of Winston at the next Sessions to answer such trespass and offences as shall be objected against him.

Marginal note: Released by proclamation 25 Apr. 1661.

71

UNLAWFUL RELIGIOUS ASSEMBLY

S3A/62

10 February 1660/1. Before Ric. Lardner, esq., Mayor, and John Timbrell, gent.

Informations

(a) Ric. Young said that this day, between 10 and 11 in the morning, there were met together in the house of Tho. Young in Portsmouth: Tho. Young, Humf. Jones, Edw. Yeomans, Sam. Funter, Wil. Chace, Rob. Smith and John Benger. He heard them speak but does not know what they said, so he had them brought to the Main Guard and afterwards they were delivered over to the Mayor. *Signed.*

(b) James Floyde of Portsmouth, soldier, *confirmed the above.*

Examinations

(a) Tho. Young, Humf. Jones, Edw. Yeomans, all of Portsmouth, Sam. Funter of Portsea, Wil. Chace and Rob. Smith of Portsmouth and John Benger of Portsea all said that they met as stated, but the end of their meeting was to serve their God.

On being asked whether they would take the oath of allegiance to the King, they all said they could not swear for conscience' sake.

Marginal note: 25 Apr. 1661. Released by the Court.

(b) Wil. Jenens said that yesterday he was in an assembly contrary to the King's laws, but it was not an unlawful assembly. Asked to take the oath of allegiance, he said he could not swear for or against any man.

(c) Jonas Goffe, Wil. Rutter, Wil. Lun and Tho. Cozens were at the meeting. They refused to take the oath, saying that for conscience' sake they could take no oath at all.

(d) Elizabeth Greene, Elizabeth Lun, Mary Found, Dorothy Rutter and Mary Lun were all at the meeting yesterday at the house of Wil. Jenens. They all said they could not take the oath of allegiance for conscience' sake.

Footnote: Released by the Court.

72

ASSAULT

S3A/63

1 March 1660/1. Before Ric. Lardner, esq., Mayor.

Recognisances

>John Hunt of St Magnus, London, mariner, in £40.
>
>Isaac Bell in £20.
>
>James Fooks of Ratcliff, Mdx, mariner, in £20.

For appearance of Hunt at the next Sessions to answer such trespasses and offences as shall be objected against him.

Footnote: Bound over for beating a boy, see Capt. Peacock's Coroner's Inquest.

Marginal note (Latin): He forfeited.

S3A/64

28 March 1661.

Certificate

Certificate by John Beere that John Hunt, late midshipman on H.M.S. Marmaduke, now belongs to H.M. Frigate Cygnet ('Signett'), commander Capt. John Beare.

73
THEFT

S3A/65

29 March 1661. Before Ric. Lardner, esq., Mayor, and John Tippetts, gent.
Examination
John Ellis of Hull, Yorks., seaman, said that between 8 and 9 last night, Wil. Somerhill, Jonathan Orrell, Tho. Williams and himself, all of H.M.S. Matthias, took the ship's boat and went to a French ship at anchor in the harbour, cut off the cable at the head of the ship, weighed the anchor and carried both away. The anchor they put on a fly-boat in the harbour, selling it to its boatswain Sam. Burroughs for 10s. The cable they took to the ship Matthias and made it fast under water to the westernmost buoy of that ship.   *Signed by mark.*
   Footnote (scored through) : To remain in prison.

25 April 1661. Before the Mayor and Recorder.
Recognisances
       John Ellis in £20.
       John Hampton in £10.
       Tho. Jones in £10.
For appearance [of Ellis] at the next Sessions.
Marginal notes :
(a) *(English and Latin)* Paid on his recognisance.
(b) *Refers to* John Hampton; *not fully legible.*

S3A/66

[29 March 1661]. Before the Mayor and Justices aforesaid (*i.e. Ric. Lardner and John Tippetts*), the day and year aforesaid.
Examination
Sam. Burroughs (*signs* Bourres) of Ipswich, Suff., mariner, said that about 8 last night four young men came in a boat to a fly-boat in Portsmouth Harbour, called the Willing Wind (*?*'Willingnind'), and brought aboard an anchor weighing about 1 cwt 3 qr which he bought for 10s.   *Signed.*

2 April (recte May?) 1661.
Recognisances
       Sam. Burres of Ipswich, Suff., mariner, in £20.
       Edw. Wilkinson of the same, mariner, in £10.
       Bart. Brome of the same, seaman, in £10.
For appearance of Sam. Burges (*sic*) at the next Sessions to answer such trespasses and offences as shall be objected against him.
   Marginal note (Latin) : He forfeited.

MICHAELMAS SESSIONS 11 October 1661

For further entry in Sessions Books see Appendix II, no. 75.

74
ASSAULT

S3A/67

10 May 1661. Before Ric. Lardner, esq., Mayor.
Recognisances
       John Munday 'of P.', maltster, in £20.
       Tho. Hart 'of P.', gent., in £20.
For appearance of Mary, wife of Henry Johnson, at the next Sessions to answer such trespasses and offences as shall be objected against her.
   Bound over for kicking Mary ('Marie'), wife of Geo. Northcotte, who now lay sick.
   Footnote : Mr Archer has been with her and she told him that the kick was not where her swelling was. On the same day.

75	S3A/68
WIFE-BEATING,	**9 July 1661.** Before Ric. Lardner, esq., Mayor.
THREATENED	*Recognisances*
ARSON AND	
DRUNKENNESS	

John Voake in £20.

Geo. Acre of Cosham in £10.

John Allum in £10.

For appearance of Voake at the next Sessions to answer such trespasses and offences as shall be objected against him.

Bound over for beating his wife and threatening to burn his goods. He has been bound over at almost every Sessions and often drunk.

Marginal note: Released by the Court.

See also nos 53, 69.

76	S3A/69
THEFT	**27 July 1661.** Before Wil. Michell, gent.
	Recognisances

Phil. Curtis of Portsea, mason, in £20.

Ric. Clapshaw of Portsea, wheelwright, in £10.

Tho. Goldfinch of Portsea, carpenter, in £10.

For appearance of Curtis at the next Sessions to answer such trespasses and offences as shall be objected against him.

Bound over for taking part of a wheat-sheaf from the land of Wil. Holmes yesterday, 26 July.

Marginal note: Released by the Court.

77	S3A/70
POPERY AND	**No date.** No name of Justice.
THEFT	*Information*

Wil. Hawley wrote (owing to lameness) to the Mayor that this same afternoon one of the Burgesses, Tho. Jones, drank the health of the Pope and Cardinal Mazarin. This made people leave the kitchen and when they were gone Jones went to the buttery and stole a goose sent to be dressed for some gentlemen the next day.

13 September 1661. Before Mr Mayor, Mr Granger, Mr Tawke, Mr Comfort, Mr Salesbury and Mr Biggs.[8]

Informations

(a) Barbara Hawley made oath that Jones drank a health to the Pope and Mazarin.

(b) Jones confessed he took away the goose.

Footnote: Committed to the Town Hall till sureties could be found.

No date. Before the Mayor.

Recognisances

Tho. Jones in £20.

Sam. Burningham in £10.

John Hampton in £10.

For appearance [of Jones] at the next Sessions.

Footnotes:

(a) (*Latin*) He acknowledged on the same day before the Mayor.

(b) Released by the Court.

---

[8] Apart from one or two cases concerning theft from the Dockyard, this is the only instance where non-justices hear an examination. In this case, only the Mayor, Ric. Lardner, was a J.P. The others were Aldermen, though with the exception of Sam. Biggs they had previously been Mayors. In October 1661, Biggs was removed from office owing to an irregular election and of the rest all except Comfort and Salesbury were removed in September 1662 under the Corporations Act, 1661 (13 Cha. II, st. 2, c.1).

EASTER SESSIONS 10 April 1662

78
ABUSING
AUTHORITY

S3A/72

22 October 1661. Before John Timbrell, esq., Mayor.
Recognisances
      Rob. Wilkins in £20.
      James Hollaway in £10.
      Ric. White in £10.
For appearance of Wilkins at the next Sessions.
Bound over 'for giving the Justices ill langauadge' at the opening of the Law-day and threatening them.
    Footnote: 'Do your worst I care not what you can doe to me'.
    Marginal note: Released at Sessions, 10 Apr. 1662.
See also App. II, no. 75.

79
Subject unknown

S3A/71

25 October 1661. Before John Timbrell.
Recognisances
      James Biggs in £20.
      David Clements in £10.
      John Shenke in £10.
For appearance of Biggs at the next Sessions and in the meantime to keep the peace towards James Edwards.
    Footnote: Released at Sessions, 10 Apr. 1662.

80
BASTARDY

D11A/16/4

15 January 1661/2. Before Fra. Holt, esq., Deputy Mayor, and Hugh Salesbury, gent.
Examination
Mary Addams of Castle Cary, Som., singlewoman, said she lived at the Unicorn in Brockenhurst ('Brockhurst') and was with child begotten by Phil. Acreman of Aller ('Auler'), Som., weaver, who promised her marriage. Further Roger Ingland of Portsmouth, soldier, who married her own natural mother had lain with her since she was with child at the Unicorn abovementioned and had knowledge of her body.
          Signed by mark.

81
BLASPHEMY

S3A/73

11 March 1661/2. Before John Timbrell, esq., Mayor, and Fra. Holt, gent.
Recognisances
      Henry Ransteed in £20.
      Tho. Gellett in £10.
      Rob. Uphman in £10.
For appearance of Ransteed at the next Sessions.
Bound over for saying that there was neither God nor Devil nor heaven nor hell and other lewd words.
    Footnote: Released by order of the Mayor.

MICHAELMAS SESSIONS 14 October 1662

82
THEFT

S3A/74

26 July 1662. Before John Timbrell, esq., Mayor, and Fra. Holt, gent.
Information
Elizabeth, wife of Tho. Ramson, Eleanor, wife of Rob. Jackson, and another woman stole wheat from the sheaves in the common fields of Portsmouth, by the oaths of John Hollawaye and Wil. Holmes.   *Signed by* T[ho.] Mullins.

83
ABUSING
THE MAYOR

S3A/76

No date. Before Wil. Michell, gent., and Hugh Salesbury, gent.

Recognisances[9]

Justinian Wyat in £20.

Henry Jenner in £10.

Simon Musgrave in £10.

For appearance of Wyat at the next Sessions.

Bound over for abusing the Mayor and threatening him about the burying of a man, and refusing to come when sent for.

Footnote: Released by the Court.

84
ABUSING
THE MAYOR

S3A/77

16 August 1662. Before Fra. Holt, gent., and Hugh Salesbury, gent.

Information

Wil. Ransteed of Portsmouth, labourer, said that on Thursday last, 14 Aug., John Allum said to Mr John Timbrell, the present Mayor, that he did not care a turd for him nor for any Constable in the town. *Signed by mark.*

Added below the signature: In the presence of the said Justices he (*i.e. Allum*) threatened that he would sue the Mayor and would sue Ransteed for pounding his hog and would make him pay for it 'and other foule speeches'.

25 August 1662. Before Hugh Salesbury.

Recognisances

John Allum in £20.

Wil. Mose in £10.

Ric. Thomas in £10.

For appearance of Allum at the next Sessions.

Marginal note (Latin): He forfeited because he did not appear.

Footnote (English and Latin): After 1 Nov. next, none to keep hogs in Town; 'drawe up an order to be sett upp'.

85
ASSAULT AND
ABUSING
THE MAYOR

S3A/78

9 September 1662. Before John Timbrell, esq., Mayor, Fra. Holt and Hugh Salesbury.

Information

Sebastian Watts had been ordered to appear before the Mayor and had failed to do so. Complaint that yesterday he offered violence to Widow Barlow, threatened to beat out her brains and threw water on her. He is known as a common disturber of the peace. Now present in Court he mocked at the Mayor.

Footnote: Christian Cray, widow, made oath she went in fear of her life for the said Sebastian Watts, 16 Sept.

S3A/79

1 October 1662. Before Ant. Haberley, esq., Mayor.

Recognisances

Sebastian Watts in £20.

Henry Warren in £10.

John Wyatt in £10.

For appearance of Watts at the next Sessions and to keep the peace, especially towards Christian Cray, widow.

Footnotes (Latin):

(a) He owes on his recognisance.

(b) Sick: his forfeiture respited until the next Sessions.

(c) He did not appear at the Sessions, 4 May 1663.

See also no. 103.

---

[9] This recognisance is headed by these memoranda probably for the Court Leet jury (no date [*circa* 1662?]):
To remember James Plover for his hogsty. Goody Byshopp for the same. Aleme for his shop. Rob. Peter for his dung ('doung').
Henty for the same.

86
THEFT

S3B/6

26 September 1662. Before John Timbrell, esq., Mayor, and Hugh Salesbury, gent.
Information
Godf. Morgan of Portsmouth, rope maker, said that on 16 Sept. he asked Mr Brown, one of the Constables of the Borough, to go with him to search for certain nails, being His Majesty's goods marked with the broad arrow,[10] according to Royal Proclamation[11] and orders given him by the Principal Officers of the Navy. On the same day in the nailer's shop of Elizabeth Bissell on the Point they found a small parcel of nails of the value of 10d or 11d, most of them (but not all) marked with the broad arrow, which they seized in accordance with the said Proclamation and orders. She asked them not to take them away, being such a small quantity.
Signed by mark.

Examination
Elizabeth Bissell of Portsmouth, widow, said that about a fortnight ago a man, whose name she did not know, brought a parcel of nails to her shop for sale, for which she gave him 6d and a cup of beer. She did not know the broad arrow or the King's mark was on them and knew nothing of the Royal Proclamation.

87
THEFT

S3A/80

27 September 1662. Before John Timbrell, esq., Mayor.
Information
Edw. Byland of Portsmouth, shipwright, said that about five weeks ago Ric. Lockier, leaving the Dockyard when men were leaving work at night, had with him a bag of chips amongst which was a parcel of spikes and nails which Byland thought must be the King's so he seized them and put them in the stores at the Dockyard. *Signed.*

27 September 1662. Before the Mayor and Wil. Michell, gent.
Examination
Ric. Lockier said that, being a block maker working in the Dockyard, he from time to time over twelve months had found spikes and nails and thrown them in a corner. About five weeks ago he took them up and put them in his bag of chips. They would have been spoiled and lost, if he had not taken them. *Signed.*

S3A/81
29 September 1662. Before John Timbrell, esq., Mayor.
Recognisances
     Ric. Lockier in £20.
     James Yeatman in £10.
     Mat. Hacker in £10.
For appearance of Lockier at the next Sessions.
Footnote: Released by the Court, 14 Oct. 1662.

EASTER SESSIONS 4 and 11 May 1663

88
ABUSING
AUTHORITY

S3A/82

18 October 1662. Before Ant. Haberley, esq., Mayor, John Timbrell, gent., Wil. Michell, gent., and Hugh Salesbury, gent.
Recognisances
     John Kent in £20.
     Tho. Delling in £10.
     Amos Jefferyes in £10.
For appearance of Kent and his wife Jane at the next Sessions.
Bound over for abusing the Jury this present Law Day.
Footnote: Kent and his wife released by the Court, 4 May 1663.

---

[10] The use of the broad arrow as a Government mark goes back to the time of Sir Philip Sidney who, as Master of Ordnance in 1583, adopted the 'pheon' or broad arrow from his coat of arms for this purpose. It is still used.
[11] See *Calendar of State Papers Domestic*, 1661–62, p. 152. Proclamation for discovery and punishment of the embezzlement of Navy stores: certain modes are to be adopted in manufacture to distinguish the King's rope, sails and pendants; other goods to be marked with the broad arrow where possible (*Proclamation collection*, p. 165).

89
ASSAULT

S3B/7

4 November 1662. By Ant. Haberley, Mayor.
Warrant for arrest
Directed to the Constables of the Borough and Liberties. To arrest and bring Rob. Parker before him and to commit him to gaol until he finds sureties. On complaint of Elizabeth, wife of Tho. Weyman, that he had that day beaten and wounded her and drawn blood, so that she goes in fear of her life and limbs.
Signed and sealed (wax seal on document: on a chevron two crossed swords, between three heads(?)).

S3A/83

5 November 1662. Before Ant. Haberley, esq., Mayor.
Recognisances
   Rob. Parker in £20.
   Ric. Joyce in £10.
   Rob. Uphman in £10.
For appearance of Parker at the next Sessions and to keep the peace, especially towards Elizabeth, wife of Tho. Weyman.

90
THEFT

S3A/84

24 March 1662/3. No name of Justice.
Recognisance
Tho. Willard bound over because on a search thirteen nails, marked with the King's mark, were found in the house of Mrs Elizabeth Lovegrove, where he lives, and three or four more nails similarly marked were taken out of a fence which he made against part of Portsea churchyard.

S3A/85

24 March 1662/3. Before Ant. Haberley, esq., Mayor, and Wil. Michell, gent.
Recognisances[12]
   Tho. Willard in £20.
   Tho. Mills in £10.
   Elizabeth Lovegrove, widow, in £10.
For appearance of Willard at the next Sessions.
Footnote: Released by proclamation at the Sessions, 4 May 1662 (*recte* 1663).

91
CONTEMPT
AND
DISLOYALTY

S3A/86

31 March 1663. Before Ant. Haberley, esq., Mayor, and Wil. Michell, gent.
Recognisances
   Art. Hawtrey in £20.
   Henry Whitehorne in £10.
   Wil. Ratten in £10.
For appearance of Hawtrey at the next Sessions.
Bound over for not obeying a warrant directed to the Constable.
Footnotes:
 (a) 4 May 1663. Committed for refusing the oath of allegiance and supremacy. Tho. Mordlin the like and disobeying a warrant directed to the Constable.
 (b) 11 May 1663. Art. Hawtrey released, having taken the oath of supremacy before the Mayor and Wil. Michell.

92
THEFT

S3A/87

2 April 1663. Before Ant. Haberley, esq., Mayor.
Information
Susan Earle was summoned before the Mayor for having some scaffolding 'cloven out' and brought to her house to the quantity of half a dozen burthens, which she said Wil. Worth brought.

---

[12] Under this recognisance are the following items (no date [*circa* 1663]):
 (i) Plea of debt. Ric. Jennance by his attorney, Rob. Uphman, claims £5 owing by Nic. Elsey of Fareham, sawyer.
 (ii) Wil. Skilton complaining against Wil. Richards in a plea of trespass on the case: a hat and hat-case lost to be brought from London, 1 Dec. 1662, worth 11s 4d; fee for release 3s 6d. Defendant promised satisfaction.

John Moody and John Colbrooke said that they saw at her house yesterday, 1 Apr., both timber and planks of the scaffold of the Garrison.

She confessed that she sells beer retail and was not bound over this Lent because she had a sick person in her house.

S3A/88

4 April 1663. Before John Timbrell, gent.
Recognisances
  Susan Earle 'of P.', widow, in £20.
  Tho. Keden, gent, in £10.
  Rob. Hawks in £10.
For appearance of Susan at the next Sessions.

Committed 1 Apr. for receiving scaffold boards and timber cleft for burning by a soldier.
  Footnote: Released by proclamation at Sessions, 4 May 1663.

MICHAELMAS SESSIONS 12 and 21 October 1663

93
ASSAULTING AUTHORITY

S3A/89

1 May 1663. Before Ant. Haberley, esq., Mayor.
Recognisances
  Zacharias Later in £20.
  John Collins in £10.
  Edm. Wormell in £10.
For appearance of Later at the next Sessions.

Bound over for beating the Beadle and saying to the Mayor that he would beat the Mayor's fool's coat and him too.
  Footnotes:
  (a) Forfeited for not appearing at Sessions, 12 Oct. 1663.
  (b) (*Latin*) It is respited until the next Sessions.
  (c) 25 May 1664, continued to the next Sessions.

94
SLANDER

D22A/1/9

15 May 1663. Before Ant. Haberley, esq., Mayor, Fra. Holt, gent., and Hugh Salesbury, gent.
Information
Matthias Wotton of Portsmouth, seaman, said that last week when he was upon the Point without Pointgate he met John Thorne, a barber living there, who asked him where he had been as he had not seen him for a long time. Thorne then told him that one of his (Wotton's) great enemies, Serg. Selman, was dead and that Capt. Whitehead had done Sir Phil. Honywood's business. He was sure Sir Phil. would never be Governor of Portsmouth for he was cashiered in Charles I's time for being a coward and afterwards was a poor planter in Barbados. Honywood later came to London in a leathern doublet and by favour of a lady of the Court became a captain of a foot company and by Sir Cha. Berkeley's favour Deputy Governor of Portsmouth. The King was sorry he had knighted him, thinking he was another brother. He was called 'the mistaken knight'. This Thorne said in the presence of Walt. Harford who asked him how he dare say such words. He answered that he would justify them at the Market Cross.   *Signed.*

S3B/40

No date. Before the Mayor and Justices aforesaid (*i.e. Ant. Haberley, Fra. Holt and Hugh Salesbury*).
Examination
John Thorne of Portsmouth, barber, said that on 23 Apr. last Matthias Wotton came to him on the Point and told him that Capt. Whitehead was come to town again and that the sergeant who accused Wotton was dead. Wotton said 'the Devill (I thinke) has carried him away, Capt. Whitehead is disbanded and I doe heare Sir Phillip is rubbed off . . . Major Burridge spoke to me to be entered into his

company againe'. Last Saturday, as Thorne heard that he was held responsible for spreading this story, he taxed Wotton about it in the presence of Mr John Arnold and Peter Haward. Wotton said he had had it from Thorne and reported it at Hawks' house and it was in all the officers' mouths. *Signed.*

S3A/90
16 May 1663. Before Ant. Haberley, esq., Mayor.
Recognisances
      John Thorne in £20.
      Tho. Gellet in £10.
      Ric. West in £10.
For appearance of Thorne at the next Sessions.
Footnotes (Latin):
(a) He forfeited.
(b) See the examinations.
See also no. 105.

EASTER SESSIONS 25 April and 2 May 1664

95
ASSAULT

S3A/91
30 October 1663. Before Henry Perin, esq., Mayor.
Recognisances
      Tho. Fiveash in £20.
      Henry Whitehorne in £10.
      John Collins in £10.
For appearance of Fiveash at the next Sessions.
Bound over for beating Henry Isemonger, wounding him in the eye, bruising and threatening him.

96
BASTARDY

S3A/92
19 December 1663. Before Henry Perin, esq., Mayor, and Wil. Michell, gent.
Recognisances
      Fra. Percivall in £40.
      James Humfry, surgeon, in £20.
      John Aldridge, chandler, in £20.
For appearance of Percivall at the next Sessions.
Bound over because Anne Barnat says she is with child by him.
Footnotes:
(a) The child being dead and the parish not chargeable, Mr Percivall was released.
(b) *(Scored through)* Remember to take 2s 6d for my fee.
(c) *(Latin)* He acknowledged on the day and year above said.
(d) Afterwards released by the Court.

97
FORNICATION
AND BRIBERY

D11A/16/5
15 January 1663/4. Before Henry Perin, esq., Mayor.
Information
John Meader of Portsmouth, block maker, said that about Christmas last he heard James Austin of Portsmouth, baker, say this. Austin was one Sunday last summer at Mr Alcorne's works in the Isle of Portsea and coming back lost his way. On looking round he at last saw Gatcombe Trees and, then knowing where he was, he leapt over a hedge on to his way. Turning about he saw a man on a maid with his breeches down. When the man saw him he pulled up his breeches and leapt into a wheatfield. The maid stood up and faced him but said nothing. The man was a mercer in Portsmouth, the initials of his name H.C. Hers were A.T. and she was daughter of a Portsmouth Mayor now dead. The man met him and took him to a tavern, gave him a pint of wine and offered him £5 to hold his tongue. Later he met the maid who jogged him in the arm to speak to him and went with him to the lane between Mr Tawk's house and Mrs Trigg's house where she offered him four half-crowns not to speak of the affair. *Signed.*

98
Subject unknown

S3A/93 (entry i)

8 February 1663/4. Before Henry Perin, esq., Mayor.
Recognisances

> Wil. Cozens in £20.
> Tho. Joyner in £10.
> James Holloway in £10.

For appearance of Cozens at the next Sessions.

99
Subject unknown

S3A/93 (entry ii)

No date [circa 8 February 1663/4]. No name of Justice.
Recognisances

> Walt. Thirman in £20.
> Ric. Young in £10.
> Edw. Cotton in £10.

100
DISLOYALTY

S3A/94

8 February 1663/4. Before Henry Perin, esq., Mayor.
Recognisances

> Tho. Ranfeild in £20.
> Edw. Flood in £10.
> John Collins in £10.

For appearance of Ranfeild at the next Sessions.
Footnote: Appeared and committed for refusing to take oaths of allegiance and supremacy.

101
ASSAULT

S3A/95 (entry i)

29 February 1663/4. Before Fra. Holt, esq., Deputy Mayor.
Recognisances

> Walt. Evans in £20.
> Ric. Joyce in £10.
> Edw. Flood in £10.

For good behaviour.
For beating Bridget Robinson on 13 Feb.
Marginal note: Released by the Court.

102
ABUSING AUTHORITY

S3A/96

20 April 1664. Before Henry Perin, esq., Mayor.
Recognisances

> Ric. Neve sen. in £20.
> Henry Jenner in £10.
> Walt. Perry in £10.

For appearance of Neve at the next Sessions.
Bound over for speaking scandalous words against Mr Salesbury.
Footnote: Released by the Court, 25 Apr. 1664.

MICHAELMAS SESSIONS 17 and 25 October 1664

103
ABUSING THE MAYOR

S3A/97

30 April 1664. Before Henry Perin, esq., Mayor.
Recognisances

> Sebastian Watts in £20.
> Henry Warren in £10.
> John Collins in £10.

For appearance of Watts at the next Sessions.
Footnote (Latin): Continued because he is in Court on execution [of the recognisance].
See also no. 85.

104
Subject unknown
	S3A/98
	6 July 1664. Before Henry Perin, esq., Mayor.
	Recognisances
	      John Norton in £20.
	      Rob. Hawks in £10.
	      Edw. Flood in £10.
	For appearance of Norton at the next Sessions.
	Footnote: Released by the Court, 17 Oct. 1664.

105
DEFAMATION
	S3A/99
	14 July 1664. Before Henry Perin, esq., Mayor.
	Recognisances
	      John Thorne in £20.
	      John Beale in £10.
	      Ric. Joyce in £10.
	For appearance of Thorne at the next Sessions.
	Footnote: Released by the Court, 17 Oct. 1664.
	See also no. 94.

106
POUNDBREACH
	S3A/100
	18 July 1664. Before Henry Perin, esq., Mayor, and Ant. Haberley, gent.
	Recognisances
	      Tho. Balch in £20.
	      Ric. Poate in £10.
	      Wil. Smith in £10.
	For appearance of Balch at the next Sessions.
	Bound over for a poundbreach on the complaint of Tho. Parks, Chamberlain.
	Footnote: Released by the Court, 19 Oct. 1664.

107
ASSAULT
	S3A/101
	4 August 1664. Before Henry Perin, esq., Mayor.
	Recognisances
	      Godf. Morgan in £40.
	      Henry Tovey in £40.
	For appearance of Katherine, wife of Rob. Rawlins, at the next Sessions.
	Bound over for fighting with and striking Eleanor Todd.
	Footnote: Katherine did not appear.

108
ASSAULT
	S3A/102
	10 (?) September 1664. Before Henry Perin, esq., Mayor.
	Examinations
	(a) [Edwa]rd Ashley 'of P.', butcher, said that on [. . .]esday last about 4 or 5 p.m. he saw Hannah Phetiplace assault and beat Avis, wife of Mr Sam. Reniger, with a great stick, strike her three or four times, and if she had not gone indoors she might have been killed.
	(b) Hannah Phetiplace said she only struck her one blow.
	(c) Avis Reniger confessed that she beat down the partition with a cleaver.
	(d) Henry Barnes and Wil. Mose said that they saw Mrs Reniger with a fire-fork in her hand at the time of this falling out.
	(e) Wil. Mose said he heard Mrs Reniger call John Collins' wife a pickpocket and that he saw Mrs Reniger beat down the partition and heard her vulgar abuse against Hannah Phetiplace and her mother.
	(f) Mrs Collens confessed that she threw boiled turnips in Mrs Reniger's face.
	Recognisances
	      Hannah Phetiplace in £20.
	      John Biffin in £10.
	      John Collins in £10.
	For appearance of Hannah at the next Sessions.
	Footnote: Released by the Court, 17 Oct. 1664.

109
ABUSE AND ASSAULT

S3A/95 (entry ii)

20 September 1664. Before Henry Perin, esq., Mayor, Ant. Haberley and Hugh Salesbury.

Recognisances
    Hannah Giles (*no sum stated*).
    Wil. Ransteed in £20.
    Edw. Grantham in £20.
For appearance of Hannah, wife of Rob. Giles, at the next Sessions.

On the same day Edw. Bedford said she called Alex. Fairhill's maid whore, fell upon Fairhill's wife and beat her, then attacked the maid and Fairhill himself, and finally she beat a seaman.

Footnote: Released by the Court, 17 Oct. 1664.

EASTER SESSIONS 7 and 21 April 1665

110
CONTEMPT AND ABUSING AUTHORITY

S3A/103

5 November 1664. Before St John Steventon, esq., Mayor, and Ant. Haberley, gent.
Recognisances
    James Heatly in £20.
    Geo. Greene in £10.
    Ric. Joyce in £10.
For appearance of Heatly at the next Sessions.
Bound over for:
(1) entertaining seamen all night contrary to orders of the Mayor and Lord Sandwich,
(2) refusing to quarter soldiers on order of the Mayor and Constables,
(3) abusing the Constable in the execution of his office.

Footnote: Released by the Court at Sessions, 6 Apr. 1665.

111
THEFT

S3A/109

27 February 1664/5. Before St John Steventon, esq., Mayor, and Henry Perin, gent.
Information
Godf. Morgan of Portsmouth, rope maker, said that this day he found in the custody of Tho. Jones in his workhouse on the Common towards the Dockyard six reels of tarred rope yarn, which he knew and believed to belong to the King. He was sure it was stolen from the King's stores, but by whom or how Jones came by it he did not know.   *Signed by mark.*
Examination
Tho. Jones of Portsmouth, rope maker, said he had six reels of tarred rope yarn which he had made up for a merchant ship in a hawser, but, being too big for that use, he took it to pieces to make smaller cord.   *Signed.*

112
THEFT

S3A/106

28 February 1664/5. No name of Justice.
Information
Chr. Stallerd informed the Commissioner that, being a waiter on the Golden Buss prize, Tho. Gouge and a Frenchman came aboard on Sunday, 19 Feb., and took a piece of the main tackle and two or three ropes without his knowing, as he was asleep. There was another waiter aboard, Tho. Money.   *Signed.*
Footnote: The Frenchman's name is Step. Houlden.   *Signed by* Rob. Starks.

S3A/107

2 March 1664/5. Before Sir Humf. Benet and Dr Perrin.
Examinations
(a) Tho. Gouge said that he took a piece of the main tackle from the Golden Buss and one piece of rope.   *Signed by mark.*
(b) Step. Alden said he was with Tho. Gouge and took a piece of the main tackle and one piece of rope.   *Signed.*

S3A/105

No date. Before Henry Perin.

Recognisances

Chr. Stallerd in £20.

For appearance at the next Sessions to give evidence against Tho. Gouge and Step. Alden concerning embezzling and taking away ropes from a prize ship called the Golden Buss. *Signed by* Henry Perin.

Recognisances

Henry Hockley, carpenter, in £10.

Sam. Smith in £10.

Step. Aulden in £20.

Dan. Gouge in £10.

Step. Gosse in £10.

Tho. Gouge in £20.

See also no. 124.

113

DISLOYALTY AND DRUNKENNESS

S3A/104

28 February 1664/5. Before St John Steventon, esq., Mayor, Henry Perin, gent., Ant. Haberley, gent., and Hugh Salesbury, gent.

Information

Sam. Smith of Portsmouth, soldier, said that in his own house on Tuesday last, 7 Feb., he heard Ric. Langley say 'Tis better to serve the Divell then to serve the King unlesse wee could have money'.

Examination

Ric. Langley said he had been drinking brandy wine and in his drink said 'If I cannot subusist, I had as good serve the Divell as serve the King'.

10 March 1664/5. Before St John Steventon, esq., Mayor.

Recognisances[13]

Ric. Langley of Southampton in £40.

Wil. Mose, barber, in £20.

Tho. Harding, joiner, in £20.

For appearance of Langley at the next Sessions.

Footnote (English and Latin): Confessed in Court that he was drunk. Ordered to pay 5s. Discharged by the Court. He owes 4s.

114

Subject unknown

S3A/108

14 March 1664/5. Before St John Steventon, esq., Mayor, Ant. Haberley and Hugh Salesbury.

Recognisances[14]

And. Lumpson in £20.

Wil. Mose in £10.

Tho. Wood in £10.

For appearance of Lumpson at the next Sessions.

Footnote: Released by the Court.

---

[13] Under this recognisance is this note: John Allom did not prosecute Edw. Deacon: Allom did not appear.

[14] Under this recognisance is the following. It is in a mixture of Latin and English.

		s	d
Bill of Costs Downer versus Croke			
warrant and arraignment		1	0
Return [of writ] and warrant of attachment		1	0
2 continuations [? of bail]			8
declaration		3	4
filing			10
bill			4
withdrawal			4
		7	6
Debt	3	7	6

115
THEFT

S3A/110

6 April 1665. At Sessions.
Recognisances
      Henry Tarrant in £20.
      Tho. Gellet in £10.
      John Collins in £10.
For appearance [of Tarrant] at the next Sessions.
Bound over for [having] nails with the King's mark.
Footnote: Released by the Court, 5 Oct. 1665.

MICHAELMAS SESSIONS 5 and 24 October 1665

116
ASSAULT

S3A/112

6 June 17 Cha. II [1665]. Before St John Steventon, esq., Mayor.
Recognisances
      Jos. Russell in £40.
      Nic. Peirson in £20.
      Ric. Hunt, baker, in £20.
For appearance of Russell at the next Sessions.
Bound over as John Cleaver said that last night about 6 p.m. Russell beat him with a stick and struck him several blows, so that his left shoulder was swollen and black and blue.
Russell being present confessed he struck him one blow.
Footnote: Released by the Court, 5 Oct. 1665.

117
SLANDER

S3A/114 (entry i)

7 June 1665. Before St John Steventon, esq., Mayor.
Examinations
(a) Ann, wife of Art. Cave, said that about six weeks ago Tho. Coker was speaking to Mary Pococke about Mrs Burridge saying that she was a good lusty trugg and that she got a suit of clothes, hat and trimmings for it from him worth 25 pieces. Mary then asked if it was done in this town or not and Coker answered 'Noe it was 100 miles away from this place'.
(b) Ann, wife of Elias Abbot, *confirmed the above.*

118
OBSTRUCTING AUTHORITY

S3A/114 (entry ii)

10 June 1665. Before Henry Perin, gent., and Wil. Michell, gent.
Recognisances
      Rob. Carpenter in £20.
      Tho. Reade of Portsea, yeoman, in £10.
      Ric. Poate of Portsea, yeoman, in £10.
For appearance of Carpenter at the next Sessions.
Bound over because yesterday, the 9th, with a bill in his hand he stopped the Mayor in person, the Alderman and Burgesses when they were riding in the usual way the circuit of the Town Liberties near Stamshaw ('Stampsey').
Footnotes:
(a) Confessed he was very sorry and would not do it again.
(b) Released by the Court, 5 Oct. 1665.

119
THEFT

S3A/113 (entry i)

13 June 1665. Before St John Steventon, esq., Mayor, and Henry Perin, gent.
Examination
John Pledger of Portsmouth, shipwright, said that before Easter last he bought of one Knight, a boatman, three elm boards ('emeboards') for which he paid 6s and landed them near the London upon the Point. He and Step. Alden were carrying them to Mrs Arnold's yards, but were stopped by Sir Humf. Bennet.
Sentence
At Commissioner Middleton's request it was ordered that John Pledger should take the boards to the Dockyard and there be laid in the stocks for two hours, which was done accordingly.

120

ASSAULT

S3A/113 (entry ii)

20 June 1665. Before St John Steventon, esq., Mayor.

Examinations

(a) Elizabeth Grover, widow, confessed that she beat Mary Gascoigne on Friday last, 16 June.

(b) Mary Gascoigne said that Elizabeth Grover beat her, scratched her and fetched the blood on her face.

26 June 1665. Before Henry Perin, gent.

Recognisances

Elizabeth Grover in £20.

Tho. Grover in £10.

Henry Tarrant in £10.

For appearance of Elizabeth Grover at the next Sessions.

Footnote: Released by the Court, 5 Oct. 1665.

121

RECEIVING STOLEN GOODS

S3A/111

24 June 1665. Before St John Steventon, esq., Mayor.

Recognisances

Henry Acton in £20.

Tho. Keden, gent., in £10.

For appearance of Ann, wife of Henry Acton, at the next Sessions.

Bound over for receiving faggots stolen from Margaret Clarke, who made oath of it at the Court, 30 May 1665.

Footnote: Paid the fees and released, 5 Oct. 1665.

122

ASSAULT

S3A/117

28 June 1665. Before St John Steventon, esq., Mayor.

Recognisances

John Knight in £20.

Tho. Merehen in £10.

Sam. Smith in £10.

For appearance [of Knight] at the next Sessions.

Footnotes:

(a) Striking Dorothy Morgan.

(b) Released by the Court, 5 Oct. 1665.

123

Subject unknown[15]

S3A/118

14 July 1665. Before St John Steventon, esq., Mayor.

Recognisances

John Morgan in £20.

Godf. Morgan in £10.

Edw. Thomas in £10.

For appearance of John Morgan and Elizabeth his wife at the next Sessions.

By the oath of John Knight and his wife.

Footnote: Released by the Court, 5 Oct. 1665, by proclamation.

124

THEFT

S3A/115

13 July 1665. Before St John Steventon, esq., Mayor.

Recognisances

Step. Alden in £20.

Jeremiah Crawley, goldsmith, in £10.

Henry Hockley, carpenter, in £10.

For appearance of Alden at the next Sessions.

See the examinations at the last Sessions.

Footnotes:

(a) Released by the Court, 5 Oct. 1665.

(b) Release: 9*d.*

---

[15] Possibly assault, connected with no. 122.

S3A/116

22 July 1665. Before St John Steventon, esq., Mayor.
Recognisances
> Tho. Goudge in £20.
> Chr. Goudge in £10.
> Edw. Flood in £10.

For appearance of Tho. Goudge at the next Sessions.
Bound over at the last Sessions. See previous examinations, etc.
Footnotes:
(a) Released by the Court, 5 Oct. 1665.
(b) Release: 5s.
See also no. 112.

125

**PLAGUE
INFECTION**

S3A/119

10 August 1665. No name of Justice.
Recognisances
> Ric. Symms in £20.
> Tho. Galpin in £10.
> Silvester Woodford in £10.

On condition [that Symms appears at the next Sessions].
Bound over for entertaining one Prangnell from Southampton, a place infected with the plague, contrary to the orders of the King, the Mayor and Justices.
Footnote: Released by the Court, 5 Oct. 1665.

126

**TRADING
IRREGULARLY**

S3A/120

11 August 1665. Before St John Steventon, esq., Mayor, and Hugh Salesbury.
Recognisances
> Tho. Triggs in £20.
> Edw. Flood in £10.
> Wil. Watts in £10.

For appearance of Triggs at the next Sessions.
Bound over for cheating a stranger of six pennyworth of mackerel.
Footnote: Released by the Court.

127

**CUSTOMS
EVASION**

S3A/121

11 August 1665. Before St John Steventon, esq., Mayor.
Recognisances
> (a) John Deane in £20.
> John Wyatt in £10.
> Ant. Hayward in £10

For appearance [of Deane] at the next Sessions.
Bound over on the complaint of Rob. Payne for cheating the Customs.
Footnote: Released by the Court, 5 Oct. 1665.
> (b) John Willis in £20.
> John Wyatt in £10.
> Ant. Hayward in £10.

For appearance [of Willis] at the next Sessions for the same offence as Deane.
Footnote as for (a).
Endorsement: Witness – the boy at the Rainbow.

128

**ASSAULT AND
DRUNKENNESS**

S3A/122

11 August 1665. Before St John Steventon, esq., Mayor.
Recognisances
> Alex. Fairehill in £20.
> John Wyat in £10.
> Art. Hayward in £10.

For appearance of Fairehill at the next Sessions.
Bound over for beating his wife and servant-maid out of doors Sunday night last. He was several times complained of and confessed to be drunk.
Footnote: Released by the Court, 5 Oct. 1665.

129
**REFUSING TO
ASSIST
CONSTABLE**

S3A/123

3 October 1665. Before Ben. Johnson, esq., Mayor.
Recognisances

John Alford of Chideock, Dors., mariner, in £20.
Rob. Payne in £10.
John Dyer in £10.

For appearance of Alford at the next Sessions.

Bound over on complaint of Nic. Peirson, Constable, for not assisting him in his office.

Footnote: Released by the Court, 5 Oct. 1665.

130
Subject unknown

S3A/124

10 October 1665. Before Ben. Johnson, esq., Mayor.
Recognisances[16]

Rob. Reynolds in £20.
John Child in £10.
James Austen in £10.

For appearance [of Reynolds] at the opening of the Law-day, 24 Oct. next.

Marginal note (English and Latin): Paid for release.

Footnote: Released by the Court.

131
Subject unknown

S3A/125

12 October 1665. Before Ben. Johnson, esq., Mayor.
Recognisances

John Gray in £20.
Fra. Gray in £10.
John Chestle in £10.

For appearance of John Gray at the opening of the Sessions on 24 Oct. next.

Marginal note (English and Latin): Paid for release.

13 October 1665. Before the same.
Recognisances

Fra. Hicks in £20.
Tho. Jones in £10.
John Collins in £10.

On condition for Hicks as above.

Marginal note (English and Latin): Paid for release.

EASTER SESSIONS 30 April, 8 and 12 May 1666

For further entry in Sessions Book see Appendix II, no. 76, and see also Appendix III, nos 7, 8.

132
BIGAMY

S3A/128 (entry i)

24 October 1665. Before Ben. Johnson, esq., Mayor.
Recognisances

Elizabeth Carricke alias Deacon, in £200.
Chr. Wynter, of Portsmouth, currier, in £100.
Peter Wilbert 'of P.', carpenter, in £100.

For appearance of Elizabeth Carrick before the Justices tomorrow at the Town Hall and not to depart without licence.

S3A/127

25 October 1665. Before Ben. Johnson, esq., Mayor, and Wil. Michell, gent.
Informations

(a) Wil. Penford (*signs* Pansfard) of Old Basingstoke, weaver, said that he knew Henry Carricke of Basingstoke, currier, but had not seen him for many years. Edw. Grantham of this town told Penford last Saturday that Henry Carricke had a wife

---

[16] For a reproduction of this recognisance see fig. 5, and for a transcript see App. I, no. 2(3).

living in Portsmouth who had another husband, Edw. Deacons. Grantham gave Penford a flagon of beer and 2*d* to send him back a letter when he got home to say whether Carricke was living there or not.   *Signed.*

(b) Edw. Grantham of Portsmouth, cutler, born at Basingstoke, said he had known Henry Carricke for a long time and knew him when he lived in Portsmouth with his wife Elizabeth about three years ago. About that time he left Portsmouth and his wife remained here and she has since been the reputed wife of Edw. Deacons for about two years. She has since had two children and is now with child again. About a year ago she asked Grantham to enquire at Basingstoke if her husband was alive, as she had not heard from him since he left. He enquired but got no news. He understood that the Grand Inquest was about to present her for having two husbands alive.   *Signed.*

(c) Edw. Deacons said he was lawfully married about two years ago to Elizabeth who was wife of Henry Carricke. Before his marriage he made diligent enquiry at Basingstoke and elsewhere, but could not hear of him.   *Signed by mark.*
Examination
Elizabeth Carricke, alias Deacons, said she had been married three times. First to John Goly, a currier of this town, by whom she had five children before he died here. The second was Henry Carricke by whom she had two children and with whom she lived till about three years ago, when being much in debt he left and she had not heard from him since. Her third husband was Edw. Deacon to whom she had been lawfully married for over two years.

Asked why she married before being assured of her husband's death, she answered that she was told by several seamen from London, particularly by Walt. Fry, cook of H.M.S. Phoenix, that her husband had gone to sea in a merchant ship to New England but sickened and died on board.

She understood that Tho. Carrick, her second husband's brother, had left his wife and children at Basingstoke, so asked Edw. Grantham to find out if her said brother-in-law had returned.   *Signed by mark.*

S3A/128 (entry ii)
1 November 1665. Before the same (*i.e. Ben. Johnson*).
Recognisances
> Elizabeth Carricke alias Deacons in £100.
> Wil. Mose in £50.
> Peter Wilbert 'of P.', carpenter, in £50.

For appearance of Elizabeth at the next Sessions.
Footnote (Latin): She did not appear.

133
Subject unknown

S3A/126
28 October 1665. Before Ben. Johnson, esq., Mayor, and Ant. Haberley, gent.
Recognisances
> Tho. Gellett in £20.
> Ric. Uthwaite in £10.
> John Upsdale in £10.

For appearance of Gellett at the next Sessions.
Footnote (Latin): He did not appear and he renounced.
Possibly related to no. 137.

134
PROFANING A HOLY DAY

S3A/129
10 November 1665. Before Ant. Haberley, gent.
Recognisances
> (a) Sam. Crutchfeild in £20.
>   Ric. Uthwait in £10.
>   Edw. Flood in £10.

For appearance of Crutchfeild at the next Sessions.
Marginal note (Latin): He did not appear.

(b) Tho. Moreing in £20.
     Rob. Uphman in £10.
     Ric. Saunders in £10.
For appearance of Moreing at the next Sessions.
Marginal note: Released by the Court, 30 Apr. 1666.
(c) John Head in £20.
     Ric. Uthwaite in £10.
     Tho. Moreing in £10.
For appearance of Head at the next Sessions.
Marginal note (Latin) against Uthwaite[17]: Dead.
Footnote: All bound over for selling drink on the last fast day in the time of divine service.

135 **ASSAULT**	S3A/130 **30 November [1665].** Before Ant. Haberley, gent.

Recognisances
(a) Fra. Gadus (*also* Gradus) in £20.
     Ric. Ridge, gent., in £10.
     John Stephens of Maldon, Essex, mariner, in £10.
For appearance of Gradus at the next Sessions.
Marginal notes (Latin):
     (a) He acknowledged, etc.
     (b) Released.
(b) Verissimo De Silvo in £20.
     Ric. Ridge, gent., in £10.
     John Stephens of Maldon, Essex, mariner, in £10.
On condition [for De Silvo] as above.
Marginal notes (Latin):
     (a) He acknowledged.
     (b) Released.
(c) (*blank*) Roche in £20.
     (*blank*) in £10.
     (*blank*) in £10.
On condition [for Roche] as above.

21 November 1665. Before Ben. Johnson, esq., Mayor, and Ant. Haberley, gent.
Information
Ferdinando de Murcedo said that Franco Gadus, Verissimo De Silvo and Roche beat him here in this town and he goes in fear of his life.

136 **REFUSING THE** **WATCH**	S3A/132 **6 December 1665.** Before Ben. Johnson, esq., Mayor, and Ant. Haberley.

Recognisances
     Phil. Elmes in £20.
     Ric. Uthwaite in £10.
     Rob. Hawks in £10.
For appearance of Elmes at the next Sessions.
Footnotes:
(a) For refusing the watch.
(b) (*Latin*) He did not appear.

137 **INCITING** **MUTINY**	S3A/135 **16 December 1665.** Before Ben. Johnson, esq., Mayor.

Recognisances
     Tho. Gellet in £40.
     Ric. Uthwait in £20.
     Rob. Hawks in £20.

---

[17] Although against this name, the note probably refers to Head, as Uthwaite appears later in no. 136.

For appearance of Gellet at the next Sessions.

Bound over for words tending to mutiny in the fleet, very prejudicial to His Majesty's present expedition.

Footnotes :

(a) (*Latin; scored through*) He did not appear.

(b) Continued.

Possibly related to no. 133.

138
THEFT

S3A/131

20 December 1665. Before Ben. Johnson, esq., Mayor, and Ant. Haberley, gent.

Recognisances

Mic. Tayler in £20.

James Holloway in £10.

Tho. Barnes in £10.

For appearance of Tayler at the next Sessions.

Bound over for stealing hoops and pipestone taken from Mr Ridge.

Footnote : Discharged by the Court, 30 Apr. 1666.

139
Subject unknown

S3A/133

29 December 1665. Before Ben. Johnson, esq., Mayor, (and Sam. Williams *scored through*).

Recognisances

Tho. Stockell (*also* Stockwell) of Newport, Isle of Wight, carrier, in £40.

Wil. English of Portsmouth, innholder, in £20.

Alex. Eastwood of Portsmouth, yeoman, in £20.

For appearance of Stockwell at the next Sessions.

Footnote : Released by the Court, 30 Apr. 1666.

140
DANGEROUS RIDING

S3A/134

29 December 1665. Before Ben. Johnson, esq., Mayor.

Recognisances

Rob. Uphman of Portsmouth, innholder, in £100.

John Tymbrell of Portsmouth, gent., in £100.

For appearance of Edw. Smaledridge at the next Sessions.

Footnotes :

(a) For riding (*one word illegible*) over children.

(b) Released by the Court, 30 Apr. 1666.

141
DRUNKENNESS

S3A/136

16 January 1665/6. Before Ben. Johnson, esq., Mayor, and Ant. Haberley, gent.

Recognisances

James Swayne in £20.

Sam. Knight jun. of the Dockyard in £10.

James Hotkins, rope maker, in £10.

For appearance of Swayne at the next Sessions and to keep the peace, especially towards Mary, wife of David Meriweather, and not to depart [the jurisdiction of] the Court without licence.

Bound over for breaking the windows of David Meryweather on Sunday night, 9 Jan., and being then drunk, so that Mary Meriweather goes in fear of her life.

Marginal notes :

(a) Released by the Court, 30 Apr. 1666.

(b) 5s to Mr Haberley for being drunk.

40

142
PLAGUE
INFECTION

S3A/137

27 January 1665/6. Before Ben. Johnson, esq., Mayor, and Ant. Haberley, gent.
Recognisances
      Rob. Hawks in £20.
      John Norton, gent., in £10.
      Tho. Challenge in £10.
For appearance of Hawks at the next Sessions.
Bound over for entertaining strangers from Southampton against the orders of the Mayor and Justices, especially a woman suspected to be infected.
    Footnote: Released by the Court, 30 Apr. 1666.

143
PLAGUE
INFECTION

S3A/138

3 February 1665/6. Before Ben. Johnson, esq., Mayor, and Ant. Haberley.
Recognisances
      Wil. White in £20.
      Edw. Brooker in £10.
      Griffin Roades in £10.
For appearance of White at the next Sessions.
Bound over for entertaining one from London without leave, against the order of the Justices, who died at his house.
    Footnote (Latin): He did not appear.

MICHAELMAS SESSIONS 15 and 25 October 1666

No papers survive except for entries in Sessions Books: see Appendix II, nos 77, 78.

EASTER SESSIONS 23 April and 6 May 1667

No papers survive.

MICHAELMAS SESSIONS 11 and 23 October 1667

No papers survive.

EASTER SESSIONS 26 March and 7 April 1668

No papers survive except for entries in State Papers Domestic: see Appendix III, nos 9, 10.

MICHAELMAS SESSIONS 8 and 26 October 1668

No papers survive except for entry in Sessions Books: see Appendix II, no. 79.

EASTER SESSIONS 22 April and 5 May 1669

No papers survive except for entry in State Papers Domestic: see Appendix III, no. 11.

MICHAELMAS SESSIONS 7 and 26 October 1669

144
ASSAULTING
A JUSTICE[18]

S3/1/5
11 October 1669. Before Grantham Wyan, Deputy Mayor.
Recognisances
        Fra. Lucas in £200.
        Ric. Ridge of Portsmouth, gent., in £100.
        Wil. Domineeke of Portsmouth, shipwright, in £100.
For appearance of Lucas at the next Sessions to answer for beating and abusing Mr Hugh Salesbury, Justice of the Peace.

145
SLANDER[18]

S3/1/4
20 October 1669. Before Grantham Wyan, Deputy Mayor.
Recognisances
        Fra. Lucas of Portsmouth, shipwright in £100.
        Wil. Domineeke of Portsmouth, shipwright, in £50.
For appearance of Lucas at the next Sessions.
Bound over for slandering Mr Salesbury and Mr Steventon.

EASTER SESSIONS 14 and 26 April 1670

No papers survive except for entry in Sessions Books: see Appendix II, no. 80.

MICHAELMAS SESSIONS 6 October 1670

146
ABUSE

S3/1/13. *Calendar number on document: 2.*
10 May 1670. Before Ant. Habberley, gent.
Recognisances
        James Swaine in £20.
        Fra. Percivall of Portsmouth in £10.
        Tho. Poate of Portsmouth in £10.
For appearance of Swaine at the next Sessions.
Bound over for abusing his daughter-in-law.
Marginal note (Latin): Discharged by the Court.

147
ABUSE

S3/1/12. *Calendar number on document: 3.*
18 May 1670. Before Sam. Burningham, esq., Mayor.
Recognisances
        Phil. Elmes in £20.
        Wil. Domineeke in £20.
For appearance of Margery, wife of Rob. Portland, at the next Sessions.
Bound over for abusing Sarah, wife of Tho. Clarke.
Footnote (Latin): Discharged by the Court.

148
ASSAULT

S3/1/3
18 July 1670. No name of Justice.
Informations
(a) John Street of Portsmouth, rope maker, said that when he was at the White Dog at the Mill near Portsmouth with Ben. Burgis and Alice Harvy alias Cleaver, widow, Alice declared that if Nic. Hammond's maid had not come into the room and taken him by the hair of the head, the said Hammond would have ravished her. She desired Burgis to go to Hammond and say she would have £10 of him and would not accept £9.19s 11¾d.

---

[18] For full details of this case about the theft of timber from the Dockyard heard before the Navy Commissioners in London see *Calendar of State Papers Domestic*, 1668–69, p. 593; ibid., 1670, pp. 14–15, 22, 25, 30–31, 73–74, 504.

(b) Elizabeth, wife of Cha. Brewer, said that Alice Harvey sent to her to come to her and said that she was to be her mistress. Alice added that Nic. Hammond drove her from place to place and had bruised her body. *Elizabeth repeated the evidence of the maid's entry and Alice's demand for £10.*

(c) Goodwife Croberd. *No entry against the name.*

<table>
<tr><td>149
THEFT</td><td>S3/1/2</td></tr>
</table>

149
THEFT

S3/1/2
3 August 1670.
Presentment (Latin)
Presents Wil. Longe lately of Portsmouth, labourer, for feloniously taking 5 lb. weight of wrought ('wrot') iron to the value of 10*d* of the goods and chattels of our Lord the King and against his peace.
Endorsements:
(a) True bill.
(b) John White, James Hobbs and Roger Githeridg: sworn.

S3/1/1
5 August 1670. Before St John Steventon, gent.
Informations
(a) John White said that on 3 Aug. last about noon, being on board 'the newe first rate shippe of his Majesty's now a building in Portsmouthe Docke', he saw Wil. Longe come on to the upper deck and after walking about for some time take up a piece of a ring bolt and thrust it between his breast and doublet. He then took up two set bolts, put them in the same place and went away with the said iron.
Signed by mark.
(b) James Hobbs *repeated the above evidence in almost exactly the same words.*
Signed by mark.
(c) Roger Githeridge *repeated the above evidence and added* that at the same time he saw Tho. Hammond, servant of Tho. Richards, plug keeper, come on board the ship and take one set bolt, put it in his doublet and take it away.   *Signed by mark.*
(d) John White and James Hobbs *repeated the evidence of the last witness about Tho. Hammond.*   *Both sign by mark.*
Examination
Tho. Hammond admitted that he took a new bolt and carried it to the plug keeper's cabin.
Wil. Long denied the allegation against him.

S3/1/10. *Calendar numbers on document:* 5, 6.
10 August 1670. Before Sam. Burningham, esq., Mayor, Hugh Salesbury, gent., and St John Steventon, gent.
Recognisances
(a) Tho. Hamond in £20.
 James Dunkinson of Portsmouth, goldsmith, in £10.
 Elizabeth Paul of Gosport, widow, in £10.
For appearance of Hamond at the next Sessions.
(b) Wil. Long in £20.
 Elizabeth Paul of Gosport, widow, in £10.
 James Dunkinson of Portsmouth in £10.
For appearance of Long at the next Sessions.
Bound over for stealing the King's goods from the Dockyard.
Footnote (Latin): He forfeited on his recognisance.
See also no. 169 (18).

150
ABUSE OF
AUTHORITY

S3/1/11
10 August 1670. Before Sam. Burningham, esq., Mayor, and St John Steventon, gent.
Recognisances
 Rob. Cooke in £40.
 Wil. Franklin of Portsmouth in £20.
 John Mason of Portsmouth in £20.
For appearance of Cooke at the next Sessions.

Bound over for abusing the jury of the Clerk of the Markets' Court[19] 'in saying that they went about a pickpocketing'.

Footnote (Latin): Discharged by the Mayor.

151
POUNDBREACH

S3/1/9. *Calendar number on document*: 7.

11 August 1670. Before Sam. Burningham, esq., Mayor.

Recognisances

    John Aylward of Kingston in £20.

    Nic. Selden of Portsmouth in £10.

For appearance of Aylward at the next Sessions to answer for making a pound-breach.

Bound over for putting his horse in the Common and taking him away from the Chamberlain.

Footnote (Latin): Discharged by the Mayor.

152
SLANDER

S3/1/8

16 August 1670. Before Sam. Burningham, esq., Mayor, Grantham Wyan and St John Steventon.

Recognisances

    Alice Osborne, widow, in £20.

    James Beare of Portchester in £10.

    Phil. Davis of Portsmouth in £10.

For appearance of Alice at the next Sessions.

Bound over for slandering Nic. Hamond.

Footnote (Latin): Discharged by the Court.

153
ASSAULT

S3/1/7

13 September 1670. Before Grantham Wyan, gent., Deputy Mayor.

Recognisances

    Amy, wife of Hendricke Lysten, in £20.

    John Childe of Portsmouth, carpenter, in £10.

    John Chivers of Portsmouth, labourer, in £10.

For appearance of Amy at the next Sessions.

Bound over for assaulting Elizabeth, wife of David Gray.

Footnote (Latin): Discharged by the Court.

154
Subject unknown

S3/1/6

15 September 1670. Before Grantham Wyan, gent., and Ant. Haberley, gent.

Recognisances

    Janura (*or* Jonura?) Mills, widow, in £20.

    Geo. Barcombe in £10.

    Wil. Saunders in £10.

To appear at the Sessions.

EASTER SESSIONS 3 May 1671

155
FORESTALLING

S3/2/1

26 April [23?] Cha. II [1671].

Presentment (Latin)

Presents Ann, wife of John Mooren of Portsmouth, cordwainer, for forestalling and buying from various persons 12 lb. of butter at the price of 7*d* in the market of Portsmouth before such butter was to be openly sold in the said market contrary to the Statute[20] and against the King's peace.   *Signed by* [Edw.] Archer.

---

[19] The Mayor was ex officio Clerk of the Market (cf. no. 299).
[20] Statute: 5 & 6 Ed. VI, c.14.

MICHAELMAS SESSIONS 5 October 1671

No papers survive.

EASTER SESSIONS 18 April 1672

156
SUSPECTED
FELONY

S3/2/12. *Calendar numbers on document:* 13, 14, 15.

20 October 1671. Before Phil. James, esq., Mayor.

Informations

(a) Wil. Nicholls of Kingston, yeoman, said that last Saturday night being with Tho. Barrow and James Crooker and several others at the Blue Anchor, Kingston, he heard Crooker ask Barrow whose were the mast and the rest of the things lying in the barn at Horsea ('Horsey'). Barrow answered that they were his. Crooker said there was one at Portchester would give 30*s* for it. Barrow answered that for aught he knew it was Mr Geales. *Signed.*

(b) Tho. Baker of Kingston *deposed as above.*

Recognisances

(a) James Crooker in £20.
Tho. Baker in £10.
Ric. Crooker in £10.

For appearance [of James Crooker] at the next Sessions.

(b) Tho. Barrow in the like sum of £20 with the same sureties on the same condition.

(c) Henry Pen in the like sum of £20 with the same sureties [on the same condition].

S3B/9. *Calendar number on document:* 13.

20 October 1671. Before Phil. James, esq., Mayor.

Recognisances

James Crooker in £20.
Tho. Baker of Kingston in £10.
Ric. Crooker of Kingston in £10.

For appearance of James Crooker at the next Sessions and not to depart [the jurisdiction of] the Court without licence.

Bound over on suspicion of felony.

Footnote: Respited till tomorrow.

See also no. 169 (13–15).

157
SERVICE

S3/2/10. *Calendar number on document:* 17.

6 November 1671. Before Phil. James, esq., Mayor, Tho. Plover and Sam. Williams.

Recognisances

Nat. Popejoy in £40.
Tho. Dismore of Lockeridge, parish of Fyfield (*recte West Overton*), Wilts., cloth-worker, in £30.

For appearance [of Popejoy] at the next Sessions.

Bound over being servant to Henry Dismore of Southwark, [Surr.], draper.[21]

Marginal note (Latin): Discharged by the Mayor.

See also no. 169 (17).

158
ASSAULT

S3/3/17. *Calendar number on document:* 9.

11 November 1671. Before Phil. James, esq., Mayor.

Information

Ann Judson said she went in fear of her life that Ant. Stratton will beat, wound or kill her.

See also no. 169 (9).

---

[21] Perhaps because unapprenticed.

159
**TRADING
IRREGULARLY**

S3/2/17. *Calendar number on document:* 10.

8 November 1671. No name of Justice.
Information
Tho. Nealer of Portsmouth, labourer, said that yesterday he bought of Humf. Fullford and Ben. Fulford at the house of Ric. Thomas, being the White Hart, one cradle rug which cost 4s. *Signed by mark.*

D11A/16/7. *Calendar number on document:* 10.

13 November 1671. Before Phil. James, esq., Mayor.
Recognisances
      Ben. Fulford of Chichester, [Suss.], in £20.
      Henry Whitehorne of Portsmouth, victualler, in £10.
      Alex. Farehill of the same, cordwainer, in £10.
For appearance of Fulford at the next Sessions.
Footnotes:
(a) Bound over as a petty chapman for selling his wares within this Liberty.
(b) Stands upon his recognisance.

S3/2/4

15 November 23 Cha. II [1671].
Presentment (Latin)
Presents Ben. Fulford of Chichester, Suss., labourer, who was and is a petty chapman and on the said day did wander from Chichester to Portsmouth and during that day sold to various subjects of the King petty wares, viz. coverlets and blankets, contrary to the Statute etc.[22]
    Endorsements:
    (a) True bill.
    (b) Tho. Bernard, James Arnold: sworn.
    (c) Bill and fine 10s.
See also no. 169 (10).

160
**TRADING
IRREGULARLY
AND
UNAPPRENTICED**

S3/2/15. *Calendar number on document:* 11.

14 November 1671. Before Phil. James, esq., Mayor.
Examination
Ben. Dennis of Winchester, chapman, said he was at dock near Portsmouth with two horses laden with goods last Saturday and yesterday but only sold one comb. *Signed by mark.*

S3/2/16. *Calendar number on document:* 11.

14 November 1671. Before Phil. James, esq., and Sam. Williams, gent.
Recognisances
      Ben. Dennis of Winchester in £40.
      Phil. Elmes in £20.
      Step. Gosse in £20.
For appearance [of Dennis] at the next Sessions.

S3/2/2

15 November 23 Cha. II [1671].
Presentment (Latin)
Presents Ben. Dennis, lately of Winchester, labourer, who was and is a petty chapman and on the said day did wander from Winchester to Portsmouth and during that day sold to various subjects of the King petty wares, viz. knives, scissors and laces, contrary to the Statute[23], in contempt of the laws and against the King's peace. *Signed by [Edw.] Archer.*

    Endorsements:
    (a) True bill.
    (b) He submits in 13s 4d.

---

[22] Statute: 1 & 2 Phil. & Mary, c.7.
[23] Statute: 1 & 2 Phil. & Mary, c.7.

S3/2/3

15 November 23 Cha. II [1671].

Presentment (Latin)

Presents Ben. Dennis of Winchester, labourer, for exercising the art, mystery or manual occupation of a comb maker in Portsmouth on 15 Nov. 23 Cha. II by selling various comb maker's wares up to the date of this inquiry, without being taught or apprenticed for seven years according to the Statute of 12 Jan. 5 Eliz. [1562/3].

Endorsement: Chr. Abin.

See also no. 169 (11).

161

THEFT

S3/2/18

15 November 1671. Before Phil. James, esq., Mayor, and Grantham Wyan, gent.

Information

Jane, wife of Jonathan Coasier, of Wigley near Romsey, yeoman, said she left her house in Portsmouth at wheat harvest last locked up securely. Last night when she returned she found a wall broken down next to the house of one Clayton and she found lost in the house a pair of bellows, four pewter dishes, a lanthorne, a pewter chamber-pot, four pewter pottingers, a dozen and three spoons which were in a blue cup, four pairs of coarse sheets, three pairs and one pillow-tie, one feather bolster, one dozen bottles, and three fir sticks for curtains to set against a half-headed bed-stead. She found in the possession of Ann, wife of John Marchant, seaman, the fir sticks and a bottle at Goodman Kyte's which he had bought of Ann. *Signed by mark.*

162

ABUSING AUTHORITY

S3/2/8

29 November 1671. Before Hugh Salesbury, Sam. Williams, gent., and Grantham Wyan, gent.

Information[24]

John Greenaway (*also* Greenway) said that about a fortnight ago, as Churchwarden of Portsmouth, he went to the house of John Moody to collect a rate for repairs to the church. Moody complained that he was rated more than Mr Mayor and added that if he paid more, his wife should sit above Mrs Mayoress and he would pull her out by the shoulders. *Signed.*

S3/2/9

4 December 1671. Before Phil. James, esq., Mayor, and Sam. Williams.

Information

Ric. Preist said that being with Mr Greenaway, one of the Churchwardens of Portsmouth, about a fortnight ago collecting a church rate, they came to the house of John Moody in Portsmouth who, being in a great passion, said that never a man in town was rated as he was and that his wife should sit above Mrs Mayoress.

Signed by mark.

163

ASSAULT

S3/2/6. *Calendar number on document:* 7.

16 December 1671. Before (*blank*) Mayor.

Informations

(a) Ric. Woolgar said that last night Henry Woolgar tried to waylay and kill Phineas Haynes and afterwards took a prong(?) to run him through.

Signed by mark.

(b) Phineas Haynes said that he was in fear of his life from Henry Woolgar and that the above evidence of Ric. Woolgar was true. *Signed by mark.*

See also nos 169 (7), 170.

164

SETTLEMENT AND BASTARDY

S3/2/7. *Calendar number on document:* 8.

No date. Before Phil. James, esq., Mayor, and Grantham Wyan.

Examination

Mary Phillipps late of Fareham, singlewoman, said that she was servant to Ric. Pescod of Fareham, victualler, three-quarters of a year and came from there about five weeks before Michaelmas last to the house of Henry Ransted, Sergeant-at-Mace, where she stayed for seven weeks and more, then stayed with friends at South

---

[24] For a reproduction of this information see fig. 6, and for a transcript see App. I, no. 3.

F

Stoneham for three weeks and then went back to Henry Ransted's house in Portsmouth where she had been since. She was begotten of child by Ric. Westbrooke of Fareham in Pescod's house. *Signed by mark.*

S3B/8. *Calendar number on document:* 8.
16 December 1671. Before Phil. James, esq., Mayor.
Recognisances
      Ric. Westbrooke of Fareham in £60.
      Tho. Bernard of Portsmouth, gent., in £30.
      Wil. Rolfe of Fareham, tanner, in £30.
For appearance of Westbrooke at the next Sessions.
Bound over for getting Mary Phillips with child.
Footnote: Respited until security given for discharging the parish.
See also no. 169 (8).

165
THEFT(?)

S3/2/11

3 January 1671/2. Before Phil. James, esq., Mayor.
Information
Ric. Smith, seaman of H.M. Frigate York, said that on Thursday night last he was with Tho. Chettle and John Adams, other seamen of the same ship, at the Blue Anchor at Kingston where they asked for lodging and supper. The tapster brought up two pigs ready dressed saying they could have which they liked and they had one for supper. *Signed.*
Examination
Ann Churles, spinster, said that last Thursday she dressed a pig brought to her by John de Lannce to be roasted, which pig was cropped in one of its ears and had a black spot about the rump. *Signed by mark.*

166
BASTARDY

S3/2/13. *Calendar number on document:* 12.
14 September 1671. Before Tho. Plover, esq., Mayor.
Examination
Margery Hopkins of Portsea, singlewoman, said she was servant to Wil. Griffin of Pudshole and came to live there last Michaelmas. She was begot with child by one Henry Wright, a seaman of the ship Resolution, who lived at St Margaret's Hill. London. She had about seven weeks to go with child. *Signed by mark,*

S3/2/14. *Calendar number on document:* 12.
9 January 1671/2. Before Phil. James, esq., Mayor.
Examination
Margery Hopkins, singlewoman, said she was begotten with child by Geo. Gray in a little room at Pudshole about 7 p.m. about a month before Lady Day when her master Griffin was coming from the said house to Portsmouth to live. The said Gray had had carnal knowledge of her body six or seven times before.
See also no. 169 (12). *Signed by mark.*

167
ASSAULT

D11A/16/6. *Calendar number on document:* 16.
14 February 1671/2. Before Phil. James, esq., Mayor.
Recognisances
      Tho. Carnell of Portsmouth, mariner, in £20.
      Rob. Cooke of the same, victualler, in £10.
      Mat. Symons of the same, victualler, in £10.
For appearance of Joan, wife of Tho. Carnell, at the next Sessions to answer such trespasses as shall be objected against her and to keep the peace, especially towards (*blank*), wife of Rob. (Tho. *scored through*) Jackson.
Footnote: Bound over for beating Tho. Jackson's wife.
See also no. 169 (16).

168
ASSAULT

S3/3/1

10 March 24 Cha. II [1671/2].

Presentment (Latin)

Presents Nic. Badcocke lately of Portsmouth, gent., who on 10 Mar. 24 Cha. II by force of arms in Portsmouth wounded and ill-treated Tho. Goddard.

    Footnote: He submitted and was fined 20s.

    Endorsements:

    (a) True bill.

    (b) Tho. Goddard, Frampton Speed, Geo. Hodely: witnesses.

169
LIST OF RECOGNISANCES

S3/2/5

[18] April 1672. Easter Sessions.

List of Recognisances since Michaelmas Sessions 1671 with reason for binding over.

  (1) Grace Costin, widow, stealing coals from Mrs Haberley.

  (2) Phil. Woolcott, rape of Margaret Chambers (?).

  (3) Simon Lucas, getting Elizabeth Merriweather with child.
     See no. 171.

  (4) Tho. Lightfoot, breaking Capt. Moore's storehouse.

  (5) Tho. Hunt, abusing Capt. Elliott.

  (6) Tho. Triggs   ⎫
      Paul Richards   ⎬ libel.

  (7) Henry Woolgar, threatening to kill Phineas Haynes.
     See nos 163, 170.

  (8) Ric. Westbrooke, getting Mary Phillips with child.
     See no. 164.

  (9) Ant. Stratton, beating and abusing Anne Judson, widow.
     See no. 158.

  (10) Ben. Fulford   ⎫
  (11) Ben. Dennis   ⎬ selling his wares within this Liberty.
     See nos 159, 160.

  (12) Geo. Gray, getting Margery Hopkins with child.
     See no. 166.

  (13) James Crooker   ⎫
  (14) Tho. Barrow   ⎬ suspicion of felony. *See no.* 156.
  (15) Henry Penn   ⎭

  (16) Tho. Carnell, for his wife to appear at Sessions for beating Goody Jackson.
     See no. 167.

  (17) Nat. Popejoy, for being servant to Henry Dismore of Southwark, [Surr.].
     See no. 157.

  (18) Wil. Long, stealing the King's iron from the Dockyard.
     See no. 149.

MICHAELMAS SESSIONS 10 October 1672

170
ASSAULT

S3/3/19. *Calendar number on document:* 2.

18 April 1672. Before Phil. James, esq., Mayor.

Recognisances

     Henry Woolgar in £20.
     Art. Hawtrey of Kingston in £10.

    For appearance of Woolgar at the next Sessions.
    Bound over anew by order of the last Sessions.

See also nos 163, 169 (7).

171
BASTARDY

S3/3/20[25]

18 April 1672. Before Phil. James, esq., Mayor.
Recognisances
      Simon Lucas of Portsmouth, shipwright, in £40.
      Tho. Pay of Portsmouth, shipwright, in £20.
      Ric. Deacon of Portsmouth, shipwright, in £20.
For appearance of Lucas at the next Sessions and meantime to give security for the keeping of a bastard child.
Bound over anew by order of the Sessions.[26]
See also no. 169 (3).

172
ASSAULT

S3/3/18. *Calendar number on document:* 3.

12 May 1672. Before Phil. James, esq., Mayor, and Tho. Plover.
Recognisances
      Nic. Badcocke of Portsmouth, gent., in £200.
      Tho. Hancocke of Portsmouth, gent., in £100.
      Raleigh Hullum of Portsmouth in £100.
For appearance of Badcocke at the next Sessions.
Bound over for beating and wounding Tho. Goddard.
Footnote: Submitted and 20s fine paid to the Mayor.

173
ABUSING
AUTHORITY

D11A/16/8

2 June 1672. Before Phil. James, esq., Mayor, and Hugh Salesbury, gent.
Examination and information
Tho. Harding, Constable, said he was with Jos. Phillpott, one of the instruments to the Commissioners for the excise of beer and ale, at the house of Edw. Brooker, Sergeant-at-Mace, about 11 p.m. yesterday. He told Phillpott to go to his lodging as it was late and, as he was going, Phillpott gave him 'very ill language' saying amongst other things that 'the Constables of Portsmouth should kiss his arse'. As it was late Harding could not take him before a Justice but secured him in the Town Prison.   *Signed.*

174
CONTEMPT

S3/3/15

23 July 1672. Before Phil. James, esq., Mayor.
Examination
Dan. Vibeard said he was pre-warned by the Mayor that he should not open his shop windows in Portsmouth to sell drapery ware.

S3/3/16

23 July 1672. Before Phil. James, esq., Mayor.
Recognisances
      Dan. Vibeard in £20.
      Wil. Palmer in £10.
      John Swaine in £10.
For appearance of Vibeard at the next Sessions.
Bound over for 'contempning' of the Mayor's order in opening his windows when he had a contrary order and calling the Mayor 'foole upon ye breath'.

175
ASSAULT

S3/3/12

16 August 1672. Before Phil. James, esq., Mayor.
Examination
Wil. Colmer of Portsmouth, rope maker, said that last Friday about 6 p.m. in the house of (*blank*) English in Portsmouth, being his quarters, he was with John Adams,

---

[25] Endorsements (this document was evidently at one time the outermost document in the bundle for these Sessions):
  (a) (*English and Latin*) Michaelmas Sessions 1672. Archer, Clerk of the Peace.
  (b) 'Here are Instruments for pound Breach and for a person refusing to be uncovered and keeping his Hatt on whilst a Proclamacion was reading'.
[26] This order for renewal and that in no. 170 were made at the Easter Sessions held on 18 Apr. 1672, but these papers were put on the file for the following Michaelmas Sessions as the cases were brought up again then.

a Dutchman, and Elizabeth, wife of Tho. Casey. Elizabeth began to abuse and beat Adams and presently the said John (*sic*) Casey came in and gave Adams several blows.   *Signed.*

S3/3/13. *Calendar number on document:* 7.
16 August 1672. Before Phil. James, esq., Mayor.
Recognisances
>   Tho. Casey and Elizabeth his wife in £20.
>   Ric. Mellish of Portsmouth in £10.
>   Ant. White of Portsmouth in £10.
For appearance of Tho. and Elizabeth Casey at the next Sessions.
Bound over for beating John Adams, a Dutchman belonging to the Unicorn.

176
BASTARDY

S3/3/14
20 August 1672. Before Phil. James, esq., Mayor.
Examination
Ann Randall, singlewoman, said that she was servant to John Williams of Horsley-down, Southwark, [Surr.], tailor, at Christmas last. She lived with him for a quarter of a year and no longer and she was with child by him.
                                                                            Signed by mark (as Ann Williams).

177
POUNDBREACH

S3/3/3
19 August 24 Cha. II [1672].
Presentment (Latin)
Presents Ellis Baker of Portsmouth, gent., who on 19 Aug. 24 Cha. II tried to remove fourteen cows doing damage in a field of twenty acres, called Havencroft, to a park at Coldharbour but Ric. Mittins of Portsmouth, yeoman, forcibly prevented this.
                                                                            Signed by [Edw.] Archer.

>   *Endorsement:* Ellis Baker, Tho. Plover.

S3/3/10
20 August 1672. Before Phil. James, Mayor.
Examination
Tho. Plover jun. said that he was with Mr Ellis Baker, Chamberlain of Portsmouth, yesterday afternoon when they were going to drive the fields. Having driven the field Havencroft, they found several cattle there and as they came back again they met Ric. Mittins in the lane beyond the fountain who stopped the cattle, prevented them from going to the pound and drove them away with the assistance of Pyle's man.
                                                                            Signed.

S3/3/11. *Calendar number on document:* 9.
22 August 1672. Before Phil. James, esq., Mayor.
Recognisances
>   Ric. Mittins in £20.
>   Ric. Ridge of Portsmouth in £10.
For appearance [of Mittins] at the next Sessions.
Bound over for a poundbreach.

178
CONTEMPT

S3/3/2
30 August 24 Cha. II [1672].
Presentment (Latin)
Presents Rob. Wilkins of Portsmouth for contempt on 30 Aug. 24 Cha. II in the Market Place in obstinately and contemptuously refusing to remove his hat in the presence of Phil. James, esq., Mayor, and in contempt of the Royal Proclamation.
                                                                            Signed by [Edw.] Archer.

Footnote: He submitted and was fined £5.
Endorsements:
(a) True bill.
(b) John Murrey, John Chapman.

S3/3/8

14 September 1672. Before Phil. James, esq., Mayor.
Recognisance
      John Morey in £20.
For his appearance at the next Sessions.
Bound over to prosecute Rob. Wilkins.

179
RIOT

S3/3/9

31 August 1672. Before Phil. James, esq., Mayor.
Recognisances
      Edw. Woolgar in £20.
      Rob. Gregge in £10.
      Jos. Softly in £10.
For appearance of Edw. Woolgar at the next Sessions.
Bound over for a riot and breaking Mr Gravett's windows.

S3/3/5

6 September 1672. Before Phil. James, esq., Mayor, and Sam. Williams, gent.
Recognisances
      Ric. Woolgar of Kingston, labourer, in £20.
      Rob. Hawkes in £10.
      Jos. Perman in £10.
For appearance of Ric. Woolgar at the next Sessions.
Bound over for a riot and breaking Mr Gravett's windows.

S3/3/6

6 September 1672. Before Phil. James, esq., Mayor, and Sam. Williams, gent.
Recognisances
      Nic. Woolgar in £20.
      Rob. Hawkes of Kingston in £10.
      Jos. Perman in £10.
For appearance of Nic. Woolgar at the next Sessions.
Bound over for a riot and breaking Mr Gravett's windows.

S3/3/7

6 September 1672. Before Phil. James, esq., Mayor, and Sam. Williams, gent.
Recognisances
      Phineas Haynes of Kingston, in parish of Portsea, labourer, in £20.
      Rob. Hawkes in £10.
      Jos. Perman in £10.
For appearance of Haynes at the next Sessions.
Bound over for a riot and breaking Mr Gravett's windows.

S3/3/4

8 October 1672. Before Nic. Peirson, esq., Mayor, Phil. James and Hugh Salesbury.
Recognisances
      Ann Clapshawe in £20.
      Phil. Elmes in £10.
For appearance [of Ann] at the next Sessions.
Bound over for a riot and breaking Mr Gravett's windows.

EASTER SESSIONS 17, 29 April, 20, 27 May and 3 June 1673
No papers survive.

For further entry in Sessions Books see Appendix II, no. 81.

180

RAPE

S3/4/4

15 July 1673. Before Nic. Peirson, esq.

Examination

Mary Penn of Kingston, singlewoman, said that about a fortnight before Midsummer last she was a servant of Jos. Peerman. About midnight he called to her to bring him some beer for the child that lay in the bed with him. She set the beer down by the bedside and her master got out of bed and took hold of her and threw her on the bed and stopped her mouth with a sheet and his hand. He said she was his servant and if she cried out he would mischief her. Before he had carnal knowledge of her body, he promised her marriage so she consented. She never disclosed this to anybody because he had promised her marriage. A week last Thursday she asked him if he would marry her but he refused. She then went to her sister Binstead at Kingston and told her. *Signed by mark.*

S3/4/3

22 July 1673. Before Nic. Peirson, esq., Mayor, and Phil. James.

Recognisances

Jos. Peerman of Kingston, parish of Portsea, victualler, in £40.

John Fussard of Kingston, victualler, in £20.

John Burrell of Kingston, labourer, in £20.

For appearance of Peerman at the next Sessions to answer Mary Penn, singlewoman.

Bound over on adjournment of charge of rape against Mary Penn.

181

THEFT

S3/4/1

19 August 1673. No name of Justice.

Information

John Brewty of the City of London, vintner, servant to Mr Wil. Tomson, said that the carrier of Godalming, [Surr.], informed his master by letter dated Saturday 16 Aug. that Jos. Jones, a person mentioned in the Gazette, was then at Godalming. His master sent him to Godalming where he heard that Jones was in Portsmouth where he found him, had him arrested and charged with feloniously stealing £45 from Mr John Walker at the Swan in Bedford. *Signed.*

Recognisance

John Brewty in £40 to appear at Bedford Assizes to give evidence.

182

ARSON

S3/4/2 (entry i)

No date [circa 19 August 1673]. No name of Justice.

Informations

(a) Rob. Kibe said that about a quarter of a year ago he found a lighted match in the furze near his dwelling, took it in and quenched it, not knowing how it came there.

(b) Henry Evans. *No entry against his name.*

(c) Susanna Sanders said that when she was abroad leasing she met (*blank*), servant of (*blank*) Roaker.

(d) Mathew Brooman said that last Wednesday she (*sic*), being leasing in the fields with Joan Pococke, servant to John Roaker, asked her 'what she done here soe early'. Joan answered she knew well enough what she had to do here and that according to her dame's command she had laid fire 'to do Goodman Kibe's business'. *Signed by mark.*

(e) Elizabeth, wife of Geo. Sturton, said that last Wednesday she was in the fields leasing with Mathew Brooman and Joan Pococke, servant to John Roaker, when the two girls fell out and in their quarrel Roaker's servant declared that for Kibe's part she would do his business as she would warrant they should all see. *Signed by mark.*

19 August 1673.
Recognisances (scored through)
  Joan Pocock in £20.
  John Roaker in £10.
  John Edwards in £10.
For appearance [of Joan] at the next Sessions.

183
TRADING
IRREGULARLY

S3/4/2 (entry ii)
No date [circa 19 August 1673]. No name of Justice.
Memoranda
 (a) 'Murray wid[ow] for selling beer without licence.'
 (b) 'Mary the wife of Roger Pascoe.'

184
Subject unknown

S3/4/5
20 August 1673. Before Nic. Peirson, esq., Mayor.
Recognisances
  Wil. Thomson of Portsmouth, soldier, in £10.
  Wil. Tanner of Portsmouth, yeoman, in £5.
  Edw. Carter of Portsmouth, yeoman, in £5.
For appearance of Elizabeth, wife of Wil. Thomson, at the next Sessions.

185
ASSAULT

D11A/16/9
12 September 1673. Before Nic. Peirson, esq., Mayor.
Informations
 (a) Joan, wife of Geo. Rogers of Portsmouth, shipwright, said that on Tuesday morning Rebecca Richards of Portsmouth, spinster, and Elizabeth Rogers, her own daughter, went into the Dockfield to lease some barley. On their return about 8 p.m. Rebecca came in 'very melancholly' and told her that John, son of Wil. Clapshawe, of Kingston, John Curtis and Geo. Light of the same place had met with her in the field and threw her down on the ground several times. Light sat down on her stomach and hands and stopped her breath several times, while Clapshawe held her feet. They used 'many unciville terms' and called Curtis to come and lie with her. She was 'much disquieted and troubled' and has been ever since. *Signed by mark.*

 (b) Elizabeth, daughter of Geo. Rogers of Portsmouth, shipwright, aged 13, said that about 3 or 4 p.m. last Tuesday she was with her sister Rebecca Richards in the common field called Dockfield near the Pesthouse. *She confirmed the above evidence, adding* that the three men tried to get Rebecca to come away from where she was working, but she refused. She laid hands on Curtis when he attempted to lie with Rebecca. He called Elizabeth a damned bitch, kicked her and threw her down almost into a deep ditch of water. The second time that they threw Rebecca down they bound her with a cord. *Signed by mark.*

 (c) Rebecca Richards of Portsmouth, spinster, aged 19, *confirmed the above evidence.* She added that there was a little boy with them, John Palm[er]. The first time she was thrown down she was held for about a quarter of an hour. They threw her down twice more. She has been 'very much disquieted and troubled', not having been well ever since. *Signed by mark.*

186
ASSAULT

S3/4/6
6 October 1673. Before Nic. Hedger, esq., Mayor, and Sam. Williams.
Information
Fra. Blake of Portsmouth said that on this day, after the Mayor and Justices had left the Court, John White took Phil. Peerson, his apprentice, by the shoulders and shoved him and struck him. *Signed by mark.*

EASTER SESSIONS 14 May 1674

No papers survive except for entries in Sessions Books: see Appendix II, nos 82, 83.

MICHAELMAS SESSIONS 15 October 1674

No papers survive.

EASTER SESSIONS 22 April 1675

187
OBSTRUCTING
AUTHORITY

S3B/10

17 December 1674. No name of Justice.

Examination

Wil. Francis of Kingston, in the parish of Portsea, husbandman, said that last Tuesday about 7 a.m. he went to Hilsea Common to cut some bushes for Ric. Alchorne, esq., carrying his scythe and hammer with him. He was to be paid by the great, i.e. 2*s* 6*d* per load. He worked there till about 12 and then went home, not feeling very well. About twilight he went to Hilsea to sell a doublet, then went to the barn where Mr Alchorne's men were still working and stayed about an hour, then to the shop of Goody Gumbe the smith to shave the hilfe of his bill and from there went home to bed. Soon after, the Constable knocked at his door saying he had come to search. He said that if the Constable would come in without his staff, or if Mr Yeomet or his wife came, they might search. He did not let them in because formerly his house had been searched for stolen goods merely through spleen and malice to impeach his credit. He heard there was a warrant against him, so thought the bailiff would come to arrest him. He told them that if they wanted to come in they must break open the door, threatening to do them a mischief. They did break open the door and searched the house and he told one Greene who came with them that if it were not for fear of the law, Greene should never clench his fist at him. *Signed by mark.*

MICHAELMAS SESSIONS 14 October 1675

No papers survive.

EASTER SESSIONS 13 April 1676

188
BASTARDY

D11A/16/10

29 December 1675. Before St John Steventon, esq., Mayor.

Information

Elizabeth, late wife of Ric. Carter of Kingston, said that her husband had been gone from her this seven years. Last harvest she bargained with Rob. Hawkes of Kingston and about the end of August Rob. Rascar, then a servant of Hawkes, had carnal knowledge of her body 'athwart ye chayres by the fireside' after Hawkes and his wife had gone to bed and again in the fields and got her with child. After that, viz. about three months ago, Mr Collins, Curate of Wymering, came to bed to her at Mr Gates' at Gatcombe, where the maid of the house was abed with her.

D11A/16/11

29 December 1675. Before St John Steventon, esq., Mayor, and Phil. James, gent.

Examination

Elizabeth, late wife of Ric. Carter of Kingston, *confirmed the above statement about her relations with Rob. Rascar.* The occasion in the fields was about a week after that in the house.

Footnote: Make a warrant to bring Jane Clapshaw.

See also nos 192, 194, 204 (2).

189
WRONGFUL
ARREST

S3B/11

No date [circa 21 April 1676]. No name of Justice.
Informations

(a) James Anderson, aged 22, said that yesterday about 3 to 4 p.m. Nic. Nosse and Jerome Overton, two bailiffs, came to Mrs Collins' house at Neptune's Court with two drummers. One bailiff went into the kitchen and arrested Mary Young as Mrs Collins. The drummers disputed whether she was Mrs Collins, and when the bailiff found the parlour locked from inside, he suspected he was mistaken in the first arrest. He tried to open the door with his stick and then took a fire-fork from the chimney to break it open. Anderson tried to prevent him as he feared they came to rob the house, but the bailiff broke the door open and arrested Mrs Collins. She sent Anderson to call some of her friends. *Signed.*

(b) Mary Young of Portsmouth, spinster, *confirmed the above evidence; she referred to James Anderson as* the tapster. *Signed.*

(c) Mary Reynolds and Alice Rumble both of Portsmouth, spinsters, *confirmed the above evidence.* They added that when the tapster desired the bailiffs to desist they swore they would break open all the doors in the house. *Both sign by mark.*

21 April 1676. Before St John Steventon, esq., Mayor.
Information
Ric. Godfrey of Portsmouth said that yesterday afternoon he was sent for to the house of Mrs Collins at Neptune's Court. He found her in the custody of Nic. Nosse and Jerome Overton of Winchester, pretended bailiffs of the County Sheriff, who had arrested her at the suit of Tho. Cornelius upon a process from the Common Pleas. He found the door out of the hook and the ward of the lock bent and the fire-fork bent almost half double. Nosse and Overton admitted that they kept her till about 10 this morning before she could procure bail. *Signed.*

S3B/12

No date. No name of Justice.
Examinations

(a) Nic. Nosse of Winchester said that yesterday afternoon he went with Jerome Overton, who is a bailiff's follower, to arrest Mrs Collins at her house. They arrested her, but he himself was not in the house when the door was broken.

(b) Jerome Overton of Winchester said he lived at Winchester and was assistant to the Sheriff's bailiff. *Record uncompleted.*

21 April 1676. No name of Justice.
Recognisances
James Anderson in £20 to appear and prosecute.
Mary Young in £20 on the said condition.
Alice Rumball in £20 on the said condition.

190
DISLOYALTY

D11A/16/12

10 June 1676. Before St John Steventon, esq., Mayor, Sam. Williams, gent., and Phil. James, gent.
Informations

(a) Henry Rainstead of Portsmouth, Sergeant-at-Mace, said that about 12 o'clock yesterday he was at the Whitehouse, the Town Prison, with Sam. Moone and heard Moone say that the Duke of York had declared himself a papist and that Moone would be the first to fight against him according to the oath of allegiance and supremacy that he had taken. *Signed.*

(b) Edw. Brooker said that yesterday about noon he was at home in the Whitehouse. *He confirmed having heard the above statement of Moone.* *Signed.*
See also App. III, no. 12.

191
ABUSING
AUTHORITY

S3B/13

24 August 1676. Before St John Steventon, esq., Mayor, and Phil. James, gent.

Informations

(a) Rob. Bishopp of Portsmouth, baker, said that last Tuesday, 22 Aug., about 10 p.m. he was ordered by Mr Etherrington, one of the Constables, to assist him when Frances, wife of Wil. Streaper, abused him, calling him rogue and knave and using indecent language. *Signed.*

(b) James Etherrington said that at the time above-mentioned he was going after a man who threatened to cause his wife's death and as he went along the street Frances, wife of Wil. Streaper, was standing at the door of Mrs (*recte Mr*) Paine railing against his wife. He asked why she was abroad at that time of night abusing her neighbours. She said she would stay there in spite of him. He went on to deal with the man threatening his wife and she followed, asking if she should be afraid to stand in the street for a Constable. *Signed.*

(c) Elizabeth (*signs* Mary) Parker, widow, said that at the above-mentioned time she was in her house and heard an outrage in the street. She went to the door and heard Frances, wife of Wil. Streaper, call Mr Etherington, the Constable, 'rascall and pittifull fellowe and that she did not care a turd for him'. *Signed.*

Recognisances

    Frances, wife of Wil. Streaper of Portsmouth, gent., in £20.
    Fra. Lucas of the same, shipwright, in £10.
    Elizabeth Dominecke of the same, widow, in £10.

For appearance of Frances Streaper at the next Sessions to answer such things as shall be objected against her.

Bound over for abusing the Constable.

Footnote: To find sureties and to appear at the next Sessions.

192
BASTARDY

D11A/16/13

5 September 1676. Before Hugh Salesbury, gent.

Examination

Elizabeth Carter said that about Midsummer 1675 she was haymaking with Tho. Barrowe, who about the middle of the day had carnal knowledge of her body in the field. About a week later being at the house of his brother, Ric. Barrowes, Tho. Barrowes again had carnal knowledge of her body on the bed. When she swore that the child was begotten by Rob. Rascar she was being threatened by her aunt Jane Clapshowe and Margaret Guilbert, both housekeepers at Kingston. She was brought abed about a week in April following with a male child. *Signed by mark.*

Recognisances

(a) Tho. Barrowe of Kingston in £10.
    John Fuzard of the same in £5.
    Tho. Hackman of the same in £5.
For appearance of Barrowe 'at His Majesty's Sessions'.

(b) Rob. Rascar in £10.
    Rob. Hawkes in £5.
    Tho. Tomes in £5.

(c) Elizabeth, wife of Ric. Carter, in £10.
    Rob. Hawkes in £5.
    Ric. Mittens in £5.

See also nos 188, 194, 204 (2).

EASTER SESSIONS 26 April 1677

193
Subject unknown

S3/5/1. *Calendar number on document:* 1.

12 October 1676. Before Sam. Williams, esq., Mayor, Sir John Biggs, Recorder, and other Justices.

Recognisances[27]

  Ant. Corps of Portsmouth, tailor, in £20.

  Wil. Clarke in £10.

  Ric. Corps in £10.[28]

For appearance [of Ant. Corps] at the next Sessions. Bound anew.

See also no. 204 (1).

194

BASTARDY

S3/5/2. *Calendar number on document:* 2.

13 October 1676. Before Sam. Williams, esq., Mayor, and Sir John Biggs, Recorder.

Recognisances[29]

  Elizabeth Carter of Kingston, parish of Portsea, in £20.

  Rob. Hawkes of the same, yeoman, in £10.

For appearance of Elizabeth at the next Sessions.

Bound over anew.

See also nos 188, 192, 204 (2).

195

REGRATING

D11A/16/14. *Calendar number on document:* 3.

4 November 1676. Before Sam. Williams, esq., Mayor, St John Steventon, gent., and Nic. Hedger, gent.

Informations

(a) Phil. James of Portsmouth, gent., said that on Saturday 28 Oct. he ordered from Nat. Harwood two joints of veal, a loin ('line') and a neck, to be sent to his house. Harwood said the veal had not come but promised to send it as soon as his calf came. He sent it and James paid 4*s* and upwards for it.   *Signed.*

(b) Tho. Heather of Havant, butcher, said that on Saturday 28 Oct. he brought a calf in the skin to this market and Nat. Harwood, butcher, bought it and paid 20*s* for it.   *Signed by mark.*

(c) Mary Wyan of Portsmouth, widow, said that on Saturday 28 Oct. she came to the market to the upper end of the butchers' shambles. Seeing some calves' legs, she asked a country butcher for some veal and he told her that he had brought a calf to market but Nat. Harwood had bought it all. As she came by Harwood's standing she saw the calf flaying ('fleaing').   *Signed.*

Examination

Nat. Harwood of Portsmouth, butcher, said that on Thursday 26 Oct. he bargained with Tho. Heather of Havant for a calf. He asked 20*s* and Harwood offered him 19*s* but he refused. He said that if he liked the calf he would give 20*s*. Heather brought the calf to market on the Saturday and he paid him 20*s* for it.

Footnote: Harwood acknowledged his examination but refused to sign as he would not have his own hand to be witness against himself.   *Signed by* R. Godfrey.

S3/5/3

4 November 1676. Before Sam. Williams, esq., Mayor, and St John Steventon, gent.

Recognisance[30]

  Tho. Heather of Havant, butcher, in £10.

For appearance at the next Sessions to give evidence against Nat. Harwood for regrating the market.

---

[27] Note of the following bond (condition not stated) is made at the foot of this recognisance:
13 April 1676. John Bye of Portsmouth, gent., bound in £10 to Tho. Brunker of Portsmouth, brazier.
[28] Ric. Corps is given as Wil. Corps in no. 204(2).
[29] On this recognisance is endorsed these memoranda:
Ellis Baker *v.* John Thomas
Jarvis Morlin *v.* Silvian Davies
Idem *v.* Tho. Clarke
[30] For a reproduction of this recognisance see fig. 4, and for a transcript see App. I, no. 2(2).

S3/5/4. *Calendar number on document:* 3.

4 November 1676. Before Sam. Williams, esq., Mayor, and St John Steventon, gent.
Recognisances
> Nat. Harwood of Portsmouth, butcher, in £40.
> James Watle of Portsmouth, butcher, in £20.
> James Harris of Portsmouth, butcher, in £20.

For appearance of Harwood at the next Sessions.
Bound over for regrating the market.

S3/5/5

4 November 1676. Before Sam. Williams, esq., Mayor, and St John Steventon, gent.
Recognisance
> Mary Wyan of Portsmouth, widow, in £10.

For appearance at the next Sessions to give evidence against Nat. Harwood.
See also no. 204 (3).

196
ASSAULT

S3/5/9

16 October 1676. Before Sam. Williams, esq., Mayor.
Information
Tho. Jacob of Portsmouth, labourer, said that about 8 p.m. last night Henry Mathewes came to the house of And. Meers at the Almshouse in Portsmouth and swore that he would break open the door. He asked for his wife, Meers' daughter, saying he was sure she was there. This brought neighbours in and Mathewes fell to fighting.   *Record uncompleted.*
Examination
Henry Mathews of Portsmouth, seaman, said that between 7 and 8 he went to the house of And. Meers, his father-in-law, to ask for his wife. He took hold of the door and presently it opened and some of the neighbours took hold of him and brought him to prison.   *Signed by mark.*

S3/5/6. *Calendar number on document:* 4.

16 October 1676. Before Sam. Williams, esq., Mayor.
Recognisances
> Henry Mathewes of Portsmouth, seaman, in £40.
> Ric. Burt of the same, yeoman, in £20.
> Tho. Allen of the same in £20.

For appearance of Mathewes at the next Sessions.
Bound over for breaking of old Meers' house.
See also no. 204 (4).

197
ASSAULT

S3/5/21

6 November 1676.
Presentment (Latin)[31]
Presents John Harwood of Kingston, parish of Portsea, yeoman, for causing an affray and beating and wounding Wil. Binsted at Kingston on 6 Nov. 1676.
   Signed by [Edw.] Archer.

Endorsements:
(a) Ignoramus.
(b) Witnesses: Tho. Hackman, Tho. Baker, Anne Mason.

S3/5/13. *Calendar number on document:* 5.

No date. No name of Justice.
Examination
John Harwood said that on Monday night he went with Tho. Hackman to Capt. Beeston's. Wil. Binsted came in while they were there and went homeward with them visiting Rob. Stayre's on the way. When they came to Widow Turner's close, within two closes of the churchyard, Hackman went to Widow Farley's and stayed there the night but Harwood only stayed about half an hour. Binsted went away, but when Harwood got home about 11 he heard a noise amongst the poultry so he went

---

[31] For a reproduction of this presentment see fig. 2, and for a transcript see App. I, no. 1.

into his skilling where he found a man stealing his poultry. He struck him with his stick in his own yard and the man ran away towards Mrs Mason. He followed the man half-way [across] the field but could not catch him and returned. *Signed.*

S3/5/11. *Calendar number on document:* 5.
8 November 1676. Before Sam. Williams, esq., Mayor.
Informations

(a) Tho. Hackman of Kingston, parish of Portsea, yeoman, said that he was at Capt. Beeston's about 6 p.m. on Monday and John Harwood was there. Wil. Bensted arrived later. Hackman and Harwood asked Beeston (*sic*) to come to town and the three of them came homewards. When they came as far as Widow Turner's close near to Widow Farley's at Fratton and within two fields of Portsea church, he left Harwood and Bensted and stayed there all night. *Signed by mark.*

(b) Tho. Baker, Constable of Kingston and Buckland, said that about 12 o'clock on Monday night John Harwood came to his house. He got out of bed and came down and Harwood told him there were thieves in his house, his hogs were turned out and his poultry crying out. He asked Harwood what he had lost but he said he could not tell. He said there was a man in his yard and he broke his stick about him. Baker found no one there and went back home. Some time after he heard somebody coming from Buckland. It was Bensted's wife who said Harwood had very much beaten her husband, so he secured Harwood with a guard at his own house till morning and Bensted confirmed that Harwood had beaten him very much the night before.

Signed by mark.

9 November 1676. Before Sam. Williams, esq., Mayor, Phil. James, gent., and Nic. Hedger, gent.
Information

Ann Mason, widow, said that on Monday night last between 1 and 2 she heard two or three blows struck and heard someone cry out 'Murther'. She went to the window and asked who they were: one answered he was Good[man] Bensted and that Harwood the other had broken his bones, so she ordered her servant to assist him and take him into the house. When she was at the window she saw a man run towards the highway with a stick in his hands. *Signed.*

S3/5/7. *Calendar number on document:* 5.
9 November 1676. Before the Mayor.
Recognisances

(a) Tho. Hackman of Kingston, parish of Portsea, in £20.
Tho. Baker in £20.
Ann Mason, widow, in £20.
For appearance [of all three] at the next Sessions to prosecute John Harwood for beating Wil. Binsted.

(b) John Harwood in £100.
Simon Coward in £50.
Tho. Upsdall in £50.
For appearance [of Harwood] at the next Sessions to answer indictment for assault and battery on Wil. Binsted.
See also no. 204 (5).

198
REGRATING

S3/5/22
7 December 1676.
Presentment (Latin)
Presents Tho. Plover of Portsmouth, butcher, for buying of Tho. Heather of Havant, butcher, on 7 Sept. last, a market day, an ox at the rate of 2*d* per lb. and selling it again at a higher rate, contrary to the Statute. *Signed by* [Edw.] Archer.
Marginal note: 5.6 E.6.14[32]
Endorsements:
(a) Ignoramus.
(b) Witnesses: Nat. Harwood, Tho. Heather.

---

[32] Marginal note refers to the Statute 5 & 6 Ed. VI, c.14.

S3/5/15. *Calendar number on document:* 6.

7 December 1676. Before Sam. Williams, esq., Mayor, and Nic. Hedger, gent.
Informations

(a) Tho. Heather of Havant, butcher, said that Mr Plover came to him at Havant about a month ago and bought a fat bullock. He took him to Langstone to see it. Plover was to send for it there and bring it to Portsmouth to kill and sell the quarters at 2*d* per lb. Heather was to have the hide and the offal. This agreement was carried out. *Signed by mark.*

(b) Nat. Harwood of Portsmouth, butcher, said that Plover sold in the Portsmouth market two or three lots of beef, being part of the said bullock, at 4*s* 6*d* per score as Mr Plover and his servants did acknowledge. *Signed.*
See also no. 204 (6).

199
ABUSING
AUTHORITY

S3/5/14. *Calendar number on document:* 7.

12 December 1676. Before Mr Mayor, Mr Steventon and Mr James.
Committal order
Tho. Hunt came into Court 'in an upbraideing manner' and told Mr Steventon that he paid more to the poor-book than he did. He gave the Court several other affronts.
Committed until such time as he finds surety.
Signed (*Latin*) *by* E[dw.] Archer, Town Clerk.

S3/5/8. *Calendar number on document:* 7.

No date. Before Sam. Williams, esq., Mayor, and Nic. Hedger, gent.
Recognisances
Tho. Hunt in £40.
Henry Lunn in £20.
A. Beacham in £20.
For appearance [of Hunt] at the next Sessions.
See also no. 204 (7).

200
BASTARDY

D11A/16/15. *Calendar number on document:* 8.

13 January 1676/7. Before Sam. Williams, esq., Mayor, and St John Steventon, gent.
Information
Ann Long of Portsmouth, singlewoman, said she lived with John Merrit of Portsmouth, block maker, and that he had carnal knowledge of her body twice, once at Michaelmas, when she came from him to live with James Lambert, the other time about a fortnight after she had been there, when she went back to Merritt's for her clothes one Sunday afternoon and there was nobody else in the house. She was now with child by Merriott. He tried 'divers times' to lie with her before. *Signed by mark.*
Recognisances
John Merrit in £40.
Edw. Brooker in £20.
For appearance [of Merrit] at the next Sessions.
Endorsement: Information against Mr Merrit about a child begotten upon Ann Long.
See also no. 204 (8).

201
ABUSE

S3/5/16. *Calendar number on document:* 9.

19 January 1676/7. Before Sam. Williams, esq., Mayor, St John Steventon, gent., and Phil. James, gent.
Informations
(a) Ric. Cresset, gent., corporal of Capt. Slingsbye's troop, said that last night about 9 p.m. he came to the house of John Thorne at the White Hart on the Point where he was lodging and went to his room with two gentlemen of the troop and called for a flagon of beer which was brought. Thorne, who was below stairs, asked what those rogues wanted. When they called for another flagon of beer Thorne, in great passion, asked whether those pitiful rogues must be waited on, so he went downstairs and asked Thorne why he abused them. Thorne then called him a rogue and

pitiful, beggarly fellow and said it was past 10 o'clock and he would go to Sir Roger Manley the Governor. *Signed.*

(b) Henry Tanner, gent., of the same troop, *repeated some of the above evidence* saying that Mr Cresset called for a flagon of beer and a faggot which were brought. They sent the boy for two flagons more but he came up and said that his master said they should only have one, so they told him to take it down again. They went downstairs and Tanner held the candle. Thorne said to him 'what are you that hold the pipe in your mouth'. He answered that he was one of His Majesty's servants. *Signed.*

S3/5/10. *Calendar number on document:* 9.

19 January [1676/7]. Before Sam. Williams, esq., Mayor.
Recognisances

John Thorne of Portsmouth, victualler, in £40.
Tho. Damarum of the same in £20.
Wil. Standen of the same in £20.
For appearance of Thorne at the next Sessions.
Bound over for abusing Mr Cresset and others.
See also no. 204 (9).

202

ASSAULT

S3/5/19. *Calendar number on document:* 13.

27 March [1677]. Before Sam. Williams, esq., Mayor, St John Steventon, gent., and Nic. Hedger, gent.
Informations

(a) John Roaker of Portsmouth said that about 4 p.m. today he was at his pump pumping when he was called to the house of Wil. Whitehead, there being some disturbance. He found Whitehead's wife and Ric. Barnes athwart the stile by the house. Barnes struck her on the head with the stick now shown him and the blood ran from her head *Signed by mark.*

(b) John Stubberfeild of Portsmouth, caster maker, said that about 3 p.m. today he was at work with Wil. Standing, the rope maker, near the house of Wil. Whitehead and, hearing John Roaker's wife crying out for help, he went there. He found Whitehead's wife and Ric. Barnes down together in the entry. The people that were there got them up and parted them and tried to quiet them. They with the other company that were in the house went into the hall. Barnes would then have left but the woman said he should not till he had paid for the broken globe and the reckoning and she thrust him back into the room. Then Barnes struck her down with his fist. Stubberfeild returned to work, but, there being further disturbance, he went back and found the two athwart the stile. Barnes then struck her with the stick now shown him and the blood came out through her head-cloth. *Signed by mark.*

S3/5/17

27 March 1677. Before the Mayor and Justices aforesaid (*i.e. Sam. Williams, St John Steventon and Nic. Hedger*).
Examination
Ric. Barnes said that he was this afternoon with some friends at the house of Wil. Whitehead, where they drank three flagons of beer and a noggin of brandy, for which he paid 10d. His friends did not follow him out, so he stayed in a field for a while before returning to the house. There he found Whitehead's wife with his friends. John Robinson and John Spereing. She demanded 2d more and payment for a globe that was broken. He said he would pay but she called him a rogue. Though he put his money on the table, she still would not let him go and fell upon him 'like to murder him twice'. He got out and seeing his stick over the stile he reached to take it and she and others fell upon him; whether he struck her or not he did not know.
Signed by mark.

S3/5/18

27 March 1677. Before Sam. Williams, esq., Mayor.
Recognisances
(a) John Roaker of Portsmouth, labourer, in £20.

For appearance at the next Sessions to give evidence against Ric. Barnes for beating the wife of Wil. Whitehead.

(b) Wil. Whitehead in £40.
     John Stuberfeild in £20.
On the same condition as the last.

27 March 1677. Before Sam. Williams, esq., Mayor, St John Steventon, gent., and Nic. Hedger, gent.

Recognisances

Ric. Barnes of Portsmouth, victualler, in £100.
Ric. Preist of the same, gent., in £50.
Tho. Gaytod of the same, victualler, in £50.[33]

For appearance of Barnes at the next Sessions and not to depart [the jurisdiction of] the Court without licence.

See also no. 204 (13).

<table>
<tr><td>203</td><td>S3/5/20</td></tr>
<tr><td>THEFT</td><td></td></tr>
</table>

26 March 29 Cha. II [1677].

Presentment (Latin; very worn)

Presents Rob. Fewter of Portsmouth, caulker, for stealing 66 lb. of the King's lead worth 10d on 26 Mar. 29 Cha. II.   *Signed by* [Edw.] Archer.

Endorsements:

(a) True bill.
(b) Witnessses: John Moore, gent., Tho. Brouncker, Ant. Charleton.

S3B/14

2 April 1677. Before Sir John Kempthorne, kt, one of the Principal Officers and Commissioners of H.M. Navy, and Mr St John Steventon.

Examinations

(a) Mr Tho. Brunker said that Rob. Fewter brought a bag into his shop and Capt. John Moore followed and asked him what the fellow had brought into the shop. He said he knew not as the bag was tied up. He never knew of lead being brought to his house, nor bargained for it, and never remembered buying anything of His Majesty's property from Rob. Fewter.

(b) Ant. Charleton, caulker, working in H.M. Yard, master of Rob. Fewter, said he did not know when or where his servant got the lead, nor of the bringing of it to his house. Fewter had served him for over six years and had always been faithful.

D11A/16/16. *Calendar number on document:* 14.

2 April 1677. Before Sir John Kempthorne kt, one of the Principal Officers and Commissioners of H.M. Navy, and St John Steventon.

Examination

Rob. Fewter confessed that part of the lead he carried to Mr Tho. Brouncker's shop he had off the keel of H.M.S. Rupert lately graved (about 30 lb.), part from H.M.S. Harwich (about 12 lb.) and the rest from several other ships in caulking 'in ye weake of ye Galleryes',[34] 66 lb. in all. He kept the lead in his master's house under the wood and his master knew nothing of it. He did not remember who advised him to take it to Mr Brouncker's shop. Mr Brouncker knew nothing of the lead till he took it to his shop.

Deposition

Capt. John Moore said that on 26 Mar. 1677 about 10 a.m. he saw Rob. Fewter, servant to Ant. Charleton, caulker of H.M. Yard, carrying a heavy bag on his shoulder. Suspecting that it contained the King's goods he followed him to Mr Brouncker's shop where he found 66 lb. of old pieces of sheeting-lead which Fewter said he picked up at several gravings of ships and had kept some of it by him for two years.

See also no. 204 (14).

---

[33] Tho. Gaytod is given as Tho. Gayton in no. 204(13).
[34] weake: Probably 'wake'. The gallery was at the stern of the ship.

G

S3/5/12

[26 April] 1677. Easter Sessions.

(1) Ant. Corps bound anew about his boy.   Wil. Clarke
                                                            Wil. Corps[35]

Marginal note (Latin): Discharged by the Court.
See no. 193.

(2) Elizabeth Carter bound anew to behaviour [for   Rob. Hawkes
bastardy].
Note placed over entry (Latin): Recognisance of Hawkes
discharged by the Court, 15 May 1677, Mr Mayor
and Mr Hedger present.
See nos 188, 192, 194.

(3) Nat. Harrwood, for regrating the market.   James Watle
                                                            James Harris

Marginal note: Ignoramus.
See no. 195.

(4) Henry Mathewes, for breaking And. Meers' door.   Ric. Burt
                                                            Tho. Allen

See no. 196.

(5) John Harwood, for assault and battery on Wil.   Simon Coward
Binsted.   Tho. Upsdall
Note placed over entry: Ignoramus.
See no. 197.

(6) Mr Plover, for regrating the market.
Note placed over entry: Ignoramus.
See no. 198.

(7) Tho. Hunt, for abusing Mr Steventon.   Henry Lunn
                                                            And. Beacha[m]

Marginal note (Latin): Discharged by the Court.
See no. 199.

(8) John Merriot, for a bastard begotten by him on his   Edward Broo[ker]
servant.
Marginal note (Latin): Discharged by the Court.
See no. 200.

(9) John Thorne, for abusing the troopers in his house.   Tho. Damarum
                                                            Wil. Standen

Marginal note (Latin): Discharged by the Court.
See no. 201.

(10) John Heather ⎤ for driving with iron-bound ⎧ Ric. Burt
                  ⎬ wheels against the   ⎨ Geo. Harwood
                  ⎪ Constitution.   ⎩
(11) Geo. Harwood ⎦   ⎧ Ric. Burt
                                                  ⎨ John Heather
                                                  ⎩

Marginal note (Latin): Discharged by the Court.

(12) John Child, for stealing 'cappsquares' from the   Henry Barnes
carriages of the King's guns at Blockhouse Point.   Tho. Roberts

(13) Ric. Barnes, for assault and battery on Ann   Ric. Preist
Whitehead.   Tho. Gayton[36]
Marginal note (Latin): Discharged by the Court.
See no. 202.

(14) Rob. Fewter, for stealing the King's lead.   Ant. Charleton
See no. 203.

---

[35] Wil. Corps is given as Ric. Corps in no. 193.
[36] Tho. Gayton is given as Tho. Gaytod in no. 193.

For further entries and copies of most of these papers in Sessions Books see Appendix II, nos 84, 85, 87–96.

205

DISSENTERS'
CONVENTICLE

D11A/16/17

14 October 1677. By Henry Beverley, Mayor, Sam. Williams, gent., and St John Steventon, gent.

Memorandum and sentence with certificate[37]

On Sunday 14 Oct. 1677 John Hickes of Portsmouth, gent., was found by the three above named Justices preaching and teaching in a seditious conventicle or meeting held at the Golden Ball, being the house of Rob. Reynolds of Portsmouth, baker, there being assembled over five persons besides those of the household, all over sixteen and subjects of this Realm. They were assembled under pretence of exercise of religion in other manner than according to the liturgy of the Church of England contrary to the Statute of 22 Cha. II.

Reynolds being on his own confession the lawful owner of the house is convicted before us of wittingly and willingly allowing the said assembly and we fine him the sum of £20. *Signed and sealed by all three Justices; wafer seals missing.*

Appended: Certificate, 24 Oct. 1677, of the record and conviction for the Sessions of 18 Oct. adjourned to 6 Nov. 1677. *Signed by all three Justices.*

D11A/16/18

14 October 1677. By Henry Beverley, Mayor, Sam. Williams, gent., and St John Steventon, gent.

Memorandum and sentence with certificate

In form similar to that above fining those attending the meeting there referred to (*unnamed*) 5s each. *Signed and sealed by all three Justices: wafer seals missing.*

Appended: Certificate, 24 Oct. 1677, of the record and conviction for the Sessions of 18 Oct. adjourned to 6 Nov. 1677. *Signed by all three Justices.*

See also App. II, nos 88, 89.

206

DISSENTERS'
CONVENTICLE

D11A/16/19 (entry i)

21 October 1677. No name of Justice.

Information

Tho. Henning and Tho. Nixon said that Ric. Drinkwater was preaching in an unlawful conventicle contrary to the Statute of 22 Cha. II, there being present about seventeen persons including:

Tho. Bolton	(*blank*) Drinkwater
Step. Knowler	Margaret Cozens
Rob. Smith	S.(?) Fishborne
Tho. Crocker	John Collier

Signed by both.

D11A/16/20

21 October 1677. By Henry Beverley, Mayor, Sam. Williams, gent., and Phil. James, gent.

Memorandum and sentence with certificate[38]

In form similar to that in no. 205, that on Sunday 21 Oct. 1677 on the oaths of Tho. Henning and Tho. Nixon, Ric. Drinkwater of Portsmouth, yeoman, was found about 11 a.m. preaching to above five persons in a house belonging to Wil. Cozens the elder, who was fined £20. *Signed and sealed by all three Justices; wafer seals missing.*

Appended: Certificate, 24 Oct. 1677, of the record and conviction for the Sessions of 18 Oct. adjourned to 6 Nov. 1677. *Signed by all three Justices.*

---

[37] There is a note added in pencil, apparently a 19th-century hand, on this document:
'Hickes was fined Twenty Pounds and was in Monmouth's Rebellion and was the cause of the execution of Lady Lisle by beheading under sentence by "Monster Jeffreys". See the fresco painting by Ward in the Lobby of the House of Commons'. There is also a note on Hickes in R. East, *Extracts from Portsmouth records*, p. 179.

[38] For a reproduction of this memorandum and sentence see fig. 7, and for a transcript, with the certificate, see App. I, no. 4.

D11A/16/21

21 October 1677. By Henry Beverley, Mayor, Sam. Williams, gent., and Phil. James, gent.

Memorandum and sentence with certificate

In form similar to that in no. 205, fining the following 5*s* each:

Tho. Boulton	(*blank*) Drinkwater
Step. Knowler	Margaret Cozens
Rob. Smith	(*blank*) Fishbourne
Tho. Crocker	John Collier

Signed and sealed by all three Justices; wafer seals missing.

Appended: Certificate, 24 Oct. 1677, of the record and conviction for the Sessions of 18 Oct. adjourned to 6 Nov. 1677. *Signed by all three Justices.*

See also App. II, nos. 90, 92.

207

ASSIZE OF BREAD

D11A/16/19 (entry ii)

No date [circa 21 October 1677]. Issued by the Justices[39]

White bread: Halfpenny loaf was to weigh 4 ounces 0 drams, penny loaf to weigh 8 ounces 1 dram and 2*d* loaf to weigh double this.

Wheaten bread: Penny loaf was to weigh 12 ounces 1 dram and the 2*d*, 3*d*, 4*d* and 6*d* loaves to weigh in appropriate multiples of this.

Household bread: Penny loaf was to weigh 16 ounces 2 drams and the 2*d*, 3*d* 4*d* and 6*d* loaves to weigh in similarly appropriate multiples.

208

DISSENTERS' CONVENTICLE

D3A/1/3

21 October 1677. By Sam. Williams, Deputy Mayor, and Nic. Hedger.

Memorandum and sentence with certificate

In form similar to that in no. 205, that Wil. Farmer and James Clifford said that Ric. Drinkewater of Portsmouth, yeoman, was found preaching in a seditious conventicle of over five persons in the house of Wil. Cozens. Cozens fined £20 for permitting such an assembly to meet a second time in his house.

Signed and sealed by both Justices; wafer seals missing.

Appended: Certificate, 24 Oct. 1677, of the record and conviction for the Sessions of 18 Oct. adjourned to 6 Nov. 1677. *Signed by both Justices.*

D11A/16/22

21 October 1677. By Sam. Williams, Deputy Mayor, and Nic. Hedger, gent.

Memorandum and sentence with certificate

In form similar to that in no. 205, *it repeats the information given above and gives the time as* 3 p.m. The following were fined (*blank*) because it was the second time:

Rob. Smith	Tho. Boulton
Step. Knowler	John Collier
Tho. Crocker	(*blank*), wife of Mic. Richardson
(*blank*) Drinkwater	

Signed and sealed by both Justices; wafer seals missing.

Appended: Certificate, 24 Oct. 1677, of the record and conviction for the Sessions of 18 Oct. adjourned to 6 Nov. 1677. *Signed by both Justices.*

See also App. II, nos 94, 95.

209

DISSENTERS' CONVENTICLE

D3A/1/2

21 October 1677. By Sam. Williams, Deputy Mayor, and Nic. Hedger.

Memorandum and sentence with certificate

In form similar to that in no. 205, that on Sunday 21 Oct. 1677 Tho. Henning, Tho. Smith, Tho. Tyler and Hen. Matthews said that John Collier of Portsmouth, tailor, was found by them about 3 p.m. on that day preaching in a seditious conventicle at a house of Wil. Cozens sen., there being assembled fifteen persons or more. Collier is fined £20. *Signed and sealed by both Justices; wafer seals missing.*

---

[39] This was done according to the Statute 51 Hen. III, c.6, amended by 22 & 23 Cha. II, c.12.

Appended: Certificate, 24 Oct. 1677, of the record and conviction for the Sessions of 18 Oct. adjourned to 6 Nov. 1677. *Signed by both Justices.*
See also App. II, no. 96.

210	D11A/16/23
DISSENTERS'	**18 November 1677.** Before Henry Beverley, esq., Mayor, Sam. Williams, gent., and
CONVENTICLE	St John Steventon, gent.

Information
Geo. Wharton and Alex. Willson, gent., said that about 3 p.m. that afternoon they found Tho. Bowes preaching to a seditious conventicle of over twenty people, including:

    John Collier   Rob. Hoocker
    Edw. Flower   (*blank*), wife of Mic. Richardson
                                                      Signed by both.

D11A/16/24
19 November 1677. By Henry Beverley, esq., Mayor, Sam. Williams, gent., and St John Steventon, gent.
Memorandum and sentence with certificate (Latin)
In form similar to that in no. 205, *it repeats information given above but gives the name of Richardson's wife as* Lydia. Each of those attending was fined 5s.
Signed by all three Justices.
    Appended: Certificate, 19 Nov. 1677, of the record and conviction for the Sessions of 18 Oct., adjourned in turn to 6, 13 and 26 Nov.

EASTER SESSIONS 11 and 23 April 1678

For further entry in Sessions Books see Appendix II, no. 86.

211	D11A/16/25
ASSAULT	**15 January 1677/8.** Before Sam. Williams, gent., Deputy Mayor.

Information
John Addams of Portsmouth, barber and Constable, said that last Saturday about 10 p.m. he went with Wil. Standen, another Constable, to the house of John Grover to drink a pot of beer. They found Tho. Wells and his wife and Dan. Collins sitting by the fire with John Grover and his wife. Before they had drunk Corporal Davis came into the room with two musketeers and asked Addams if he lodged there. He answered Davis that he knew he did not. Davis then said Addams should come and lie at his house but on the boards not on a bed. Addams refused to go and the corporal laid hold of him and made the musketeers hold him too. He asked to go home and shut up his shop; this he did and shut the door but the corporal broke in, seized his constable's staff and tried to break it. *Signed.*

MICHAELMAS SESSIONS 18 October 1678

212	S3B/15
BASTARDY	**20 April 1678.** Before Nic. Hedger, gent.

Information
Sarah Long, spinster, said she is now servant to Edw. Flower of Kingston, entering his service on Friday of Easter week and agreeing to serve him till Midsummer. Before she came to him she lived for three and a quarter years with Wil. Badcocke of Portsmouth, mariner, and she was there begotten with child about six months ago by Badcocke her master. *Signed by mark.*

213
BASTARDY

D11A/16/26. *Calendar number on document:* 6.

17 June 1678. Before Nic. Hedger, gent.
Information
Mary Gibbins, spinster, said she had lived with John Clifford of Portsmouth, victualler, since 26 Mar. last. She did not know whether she was with child or not, but confessed that he had had carnal knowledge of her body several times. If she was with child, he was the father.

Signed by mark; countersigned by witnesses Tho. Hayes, James Archer.
Recognisances
    John Clifford of Portsmouth in £20.
    Mat. Gibbins of the same, labourer, in £10.
For appearance of Clifford at the next Sessions and not to depart [the jurisdiction of] the Court without licence.

EASTER SESSIONS 1 May 1679

214
ABUSING
AUTHORITY

S3/6/51

14 November 1678. Before John Moore, Mayor.
Recognisances
    Tho. Hamond of Portsmouth in £20.
    Ric.(?) Preist of the same in £10.
    Ric. Barnes of the same in £10.
For appearance of Hamond at the next Sessions and not to depart [the jurisdiction of] the Court. Bound over for abusing the Mayor.
Note (Latin) against Hamond's name: He came.
Footnote: 25 Jan. 1678/9. Discharged by Rob. Shales, esq., Mayor, and Mr Nic. Hedger(?), gent. Tho. Ham[ond] not to be put on the next jury.

215
POPERY AND
SETTLEMENT

S3/6/52

17 December 1678. Before Henry Beverley, Deputy Mayor, and Nic. Hedger, gent.
Recognisances
    Fra. Perkins of Kingston, parish of Portsea, gent., in £200.
    Winifred Yeomett of the same, widow, in £100.
    John Betworth of the same, yeoman, in £100.
    John Pearson of Milton, yeoman, in £100.
For appearance of Perkins at the next Sessions for refusing to take the oaths of supremacy and allegiance. He was not to pass more than five miles from the house of Mrs Winifred Yeomett in Portsea being the place of his abode, and not to depart [the jurisdiction of] the Court without a licence. Suspected to be a Papist.
Footnote: Discharged by the Court on his promise to depart out of this Liberty to the New Forest and not to return here again.

S3/6/4

No date. Before Rob. Shales, esq., Mayor, and other Justices.
Recognisances
    Fra. Perkins, gent., in £100.
    John Betsworth, of Portsea, yeoman, in £50.
For removal of Perkins from the house of Mrs Yeomett in the parish of Portsea to Brook in the parish of Bramshaw ('Brambleshawe') before Wednesday next with licence to depart and not to return to Portsea without licence.

216
SERVICE

S3/6/1

28 December 1678. Before John Moore, esq., Mayor, and Nic. Hedger, gent.
Informations
    (a) Henry Rainsted, one of the Sergeants-at-Mace of the Borough, said that he was sent this day by the Mayor and Mr Hedger to the house of Mr St John Steventon to speak with Ann Olding to require her to go before the Justices of the Peace to

show cause why she absented herself from her service. He asked to see Mrs Steventon and the maid said she would go and tell her mistress. She came back and said that her mistress had locked up Ann in a chamber for a week and was resolved that Ann should not go to Mr Mayor's to live. When her mistress was well she would come and speak to Mr Hedger. *Signed.*

(b) Tho. Staines (*signs* Stean[. . .]), one of the Constables of the Borough, said that yesterday, having received a warrant from the Mayor and Mr Hedger to arrest Ann Olding, he went to the house of Mr Steventon and asked for Ann. He met Mrs Steventon who told him she had locked her up and would not let her go. She herself would wait upon Mr Hedger if he so wished. *Signed.*

6 January 1678/9. Before the same Justices.

Information

John Blakely of Portsmouth, mercer, said that on Saturday last, 4 Jan., with a warrant for bringing Ann Olding before the Mayor or a Justice, he went to the house of Mr Steventon where he found Tho. Staines, another Constable, Elizabeth, wife of Mr Steventon and Ann Olding, together with others in a room. Mr Staines went out, then Mrs Steventon following, Ann went to go too, so Blakely tried to stop her and told her she must go with him. Mrs Steventon seeing this rescued Ann by thrusting him aside and pulling Ann into a closet and fastening it. *Signed.*

S3B/16

No date.[40]

Case for counsel's opinion

Complaint was made by Mr Mayor to Mr Nic. Hedger and the rest of the Justices that Ann Olding had agreed to serve him from St Thomas' day[41] last for a whole year and had absented herself. A warrant was issued for the Constables to bring her before the Justices.

Tho. Staines, one of the Constables, found Ann at the house of Mr St John Steventon and meeting Elizabeth, Steventon's wife, asked for Ann, but she said she had locked her up and would not let her go with him.

Mr Hedger sent Henry Rainsted, one of the Sergeants-at-Mace, to the house to see Ann and require her to come before the Justices. A maid said that her mistress had locked Ann up and would not let her go to the Mayor to live but that her mistress would speak to Mr Hedger when she was well.

Mr Hedger then wrote to Mrs Steventon, sending the letter by Mr Archer, asking her to let Ann come or there would be further trouble. Her husband on seeing the letter promised that Mrs Steventon would go to Mr Hedger on that day or the next, but she failed to go.

A new warrant was issued and another of the Constables, John Blakely, found Tho. Staines there, but Mrs Steventon prevented their arresting Ann by rescuing her and locking her in a closet.

Queries:

(1) Can Mrs Steventon for her action be compelled to find sureties to appear at the next Sessions to answer for the contempt and rescue?

(2) Mr Steventon was sworn a Justice on 20 Oct. last but has not taken the Sacrament nor taken the statutory oaths. Can he act? If not, can the Corporation proceed to a new election and may he stand for such election with the rest of the aldermen?

Mr Steventon now sponsors the quarrel. Mrs Steventon has locked up all the maid's clothes since St Thomas' day and threatens to burn them if she leaves.

The maid at Michaelmas last bargained with Mrs Steventon to serve her till St Thomas' day. After about a fortnight they quarrelled and the maid went to Mr Mayor to bargain with him. Mr Steventon protested to the Mayor and Justices that she was his servant and the Mayor sent her back. Some time after, the maid came

---

[40] Pencil note, '1678'.
[41] St. Thomas' day: 21 Dec.

again and agreed with the Mayoress to come at St Thomas' day, when her quarter would have expired. Nevertheless, though the maid had served her time, Mrs Steventon would not let her go.

Query:

(3) Of which is she the servant according to law?

13 January 1678/9. From J. Peachy.

Counsel's opinion

(1) The matter of the retainer of the servant is for the Justices to decide and they are right in issuing their warrant. Mrs Stephenton (*sic*) having obstructed the execution and rescued the party she may be bound to be of good behaviour and to appear at the next Sessions without any respect to the validity of the retainer. She could be fined for her obstruction.

(2) If Mr St John Stephenton receive not the sacrament and take not the oaths, he cannot act as a Justice. If he does act, it is void and he incurs a £500 penalty. The Corporation may go to a new election as in case of death, but ought not to put him in the election.

(3) A servant may be retained for a quarter of a year and may within that time contract with another to begin at the end of that quarter. I take the Statute of 5 Eliz. as to retainer for a year to extend to labourers and servants in the trades therein mentioned.

Signed.

217 **CONTEMPT**	S3/6/53

11 January 1678/9. Before Nic. Hedger, gent.

Recognisances

  Simon Lawrence of Portsmouth in £20.
  Wil. White sen. of the same, victualler, in £10.
  Nic. Lawrence of the same, gardener, in £10.

For appearance of Simon Lawrence at the next Sessions and not to depart [the jurisdiction of] the Court without licence.

Bound over for contempt of Court.

218 **Subject unknown**	S3/6/56

21 January 1678/9. Before John Moore, esq., Mayor, Henry Bev[er]ley, gent., Sam. Williams, gent., and Nic. Hedger, gent.

Recognisances

  John Blackeley in £20.
  Lewis Barton in £10.

For appearance [of Blackeley] at the Sessions.

219 **ASSAULT AND BATTERY**	S3/6/54

17 April 1679. Before Phil. James, gent.

Recognisances

  Nic. Roaker of Portsmouth, husbandman, in £50.
  John Child of the same, house-carpenter, in £20.

For appearance of Roaker at the next Sessions on indictment for assault and battery.

For assaulting Mr Rob. Holloway.

220 **FAILING TO PROSECUTE**	S3/6/55

17 April 1679. Before Nic. Hedger, gent., and Phil. James, gent.

Recognisances

  Katherine, wife of Tho. Rudge of Portsmouth, victualler, in £100.
  Tho. Colecut of Winchester, gent., in £50.
  Tho. Rudge of Portsmouth, victualler, in £50.

For appearance of Katherine at the next Sessions for not prosecuting Tho. Goodier but concealing ('cealeing') his robbery.

S3/6/17

23 April 1679.
Presentment (Latin)
Presents John Adams of Portsmouth, barber, for beating and wounding Mat. Footes
on 23 Apr. 1679. *Signed by* [Edw.] Archer.

Footnote: He confesses the indictment because he does not wish to oppose the King.
3s 4d.
Endorsements:
(a) Witness: Mary Badcocke sworn.
(b) True bill.

S3/6/3

1 May 1679. Before Nic. Hedger, gent.
Informations
(a) Mary, wife of Wil. Badcocke of Portsmouth, mariner, said that about 22 Apr.
last some youths were playing before her husband's door on the Point, taking great
clods of earth from the works and throwing them at each other. Mat. Footes, a
soldier, seeing this, took a stick and went out of doors to strike the boys and send
them away from the works. In the meantime John Adams passed by him and presently
came back and having a cane in his hands fell upon Footes and struck him several
blows about his head and shoulders and beat at the door. Footes has been sick ever
since and spits blood. *Signed by mark.*

(b) Osmond Branstone, soldier under the command of Capt. Seamer, said that
about Easter Tuesday last he was at the shop of Goodman Knowler on the Point and
saw several boys before the house of Wil. Badcocke and heard them quarrel, curse and
swear saying that if the son of a whore came out they would thrash his bones. Mat.
Footes, a soldier, came out of the house and one of the boys came at him and closed
with him. By the time Footes had got clear of the boy, John Adams came and fell foul
of him and struck him several blows with his cane about the head and shoulders.
Signed by mark.

Examination
John Adams said that on Easter Tuesday last by the house of Wil. Badcocke several
boys were playing at 'chucke bullett' and a soldier amongst them. He found that
there was a difference between the boys and the soldier, who went in to Badcocke's
house, fetched a stick and fell foul of the boys, who closed with him. Seeing his
neighbours' children beaten he struck the soldier who struck him back, so he took
the stick out of the soldier's hands and left him. Persuaded by another soldier, he
gave the stick to the servant to return to him. *Signed.*

1 May 1679. Before the Mayor and Justices in open Sessions.
Recognisances
(a) John Adams in £40.
John Grover in £20.
Henry Ransted in £20.
For appearance of Adams at the next Sessions.
(b) Mat. Footes soldier in £10 to prosecute against Adams.
See also no. 232 (1).

S3/6/2

No date [circa April 1679].
A list of names, each marked as sworn ('Jur[atur]'):

Wil. Terrill	Tho. Hayer	Rob. Bishoppe
Sam. Ingram	John Lewen	Sam. Barlowe
John Thorne	Hugh Grove	Dan. Collins
John Cotten	Tho. Triggs	Ric. Neave

Footnote (Latin): Geo. Clarke was sworn for the defence.
Endorsement:

traverse	x s		
summoning jury	viij s		
swearing three witnesses	j s		
verdict	iij s	iiij	d
£1	2	4	

223
ASSAULT

S3/6/18

3 June 1679.
Presentment (Latin)
Presents Mic. Russell of Portsmouth for beating and wounding Elizabeth, wife of Wil. Griffen of Portsmouth, shipwright, on 3 June 1679.   *Signed by* [Edw.] Archer.
    Footnote: He confesses the indictment because he does not wish to oppose the King. Fined 3s 4d.
        Endorsements:
        (a) Eliza Griffin sworn.
        (b) True bill.

S3/6/5

4 June 1679. Before Rob. Shales, esq.
Recognisances
        Mic. Russell of Portsea, mason, in £20.
        John Burrell in £10.
        Henry Pen in £10.
    For appearance of Russell at the next Sessions and to keep the peace especially towards Eliza, wife of Wil. Griffin.
See also no. 232 (2).

224
ASSAULT

S3/6/6

6 June 1679. Before Rob. Shales, esq., Mayor.
Information
Ralph Heather of Gosport, rope maker, said that about 6 a.m. this morning he was at work at the King's rope-house at the Dock when Ben. Watson and others came to work. As Heather had lost a bottle of beer that he had brought with him, he challenged Watson for his beer (Watson having some time before taken his victuals and drink). Watson denied it and when some were ordered to go to the other end of the rope-house 'to goe to laying', Watson would have him go but he refused. They fell out and there were ill words, Watson came and kicked him, struck him on the face and threatened to beat him worse.   *Signed.*

225
THEFT

S3/6/7

8 June 1679. Before Rob. Shales, esq., Mayor.
Recognisances
        Mat. Holt of Portsmouth in £100.
        Nic. Roaker of the same, husbandman, in £50.
        Wil. Easton of the same, victualler, in £50.
    For appearance [of Holt] at the next Sessions and not to depart [the jurisdiction of] the Court without licence.
    Bound over on suspicion of stealing sacks of wheat from the Navy victuallers.
See also no. 232 (3).

226
SERVICE

S3/6/8

25 June 1679. Before Nic. Hedger, gent.
Information
John Heddy of Dorset, husbandman, said that Fra. Pratt, being a servant of Step. Olding, declared in his presence that he would take his shirt and run away from his master.   *Signed by mark.*
    Footnote: Mr Hedger ordered the servant to go to his master which he promised to do and was discharged.

227
SERVICE AND
ASSAULT

S3/6/9

15 July 1679. Before Sam. Williams, gent., Deputy Mayor, and Nic. Hedger, gent.
Information
Joan Gates of Portsmouth, spinster, servant to Goodwife Long, said that she got leave of her dame to attend Elizabeth Crispe in her sickness and her dame would not take

her back. Elizabeth gave her leave to stay with her until she had a new service. One night whilst she was there Geo. Guy came to bed to them and when she told this next day, Elizabeth fell upon her and beat her making her spit blood.

Signed by mark.

228
THEFT

S3/6/19
28 July 1679.
Presentment (Latin)
Presents Tho. (*sic*) Wooldrige of Portsmouth, labourer, for stealing £10, the personal property ('de pecuniis propriis mune[rariis]') of Tho. Chadborne of Portsmouth, gent.

Signed by [Edw.] Archer.

Note against Wooldrige's name: Non cul.
Endorsements:
(a) Tho. Chadborne sworn.
(b) True bill.

S3/6/10 (entry i)
31 July [1679]. Before Nic. Hedger, gent.
Information
Tho. Chadborne, master and gunner of the ship Edgar, said that John Wooldrige, his servant, was usually entrusted by him with money and other things. Last Tuesday afternoon he missed some money he had left in a locker and, missing his servant, made search for him. He found him with some money about him which he supposed was his money.

Signed by mark.

Recognisance
Tho. Chadborne in £20.
For appearance at the next Sessions to give evidence against John Wooldrige for stealing money from him.
Examination
Wooldrige (*signs* Woolderidg) said that his master and mistress went ashore and left him to make up the bed in the cabin. He found some money on the bed wrapped up in a handkerchief. His master owed him money and he wanted some clothes, so he took the money, went ashore and bought clothes. His master had the rest back.

Signed.

S3/6/11
8 August 1679. Before Nic. Hedger.
Recognisances
John Wooldridge of Portsmouth, yeoman, in £40.
Jonathan Ridge in £20.
Tho. Triggs in £20.
For appearance [of Wooldridge] at the next Sessions to answer indictments made against him by Tho. Chadborne.
See also no. 232 (4).

229
ABUSE

S3/6/10 (entry ii)
31 July 1679. Before Nic. Hedger, gent.
Recognisances
James Yatman of Portsmouth, baker, in £10.
Wil. Tanner in £5.
Jonathan Ridge in £5.
For appearance of Yatman at the next Sessions.
Bound over for abusing Mr Ridge.
See also no. 232 (5).

230

REGRATING

S3/6/20

28 August 1679.

Presentment (Latin)

Presents Tho. Damarum of Portsmouth, rope maker, for buying in the public market on 28 Aug. from a person unknown twenty salt fish to the value of 10s and immediately selling them in the market at a higher price contrary to the Statute.

Signed by [Edw.] Archer.

Marginal note: 5: 6: Ed: 6: 14.[42]

Endorsements:

(a) Witnesses, Nic. Selden, Isaac Hancocke, Wil. White, sworn.

(b) Ignoramus.

S3/6/12

2 September 1679. Before Rob. Shales, esq., Mayor, Henry Beverley, gent., Sam. Williams, gent., Nic. Peirson, gent., and Phil. James, gent.

Informations

(a) Wil. White, Beadle, said that about a fortnight ago a master of a vessel whose name he has forgotten came to him and asked him to cry some fish at 14d and the best at 18d a couple. Afterwards he came to the master and asked him for the Mayor's due. He answered he would haul the vessel to Mr Gyles' quay for they were sold to Mr Damarum. Afterwards Mr Damarum ordered him to cry the said fish in his own name, some at 14d and others at 22d a couple. *Signed by mark.*

(b) Nic. Selden said that about a fortnight ago he asked the master of the vessel that had fish if he would sell any and he said he would not until they were cried.

Signed.

(c) Isaac Hancock said that about the beginning of August as he came from the Dock he went on board a vessel that was at the Town Quay and asked them if they had any fish to sell. They said not till next morning when they would open the hatches and he should have them at 18d a couple. *Signed.*

2 September 1679. Before the Mayor.

Recognisances

(a) Tho. Damarum in £40.

Rob. Gyles in £20.

Wil. Franklin in £20.

For appearance of Damarum at the next Sessions.

(b) Nic. Selden in £10.

Isaac Hancocke in £10.

Wil. White in £10.

For appearance at the next Sessions to give evidence against Tho. Damarum.

Footnote: Tho. Damarum did in the presence of the Justices confess that he bought the fish of the master of the vessel.

See also no. 232 (6).

231

THEFT

S3/6/16

30 August 1679.

Presentment (Latin)

Presents Wil. Jefferyes, John Hargood and John Beedle, all of Portchester, labourers, for stealing on 30 Aug. 1679 seven leather buckets of the King's goods value 11d.

Signed by [Edw.] Archer.

Endorsements:

(a) Step. Woolgate, John Small, Alex. Hubbard, John Nichoalson, sworn.

(b) Ignoramus.

S3/6/13

9 September 1679. Before Rob. Shales, esq., Mayor.

Information

Step. Woolgate said that about two months ago he was ordered to search for leather buckets (by Sir John Kempthorne) and searched the chest of Wil. Jefferyes and found there two or three pieces of the King's leather buckets. *Signed.*

---

[42] This is a reference to the Statute 5 & 6 Ed. VI, c.14.

S3/6/14

9 September 1679. Before Rob. Shales, esq., Mayor.

Recognisances

   (a) Wil. Jefferyes in £20.

       Rob. Sparkes in £10.

For appearance [of Jefferyes] at the next Sessions.

   (b) John Hargood in £20.

       Tho. Henslow in £10.

For appearance [of Hargood] at the next Sessions.

   (c) John Beadle in £20

       Rob. May of Portchester in £10.

For appearance [of Beadle] at the next Sessions.

   (d) Step. Woolgate in £10.

For appearance at the next Sessions to prosecute Wil. Jefferyes, John Hargood and John Beadle for stealing the King's goods.

See also no. 232 (7).

232
CALENDAR[43]

S3/6/15

20 October 1679. Michaelmas Sessions.

(1)	John Adams, for assaulting Mat. Foots.	John Grover Henry Ransted
	See no. 221.	
(2)	Mic. Russell bound over to keep the peace [for assault].	John Burrell Henry Penn
	See no. 223.	
(3)	Mat. Holt bound over to the behaviour [for theft].	Nic. Roaker Wil. Easton
	See no. 225. *Marginal note (Latin):* Discharged by the Court.	
(4)	John Wooldridge, apprentice to Tho. Chadborne, suspected of taking away his master's money. *See no.* 228.	Jonathan Ridge Tho. Triggs
(5)	James Yattman to the behaviour.	Wil. Tanner Jonathan Ridge
	See no. 229. *Marginal note (Latin):* Discharged by the Court.	
(6)	Tho. Damarum, for a regrator.	Rob. Gyles Wil. Franklin
	See no. 230.	

  (7) Wil. Jefferyes } for cutting the King's leather buckets and stealing
       John Hargood } the leather.
       John Beadle }

     See no. 231.

     Footnote (Latin): Ordered by the Court that John Small shall appear to give evidence against Wil. Jefferyes.

EASTER SESSIONS 22 April 1680

233
TRADING
UNAPPRENTICED

S3/6/21

[October 1679].

Presentment (Latin)

Presents John Garrett of Portsmouth, mariner, and Elizabeth his wife for carrying on the business of a mercer in Portsmouth on 10 Oct. 30 Cha. II [1678] by selling mercer's wares and continuing for twelve months to the date of this inquiry, neither having been

---

[43] The cases have no numbers on the original Calendar. For a reproduction of this Calendar see fig. 1.

instructed in the art by practice or apprenticeship for seven years contrary to the statute.[44] *Signed by* [Edw.] Archer.

Note against Garrett's name: Non cul.
Endorsements:
(a) John Adams, John Grover, sworn.
(b) True bill.

S3/6/22
20 October 1679. No name of Justice.
Recognisance
John Garrett in £20.
To prosecute his traverse.
See also no. 256 (1).

234
Subject unknown

S3/6/24 (entry i)
20 October 1679. Before Sam. Williams, gent., Deputy Mayor, Sir John Biggs, Recorder, Nic. Peirson, gent., and Nic. Hedger, gent.
Recognisances
John Small in £100.
Wil. Francklin of Portsmouth in £50.
Ric. Matthewes of Gosport in £50.
For appearance of Small at the next Assizes and General Gaol Delivery for Hampshire.
Certificate: That examination of John Small taken by Rob. Shales was seen, but the Justices, finding the evidence not positive, have taken bail as above.

235
Subject unknown

S3/6/24 (entry ii)
21 October 1679. Before Sam. Williams and others as above.
Recognisances
Wil. Whitehead in £20.
David Guost in £10.
Elias Hubbard of Portsmouth, cordwainer, in £10.
For appearance of Ann, wife of Wil. Whitehead, at the next Sessions.

236
CONTEMPT

S3/6/50
21 October 31 Cha. II [1679].
Presentment (Latin)
Presents John Chapman of Portsmouth, one of the Overseers of the Poor, for refusing to obey orders of the Justices. *Signed by* [Edw.] Archer.
Note against Chapman's name: Non cul.
Endorsements:
(a) Mic. Gray, James Arnold, sworn.
(b) True bill.

S3/6/23
23 October 1679. Before Nic. Peirson, gent.
Recognisances
John Chapman in £20.
John Butcher in £10.
John Garret in £10.
For appearance of Chapman at the next Sessions.
Bound over for disobeying the order of Mr Hedger, [Chapman being] one of the Overseers of the Parish.
See also nos 256 (2), 270 (2).

---

[44] Statute: 5 Elizabeth I, c.4.

237
TRADING
IRREGULARLY

S3/6/25
10 November 1679. Before Nic. Hedger and Nic. Peirson.
Recognisance
    Henry Alford of Gosport in £20.
For appearance at the next Sessions.
Bound over for selling hats on the Point.
Footnote: Paid 4s.
See also no. 256 (3).

238
TRADING
IRREGULARLY

S3/6/26
5 December 1679. Before Nic. Peirson, gent., and Nic. Hedger, gent.
Examination
Wil. Peagan of Newgate St., London, servant to Mr John Carter, linen-draper of the Hand in Hand in Newgate St., said he was a Scotsman born in Dumfries and was apprenticed to Mr John Carter. He lived with him for about a year and a half and came from there about a fortnight ago travelling with a pack of linen ware to Guildford, Godalming, [Surr.], and Chichester. From there he came here to Portsmouth to dispose of his goods. He sold at Portsmouth about 4 yds of blue linen. He called at several houses to sell his wares before he sold this.   *Signed by mark.*

S3/6/27
6 December 1679. Before Nic. Peirson, gent., and Nic. Hedger, gent.
Recognisances
    Wil. Pegan of Newgate Market, London, linen-draper, in £10.
    Edw. Brooker in £5.
For appearance of Pegan at the next Sessions.
See also no. 256 (4).

239
DRUNKENNESS

S3/6/28
12 December 1679. Before Nic. Hedger, gent.
Information
Sarah, wife of Tho. Goudge of Portsmouth, shipwright, said that on the day Mr Hull was buried, 25 Nov. last, (*blank*) Day of Portsmouth, joiner, was very drunk and came into church reeling.   *Signed.*

240
SETTLEMENT

S3/6/29
15 December 1679. Before Nic. Hedger, gent.
Information
Rob. Henty (*signs* Hentie), one of the Constables of the Borough, said that he found that day a man leaning over Good[man] Bishopp's pales and he asked him if he was the man placed on Tho. Alford last Saturday. He said he was, so he took him to Alford's house and said to Alford 'You know that the Justices ordered you to take in this man and to keepe him untill that he was sent away by a passe, if not your lycence will be taken away'. Alford answered 'Ye divell take ye lycence'.   *Signed.*

241
BASTARDY

S3/6/30
1 January 1679/80. Before Nic. Hedger, gent.
Recognisances
    Henry Bird in £20.
    Wil. Foster in £10.
For appearance of Henry Burd (*sic*) at the next Sessions to answer the Church-wardens and Overseers of Woolwich, [Kent], concerning maintenance of a female bastard born of Rebecca Mosse, deceased.
Examination
Henry Burd (*signs* Bird) of Woolwich, Kent, shipwright, acknowledged that the child born of Rebecca Mosse about the middle of Nov. 1678 was his.   *Signed.*

242

Subject unknown

S3/6/31

26 January 1679/80. Before Sam. Williams, gent., and Nic. Hedger, gent.

Recognisances

> Rob. Baxter, gent., in £200.
> John Marsham, gent., in £100.
> Ric. Hovell, gent., in £100.
> Henry Harris, gent., in £100.

For appearance of Baxter before the Court of the King's Bench at Westminster on Monday 9 Feb. next.

243

NEGLECT OF DUTY

S3/6/32

26 January 1679/80. Before Sam. Williams, gent., and Nic. Hedger, gent.

Recognisances

> Joshua Whitehorne in £20.
> Edw. Chapman in £10.
> Ric. Preest in £10.

For appearance [of Whitehorne] at the next Sessions.

Bound over for not doing his duty as Constable and not executing the Lord Chief Justice's warrant.

Marginal note against Chapman's name (Latin): He owes on his recognisance 5*s*.

See also no. 256 (5).

244

CONTEMPT OF COURT

S3/6/33

4 February 1679/80. Before Sam. Williams, gent.

Recognisances

> Wil. Carey of South Petherton, Som., cordwainer, in £20.
> Mar. Richards of Gosport, cordwainer, in £10.
> Jos. Joanes of Portsmouth, cook, in £10.

For appearance of Carey at the next Sessions.

Bound over for contempt of Court.

See also no. 256 (6).

245

ASSAULT

S3/6/49

10 February 32 Cha. II [1679/80].

Presentment (Latin)

Presents Wil. Terrell of Portsmouth, gent., for assault at Portsmouth of Tho. Hunt.

> *Signed by* [Edw.] Archer.

Note over Terrell's name: Non cul.

Endorsements:

(a) Tho. Hunt, Elizabeth Munday, Walt. Stayner.

(b) True bill.

S3/6/34

10 February 1679/80. Before Theo[philus] Curtis, esq., Mayor, and Nic. Hedger, gent.

Information

Tho. Hunt of Cosham, husbandman, said that last Monday a parcel of wines supposed to be French was stopped at Cosham. He informed Col. Norton who gave him a letter to the Customs office at Portsmouth to deliver to Mr Grannt. He met Mr Salisbury there who, as the letter was directed to Mr Grannt or any other of the Customs, opened it. As he was riding home at the Point at Portsmouth two men, Mr Terrell and one he did not know, beat him off his horse calling out 'rogue, he is an informer, kill him'. They followed him to the upper end of the High Street of Portsmouth where he was forced to go into a shop. Mr Terrell said to the man in the shop to turn him out for he was a rogue and he pursued after him. *Signed by mark.*

23 February 1679/80. Before Nic. Hedger, gent.
Recognisance
> Wil. Terrell of Portsmouth, gent., in £20.

For appearance at the next Sessions.

S3/6/43

16 April 1680. Before Nic. Hedger, gent.
Recognisance
> Tho. Hunt in £10.

For appearance at the next Sessions to prosecute against Wil. Terrell for breach of the peace.
See also no. 256 (7).

246
RECEIVING
STOLEN GOODS

S3/6/35

11 February 1679/80. Before Theo[philus] Curtis, esq., Mayor, Rob. Shales, gent., and Nic. Hedger, gent.
Examination
Elizabeth Morley, a parish-child, being servant to Bridget, wife of Henry Etherington, a month ago took a shirt out of several brought to her mistress to wash, and unknown to her mistress sent it to Goodwife Clyfford, who had spoken to her for it some time before and afterwards sent her daughter to fetch it. For this she had a penny. About two months ago Goodwife Jacob spoke to her to bring her a shirt which she did and was given some apples. Afterwards she took a long neckcloth, a dressing and a forehead binder for which she was given some more apples. Also she took Joan Hawkins, lately servant to Harry Ranstead, one shirt which Joan spoke for and Joan gave her a penny. Afterwards she saw the said Joan take from the hedge in Henry Etherington's garden one Holland 'pillowber'. *Signed by mark.*
Recognisances
> Tho. Jacob in £5.
> Joan Hawkins in £5.
> Tho. (Clyfford *scored through*) Jacob in £5.

For appearance of Goodwife Jacob, Joan Hawkins and Goodwife Clyfford at the Sessions to answer indictments.
See also no. 256 (8).

247
ASSAULT

S3/6/36

25 February 1679/80. Before Sam. Williams, Deputy Mayor, and Nic. Hedger, gent.
Information
Phil. Lavis of Portsmouth, block maker, said that yesterday about 6.30 p.m. he was going home and was within ten doors of his own house when he met Lieut. Ric. Crofts in the open street a little above Capt. Williams' door. Lavis had a pump-hook about 7 ft long on his shoulder and after he had passed the lieutenant called 'damn him what is y^t you have upon your shoulder?' He answered that if he pleased to come back he might see. The lieutenant when he saw it swore that it had a screw at the end of it and 'was valuefull for him to carry' and he would have it. When Lavis maintained it was his own, the lieutenant swore that he should bring it to him but Lavis told him he might come and see it again. The lieutenant swore and drew his sword, thrust him through the coat and cut his hand which is disabled. *Signed by mark.*
> *Footnote (Latin):* The parties agree.

248
TRADING
IRREGULARLY
AND
SETTLEMENT

S3/6/42

2 March 1679/80. Before Sam. Williams, gent., Deputy Mayor, and Nic. Hedger.
Information
Rob. Hentie, a Constable of the Borough, said that he saw John Allen this afternoon go in to Mrs Franklin's. When he followed he found John showing some cloth called muslin. He asked 10 groats for it and she bid him 2s. John answered that he had sold it dearer at the other house just before and also some lace. *Signed.*

Examination

John Allen, a Scotsman now of Heyshott, Suss., petty chapman, said he had lived at Heyshott for two years. He came from there last Saturday and was going on to the Isle of Wight. His business was to sell linen cloth, lace and other goods where he could. He was only a sojourner and did not pay scot nor lot and had no testimonial for his travel.   *Signed by mark.*

249
THEFT

S3/6/47

10 March 32 Cha. II [1679/80].

Presentment (Latin)

Presents Jos. Card of Portsmouth, carpenter, for theft of a thin paving stone value 4*d* the property of Tho. Fitch, mill[er], and John Fitch.   *Signed by* [Edw.] Archer.

Endorsements :
(a) Tho. Tomes sworn.
(b) Ignoramus.

S3/6/37

10 March 1679/80. Before Nic. Hedger, gent.

Information

Tho. Tomes of Gosport, mason, said that this morning he was at the work by the Square Tower and saw Jos. Card coming towards the stones but when he saw him Card turned away and went out of the gate. One of the gunners looked over the wall and said that there was a man with a stone on his back, so Tomes followed him as far as God's House. When Card saw him, he dropped the stone and left it, which stone he said was belonging to his master.   *Signed.*

Examination

Jos. Card said that this morning he was at the Point, intending to go on the backside of the water house, but the sentry would not let him pass. He was forced to go back and turn on the other side and went on the Point intending to go towards Southsea Castle to see if he could find anything driven up on the shore. Finding a stone, he took it up and carried it homeward.   *Signed.*

Recognisances
(a) Jos. Card in £20.
    Simon Lawrence in £10.
    Tho. Card, painter, in £10.
For appearance of Jos. Card at the next Sessions.
(b) Tho. Tomes in £10.
To prosecute and give evidence.
See also no. 256 (9).

250
APPRENTICESHIP
OR PARISH-
CHILD(?)

S3/6/38

13 March 1679/80. Before Nic. Hedger, gent.

Recognisances
    John Tayleur, gent., in £20.
    Phil. Fetherstonhaugh, gent., in £10.
    John Higgin, cordwainer (?), in £10.
For appearance of Tayleur at the next Sessions to answer for putting away Ben. Knowles whom he undertook to breed.
See also no. 256 (10).

251
BASTARDY

S3/6/39

16 March 1679/80. Before Sam. Williams, gent., Deputy Mayor, and Nic. Hedger, gent.

Information

Elizabeth Clarke of Portsmouth, singlewoman, said that on Whit Sunday last Wil. Etherington had carnal knowledge of her body and the said Etherington was the father of the female child born to her.   *Signed by mark.*

252
ABUSE

S3/6/40

18 March 1679/80. Before Sam. Williams, Deputy Mayor, and Nic. Hedger, gent.
Information
Elizabeth, wife of Wil. Terrill of Portsmouth, gent., said that last night she was very much abused by Mr Henry Holt and goes in fear of her life that he beat, wound or kill her. *Signed.*

253
ASSAULT

S3/6/46

29 March 32 Cha. II [1680].
Presentment (Latin)
Presents Walsingham, wife of Edw. Edwards of Portsmouth, for assaulting Margaret Broughton, widow. *Signed by* [Edw.] Archer.

> *Footnotes:*
> (a) She confesses the bill because she does not wish to oppose the King.
> (b) No fine paid because she is a pauper.
> *Endorsements:*
> (a) Margaret Broughton, Joan Laming, sworn.
> (b) True bill.

S3/6/41

1 April 1680. Before Sam. Williams, gent., Deputy Mayor.
Information
Margaret Broughton, widow, said that last Monday Walsingham, wife of Edw. Edwards, fell upon her and struck her three blows which made her bleed, tore her hood and took away both it and her handkerchief, which cost her 17s. She went in fear of her life that she would either beat or wound her. *Signed by mark.*
Recognisance
> Margaret Broughton in £10.
To prosecute and give evidence against Walsingham Edwards.
See also no. 256(11).

254
TRADING UNAPPRENTICED

S3/6/48

[April 1680].
Presentment (Latin)
Presents Geo. Soames of Portsmouth, butcher, for exercising the art, mystery or occupation of a butcher for over a year from 1 Apr. 1679 without education or apprenticeship. *Signed by* [Edw.] Archer.

> *Note over Soames' name:* Non cul.
> *Endorsements:*
> (a) Nat. Harwood, James Wattle, John Higgen, John Frost, sworn.
> (b) True bill.
See also nos 256 (12), 270 (1).

255
Subject unknown

S3/6/44

22 April 1680. No name of Justice.
Recognisance
> Wil. Stayner of Portsmouth, cordwainer, in £10.
For appearance at the Court to give evidence for the Crown.

256
CALENDAR[45]

22 April 1680. Lady-day Sessions.
(1)   John Garret and Elizabeth his wife to prosecute
their traverse, [for trading unapprenticed].
See no. 233.
Marginal note (Latin): Writ of certiorari issued.

---

[45] The cases have no numbers on the original Calendar.

(2)	John Chapman one of the Overseers of the Poor, for disobeying the Justices' order. See nos 236, 270 (2). Note against Chapman's name: 'Bil'.	John Butcher John Garret
(3)	Henry Alford, for selling hats [and thus trading irregularly]. See no. 237. Marginal note (Latin): Discharged by Justice Nic. Hedger.	
(4)	Wil. Pegan a Scottish pedlar, [for trading irregularly]. See no. 238.	Edw. Brooker
(5)	Joshua Whitehorne, Constable, for not executing the Lord Chief Justice's writ. See no. 243. Marginal note (Latin): Discharged by Justice of the Peace.	Edw. Chapman Ric. Preist
(6)	Wil. Carey, for contempt of Court. See no. 244. Marginal note (Latin): Discharged by the Court.	Martin Richards Jos. Jones
(7)	Wil. Terrill, for assaulting Tho. Hunt. See no. 245. Marginal note: 'Bil'.	
(8)	Goodwife Jacob Joane Hawkins Good[wife] Clyfford } for receiving stolen goods from Elizabeth Morley See no. 246.	Tho. Jacob
(9)	Jos. Card, for stealing a stone. See no. 249. Marginal note: 'Bill'.	Simon Lawrence Tho. Card
(10)	John Taylear [concerning apprenticeship or parish-child]. See no. 250. Marginal note (Latin): Discharged by Justice of the Peace.	
(11)	Walsingham Edwards for assaulting Margaret Broughton, widow. See no. 253. Marginal note: 'Bill'.	
(12)	Geo. Soames, for using the trade of a butcher [and thus trading unapprenticed]. See nos 254, 270 (1). Marginal note: 'Bill'.	

MICHAELMAS SESSIONS 14 October 1680

257
DESERTION OF WIFE

S3B/18

1 May 1680. Before Theophilus Curtis, esq., Mayor, Sam. Williams and Nic. Peirson.

Informations

(a) Emm, wife of Geo. Harwood of Portsmouth, waterman, said that her husband had often threatened to desert her and leave her to starve. That morning he put up his money, which she judged to be about £100, got his clothes and tried to go away, leaving her no money. The Constable, having a warrant, stopped him. *Signed by mark.*

(b) Joshua Whitehorne said he heard Geo. Harwood say in the presence of Mr Peirson that he would pay nothing for maintenance of his wife, but would rather go to gaol for life. Mr Peirson committed him to gaol. *Signed.*

258

THEFT

S3/7/2

7 May 32 Cha. II [1680].
Presentment (Latin)
Presents Geo. Langerish of Portsmouth, victualler, for stealing 5 lb. of gunpowder of the King's goods worth 10*d*.   *Signed by* [Edw.] Archer.
   Endorsements:
   (a) Tho. Wakefeild, James Passenger, sworn.
   (b) Ignoramus.

S3B/19. *Calendar numbers on document:* 3, 4.
7 May 1680. Before Nic. Peirson, gent., and Nic. Hedger, gent.
Informations
   (a) Tho. Wakefeild of Portsea, gunner, said that yesterday about 2 p.m. a certain cart came which they suspected had in it prohibited goods. With his authority he made some soldiers at Portsbridge ('Postbridge') search it, when they found a bag of cut tobacco and three cartridges of gunpowder, which John Passenger admitted to be his.   *Signed by mark.*

   (b) John Passenger said that being at the house of Geo. Langridge in company with (*blank*) Soane, Langridge told him that he had a parcel of powder, about 5 lb., which he wanted him to take and dispose of or keep at his house till Langridge came. Going out of Portsbridge ('Postbridge'), it was seized.   *Signed.*

   (c) Geo. Langerish added that the powder was left at his house for debt by persons unknown.   *Signed.*
Recognisances
   (a) John Passenger of Westbourne, [Suss.], tailor, in £10.
For appearance at the next Sessions to give evidence against Geo. Langrish concerning powder suspected to be the King's.
   (b) Geo. Langrish of Portsmouth, victualler, in £20.
      Rob. Shorter of the same, victualler, in £10.
For appearance of Langrish at the next Sessions and not to depart [the jurisdiction of] the Court without licence.
See also no. 270 (3, 4).

259

ASSAULT

S3/7/17

10 May 1680. Before Theophilus Curtis, esq., Mayor, Nic. Peirson, gent., and Nic. Hedger, gent.
Informations
   (a) Tho. Redman of Portsmouth, baker, said that about 8 p.m. yesterday Henry Seagar sent him to the bake-house to light a candle and on coming out he saw a light in the yard of Mr Vyneing's tenements. He asked those there to light a candle. Then Mr Greene struck him over the pate and leapt over the pale after him and drove him into the street and struck him several blows. He met Seagar and told him what had happened. He heard Mr Greene swear he would be revenged of Seagar four times at the least.   *Signed.*

   (b) Henry Seagar said that about 8 p.m. yesterday he met Tho. Redman coming out of the yard and Mr Greene in the yard who asked Seagar what he meant there and whether he came to 'vindicate' Redman. He answered that he had as much right to be there as Greene had. Greene then thrust at him twice, missed his face but struck his hat off. Then he struck him twice again over the head and pursued him into the bake-house swearing he would perish in hell-fire rather than take that abuse.   *Signed.*

   (c) Jos. Thompson and Elizabeth Woolvin *confirmed the above evidence.*
                  Signed by both (Elizabeth Woolvin by mark).

260

TRADING IRREGULARLY

S3/7/16. *Calendar numbers on document:* 5, 6.
26 June 1680. Before Theophilus Curtis, esq., Mayor, Mr Peirson and Mr Hedger.
Information
Tho. Cooke of Portsmouth, soldier, said that about 1 p.m. this afternoon he bought a pound of tobacco of Elizabeth, wife of Laur. Clarke of West Cowes [I.W.]. She weighed it out for him and he paid 6*d* to another woman for it which she passed on to

Elizabeth. Yesterday he bought another pound of tobacco of Elizabeth, wife of Wil. Bolley of West Cowes, tobacco-pipe maker, and gave her 6*d* for it, which she confessed in her examination. *Signed by mark.*

Recognisances
    (a) Tho. Cooke in £10.
For appearance at the next Sessions to give evidence against Elizabeth Clarke and Elizabeth Bolley.
    (b) Roger Upsdall in £10.
For appearance of Elizabeth Clarke at the next Sessions.
    (c) The same Roger Upsdall in £10.
For appearance of Elizabeth Bolley at the next Sessions.
See also no. 270 (5, 6).

261
Subject unknown

S3/7/15. *Calendar number on document:* 7.
2 June 1680. Before Nic. Hedger, gent.
Recognisances
        Henry Woollgar of Kingston, labourer, in £10.
        Tho. Goldfinch, house-carpenter, in £5.
For appearance of Woollgar at the next Sessions.
See also no. 270 (7).

262
ASSAULT

S3/7/12
3 July 1680. Before Nic. Hedger, gent.
Information
Wil. Gregory of Portsmouth, seaman, said that on the same afternoon Fra. Mersh came to his house and broke his windows, threatening to break them all.
Signed by mark.

263
THREATENED ASSAULT

S3B/20
2 July 1680. Before Nic. Hedger, gent.
Informations
    (a) Wil. Fisher of the parish of Leadenhall, London, bricklayer, said that Henry Morgin came to Redbridge where he was drinking and followed him to Southampton and then to Portsmouth. He threatened to take his wife away from him dead or alive and used other threats, which put him in fear of his life. *Signed by mark.*
    (b) John Dale said that last night Henry Morgin with several others came to enquire for Wil. Fisher and his wife. Dale said the Fishers were in the next room, but as Morgin and his company had sticks in their hands he would not let them in. However they pursued the Fishers and said they would have them down. *Signed.*
Recognisances
        Wil. Fisher in £10.
        John Dale in £10.
For appearance at the next Sessions to prosecute and give evidence against Henry Morgin.

S3/7/14. *Calendar number on document:* 8.
7 July 1680. Before Nic. Hedger, gent.
Recognisances
        Henry Morgin of Salisbury ('Sarum'), shoemaker, in £20.
        Edw. Brooker in £10.
        Jonathan Ridge in £10.
For appearance [of Morgin] at the next Sessions to answer indictments preferred against him by Wil. Fisher.
Footnote: Brooker promised payment.
See also no. 270 (8).

264
**TRADING
IRREGULARLY**

S3/7/5

19 July 1680. Before Nic. Hedger, gent.
Informations

(a) Sam. Critchell of Portsmouth, cordwainer, said that a week ago today in the morning he was at the house of Wil. Whitehead on the Point and called for a flagon of beer which was brought to him by Jane, the servant of the house, and he paid *2d* for it. *Signed by mark.*

(b) Tho. Alford said that Jane Webb, servant to Wil. Whitehead, told him and his wife that Mr Henry Beverly and his wife had taken a false oath whereby her master had been put by selling beer since the Friday before these words were spoken, i.e. about eight or ten days ago. *Signed by mark.*

(c) Rob. Hentie said that on Thursday 8 July, by order of Rob. Shales and Nic. Hedger, Justices, he forbade Wil. Whitehead and his wife to sell beer and ale in the house they lived in after that day. *Signed.*

265
ASSAULT

S3/7/11

10 March 1679/80. Before Sam. Williams, gent., Deputy Mayor, and Nic. Hedger, gent.
Information

James Etherington said that about 7 p.m. yesterday he was sitting on a bench outside the Pointgate, called Pennyless Bench, talking with Mrs Jones when Tho. Smith, who was in company with three others, left his companions and fell across his legs, so he called him a saucy fellow for coming so near. A neighbour then told him that Smith on going to the Platform said he would go home and fetch a stick to beat him. A quarter of an hour later when Etherington left and was going home, Smith with his coat off came with three other men, some carrying sticks, to the corner shop, passing by where he had sat before. He said, that rogue Etherington is not here, and so returned to the street to Widow Farehill's. When Etherington saw them go in, he went into the house of Wells the cooper and sent for Mrs Farehill. She denied that they were in the house. He went out with her and Wells and saw Smith standing in Mrs Farehill's shop. She said she did not know they were there. *Signed.*

S3/7/10. *Calendar number on document:* 9.

27 July 1680. Before Nic. Peirson, gent., Deputy Mayor.
Recognisances

Tho. Smith in £20.
Mary Farehill, widow, in £10.

For appearance of Smith at the next Sessions to answer indictments preferred by James Etherington.
See also no. 270 (9).

266
ASSAULT

S3B/17

23 March 1679/80. No name of Justice.
Information

Tho. Johnes said he received when drunk great abuse from one of his own ship's companions, John Shilling, who broke his head in two places with a barrel staff and beat him heavily with the heels of his shoes. His shirt and waistcoat were pulled off and cut in pieces and then a second one taken off him and locked up by Shilling in his chest and worn by him since. Later Shilling beat his naked body with a billet of wood. He then took the cook's axe and would have killed him had not others come to his help. *Signed by* Henry Thomson, Abraham Right (*by mark*) *as witnesses.*

S3B/21

24 August 1680. By [Sir Wil.] Scroggs, [Lord Chief Justice].
Warrant for arrest
Directed to all Mayors, Sheriffs, Bailiffs, Constables and all other officers and ministers whom these may concern.

To arrest John Shilling alias Lane to give security to preserve the peace, especially against Tho. Jones of London, mariner, who alleges that Shilling threatened to murder him, so that he goes in fear of his life.

Signed and sealed (wafer seal: a cross between four cinquefoils).

S3/7/8. *Calendar number on document:* 10.
5 September 1680. Before Theophilus Curtis, esq., Mayor, and Nic. Peirson, gent.
Recognisances
> John Shilling alias Lane in £40.
> Rob. Holloway, gent., in £20.
> John Dane of Portsmouth, shipwright, in £20.

For appearance of Shilling at the next Sessions and especially to keep the peace towards Tho. Jones, mariner.

S3/7/9
6 September 1680. Before Nic. Peirson, gent.
Information
Tho. Jones of the City of London, mariner, said that on 23 Mar. last he was at Port Mahón ('Port Mahoon') in the Straits [of Gibraltar] and John Shilling alias Lane who was with him fell upon him and beat him. Afterwards he tore his waistcoat and shirt off his back and took a hatchet and cut them to pieces and swore that he would kill him so that he goes in fear of his life. *Signed by mark.*
Recognisance
> Tho. Jones of Deptford, mariner, in £20.

For appearance at the Sessions to give evidence against John Shilling alias Lane.
See also no. 270 (10).

267
THEFT

S3/7/3
23 September 32 Cha. II [1680].
Presentment (Latin)
Presents Wil. Brickleton of Portsmouth, labourer, for stealing 8 lb. of lead worth 10d.
Signed by [Edw.] Archer.

Endorsements:
(a) Witness Edw. Archer, gent.
(b) Ignoramus.

S3/7/7. *Calendar number on document:* 11.
23 September 1680. Before Rob. Shales, gent.
Examination
Wil. Brickleton of Portsmouth, labourer, said that last Monday morning he brought from H.M. Dockyard a parcel of old lead which he sold to Joshua Whitehorne.
Signed by mark.

27 September 1680. Before (*blank*) 'one of the Justices'.
Recognisances
> Wil. Brickleton in £20.
> John Hillman of Portsmouth, gunner, in £10.

For appearance of Brickleton at the next Sessions.
See also no. 270 (11).

268
ASSAULT

S3/7/6. *Calendar number on document:* 12.
27 September 1680. Before Nic. Hedger, gent.
Informations
(a) Joan, wife of Walt. Clarke of Portsmouth, said that last Saturday Sarah Land (*or Laud?*), wife of John Land of Portsmouth, soldier, brought two soldiers to the house of the said Joan where Tho. Lutman her landlord was. Sarah thrust one of the soldiers to her landlord and then struck her landlord in the face and drew blood.
Signed by mark.

(b) Tho. Lutman of Gosport, tallow-chandler, said that last Saturday when he came to his house in Portsmouth in which Walt. Claston (*recte Clarke?*) was living he questioned Sarah Land's boy as to how the walls of his house came to be broken down. The boy called his mother and he asked her the reason of it. She abused him and told him there were some coming behind who would do his business for him. Two soldiers came and she put them forward and stepped between them and struck him in the mouth which ran with blood. Then she took a great bone and threw it at his head.

Signed.

Recognisances

        Tho. Lutman in £10.

        Joan Clarke in £10.

For appearance at the next Sessions to give evidence against Sarah Land.

28 September 1680. Before Theophilus Curtis, esq., Mayor, and Nic. Peirson, gent.

Recognisances

        Wil. Warren of Portsmouth, glover, in £10.

        Alex. Wright of the same, gardener, in £10.

For appearance of Sarah, wife of John Land, at the next Sessions to answer indictment preferred by Tho. Lutman.

See also no. 270 (12).

269
ASSAULT

S3/7/1

2 July 32 Cha. II [1680].

Presentment (Latin)

Presents Jos. Condit of Portsea, tailor, for assaulting Joan Hills, spinster, at Buckland.

Signed by [Edw.] Archer.

Endorsements:

(a) Witnesses Joan Hill, Mary Peirson, Tho. Brigsdale, John Skinner, sworn.

(b) Ignoramus.

S3/7/13. *Calendar number on document:* 13.

3 July 1680. Before Nic. Peirson, gent.

Information

Joan Hills, spinster, said that yesterday afternoon, a little before sunset, she was at work in a meadow belonging to Mrs Yeomett haying with others. Jos. Cundit came into the meadow and laid hold of Mary Pearson who was at work with her and threw her down so that she called for help. When she came to them Cundit took the rake she had in her hand and broke it and threw her down and made a cock of hay upon her. She got up and told him that she would go and tell her mistress; when she had gone a little way Cundit threw a piece of the handle at her and struck her in the face so that blood dashed out and her handkerchief and apron were soon all blood.

Signed by mark.

Recognisances

(a) (*scored through*) Jos. Condit in £20.

        John Harmesworth of Buck[land], tailor, in £10.

        Bart. Stubber of B[uckland], yeoman, in £10.

For appearance [of Condit] at the next Sessions.

(b) Jos. Condit of Kingston, tailor, in £20.

        John Harmesworth of the same, tailor, in £10.

        Bart. Stubber of the same, yeoman, in £10.

For appearance of Condit at the next Sessions to answer indictment preferred against him by Joan Hills.

See also no. 270 (13).

S3/7/4

[**14 October**] **1680.** Michaelmas Sessions.

(1) Geo. Soames 'to prosecute his traverse', for using the trade of a butcher, not being bound apprentice. *See nos* 254, 256 (12).

(2) John Chapman 'to prosecute his traverse', for disobeying the Justices' order. *See nos* 236, 256 (2). *Marginal note* (*Latin*) : Writ of certiorari issued.

(3) John Passenger of Westbourne, [Suss.], for a parcel of powder taken at Portsbridge of the King's goods.   Rob. Shorter

(4) Geo. Langrish, for the same.   Rob. Shorter *See no.* 258. *Marginal note* (*Latin*) : Discharged by the Court.

(5) Elizabeth Clarke of Cowes, for selling tobacco in town.   Roger Upsdall *Marginal note* (*Latin*) : Discharged by the Court.

(6) Elizabeth Bolley, for the like.   Roger Upsdall *See no.* 260. *Marginal note* (*Latin*) : Discharged by the Court.

(7) Henry Woolgar for the behaviour.   [Tho.] Goldfinch *See no.* 261. *Marginal note* (*Latin*) : He submitted.

(8) Henry Morgan for the behaviour, [for   Edw. Brooker threatened assault].   Jon[athan] Ridge *See no.* 263.

(9) Tho. Smith, for assaulting James Etherington sen.   Mary Farehill *See no.* 265. *Marginal note* (*Latin*) : He submitted under protest.

(10) John Shilling alias Lane, for assaulting Tho. Jones.   Rob. Holloway   John Dane

See no. 266. *Marginal note* (*Latin*) : Discharged by the Court.

(11) Wil. Brickleton, for stealing some old lead of the   John Hillman King's goods. *See no.* 267. *Marginal note* (*Latin*) : Discharged by the Court.

(12) Sarah Land (*or* Laud?), for assaulting Tho. Lutman.   Joan Clarke *See no.* 268.

(15) Jos. Cundit, for assaulting Joan Hills.   John Harmsworth   Bart. Stubber

See no. 269. *Marginal note* (*Latin*) : Discharged by the Court.

EASTER SESSIONS 14 April 1681

S3/8/12

15 October 1680. Before John Grundy, esq., Mayor, Theophilus Curtis and Nic. Peirson, gent.

Informations

(a) Edm. Ward of Portsmouth, victualler, said that Elizabeth, wife of Almond Gutteridge, asked Sergt Cary not to lodge any longer in Ward's house as she would fire the house and burn him and his wife in bed.   *Signed by mark.*

(b) Wil. Carew said that between 8 and 9 p.m. yesterday he was at the house of Almond Gutteridge when Almond's wife came in and said she had been informed that Mr Ward's wife had abused her. She could afford to fire his house, or words to that effect. *Signed.*

Examination

Elizabeth Gutteridge confessed she said that, if it were not to damage the town and her landlord she could afford to fire Ward's house. *Signed by mark.*

Recognisances

  Tho. Blankeley in £10.

  Ric. Butcher, shoemaker, in £10.

See also no. 282 (4).

272
ABUSING
AUTHORITY
	S3/8/13
	
	15 October 1680. Before the Mayor and Justices.
	Information
	John Hoskins (*signs* Hodgkin), gent., said that when he was in Court he heard Mr Thorne say he would not be huffed ('huft') by a parcel of swordsmen and dock men, a crew of rascally, beggarly fellows. *Signed.*
	Recognisances
	  John Thorne in £20.
	  Rob. Harford in £10.
	  Edw. Pitt in £10.
	For appearance [of Thorne] at the next Sessions.
	Marginal note (Latin) : 22 Feb. 1680/1. Discharged by the Mayor and one Justice of the Peace.
	
	15 October 1680. Before John Grundy, esq., Mayor, Theophilus Curtis, gent., and Nic. Peirson, gent.
	Information
	Step. Woolgate (*signs* Wollgate) of Portsmouth, gent., said that yesterday afternoon when Mr Arnold came into the court-house and asked the Mayor to take off his fine, John Thorne who was present called him 'fool' and said he would have paid 20 marks before he would have asked forgiveness. He said that we shall be well kept if we are governed by a crew of fools and rascally fellows, swordsmen and dock men, with several other reproachful expressions. *Signed.*

273
ABUSE
	S3/8/10
	
	No date. Before John Grundy, esq., Mayor, and Nic. Hedger, gent.
	Information
	Wil. Lloyd said that last night he was at the house of John Tayler on the Point to look after the boat's crew. Tayler called Capt. Skelton 'fool' three or four times saying he would give him his belly-ful. *Signed.*
	Examination
	John Tayler denied he ever said these words.
	Recognisances
	  John Tayler in £20.
	  John Carter in £10.
	  John Grover in £10.
	For appearance of Tayler at the next Sessions.
	Marginal note (Latin) : Discharged by the Court.
	See also no. 232 (3).

274 **BASTARDY**	S3/8/11 **23 October 1680.** Before John Grundy, esq., Mayor, and Nic. Peirson, gent. *Examination* Elizabeth Munday of Portsmouth, spinster, said she was now with child and John Coombes of Portsmouth, labourer, was the father. He had had carnal knowledge of her body several times and no other person. *Signed by mark.*

Information

Elizabeth Hawkes, widow, said that this morning, there being some question about his clothes, John Coombes went to Elizabeth Munday her maid and said 'Betty, art thou with child?' and 'if thou art, I will owne it and keepe ye child'.

30 November 1680. Before Nic. Peirson, gent.

Recognisances

      John Coombes in £40.

      Tho. Bowes of Portsea, yeoman, in £20.

For appearance of Coombes at the next Sessions.

275
ASSAULT

S3/8/9

2 March 1680/1. Before John Grundy, esq., Mayor.

Informations

(a) Wil. Coward of Portsea, joiner, said that Nic. Roaker told him that last Friday he took a pickaxe and shovel from the land of Tho. Burt and Wil. Cleverley and threw it into the middle of the mud and water and dug up the 'burnney' or watercourse laid with brick and planked over. On Tuesday last about 2 p.m. Nic. Roaker came out of the house of John Roaker with a stick in his hand as big as his arm and John Roaker, his wife Mary and John Poate came after him. He held up his stick at Sarah, wife of Tho. Burt.   *Signed.*

(b) Elizabeth Kill, spinster, said that yesterday afternoon Nic. Roaker and John Roaker, having sticks in their hands, came with John Poate and Mary Roaker up to the end of the pales of Tho. Burt in the parish of Portsea. Sarah, wife of Tho. Burt, was there and Poate struck her and hauled her along by the side of the bank into the dirt. Nic. Roaker broke a wheelbarrow of her mistress in pieces. *Signed by mark.*

(c) Wil. Pritchett of Portsmouth, soldier, *confirmed what Elizabeth Kill said.* He added that it took place at 2 p.m. when they were working for Tho. Burt and Wil. Cleverley.   *Signed by mark.*

Recognisances

(a) Nic. Roaker in £20.

      Jos. Cunditt in £10.

      John Roaker in £20.

      Jos. Cunditt in £10.

      John Poate in £20.

      Jos. Cundit in £10.

For appearance [of the Roakers and Poate] at the next Sessions.

(b) Tho. Burt in £20.

      Wil. Cleverley in £20.

For appearance to give evidence.

Note against names of both Nic. and John Roaker and Poate (Latin): Discharged by the Mayor.

276
TRADING
IRREGULARLY

S3/8/8

7 March 1680/1. Before John Grundy, esq., Mayor.

Examinations

(a) Mary Howard of Portsmouth, spinster, said that on Tuesday or Wednesday last she came to the house of Mr Tho. Plover of Portsmouth, butcher. She spoke to Mrs Plover and asked her for a leg of mutton for Mr Bev[er]ley. She was given this and was asked 22d. Mary took it to Goodman Lane where it was dressed. She confessed that she went to Mr Plover's house in the name of Mr Beverley without his consent. She was advised to fetch the mutton by the advice and persuasion of Sam. Winter of Portsmouth, soldier.   *Signed by mark.*

(b) Sam. Winter of Portsmouth, soldier, said he was with Mary Howard at the house of Goodman Lane last Wednesday or Thursday where they had a leg of mutton for dinner which Mary said had cost her 22d.   *Signed by mark.*

277
RECEIVING STOLEN GOODS

S3/8/7

26 March 1681. Before John Grundy, esq., Mayor.

Informations

(a) Elizabeth Fisher of Portsmouth, spinster, said she was servant to Capt. Fra. Collingwood. There were lost from the captain's garden about 15 Jan. last four Holland shifts, some of them laced, and two diaper table-cloths, three of which shifts are those now shown her. *Signed.*

(b) John Nicholson of Portsmouth, soldier, said he had lodged at the house of Henry Comings of Portsmouth for half a year and Adam Hanny lodged in the same room with him. About two months ago he found under his bed a 'snapsacke'. In it were the three shifts now shown him and a table-cloth or a sheet with three breadths in it. He told his landlord that he had found such things. *Signed by mark.*

(c) Adam Hanny of Portsmouth, soldier in Capt. Harris' Company. *No entry against the name.*

(d) Wil. Butcher (*signs* Bocher), soldier in Capt. Harris' Company, said that John Mountgomery, a soldier under the command of Capt. Lyttleton, about seven weeks ago called on him 'being there upon ye mayne Cort of guard' to give him a pot of beer at the Five Bells. Mountgomery had a parcel of linen under his company coat; it contained two table-cloths which he left with the woman at the Five Bells for his reckoning (1s). Then Mountgomery and he went to the house of Henry Cummings his landlord and borrowed 12d to redeem the said linen. He sold the two table-cloths to Cummings for 5s. *Signed.*

Recognisances

(a) Wil. Butcher in £10.
    Elizabeth Fisher in £10.
    John Nicholson in £10.
To prosecute Cummings.

(b) Henry Cummings in £40.
    Tho. Hughes in £20.

For appearance of Cummings at the next Sessions for stealing parcels of linen from Capt. Collingwood.

See also nos 282 (2), 283.

278
CONTEMPT

S3/8/5

2 April 1681. Before Sam. Williams, gent.

Recognisances

    Wil. Lyon in £10.
    John Butcher in £5.
    Edw. Brooker in £5.

For appearance of Lyon at the next Sessions.

Bound over for saying before Sarah Blowes, spinster, that if Mr Mayor had anything to say to him he might come to Lyon, for he would not go to Mr Mayor.

Marginal note (Latin): Discharged by the Court.

See also no. 282 (1).

279
ILLICIT GAMING

S3/8/2

6 April 33 Cha. II [1681].

Presentment (Latin)

Presents Simon Coleman of Portsmouth, victualler, for on 6 Apr. 33 Cha. II and at certain times before and after keeping 'a common house and place for game and play' to his own profit, viz. dice, playing-cards and other illicit games. *Signed by* [Edw.] Archer.

Note against Coleman's name: Non cul.
Endorsements:
(a) John Shackelwell sworn.
(b) True bill.

280
ASSAULT

S3/8/6

11 April 1681. Before John Grundy, esq., Mayor.
Information
Tho. Alford said that on Friday night last Wil. Turnepenny and his wife fell upon him in his own house and beat him. *Signed by mark.*
Recognisances
    (a) Tho. Alford in £10.
    For appearance at the next Sessions to give evidence against Wil. Turnepenny and his wife.

    (b) Wil. Turnepenny in £10.
        John Sowill in £5.
    For appearance of Turnepenny at the next Sessions.
See also no. 282 (5).

281
ILLICIT GAMING

S3/8/1

12 April 33 Cha. II [1681].
Presentment (Latin)
Presents Henry Smith of Portsmouth, victualler, for keeping a public place from 1 Mar. to 12 Apr. 33 Cha. II for playing for money illegal games called 'closhcales or kettlepins' contrary to the Statute of 33 Hen. VIII. *Signed by* [Edw.] Archer.
    Note against Smith's name: Non cul.
    Endorsements:
    (a) John Snelling, James Lord, John Thorne, sworn.
    (b) True bill.

282
CALENDAR[46]

S3/8/4 (entry i)

[14 April] 1681. Lady-day Sessions.

(1)	Wil. Lyon to the behaviour, [for contempt].	John Butcher Edw. Brooker
	See no. 278. *Marginal note (Latin):* Discharged by the Court.	
(2)	Henry Cummings, for buying stolen goods. *See nos* 277, 283.	Tho. Hughes
(3)	John Tailer to the behaviour, [for abuse].	John Carter John Grover
	See no. 273. *Marginal note (Latin):* Discharged by the Court.	
(4)	Elizabeth Gutteridge, widow, for saying she could afford to fire the house of Edm. Ward. *See no.* 271. *Marginal note (Latin):* Discharged by the Court.	Tho. Blankley Ric. Butcher
(5)	Wil. Turnepenny, for assault and battery on Tho. Alford. *See no.* 280. *Marginal note (Latin):* Discharged by the Court.	John Salt

283
RECEIVING STOLEN GOODS

S3/8/4 (entry ii)

[14 April] 1681. At the Sessions.
Recognisances
    Henry Cummings in £20.
    Wil. Lyon in £10.
    For appearance [of Cummings] at the next Sessions.
See also nos 277, 282 (2).

---

[46] The cases have no numbers on the original Calendar.

MICHAELMAS SESSIONS 6 October 1681

284
TRADING
UNAPPRENTICED

S3/8/3

No date [circa May 1681].

Presentment (Latin)

Presents Wil. Cozens jun. of Portsmouth, house-carpenter, for exercising the art and practice of stonemason and bricklayer from 1 Sept. 32 Cha. II [1680] for six months and more, i.e. up to the date of this inquiry, without being trained or apprenticed for seven years.[47]   *Signed by* [Edw.] Archer.

    Note against Cozen's name: Non cul.

    Endorsements:

    (a) Ric. Hunt, John Smith, Rob. Sheppard, John Harris, witnesses.

    (b) True bill.

EASTER SESSIONS 27 April 1682

No papers survive.

MICHAELMAS SESSIONS 5 October 1682

285
ASSAULT

S3/9/15

7 May 1682. Before *(blank)*.

Informations

    (a) Henry Hamblen of Portsmouth, soldier, said that last night about 12 he and Wil. Butcher, both being on the guard, saw a light at the house of Mr Wil. Terrell in Portsmouth. The doors being open they went in to drink a pennyworth each. After the beer was drawn they laid their money on the table and Hamblen went out to go into the house of office. Just as he was coming from there, Henry White the tapster met him, struck him down, beat and wounded him and he lay as dead upon the ground till Butcher and another man brought him into the house.   *Signed by mark.*

    (b) Wil. Butcher said that last night about 12 he and Henry Hamblen went into the Red Lion to spend a penny each. They had two flagons of beer. Hamblen went out to the house of office and as he stayed longer than ordinary he asked why his comrade was so long. Henry White the tapster hearing this said 'you were best to goe and looke after him for I have given him a blowe or two and he lyes without'. He went out and found Hamblen lying on the ground almost dead and he and another man brought him indoors.   *Signed.*

S3/9/14. *Calendar number on document:* 3.

7 May 1682. Before Tho. Hancocke, esq., Mayor.

Recognisances

        Henry Hamblen in £10.

        Wil. Butcher in £10.

For appearance [of both] at the next Sessions to prosecute and give evidence against Henry White for beating and wounding Hamblen.

10 May 1682. No name of Justice.

Recognisances

        Henry White of Portsmouth, labourer, in £30.

        Henry Barnes in £10.

For appearance of White at the next Sessions to answer for beating and assaulting Henry Hamblen and not to depart [the jurisdiction of] the Court without licence.

---

[47] This refers to the Statute 5 Elizabeth I, c.4.

286
ASSAULT

S3/9/13

11 May 1682. Before Tho. Hancocke, esq., Mayor.
Information
Joan Tanner, widow, said that James Lord had often assaulted her and broken open the door threatening to kill her. She feared the said Lord would either beat, wound or kill her and went in fear of her life. She prayed that the said Lord might find sureties to keep the peace. *Signed.*

287
ABUSING AUTHORITY

D11A/16/27

23 May 1682. Before John Grundy, gent., Sam. Williams, gent., and Nic. Peirson, gent.
Information
Eleanor, wife of James Thompson, said she went to Dan. Clay, collector of the hearth money, by the order of the Mayor and demanded the surplus of what she had paid for chimney money. At the same time Widow Carde demanded one shilling which she had paid more than her due. Clay said he would not return any and when they said they would complain to the Mayor he said he did not care a fart for the Mayor.
Signed by mark.
Footnote: Jane Cardife, widow, and Elizabeth Skipper, widow, both have deposed to the truth of the above. *Both sign by mark.*

288
WIFE-BEATING

S3/9/11. *Calendar number on document:* 5.

27 May 1682. Before Tho. Hancocke, esq., Mayor.
Recognisances
     Rob. Stripe in £20.
     Tho. Barrow in £10.
     Edm. Stripe in £10.
For appearance of Rob. Stripe at the next Sessions and to keep the peace, especially towards his wife.
Bound over for beating and abusing his wife.

289
ABUSE

S3B/23

1 June 1682. Before Tho. Hancock, esq., Mayor, Theophilus Curtis, gent., and Sam. Williams, gent.
Informations
   (a) Mary Cockes said that when she went to John Read and asked him for the money he owed her, he said he would not pay and that her husband was a cheat. When she said she would complain to Mr Peirson, he answered with obscenity that he did not care anything for him. *Signed by mark (as* Elizabeth Cockes*).*
   (b) Susan Widgger was with Mary Cockes *and confirmed the above evidence.*
Signed by mark.

S3/9/12. *Calendar number on document:* 4.

1 June 1682. Before Tho. Hancocke, esq., Mayor.
Recognisances
     John Read in £20.
     Ric. Stoe in £10.
     Rob. Bushoppe in £10.
For appearance of Read at the next Sessions and not to depart [the jurisdiction of] the Court without licence.

290
ASSAULT

S3/9/10. *Calendar number on document:* 6.

20 June 1682. Before Tho. Hancocke, esq., Mayor.
Informations
   (a) John Martin of Havant, bricklayer, said that about 8 p.m. yesterday he met Tho. Freeman on the road a little beyond the Rose and Crown. They went back there and drank two bottles of ale at the door. John Balch, owner of the house, drank with them. He was talking with Balch when he asked him to come in, and, as soon as they were in, Balch fell upon him, threw him down and struck several blows. *Signed.*

(b) Tho. Freeman *confirmed the above evidence and further* said that after Balch had beaten Marten, Balch took up a spit and ran at him saying he would kill him. To avoid it he ran into the street and he had to get into a neighbour's house to save himself. *Signed by mark.*

Recognisances

    (a) John Marten in £10.
        Tho. Freeman in £10.
        Henry Woolgar in £10.
        Tho. Mihell in £10.
        John Harwood in £10.

For appearance at the next Sessions to prosecute and give evidence against John Balch.

    (b) John Balch in £20.
        David Ghost of Portsmouth in £10.
        John Doe in £10.[48]

For appearance of Balch at the next Sessions to answer for assaulting John Marten and Tho. Freeman and to keep the peace, especially towards them.

291

ASSAULT

S3/9/9. *Calendar number on document:* 8.

3 July 1682. Before Tho. Hancocke, esq., Mayor.

Informations

    (a) Rob. Williams of Southampton, pewterer, said that about 2 p.m. that day, as he was coming from Kingston to Portsmouth, he called at Kemp's house to see if he wanted anything. As he was talking to the people of the house, he heard Roger Pascoe cry out to John Poat 'you rogue goe about your business and if you will not I will goe and fetch a sticke and break your limbes'. Pascoe went in and got a stick and Mary Roaker asked him where he was going and told him not to strike the man. He said 'Yes I will, you whore and you too', and struck Mary several blows. Then Pascoe and his wife fell on Poat and beat him too. *Signed by mark.*

    (b) John Poat (*signs* Poett) *confirmed the evidence of Rob. Williams.* *Signed.*

Recognisances

    (a) Rob. Williams in £10.
        John Poat in £10.

For appearance of Mary, wife of John Roaker, Rob. Williams and John Poat at the next Sessions to prosecute Roger Pascoe and Mary his wife.

    (b) Roger Paschoe in £20.
        Ric. Uthwatt in £10.

For appearance of Paschoe and Mary his wife at the next Sessions to answer Mary Roaker and John Poat and not to depart [the jurisdiction of] the Court without licence.

292

ASSAULT

S3B/22

15 May 1682. Before Tho. Hancock, esq., Mayor.

Informations

    (a) Jos. Conduit (*signs* Cunditt) said that yesterday about 7 p.m. he and his wife were coming from Cosham to bring Geo. Gittins and his wife, Wil. Binsted and his wife and Goodwife Pen homewards towards Kingston in the parish of Portsea. As they walked in the footway in the marsh, Tho. Adams overtook them riding on the highway. He called out 'you are a rascal, and if I could come at thee I would slash thee'. Adams also called him son of a whore and drew his sword half out. He rode on to Portsbridge, got off, tied up his horse at the bridge and came towards the stile from the marsh. Geo. Gittins came over the stile first and Adams drew his sword and made several passes at him. Conduit then called the sentry and the soldiers came and took Adams in custody to Portsmouth to the Governor. *Signed.*

    (b) Geo. Gittins of Portsea, rope maker, Henry Wasker of Havant, cordwainer, and John Horne of Kingston, *confirmed the evidence of Cunditt.*

    (c) Tho. Adams said he went in fear of his life that Jos. Cundit would beat, wound or kill him. *Signed.*

---

[48] For note on John Doe see Introduction, p. xiv.

I

Recognisances
(a) Jos. Cundit in £10.
Geo. Gittins in £10.
Henry Wasker in £10.
John Horne in £10.
For appearance at the next County Sessions to prosecute and give evidence against Tho. Adams.
(b) Tho. Adams in £20.
Rob. Shorter in £10.
For appearance [of Adams] at the next County Sessions to answer indictments preferred against him by Geo. Gittins.
(c) Jos. Cundit in £20.
On condition (*blank*).

S3/9/8. *Calendar number on document:* 7.
8 July 1682. Before Tho. Hancocke, esq., Mayor.
Recognisances
Jos. Cunditt in £20.
John Tayleur in £10.
For appearance [of Cunditt] at the next Sessions to answer Tho. Adams and to keep the peace, especially towards Adams.

293
WRONGFUL
IMPRISONMENT

S3B/24. *Calendar number on document:* 9.
9 August 1682. Before Tho. Hancock, csq., Mayor.
Information
Dorothy, wife of James Hobbs, said that at the request of Jane, wife of Henry Beare, about 8 or 9 on that morning she went to the Dock to fetch a burthen of junk from the nail-shop pen. She went into the pen and, while she was there, Wil. Mellersh came out of the nail-shop and locked her in the pen and kept her there over half an hour. A maid came to the shop and asked why she was imprisoned. Mellersh answered that it was for a whore's trick. *Signed by mark.*
Recognisances
Wil. Mellersh in £20.
John Perin in £10.
For appearance of Mellersh at the next Sessions.

294
HOUSEBREAKING

S3/9/5
7 September 1682. Before Tho. Hancock, esq., Mayor, and Sam. Williams.
Information
Elizabeth Colebrooke of Portsmouth, spinster, said that Tho. Small of Portsmouth, tailor, between 12 and 1 last night broke the lower kitchen window of her father's house and came in up the stairs and into her room. She asked who it was. He said 'it is I' and took hold of her but she went by him down to her father's room.
Signed by mark.

Examination
Tho. Small said (*blank*).

295
SETTLEMENT

S3/9/4
14 September 1682. Before Tho. Hancocke, esq., Mayor.
Examination
Ann Whore (*signs* Haore) of Portsmouth, spinster, said she had been in Portsmouth for six to eight weeks lodging with Widow Whitmarsh, where she asked for one night's lodging, but, falling sick, was enforced to stay for three weeks. Then she went to the house of John Ham for three nights and then moved to Horne Court for one night (she did not know the name of the woman). Then she went to Hayling Island to her father-in-law Wil. Payne and stayed about a fortnight. Last Saturday she came back to Portsmouth, but returned to her father-in-law for the night. On Monday she came to Gosport and spent the night at the house of Mary Warre alias Philip. On Tuesday she came here and lodged for two nights with Benedicta Whitehorne, widow. She had no estate to live on except what she can earn with her needle. *Signed.*

15 September 1682.
Recognisances
> Ann Hoare in £20.
> Wil. Wheeler of Portsmouth, gent., in £10.
> Wil. Terrell of the same, innholder, in £10.
> For appearance of Ann at the next Sessions.

296
ROBBERY

S3/9/7

21 September 1682. Before Tho. Hancock, esq., Mayor.
Examination
Adam François du Maine of Caen, Normandy, said that about three months ago he came from France to London where he lodged with a soldier's wife; he did not know her name, nor the name of the street. He left London for Southampton about a fortnight ago and had been at Hampton, where he intended to settle, ten days. He came to Portsmouth yesterday to see the town.   *Signed.*

S3/9/6

25 September 1682. Before Tho. Hancocke, esq., Mayor.
Information
Jonathan Powell was sent by his master, the Hon. Henry Bronncker, from London to prosecute Adam François du Maine, a Frenchman, for robbing the said master of watch, plate and guineas to the value of £100. Du Mane was arrested on a letter from his master to the Deputy Governor of Portsmouth. Jonathan Powell confirmed that Du Maine was not the man who robbed his master.   *Signed.*

297
DISSENTERS'
CONVENTICLE

S3/9/2

22 September 1682. Borough of Portsmouth and Vill of Gosport. Before Tho. Hancock (*signs* Hancock), esq., Mayor, Nic. Peirson, Mayor-elect, and Sam. Williams, gent.
Information and sentence (Latin)
Tho. Harwood and Sir And. Cooke, kt, said that Theophilus Lloyd of Gosport on 17 Sept. last preached or taught at a meeting in the house of Step. Locke in Gosport consisting of fifty persons, in addition to the said Locke's family and servants, over the age of sixteen contrary to the Statute.[49] For this, Lloyd's first offence, he has forfeited £20 to be levied on his goods and chattels, for such preaching was not in accordance with the Liturgy of the Church of England.
Signed and sealed by all three Justices (Hancock signs with a hand-stamp) 23 Sept. 1682;
papered seals appended (impressions indistinct).

298
ASSAULT

S3/9/1

2 October 34 Cha. II [1682]. Borough of Portsmouth and Vill of Gosport.
Presentment (Latin)
Presents Wil. Munday lately of Gosport, parish of Alverstoke, cook (*sic*), for assault on Jane Harwood.   *Signed by* [Edw.] Archer.
Footnote: He submitted under protest because he did not wish to oppose the King and paid a fine of 3s 4d.
Endorsements:
> (a) Witness Jane Harwood.
> (b) True bill.

S3/9/3

4 October 34 Cha. II [1682]. Before Sam. Burningham, gent.
Recognisances
> Wil. Munday of Gosport, cooper (*sic*), in £10.
> Tho. Fleet of the same, shipwright, in £5.
> For appearance of Munday at the next Sessions to answer for assault on Jane Harwood.   *Signed by the Justice.*

---

[49] Statute: 22 Cha. II, c.1.

299
ABUSE

S3/10/19

23 October 1682. Before Nic. Peirson, esq., Mayor.
Information
James Etherington sen. said that about a month ago he was at the house of Rob. Shorter in Portsmouth with Mr Tiddiman, Mr Berry, Mr Leverett and others.[50] There was some discussion and Mr Shorter fell upon him and called him knave and great knave. He asked why, and the reply was for making him pay 10 groats for short pots. He answered it was always paid since he did know what belonged to a jury and if Shorter was troubled he should go to the Mayor and Justices. Shorter then said 'you are a company of fools to put such a fellow in office' and that there were some pitiful fellows amongst them. *Signed.*

300
THREATENED
ASSAULT

S3/10/20. *Calendar number on document:* 1.

31 October 1682. Before Nic. Peirson, esq., Mayor.
Informations
(a) John Mills of Portsmouth, joiner, said that on Wednesday 25th inst. John Poat was driving a cart full of dung by the house of Mr Fra. Winter, who asked him to drive further away from the house. Poat said 'put up a post, and be damned if I shall not drive neere your house'. He afterwards took his prong out and pointed it at Mrs (*recte Mr*) Winter and swore that if he came near him he would run his prong into him. *Signed.*
(b) Ric. Middleton and Edw. Ansell declared that what John Mills said was true. *Signed by both.*

31 October 1682. Before Nic. Peirson, esq., Mayor, Tho. Hancocke, gent., Sam. Burningham, gent., and Rob. Shales, gent.
Recognisances
John Poate in £20.
John Roaker in £10.
Ant. Colebrooke in £10.
For appearance of Poate at the next Sessions to answer indictments preferred by Mr Fra. Winter.
See also no. 326 (1).

301
ASSAULT

S3/14/23

3 November 34 Cha. II [1682]. Borough of Portsmouth and Vill of Gosport.
Presentment (*Latin*)
Presents John Softley of Forton in Alverstoke, butcher of Gosport, for beating and wounding Tho. Silver of the same with a dung-fork value 2d. *Signed by* [Edw.] Archer.
Footnote: He submitted to the Court under protest because he did not wish to oppose the King and paid a fine 6s 8d.
Endorsements:
(a) Witnesses Tho. Silver, Step. Carver, John Day, Simon Young, sworn.
(b) True bill.

302
ABUSE

S3/10/18. *Calendar number on document:* 2.

12 November 1682. Before Nic. Peirson, esq., Mayor, Tho. Hancock, gent., and Rob. Shales, gent.
Informations
(a) Mary, wife of Mic. Richardson, said that last Saturday 11th inst. about 6 or 7 p.m. James Harrison, an apprentice of her husband's, came and abused her, calling her whore, bitch and such like. *Signed by mark.*
(b) Tho. Wayman said he had heard James Harrison call the said Mary whore several times. *Signed by mark.*

---

[50] These four men could be the Clerk of the Market's jury (cf. no. 150). Etherington and Leverett were burgesses. Tiddiman was on the Court Leet jury, Oct. 1681, and Leverett on the Court Leet jury, Oct. 1682.

13 November 1682. Before Nic. Peirson, esq., Mayor.
Recognisances
> James Harrison of Portsmouth in £20.
> John Stubbs of the same, victualler, in £10.

For appearance of Harrison at the next Sessions and not to depart [the jurisdiction of] the Court without licence.
See also no. 326 (2).

303
ASSAULTING AUTHORITY

S3/14/24

9 November 34 Cha. II [1682]. Borough of Portsmouth and Vill of Gosport.
Presentment (Latin)
Presents Wil. Kneller of Gosport, shipwright ('naufragius'), for assaulting Cuthbert Bembridge, Churchwarden of Alverstoke, in the execution of his office.

> *Signed by* [Edw.] Archer.

Footnote: He confesses the accusation under protest because he does not wish to oppose the King and is fined 13s 4d.

Endorsements:
(a) Cuthbert Bembridge, Humf. Stot, sworn.
(b) True bill.
See also no. 326 (3).

304
DISSENTERS' CONVENTICLE

D11A/16/28

20 November 1682. Before Nic. Peirson, esq., Mayor, Tho. Hancock, gent., Sam Williams, gent., and Rob. Shales, gent.
Informations

(a) Humf. Scott, Constable of the Vill of Gosport, said that about 11 a.m. last Sunday, 19 Nov., by notice of a warrant from the Mayor he took with him some of the inhabitants to suppress an unlawful meeting. He knocked two or three times before the door was opened and when he came in he found a Mr Lloyd in the pulpit. He called him in the King's name to come down. He replied that it was contrary to the Act of Parliament to execute a warrant or disturb the King's peace on the Sabbath day and called to the assembly of about a hundred people to sing the first two staves of the second Psalm and then he said a prayer. In the assembly were John Ernee(?), James Elliate and John Baker. *Signed.*

Humf. Scott further said that about 3 p.m. on the same Sunday he, with some of the inhabitants, went to the same conventicle and breaking open two doors they found an assembly of two hundred or more and, finding no preacher, they dispersed them. About 5 p.m. on the same day he went again and found about two hundred people there who immediately dispersed. About an hour later he went again with his assistants and some soldiers, thinking they might have returned, but found the doors shut, so could not say if there was a meeting then. *Signed.*

(b) The following persons confirmed that on going again after the 5 o'clock dispersal they could not break open the door so could not say if there was a congregation there, but truly believed that there was. *Signed by:* Ric. New
> Cuthbert Bembridge
> John Hull
> Tho. Hoopper (*by mark*)

(c) The following persons deposed that they were with the Constable at 3 p.m. *and confirmed the Constable's deposition on the 3 o'clock entry.*
Signed by: Tho. Cheesman   Step. Thomas
> John Bernitt(?)   Tho. Haberley
> John Courtney   Fra. Chandler

305
BASTARDY

S3/10/17

12 December 1682. Before Nic. Peirson, esq., Mayor, Tho. Hancock, gent., and Sam. Williams, gent.
Examination
Eleanor Hasham of Portsmouth, singlewoman, said she was begotten with child by John Chapman, gunner of H.M.S. Dartmouth, when she lived with John Stayner at

the sign of the London nine months ago in the room there called the Crown. Chapman had carnal knowledge of her body twice and no one else had and he was father of the child. *Signed by mark.*

306
ABUSE

S3/10/16. *Calendar number on document: 4.*

19 December 1682. Before Nic. Peirson, esq., Mayor.
Information
John Smith of Portsmouth, soldier, said that last Saturday he was at the house of Mr John Grandy in Portsmouth where he heard Wil. Hooper of Portsmouth, labourer, call Mr Grandy rogue and rascal and son of a whore, with several other names. *Signed by mark.*
Recognisances
    (a) John Smith in £10.
For appearance at the next Sessions to give evidence against Wil. [Hooper].
    (b) Wil Hooper in £20.
        Ant. Colebrooke in £10.
For appearance [of Hooper] at the next Sessions.
See also no. 326 (4).

307
BASTARDY

S3/10/15

10 January 1682/3. Borough of Portsmouth and Vill of Gosport. Before Nic. Peirson, esq., Mayor.
Information
Mary Morris of Gosport, singlewoman, said that seven or eight weeks ago, being servant of Mr Simon Young, who keeps the tavern at Gosport called the Sovereign, Fra. Walker, coxswain of H.M.S. Kingfisher ('Kings Fisher'), lodged there. She warmed his bed for him every night and several times he had carnal knowledge of her body. Believing she was now with child by him, he promised to marry her. No other person had had carnal knowledge of her body. *Signed.*

308
ASSAULT

S3/10/14

19 January 1682/3. Borough of Portsmouth and Vill of Gosport. Before Nic. Peirson, esq., Mayor, Tho. Hancock, gent., and Sam. Williams, gent.
Information
Cha. Saunders, seaman of H.M.S. Kingfisher ('Kings Fisher'), said that about Friday or Monday 15th he came ashore at the Dock with Ric. Harper, Tho. Aldridge, Nic. Purdue, Ric. Steele and others. When they came without the Dockgate towards Portsmouth Aldridge said to Harper 'you have beat me several tymes and if you can beat me now I will forgive you, if not, I will beat you'. Harper asked for time to take off his clothes, which he did. They then went together by the ears, but who struck first he could not say. He went to part them but Purdue and Steele took hold of him. *Signed by mark.*
    Footnote: Abraham Lewis, John Brookes, witnesses.

20 January 1682/3. No name of Justice.
Information
Abraham Lewis (*signs* Lues) said that as he and others were coming out of the Dock last Monday he saw Ric. Harper and Tho. Aldrige together. Harper asked Aldrige to let him alone as he was not in a condition to fight. They presently went together by the ears: Harper was much beaten, but who struck first he could not say. *Signed.*

S3/10/13

20 [January] 1682/3. Before Sam. Williams, gent.
Information
Ric. Harper said that he went on board H.M.S. Harwich on Monday last, 15 Jan., to muster and as he came back by boat Tho. Aldred, Nic. Purdue and Ric. Steele followed him in another boat. When he came through the Dockyard he found them in the way. As soon as Aldred saw him he began to strip and said 'Stay, I have some-what to say to you Richard Harper you shall beat me or I'll beat you before you goe

from this place'. He answered that he had been sick, had taken physic yesterday and was not in a condition to fight and asked to be let alone till some other time. Aldred replied 'I will doe it now, for if I cannot doe it here are some others will helpe me'. Aldred fell upon him and Cha. Saunders standing by would have parted them but the others held him. So Aldred beat him and cut his nose and both eyes and he has been ill ever since.   *Signed.*

309
ASSAULT

S3/10/12 (entry i)

26 January [1682/3]. Borough of Portsmouth and Vill of Gosport. Before Nic. Peirson, esq., Mayor.
Information
Tho. Hancock said that between 11 p.m. and 12 last night four or five persons came to his house in a riotous manner, including Wil. Hale, servant of Mr Wil. Terrell. They broke down some boards of the shop and threw them in the street. He thought the house was breaking up and looked out of the window asking who was there. They answered 'What loggerhead is there' and used other scurrilous words. He replied that he knew them and the Governor should know tomorrow. They cried out 'Hancocke is a cuckold'. He said they were a company of drunken sots and should be at home. They then threw stones at his window.   *Signed with a hand-stamp.*
Examination
Wil. Hale said that about 11 or 12 last night he lighted some gentlemen home to their lodging but did not know their names or their lodgings.

310
Subject unknown

S3/10/12 (entry ii)

29 January 1682/3. Before Edw. Archer, notary public.
Affidavit
John Ralleure, steersman, and the mariners of the said ship acknowledged that the above attestation is true. *No attestation and no signatories.*

311
ASSAULT

S3/10/11

1 February 1682/3. Before Nic. Peirson, esq., Mayor.
Information
   (a) Isabel, wife of Peter Gamon, said that this morning as she came from market she met Margaret, wife of Wil. Josline of Portsmouth, soldier, and as she was going into her own door Margaret threw dirt at her and took up a brickbat and threw it, striking her on the back. She then took from the lap of Ann Isemonger, a girl who was bringing some things home for her, half a pound of butter and some cheese and threw it into the dirt.   *Signed by mark.*
   (b) Ann Isemonger *confirmed the above.*

312
Subject unknown

S3/10/7. *Calendar number on document: 5.*

6 February 1682/3. Before Tho. Hancock, gent.
Recognisances
         John Johnson in £20.
         John Symes, mariner, in £10.
         Ric. Eeling, mariner, in £10.
   For appearance of Johnson at the next Sessions and to keep the peace, especially towards John Adams.
See also no. 326 (5).

313
ABUSING
AUTHORITY

D11A/16/29

8 February 1682/3. Before Nic. Peirson, esq., Mayor.
Information
Dorothy, wife of James Etherington jun., said that last Sunday, 4 Feb., she came to the house of Basilia ('Bazell') Hull, widow, for a pint of beer. She saw Mr Cha. Chapman and heard him ask why did they make such a man Mayor as Mr Hancocke, who had 'more need goe to blouding and shoeing of horses'. He swore by his maker that Hancocke was no more fit to be Mayor than his stick was: he would as soon pull off

his hat to a turd as to Mr Hancock and became obscene. Mrs Hull seemed to check him saying that Mr Hancock had done a great deal of good bringing the Charter to town. She told him he was young and foolish and that when he was old he would have more wit than to abuse an ancient man. *Signed by mark.*

314
THEFT

S3/10/9

8 February 1682/3. Before Tho. Hancoke, gent.
Information
Elizabeth, wife of Tho. Reevly, said that on 30 Jan. last Ann Hoare brought her an apron and asked her to sell it for her. She sold it to the wife of Tho. Crispe for 14*d*. Ann said she would give her a pair of black shoes if she sold it. Shoes and apron were the property of Barbara Woollgar, widow. *Signed.*

315
THEFT

S3/10/10

12 February 1682/3. Before Nic. Peirson, Mayor, and Tho. Hancock, gent.
Informations
(a) John Perrin of Portsmouth said that on last Saturday, the 10th, David Alldridge, rope maker, came to his house and left a bag with a bundle of clothes and asked him to deliver it to John Hall and be careful not to wet the clothes. What was in the bag he did not know. Two hours later Hall came and he delivered the bag and clothes. *Signed by mark.*
(b) John Hall of Fareham said that on Saturday last, the 10th, David Alldridge, rope maker, came to him on his hoy and asked him to go to John Perrin to fetch a bag and bundle of clothes and bring them to Fareham and he would come and fetch them from him. He neither saw nor knew what was in the bag till it was opened on the hoy.

316
THEFT

S3/10/8. *Calendar numbers on document: 6, 7.*

10 March 1682/3. Borough of Portsmouth and Vill of Gosport. Before Nic. Peirson, esq., Mayor.
Information
John Jent, servant of Hugh Swettingham of Gosport, mariner, said that about 9 p.m. last night he came on board his master's hoy and found [Edw.] Reaby and Peter Staning and asked them what they were doing there; they answered that they came to get a little drink. On that he lit a candle and found they had cut off a piece of Cheshire cheese which they had thrown under the iron that lay in the vessel. Staning afterwards fetched the cheese from there. He therefore took hold of Staning and said he must keep him there all night. Staning drew a knife. The other, seeing the guard-boat coming, took a boat and went away. The guard-boat took Staning and Reaby and kept them all night. *Signed by mark.*
Recognisances
    Hugh Swettingham in £10.
    John Jent in £10.
For appearance of Jent at the next Sessions to prosecute and give evidence against Peter Stoneing and Edw. Reaby for taking 4 lb. of Cheshire cheese of Hugh Swettingham and not to depart from [the jurisdiction of] the Court without licence.

10 March 1682/3. Before Nic. Peirson, esq., Mayor, Tho. Hancocke and Sam. Burningham.
Examinations
(a) Edw. Reaby, servant of Roger Pigget of Gosport, said that he and Peter Staning were on board Hugh Swettingham's hoy last night to get a little drink 'of his country boy'. John Gent came on board presently and took Staning and beat him and made him fast to the windlass of the boat. *Signed by mark.*
(b) Peter Staning confessed the above evidence to be true. *Signed by mark.*
See also no. 326 (6, 7).

317
Subject unknown

S3/10/6. *Calendar number on document:* 8.

13 March 1682/3. Borough of Portsmouth and Vill of Gosport. Before Nic. Peirson, esq., Mayor.
Recognisances
  Edm. Ward in £20.
  John Dale in £10.
For appearance of Elizabeth, wife of Edm. Ward, at the next Sessions.
Bound over on complaint of Katherine, wife of Boatswain Tho. Clements.
See also no. 326 (8).

318
THEFT

S3/10/4. *Calendar number on document:* 9.

29 March 1683. Borough of Portsmouth and Vill of Gosport. Before Nic. Peirson, esq., Mayor.
Information
Sarah, wife of John Land (*or* Laud?), said that Wil. Joslin and Margaret his wife lived in the house with her husband and herself for eleven weeks and paid 12*d* a week for the use of her house and goods and left on Saturday week last. While she was with them she stole from the house two porringers and bought two new ones offering them instead. Afterwards she stole a small porringer and a quartern pewter pot and sold it to Mr Tho. Brounker.   *Signed by mark.*
Recognisances
  John Land in £10.
  Roger Bolds in £10.
For appearance of Land and his wife and Roger Bolds at the next Sessions to prosecute and give evidence against Margaret Joslin.

29 March 1683. Before Tho. Hancocke, gent.
Recognisances
  Wil. Joslin in £20.
  Moses Linvell in £20.[51]
  Wil. Deacon in £10.
For appearance of Margaret Joslin at the next Sessions to answer indictments preferred by Sarah, wife of John Land.
See also no. 326 (9).

319
CONTEMPT

S3/10/1

11 April 1683. Borough of Portsmouth and Vill of Gosport. Before Nic. Peirson, esq., Mayor, and Tho. Hancocke, gent.
Recognisances
  Albion ('Abbine') Knapton of Gosport, gent., in £40.
  Step. Carver in £20.
  Wil. Libett in £20.
For appearance of Knapton at the next Sessions to answer for contemptuous words spoken against the Mayor and Justices and not to depart [the jurisdiction of] the Court without licence.
See also no. 326 (10).

320
ASSAULT

S3/10/2 (entry i). *Calendar number on document:* 11.

17 January 1682/3. Before Sam. Burningham, gent.
Recognisances
  (a) John Softly in £20.
   Wil. Bevis in £10.
   John Isger in £10.
For appearance of Softly at the next Court.
Bound over for wounding Tho. Silver.
  (b) Tho. Silver in £20 to prosecute.
See also no. 326 (11).

---

[51] Linvell is Lynfeild in no. 326(9).

321
Subject unknown

S3/10/2 (entry iii). *Calendar number on document:* 12.

7 April 1683. No name of Justice.
Recognisances
    John Dunmore in £10.
    Jos. Knapton in £10.
For appearance of Dunmore at the next Sessions.
Footnote: Released by consent.
See also no. 326 (12).

322
Subject unknown

S3/10/2 (entry ii). *Calendar number on document:* 13.

21 March 1682. No name of Justice.
Recognisance
    Step. Carver in £10.
For appearance of Jane, wife of Hugh Sweetingham, at the next Sessions.
Footnote: Released by consent.
See also no. 326 (13).

323
SETTLEMENT

S3/10/3

No date [circa April 1683]. Before Nic. Peirson, esq., Mayor, and Tho. Hancocke, gent.
Examination
Elizabeth, wife of John Robinson, late of Whitechapel, Mdx, shipwright, said she was the daughter of Henry Walker, labourer, who lived in Bell Yard, Whitechapel, and died there about eleven years ago. About seven years ago she married John Robinson at Whitechapel and lived with her husband at Bell Yard till Easter last. They rented a house there of Mr Tho. Stoner. About Easter last they went to Dover and her husband took a lodging in St Mary's parish of Mr Wil. Williams at the sign of the Ship and stayed till she was sent away with a pass. Her husband left her at Dover seventeen weeks ago. She had not been in Portsmouth for forty years and does not know anyone there but she heard her father say that she was born there and brought away aged three. *Signed by mark.*

324
REGRATING

S3/14/25

18 April 35 Cha. II [1683]. Borough of Portsmouth and Vill of Gosport.
Presentment (Latin)
Presents Edw. Chapman sen. of Portsmouth, glover, for regrating the market by buying 10 lb. of butter priced at 5*s* per lb. and reselling in the public market.
    Footnote: He submitted under protest because he did not wish to oppose and paid a fine 13*s* 4*d*.
    Endorsements:
    (a) Tho. Hancocke, Elizabeth Alford, sworn.
    (b) True bill.

325
OBSTRUCTING THE HIGHWAY

S3/14/26

18 April 35 Cha. II [1683]. Borough of Portsmouth and Vill of Gosport.
Presentment (Latin)
Presents Cuthbert Bembridge of Gosport, gent., and John Chivers of Alverstoke, victualler, for placing and leaving a laystall or dunghill on the King's highway running from the south to the north of a field in the parish of Alverstoke called Windmill Field.
    Footnote: He confesses the bill under protest because he does not wish to oppose the King and paid 3*s* 4*d* of a total fine of 6*s* 8*d*.
    Endorsements:
    (a) Witness Rob. Reeves, sworn.
    (b) True bill.

S3/10/5

[**19 April**] **1683.** Lady-day Sessions.

(1)[52] [John Poate, for threatened assault].   John Roaker
                                                        Ant. Colebrooke

See no. 300.

(2) [James Harrison], for abusing Mary, wife of Mic.   John Stubbs
    [Ri]chardson.
    See no. 302.

(3) Wil. Kneller, for assaulting the Churchwardens and Tho. Crewes
    Overseers of Gosport and disturbing the meeting.   Nic. Hawksworth
    See no. 303.
    Marginal note (Latin): Discharged by the Court.

(4) Wil. Hooper, for abusing Mr John Grundy.   Ant. Colebrooke
    See no. 306.
    Marginal note (Latin): Discharged by the Court.

(5) John Johnson to keep the peace.   John Symes
                                                        Ric. Eeling
    See no. 312.

(6) Edw. Reaby, for stealing 4 lb. of cheese of   Roger Smith
    Hugh Swettingham.   Wil. Paye
    See no. 316.
    Marginal note (Latin): Discharged by the Court.

(7) Peter Staning, for the same offence.   The like bails.
    See no. 316.
    Marginal note (Latin): Discharged by the Court.

(8) Elizabeth, wife of Edm. Ward, bound to the   Edm. Ward
    behaviour.   John Dale
    See no. 317.
    Marginal note (Latin): Discharged by order of Mr Mayor.

(9) Margaret, wife of Wil. Jostlin, for petty larceny. Wil. Jostlin
                                                        Moses Lynfeild
                                                        Wil. Deacon
    See no. 318.

(10) Albion Knapton bound to the behaviour, [for   Step. Carver
     contempt].   Wil. Lybett
     See no. 319.
     Marginal note (Latin): Discharged by order of the Mayor.

(11) John Softly, for beating and wounding Tho. Silver. Wil. Bevis
                                                         John Isger
     See no. 320.
     Marginal note (Latin): He submitted and paid a fine.

(12) John Dunmore, bound to the behaviour.   Jos. Knapton
     See no. 321.
     Marginal note (Latin): Discharged by Mr Burningham.

(13) Jane, wife of Hugh Swettingham, bound to the   Step. Carver
     behaviour.
     See no. 322.
     Marginal note (Latin): Discharged by Mr Burningham.

---

[52] Parts of items (1) and (2) are missing.

327
MISBEHAVIOUR
IN COURT

S3/11/1. *Calendar number on document:* 1.

19 April 1683. Borough of Portsmouth and Vill of Gosport. Before Nic. Peirson, esq., Mayor, and others.

Recognisances

        Tho. Silver of Gosport, butcher, in £20.

        Nat. Bunch of Portsmouth, gent., in £10.

        Hugh Swettingham of Gosport, sailor, in £10.

    For appearance of Silver at the next Sessions.

    Bound over for misbehaviour in Court at the Sessions.

See also no. 345 (1).

328
SETTLEMENT

S3/11/3

28 April 1683. Borough of Portsmouth and Vill of Gosport. Before Tho. Hancocke, gent.

Examination

Henry Sutton late of Portchester, metal-man, said that about six years ago he came to Portchester and whilst he was there his wife Mary came to him great with child and was delivered within 24 hours. His wife died within half a quarter of an hour after the birth; he stayed for three or four days and then went away. The minister of the parish baptised the child with the name Henry.   *Signed by mark.*

329
BASTARDY

S3/11/2

5 May 1683. Borough of Portsmouth and Vill of Gosport. Before Tho. Hancocke, gent.

Examination

Margaret Right of Portsmouth, widow, said she was with child begotten by Edw. Alford, seaman of H.M.S. America. She had lived with him as his wife at the house of Henry Comeings at the Point since last Christmas. He was the father and no other.   *Signed by mark.*

330
BASTARDY

S3/11/4

18 May 1683. Borough of Portsmouth and Vill of Gosport. Before Nic. Peirson, esq., Mayor, and Tho. Hancocke, gent.

Examination

Elizabeth Bennett of Portsmouth, singlewoman, said that about the middle of August last Tho. Mosse of Deptford, [Kent and] Surr., mariner, twice had carnal knowledge of her body at the house of John Ham of Portsmouth, victualler. On Tuesday 17 Apr. last she was delivered of a female child and Tho. Mosse was the father.   *Signed by mark.*

331
APPRENTICESHIP
AND THEFT

S3/11/6

26 May 1683. Before Tho. Hancocke, gent.

Information

Nat. Bunch of Portsmouth, gent., said that Ben. Watson, his apprentice, had several times run away for several days and nights, absenting himself unlawfully and taking away some of his master's goods.   *Signed.*

332
CONTEMPT

S3/11/5. *Calendar number on document:* 3.

28 May 1683. Before Tho. Hancocke, gent.

Information

Tho. Godden, one of the Constables, said that last Saturday about 9 p.m. he came to the house of Tho. Tyley of Portsmouth, victualler, and demanded lodging for vagrant persons sent with a pass. Tyley said they had no lodging but Godden said they must lodge there. He went to take them indoors and the door was locked. He went to

---

[53] Evidence for this adjournment only to be found in no. 346.

another door and got in but Tyley got hold of him and shut the door. He said 'dont keepe me heere a prisoner'. Tyley answered 'I scorn that' and let him out.   *Signed.*
Recognisances
    (a) Tho. Tyley of Portsmouth, house-carpenter, in £20.
        Tho. Barton in £10.
For appearance of Tyley at the next Sessions to answer indictments preferred by Tho. Godden.
    Marginal note (Latin): Discharged by the Court.
    (b) Tho. Godden in £10.
    To prosecute and give evidence against Tho. Tyley.
See also no. 345 (3).

333
ASSAULT

S3/11/20
1 June 35 Cha. II [1683]. Borough of Portsmouth and Vill of Gosport.
Presentment (Latin)
Presents Mary Brimston of Portsmouth, widow, for assaulting Rebecca, wife of John Prince, on 1 June 35 Cha. II by causing an affray and striking and wounding her so that she despaired of her life.   *Signed* 'pro [Edw.] Archer'.
    Footnote: She submitted under protest because she did not wish to oppose the King in the matter of the fine.
    Endorsements:
    (a) Rebecca Prince sworn.
    (b) True bill.

S/3/11/7. *Calendar number on document*: 4.
1 June 1683. Borough of Portsmouth and Vill of Gosport. Before Nic. Peirson, esq., Mayor.
Recognisances
    (a) Mary Brimson, widow, in £10.
        James Thomson, sailor, in £5.
For appearance of Mary at the next Sessions to answer all trespasses and indictments for assaulting, beating and wounding Rebecca, wife of John Prince, and to keep the peace, especially towards the said Rebecca.
    Marginal note (Latin): She owes for her recognisance 2s 6d.
    (b) John Prince in £10.
For appearance of John Prince and Rebecca his wife at the next Sessions to give evidence and prosecute Mary Brimson.
    Footnote: Bound over to keep the peace, the said Mary having confessed the fact before Mr Mayor.
See also no. 345 (4).

334
Subject unknown

S3/11/8. *Calendar number on document*: 5.
2 June 1683. Before Tho. Hancock.
Recognisances
        Geo. Hodgies of Gosport in £20.
        Ann Morlin of the same, widow, in £10.
        Tho. Seymor of the same in £10.
For appearance of John Hodges at the next Sessions to answer indictments preferred by Tho. Crow.

1 June 1683. Before Nic. Peirson, esq., Mayor.
Recognisance
        Tho. Crow in £10.
For appearance at the next Sessions to prosecute Geo. Hodges.
    Footnote: Recognisances respited until the end of the Sessions.
See also no. 345 (5).

335
Subject unknown

S3/11/9

4 June 1683. Before Nic. Peirson, esq., Mayor.
Recognisances

    (a) Humf. Thompson of Portsmouth in £10.

        Ant. Mitchell of the same in £5.

For appearance of Thompson at the next Sessions to answer indictments preferred by Margaret Thompson and not to depart [the jurisdiction of] the Court without licence.

    (b) Margaret Thompson in £5.

For appearance at the next Sessions to give evidence against Humf. Thompson and not to depart [the jurisdiction of] the Court without licence.

Marginal note (Latin): Discharged by the Mayor and Justices of the Peace of the Borough and Vill aforesaid.

336
**THREATENED
MURDER**

S3/11/19

20 June 1683. Before Sam. Burningham, gent.
Information

John Barnett of Gosport said that on 17 June he heard John Collins of Gosport, mariner, swear several times that he would murder Gardner Brookes the first time he met him in a place where he could have the advantage.   *Signed.*

23 June 1683. No name of Justice.
Recognisances

      Wil. Collins in £10.

      James Smith in £10.

For appearance of John, son of Wil. Collins, at the next Sessions.
Bound over for threatening Gardner Brookes.

337
THEFT

S3/11/10

18 July 1683. Borough of Portsmouth and Vill of Gosport. Before Tho. Hancock, gent., Deputy Mayor.
Informations

(a) Margaret Easton of Portsmouth, spinster, said that about three weeks ago she was with the wife of Geo. Stebbens, who was cutting to pieces a Holland shirt. She asked her where she got it and she replied from John Shaw, under-ostler to Mr Terrell. She added that she had been several times at Stebbens' room with John Shaw, where they had been very merry with wine and victuals, but she did not know where Stebbens got the shirt.   *Signed by mark.*

(b) Mary, wife of John Chandles of Portsmouth, victualler, said that this morning Joan Rabnutt (*or* Rabunnt?) came to her and told her that there were three young pullets brought down from Geo. Stebbins' chamber.   *Signed by mark.*

(c) Geo. Stebens of Portsmouth said that the fowl now shown him he had received yesterday about 3 or 4 p.m. from John Shaw, Mr Terrell's ostler, and that the two napkins and two knives found in his chamber the said Shaw had given him at other times with some victuals.   *Signed.*

(d) John Shaw of Portsmouth, labourer, said (*blank*).

S3/11/11. *Calendar number on document:* 6.

21 July 1683. Borough of Portsmouth and Vill of Gosport. Before Sam. Williams, gent., Deputy Mayor.
Recognisances

    (a) John Shaw of Portsmouth, husbandman, in £20.

        Roger Smith of the same in £10.

        Ric. Page of the same in £10.

For appearance of Shaw at the next Sessions to answer indictments preferred by Wil. Terrell for stealing several chickens and other goods of Terrell and not to depart [the jurisdiction of] the Court without licence.

Marginal note (Latin): He owes for his recognisance.

(b) Wil. Terrell of Portsmouth in £10.

For appearance at the next Sessions to prosecute and give evidence against John Shaw and not to depart [the jurisdiction of] the Court without licence.

See also no. 345 (6).

338
BASTARDY

S3/11/12

13 August 1683. Borough of Portsmouth and Vill of Gosport. Before Nic. Peirson, esq., Mayor, and Tho. Hancocke, gent.

Informations

(a) Ann Hoare, spinster, said that the child that she was lately brought to bed with was the child of Mr Wil. Terrell of Portsmouth, innholder, begotten by him at the house on the Point of the woman called Widow Englishes (now remarried) two or three days before or after 5 Nov. last. Further he had several times before had carnal knowledge of her body at one John Thompson's at the Mill.   *Signed.*

(b) Ann Upsdall of Fratton, parish of Portsea, widow, said that on 24 July last she, being a midwife, was called to Ann Hoare, who lodged at the house of John Balch, and about 9 or 10 a.m. of that day she was delivered of a male child. Ann had told her that Mr Terrell was the father.   *Signed by mark.*

S3/11/13

13 August 1683. Before Nic. Peirson, esq., Mayor.

Information[54]

Susan, wife of Humf. Widgier (lately Susan English, widow), said that about six weeks before Christmas last Ann Hoare, a stranger to her, was brought to her house by Wil. Jellett, a seaman of H.M.S. Bristol, who asked for a pot of beer to drink with her (who he pretended was his countrywoman). They went up into the chamber and he spent 14d on her in faggots and beer. Then they both went out by different doors. The next day Ann came to her house again and asked for Wil. Gellett and he being in, spoke to her slightingly and they both went away. Three or four days later she came again with Mr Browne, corporal of the Kingfisher ('Kings Fisher'); they were in a public room for some time. Then Ann went to Mr Seamar's of Gosport but she did not know how long for. About a month later – a fortnight before Christmas – she came again and was above in the chamber with some company. Mr Wil. Terrell, being very much in drink, came and asked for a pot of beer. Ann hearing his voice came down and she left them together. When she came again they had gone up to the chamber where they stayed very little time. Mary, wife of Henry Charvell, had a room opposite and had her door open all the time. They had never been in her house, except as she had stated.   *Signed by mark.*

339
Subject unknown

S3/11/15

16 August 1683. Borough of Portsmouth and Vill of Gosport. Before Tho. Hancocke, gent.

Recognisances

  John Balch of Kingston in £20.
  David Ghost of Portsmouth in £10.
  John Williams of Portsea, mason, in £10.

For appearance of Balch at the next Sessions to answer any indictments.

  Bound over for (*blank*).

See also nos 345 (7), 346.

340
Subject unknown

S3/11/16

5 August 1683. Before Tho. Hancocke, gent.

Recognisances

  Henry Comeings of Portsmouth, barber, in £20.
  John Young in £10.

---

[54] The following memoranda are added at the foot of this information:
 (i) Margaret, wife of Roger Gouldocke. She had a ring from Mr Chapman, gunner of the Dartmouth.
 (ii) The wife of John Johnson will swear that Sam. Foster lay with her at her house.

For appearance of Comeings at the next Sessions to answer objections against him by Capt. Cha. Skelton.

Footnote (*Latin*) : Discharged by the Court.

See also no. 345 (8).

341
Subject unknown

S3/11/14

21 August 1683. Before Nic. Peirson, esq., Mayor, and others.

Recognisances

John Taylor in £100.
Tho. Goudge in £50.
Geo. Gray in £50.

For appearance of Taylor at the next Sessions to answer indictments preferred against him.

Marginal note (*Latin*) : Discharged by the Mayor and Justices of the Peace of the Borough and Vill aforesaid.

342
ASSAULT

S3/11/17

21 September 1683. Before Nic. Peirson, esq., Mayor.

Information

Avice Luckham, spinster, said that this morning about 9 o'clock Elizabeth, wife of Wil. Urline, ran at her with a naked knife aimed at her breast. She warded it off with her hand and her arm was cut. *Signed by mark.*

Recognisance

Avice Luckham in £10.

For appearance at the next Sessions to prosecute Elizabeth Urline.

343
ASSAULT

S3/11/21

4 October 35 Cha. II [1683]. Borough of Portsmouth and Vill of Gosport.

Presentment (*Latin*)

Presents Sarah, wife of Griffith Williams of Portsmouth, sailor, for assaulting Elizabeth Sturt, servant of John Leverett, by causing an affray and striking and wounding her, so that she despaired of her life. *Signed* 'pro [Edw.] Archer'.

Footnote : She submitted under protest because she did not wish to oppose the King and paid a fine 3s 4d.

Endorsements :

(a) Step. Leverett, Elizabeth Sturt, sworn.

(b) True bill.

See also no. 345 (9).

344
ASSAULT

S3/11/22

1 October 35 Cha. II [1683]. Borough of Portsmouth and Vill of Gosport.

Presentment (*Latin*)

Presents John Ironmonger of Portsmouth, spurrier, for assaulting Sarah, wife of Edw. Carter, by causing an affray and striking and wounding her so that she despaired of her life. *Signed* 'pro [Edw.] Archer'.

Footnote : He submitted under protest because he did not wish to oppose the King in the matter of a fine 6s 8d.

See also no. 345 (10).

345
CALENDAR

S3/11/18 (entry i)

[4 and 23 October] 1683. Michaelmas Sessions.

(1) Tho. Silver to the behaviour, [for misbehaviour in Court]. Nat. Bunch
Hugh Swettingham

See no. 327.

(2) Tho. Brouncker to the peace. Lewis Barton
John Doe

Marginal note (*Latin*) : Discharged by the Court.

Note under entry : Against Dallerose for not prosecuting.

(3)	Tho. Tyley to the behaviour [for contempt].	Tho. Barton John Doe
	See no. 332. *Marginal note (Latin):* Discharged by the Court.	
(4)	Mary Brimston, widow, to the peace [for assault].	James Thompson John Doe
	See no. 333. *Marginal note (Latin):* Discharged by the Court.	
(5)	Geo. Hodges to the peace.	Ann Morlin, widow Tho. Seamer
	See no. 334 *Note under entry (English and Latin):* Recognisances respited by the Court.	
(6)	'John Shawe for ye' (*scored through*), [for theft].	Roger Smith Ric. Page
	See no. 337.	
(7)	John Balch to the behaviour.	David Ghost John Williams
	See nos 339, 346. *Note under entry:* Bound anew.	
(8)	Henry Comings to the behaviour.	John Young John Doe
	See no. 340. *Marginal note (Latin):* Discharged by the Court.	
(9)	Sarah, wife of Griffith Williams, indicted by John Leveret for assaulting Elizabeth Sturt, his serving-maid. *See no. 343.*	
(10)	John Ironmonger indicted for beating and wounding Sarah, wife of Edw. Carter. *See no. 344.*	

346
Subject unknown

S3/11/18 (entry ii)

No date [4 October 1683]. By the Court.
Recognisances
> David Ghost in £10.
> John Williams in £10.

For appearance of John Balch at the next Sessions to answer indictments against him.
> *Footnote:* Sessions adjourned to Tuesday, 23 Oct.

See also nos 339, 345 (7).

EASTER SESSIONS 10 April 1684

No papers survive.

MICHAELMAS SESSIONS 21 October and 4 November 1684

No papers survive.

EASTER SESSIONS 30 April 1685

347
LIBEL

S3/12/16. *Calendar number on document:* 1.

7 October 1684. Before Henry Beverley, gent.
Recognisances
> Wil. Brogden of Portsmouth in £10.
> John Thorne of the same, innholder, in £5.
> Lewis Barton of the same, goldsmith, in £5.

For appearance of Brogden at the next Sessions to answer such trespasses and misdemeanours as shall be objected against him.

Bound over on the complaint of Capt. Skelton for writing a letter for Mrs Rooke to Capt. Rooke in which he reflected on Capt. Skelton and his wife.

348
THEFT

S3/12/2. *Calendar number on document: 2.*

29 October 1684. Before Nic. Peirson, gent.
Examinations

(a) Ric. Brett of Portsmouth, barber, said that about a fortnight ago he was at his father's house at the Dolphin and a cock chick came in at the back gate; it was in the yard for four or five days and then flying up to the loft he took it. Meeting Cha. Perkins, he asked him to carry it into the country and put it out to keeping, promising he should have half for his pains. *Signed.*

(b) Cha. Perkins said that a week ago last Sunday he was standing at John Starke's door when his master, Ric. Brett, came to him and gave him the chick as above.
Signed by mark.

(c) Giles Brignell said that riding out to Kingston to water his master's horse he saw one of his master's cocks in a walk in the ground of Geo. Perkins of Kingston, which he took up and brought home. *Signed.*

Recognisances

(a) Geo. Perkins in £10.
Geo. (*sic*) Brignell in £10.
For appearance to give evidence against Ric. Brett for stealing a cock chick belonging to Maj. Slingsby.

(b) Tho. Blankley of Portsmouth, victualler, in £10.
Geo. Backham jun. of the same, barber, in £10.
For appearance of Ric. Brett at the next Sessions to answer indictments preferred against him.

349
ABUSING
AUTHORITY

S3/12/9. *Calendar number on document: 3.*

4 November 1684. Before Wil. Legg, esq., Mayor, and others at the Sessions.
Recognisances

Tho. Triggs of Portsmouth, barber, in £10.
Joshua Whitehorne of the same, chandler, in £5.
John Stubs of the same, victualler, in £5.
For appearance of Triggs at the next Sessions.
Bound over for abusing Mr Peirson in the execution of his office as Justice.
Marginal note (Latin) against Whitehorne's name: He owes for his recognisance.

350
THEFT

S3/12/1

23 October 1684. Before Isaac Betts, gent., Deputy Mayor, Sir John Biggs, Recorder, and others.
Informations

(a) Tho. Burry of Chichester, Suss., innholder, said that about the 25, 26 or 27 Aug. last a trunk was broken up at his inn, the Swan in Chichester, and the following were taken away: a buff belt with silver buckles, two pairs of shoe buckles with stones inlaid in prince's metal and several other goods which he suspects were feloniously taken by Geo. Wells of Portsmouth, gent. *Signed.*

(b) Henry Howes of Badworth Park, Lyminster, Suss., gent., said that on 26 or 27 Aug. last he was at the Black Dog in Havant, where he met the person now at the bar who called himself Geo. Wells. He had on at the time a buff belt with silver buckles and showed in his hand one pair of shoe buckles of prince's metal inlaid with stone which he offered to sell to Mr Goodwins Clarke.[55] As Wells was unbraced he could see that he had a good shirt on but could not say if it was Holland. *Signed.*

---

[55] The original is ambiguous. It could be 'Mr Goodwins Clarke' or 'Mr Goodwin's clerk'.

Recognisances
>Tho. Burry of Chichester, Suss., innholder, in £10.
>
>Henry How of Badworth Park, Lyminster, Suss., gent., in £10.

For their appearance at the next Assizes and General Gaol Delivery for Hampshire to give evidence against Geo. Wells as above.

22 November 1684. Before Isaac Betts, gent., Deputy Mayor.
Recognisances
>Geo. Wells of Portsmouth, gent., in £40.
>
>David Tayler of the same, shipwright, in £20.
>
>James Bartlett of Marlborough, Wilts., brazier, in £20.

For appearance of Wells at the next Assizes and General Gaol Delivery for Hampshire to answer indictments for breaking a chest and carrying away goods as above, the property of (*blank*) Greene.

351
THEFT

S3/12/4

24 November 1684. Before Isaac Betts, gent., Deputy Mayor.
Information
John Tailer of Gosport, caulker, said that last Saturday night he found in the chest of his apprentice, Hub. Bessent, in his house stage ropes he thought worth 4*s*, a set bolt and a few nails to the value of 6*d*, which were the King's goods and which Bessent had stolen.   *Signed by mark.*

Examination
Hub. Bessent (*signs* Heuburd Bezzent), apprentice of the above John Tailer, said that the ropes his master found were not in his chest but under his bed. He found them in his master's wood-house but who brought them there he did not know. About a month ago he brought them into the house thinking that some time he might have occasion for them. The bolt he found astern of the new ship amongst the chips and sea ore, the nails he found in his master's house on the shelves. His master made him take home a piece of plank from H.M.S. Kingfisher ('Kings Fisher') when she lay by the jetty-head and several pieces of quarters since then.   *Signed.*

352
ASSAULT

S3/12/25

4 December 36 Cha. II [1684].
Presentment (*Latin*)
Presents Henry Comeings of Portsmouth, barber, for assault on Ann Spashot.
                                                         Signed by [Edw.] Archer.

   Footnote: He submits under protest because he did not wish to oppose the King and is fined by the Court 10*s*.

S3/12/3. *Calendar number on document:* 4.

8 December 1684. Before Nic. Peirson, gent.
Information
Ann Spashot of Portsmouth, spinster, said that last Thursday afternoon she was in the house of her mistress, Ann Crowcher, in the wash-house washing clothes. Henry Cumings came and asked her why she abused his wife. She said she did not and asked him to go. He would not but came and struck her three blows; she threw a stick at him and then he tried to put her into the tub of water but could not and then dragged her about the house by the hair of her head till she was almost dead.   *Signed by mark.*
Recognisances
>(a) Ann Spashot in £5.

For appearance at the next Sessions to give evidence against Henry Cumings.
>(b) Henry Comings in £10.
>
>Henry Linton of Portsmouth, mariner, in £5.

For appearance of Comings at the next Sessions and to keep the peace, especially towards Ann Spashot.

S3/12/24

3 December 36 Cha. II [1684].

Presentment (Latin)

Presents Dan. Lawrence lately of Portsmouth, soldier, for theft of one cheese value 10*d* from Henry Seagar.   *Signed by* [Edw.] Archer.

   Footnote: He confesses the indictment in full Court.

   Endorsements:

   (a) Witnesses, Henry Seager, Dan. Collins, sworn.

   (b) True bill.

S3/12/21

13 December 36 Cha. II [1684].

Presentment (Latin)

Presents Tho. Morgan lately of Portsmouth, soldier, for assault on Dan. Collins, Deputy Constable, in the execution of his office.   *Signed by* [Edw.] Archer.

   Footnote: He submitted under protest because he did not wish to oppose the King and is fined 2*s* 6*d*.

   Endorsements:

   (a) Witnesses, Dan. Collins, Henry Seager, sworn.

   (b) True bill.

S3B/25

16 December 1684. No name of Justice.

Informations

   (a) Henry Seager said that last Saturday about 8 p.m. he lost two Cheshire cheeses out of his shop window. He went straight to Mr Peirson for a warrant which he passed to Dan. Collins the Constable, who took Tho. Dobbins to assist him. They went to the house of Tho. Morgan, at the sign of the Scotch Cross at the Point, who refused entrance and threatened the Constable and his assistant that he would be the death of them. Seager broke open the door and they found one of the cheeses in a chest which they said belonged to Elizabeth Sistons (*also* Sistense), widow. Morgan struck the Constable in the execution of his office. They found the other cheese at the empty house of Mrs Harwood beyond the Mill.   *Signed.*

   (b) Dan. Collins, Constable, *confirmed the above evidence.*   *Signed.*

   (c) Tho. Dobbins *repeated the evidence*, adding that Morgan fell to swearing and asked them how they dare search his house, he being the King's soldier.

   (d) Ant. March said that last Saturday night he called at the Scotch Cross to drink a flagon of beer and when he left Dan. Lawrence and Elizabeth Sistence went with him to his house by the Mill and Elizabeth carried something in her lap which he found to be a cheese. When they came to his house they drank 8*d* in beer and then Lawrence offered to sell him a Cheshire cheese for 3*s* (*or* 3*d*?); his wife said it was stolen, so he would not buy it and Lawrence and Elizabeth went away with the cheese. After he was in bed they came back and lodged for the night, going away in the morning before he was up. Afterwards the cheese was found by Henry Seager in an empty house of Mrs Harwood's at the top of the ceiling.   *Signed by mark.*

16 December 1684. Before Isaac Betts, Deputy Mayor, and Nic. Peirson, gent.

Recognisances

      Henry Seager in £10.

      Dan. Collins in £10.

      Tho. Dobins in £10.

      Ant. March in £10.

      Tho. Morgan in £10.

      Elizabeth Sistence, widow, in £10.

For appearance at the next Assizes and General Gaol Delivery for Hampshire to prosecute and give evidence against Dan. Lawrence, Tho. Morgan and Elizabeth Sistence for taking a Cheshire cheese value 20*s*.

S3B/26. *Calendar number on document: 4.*[56]

16 December 1684. Before Isaac Betts, gent., Deputy Mayor, and Nic. Peirson, gent.
Examinations

(a) Dan. Lawrence of Portsmouth, soldier, confessed that being in drink he took two cheeses from the bulk of Henry Seager, baker, living on the Point, took them to Tho. Morgan's house, Scotch Cross, and put them in a chest in a room rented by Elizabeth Sistense. The other cheese he took to the house of Ant. March by the Mill near Portsmouth and offered to sell it to him. He refused, so he left it in an empty house near the March's. He told Elizabeth that it was March's cheese. *Signed by mark.*

(b) Tho. Morgan of Portsmouth, soldier, said that the cheese found in his house was in a room let to Elizabeth Sistence, widow. How it came there he did not know.
Signed by mark.

Information

Elizabeth Sistence said she did not know how the cheese got into her room, but supposed that Dan. Lawrence laid it there while she was at the White Hart. Ant. March was at her landlord's house, and, finding him in drink, she went home with him. When they came almost to the Mill, Lawrence overtook them with a cheese under his arm and said to March 'you have left your cheese behind' and gave her the cheese to take to March's house. When they got there Lawrence took it from her.
Signed by mark.

Recognisances

> Tho. Morgan in £10.
> Elizabeth Sistence in £10.

To appear and prosecute Dan. Lawrence for stealing.
Footnote (Latin) : He owes for his recognisance.

18 December 1684. No name of Justice.
Recognisances

> Tho. Morgan in £10.
> Wil. Francklin in £5.
> John Brimblecombe in £5.

For appearance of Morgan at the next Sessions and to keep the peace, especially towards Dan. Collins and Tho. Dobbins.
Footnote (Latin) : He owes for his recognisance.

S3/12/6. *Calendar number on document: 5.*

18 December 1684. Before Isaac Betts, gent., Deputy Mayor, and Nic. Peirson, gent.
Recognisances

> Tho. Morgan of Portsmouth in £10.
> Wil. Francklin of the same in £5.
> John Bramblecombe of the same, mason, in £5.

For appearance of Morgan at the next Sessions and to keep the peace, especially towards Dan. Collins and Tho. Dobins.

Bound over for abusing Dan. Collins, Deputy Constable, in the execution of his office.

S3/12/5

27 December 1684. Before Isaac Betts, gent., Deputy Mayor.
Recognisances

> Dan. Lawrence of Portsmouth, soldier, in £40.
> Ant. Marsh of the same, yeoman, in £20.
> John Thomson of the same, yeoman, in £20.

For appearance of Lawrence at the next Sessions to answer indictments preferred against him by Henry Seagar for feloniously taking two cheeses of his and not to depart [the jurisdiction of] the Court without licence.

---

[56] The calendar number on this document is a mistake as it has no relation to the case mentioned in no. 352. Calendar number 5 or 6 probably intended.

354
ASSAULT

S3/12/18. *Calendar number on document:* 7.

No date. Before Isaac Betts, gent., Deputy Mayor.
Information
Tho. Grover of Portsmouth said that last night when he came home Chr. Warren, his servant, and his wife fell upon him and beat him. *Signed.*

No date. In full Court.
Recognisance
      Tho. Grover, in £10.
  For appearance at the next Sessions to prosecute and give evidence against Chr. Warren.

15 January 1684/5. Before Nic. Peirson.
      Chr. Warren of Portsmouth, gingerbread-baker, in £10.
      Ric. Smith of the same, victualler, in £5.
      Dan. Loe of the same, joiner, in £5.
  For appearance of Warren at the next Sessions and to keep the peace, especially towards Tho. Grover.
  Bound over for abusing and beating Grover.

355
SEDITION

S3/12/8. *Calendar number on document:* 8.

7 February 1684/5. Before Nic. Peirson, gent.
      Tho. Barret of Gosport in £20.
      Step. Thomas of the same, surgeon, in £10.
      Tho. Crews of the same, shipwright, in £10.
  For appearance of Barret at the next Sessions.
  Bound over on the information of Lieut. Mullins for speaking false and scandalous reports that the King was dead and that the Garrison of Portsmouth was in arms.

356
ASSAULT

S3/12/11. *Calendar number on document:* 9.

10 February 1684/5. No name of Justice.
Informations
  (a) Mary, wife of Tho. Williams of Portsmouth, said that about 7 o'clock yesterday she was at the house of James Bartlet in Gosport when suddenly without saying anything he fell on her and kicked her on the hip so that she was not able to stir. *Signed.*
  (b) Tho. Squier of Gosport, blacksmith. *No entry against the name.*

No date. In full Court.
Recognisances
  (a) Tho. Williams in £10.
  For appearance of Mary Williams at the next Sessions to prosecute and give evidence against James Bartlet.
  (b) James Bartlet of Gosport in £10.
      Rob. Reeves of the same in £5.
      Mat. Gatchcombe of the same in £5.
  For appearance of Bartlet at the next Sessions to answer indictment preferred against him for beating Mary Williams and to keep the peace, especially towards her.

357
CONTEMPT

S3/12/10. *Calendar number on document:* 10.

17 February 1684/5. Before the full Court.
Information
Jane, wife of Ric. Chapman (*signs* Ann Chagman), said that she went to Wil. Tooth and demanded the money that was ordered her by Mr Shales for keeping Leonard Little's child. Tooth said he did not care what Shales had said. *Signed.*
Recognisances
      Wil. Tooth of Portsmouth, victualler, in £10.
      Ric. Smith in £5.
      Nic. Mellish in £5.
  For appearance [of Tooth] at the next Sessions.
  Marginal note (Latin): He owes for his recognisance 2s 6d.

358
ASSAULT

S3/12/7

18 February 1684/5. No name of Justice.

Information

Wil. Urlene of Portsmouth, cordwainer, said that last Tuesday night he was at work in his shop and Fra. Treblecocke, his apprentice, was with him when Treble-cocke told him he had a cock. Asked what he would do with it, he replied that he had barley from Ric., Mr White's man, to keep it. He told Treblecocke that the barley was for him and what right had he to take it to his mother. Treblecocke asked if he had to give his master everything anyone gave him and then began to prate and talk. Urline told him to hold his tongue but he said he would not and then being boxed on the ear, Treblecocke caught up a knife and stabbed at him three or four times and cut his apron. *Signed by mark.*

359
POPERY

D11A/16/30. *Calendar number on document:* 14.

6 March 1684/5. Before Ric. Ridge, esq., Mayor, and Nic. Peirson.

Informations

(a) Tho. Wood of Portsmouth, gunner, said that last Tuesday afternoon he was at the house of Nic. Selden in Portsmouth drinking with Edm. Ward, Wil. Wood and Edw. Pickering. Geo. Wassell, gunner of H.M.S. Harwich, came and sat down to drink with them. Having a glass in his hand, Wassell drank the King's health and then the Queen's. He then began a health to the Pope, and Wood and the rest of the company refused to pledge it. Ward took the glass and drank confusion to the Pope, whereupon Wassell said that the Church of England was almost at an end. *Signed.*

(b) Edm. Ward *confirmed the above evidence.* *Signed by mark.*

(c) Edw. Pickering of Portsmouth, gunner, *confirmed the above evidence* except the drinking of confusion to the Pope, which he did not remember. Wil. Wood drank a health to the prosperity of the King and the Church of England. Wassell refused to pledge prosperity to the Church and said the Church of England would not stand long. *Signed.*

(d) Wil. Wood *confirmed the evidence of Edw. Pickering* except the words that the Church of England would not stand long, which he could not remember Wassell saying. *Signed.*

Recognisances

(a) Edm. Ward in £20.
Tho. Wood in £20.
Wil. Wood in £20.
Edw. Pickering in £20.

For appearance at the next Sessions to prosecute and give evidence against Geo. Wassell.

(b) Geo. Wassell of Portsmouth, gunner, in £40.
Tho. Harlen of the same, labourer, in £20.
John Gumb of the same, barber, in £20.

For appearance of Wassell at the next Sessions to answer such bills of indictment and other proceedings as shall be preferred against him and not to depart [the jurisdiction of] the Court without licence.

360
THEFT

S3/12/23

3 March 1 James II [1684/5].

Presentment (Latin)

Presents Elizabeth Beach of Portsmouth, spinster, for stealing a piece of linen value 10d from Frances Langridge. *Signed by* [Edw.] Archer.

Footnote: She confesses the indictment in full Court.

Endorsements:

(a) Witness Frances Langridge sworn.
(b) True bill.

S3/12/12.[57] *Calendar number on document:* 11.

10 March 1684/5. Before Ric. Ridge, esq., Mayor.

Information

Frances Langridge of Portsmouth, widow, said that about five months ago she hired Elizabeth Beach, spinster, to be her servant and last Tuesday, being Shrove Tuesday, Elizabeth left at night and feloniously took several parcels of small linen to the value of 10*d*. Last Friday they were found on her at the powder-houses on the Common.

Signed by mark.

Recognisance

   Elizabeth Langridge in £10.

 For appearance of Frances Langridge at the next Sessions to prosecute and give evidence against Elizabeth Beach.

361

ASSAULT

S3/12/14

28 March 1685. Before Ric. Ridge, esq., Mayor, Nic. Peirson, gent., and Henry Beverley, gent.

Informations

 (a) James Moore (*signs* More) of Hastings, Suss., mariner, said that yesterday afternoon Geo. Stuckey and Rob. Matthewes called on him to pay him for ballasting his vessel (they were then on the Stoes' quay). Abraham Mounsier, who had come from Southampton, was then on the quay and he asked Mounsier why he broke his mizzen-yard. Mounsier gave him ill language and took him by the collar. He refrained from striking back and entered the house of Ric. Stoes. Mounsier followed, took him by the collar and struck him in the face. He went into another room, but Mounsier followed, broke open the door and threw two flagons of beer at him.

Signed.

 (b) Geo. Stuckey, Rob. Matthewes and John Dawes, all of Portsmouth, *confirmed the evidence of Moore.* *Signed by all three (Stuckey by mark).*

Recognisances

   John Dawe in £10.

   Geo. Stuckey in £10.

   Rob. Matthewes in £10.

 For appearance at the next Sessions to prosecute and give evidence against Abraham Mounsier.

362

ASSAULT

S3/12/20

13 April 1 James II [1685].

Presentment (Latin)

Presents Elizabeth, wife of Edw. Bedford of Gosport, victualler, and Elizabeth, wife of Tho. Bramble of the same, soldier, for assault on Eleanor Mills.

Signed by [Edw.] Archer.

 Footnote: They submitted under protest because they did not wish to oppose the King. They each paid a fine of 2*s* 6*d*. Total 5*s*.

Note against both names: Non cul.

Endorsements:

(a) Witness Eleanor Mills sworn.

(b) True bill.

S3/12/15. *Calendar numbers on document:* 12, 13.

14 April 1685. Before Ric. Ridge, esq., and other Justices in full Court.

Information

Eleanor, wife of Nic. Mills of Gosport, seaman, said that yesterday morning Elizabeth, wife of Tho. Bramble, called her into her chamber where she found Elizabeth, wife

---

[57] The following memoranda are added at the foot of this document:

Parliamentary Election (i) The Mayor has a precept from Sir John Mill Bt., High Sheriff of the County, for electing two Burgesses of the Borough to serve in Parliament to be held at Westminster on 19 May next.

Contract (ii) Tho. Bridger of Liphook, wagoner, to enter into a contract to carry the goods of the Burgesses who live in town from Lady Day to Michaelmas at 3*s* 4*d* per cwt and for the rest of the year at 4*s* per cwt.

(iii) Jos. Gardner of Capt. Fox's Company. *No entry against the name.*

(iv) Jane Mishman of Minstead in the New Forest, spinster. *No entry against the name.*

of Edw. Bedford, who scratched her hand with a pin drawing blood and afterwards Elizabeth Bramble held her whilst the other woman drew blood from her face.

Signed by mark.

Examination
Elizabeth, wife of Edw. Bedford, confessed that she scratched Eleanor and drew blood.
Recognisances
      Edw. Bedford of Gosport in £10.
      Ric. Knapton of the same in £10.
For appearance of Elizabeth Bedford at the next Sessions to answer indictments and to keep the peace, especially towards Eleanor Mills.
      They are likewise bound for Elizabeth Bramble.

363
ABUSE

S3/12/13

16 April 1685. Before Nic. Peirson, gent.
Information
Wil. Male of Gosport, cooper, said that on Saturday last he heard Elizabeth, wife of James Powell, say that Mary, wife of Wil. Creed, was a murderous and a beggarly whore. *Signed.*

364
Subject unknown

S3/12/17. *Calendar number on document:* 15.

27 April 1685. Before Ric. Ridge, esq., Mayor.
Recognisances
      Wil. Terrell in £100.
      John Grundy, gent., in £50.
      Fra. Weaver, gent., (Wil. Workley *scored through*) in £50.
For appearance [of Terrell] at the next Sessions and to keep the peace, especially towards Elizabeth his wife.

365
ASSAULT

S3/12/19

28 April 1685. Before Nic. Peirson.
Recognisances
    (a) Rob. Matthews of Portsmouth in £10.
        Geo. Stuckey of the same, sailor, in £10.
        Ric. Stoe of the same, victualler, in £5.
        John Tiddiman of the same in £5.
For appearance of Stuckey and Matthews tomorrow morning at 9 o'clock to answer indictments.
    (b) John Dove of Brading, [I.W.], in £10.
To prosecute Geo. Stuckey and Rob. Matthews.
See also no. 388 (1), (2).

MICHAELMAS SESSIONS 8 October 1685

For entry in Sessions Book see Appendix II, no. 97.

366
RIOT

S3/13/6. *Calendar numbers on document:* 4, 5, 6, 7, 8.

10 May 1685. Before Ric. Ridge, esq., Mayor.
Recognisances
    (a) John Stevens of Gosport in £20.
        Ric. Stephens of the same, shipwright ('nafrangius'), in £10.
        Edw. Armorer of Portsea, rope maker, in £10.
For appearance of John Stephens at the next Sessions to answer all such riots, routs, contempts and other misdemeanours committed by him and others.
    (b) Tho. Guy of Gosport in £20.
        John Taileur of Portsmouth, innholder, in £10.
        Rob. Martin of the same, butcher, in £10.
On the same condition for Guy.

(c) Tho. Wood of Gosport, shipwright ('nafrangius'), in £20.
      Geo. Renalls of the same, sailor, in £10.
      John Santloe of the same, sailor, in £10.
On the same condition for Wood.

(d) John Abbot of Gosport in £20.
      Henry Tilden of the same, carpenter, in £10.
      Tho. Toomes of the same, mason, in £10.
On the same condition for Abbot.

(e) Rob. Batt of Gosport in £20.
      John Estwood of the same, shipwright ('nafragius'), in £10.
      Tho. Crews of the same, shipwright ('nafragius'), in £10.
On the same condition for Batt.

S3B/34
15 September 1685. Before Ric. Ridge, esq., Mayor.
Recognisances
        Mat. Gatchcombe in £40.
        Geo. Mills in £20.
To appear at the next Sessions to prosecute and give evidence against John Stephens,
Tho. Guy, Tho. Wood, John Abbott, Rob. Batt, and John Hill for riot on 1 May last.
See also no. 388 (4)–(8).

367
ABUSE

S3/13/5 (entry i). *Calendar numbers on document:* 9, 10.
15 May 1685. Before Ric. Ridge, esq., Mayor, and Sam. Williams, gent.
Information
Prudence, wife of Peter Pogson of Portsmouth, said that about 5 o'clock that afternoon she left the house of James Burnet and, while returning to her house in Warblington St., she heard Mrs Goudge say, this little rascal Ensign Lieut. Games took a false
oath for the soldier and so they are rogues alike. She also said that Alice, wife of
John Brimblecombe, yesterday morning said that the officers were all rogues and
that they cheated both King and country and had not above sixteen men in a
company.   *Signed by mark.*
Recognisances
    (a) Nic. Mellersh of Portsmouth in £20.
          Joanna Parnell (*also* Purnell) of the same, widow, in £20.
For appearance of Sarah, wife of Tho. Goudge, to answer indictments.
Marginal note (Latin): Discharged by the Mayor.
    (b) Nic. Mellersh of Portsmouth in £20.
          Edm. Lowance in £20.
For appearance of Alice, wife of John Brimblecombe, at the next Sessions to
answer indictments.
    Bound both over upon the complaint of Capt. Foxe and Lieut. Games.
Marginal note (Latin): Discharged by the Mayor.
    (c) Wil. Games in £20.
For appearance at the next Sessions to prosecute and give evidence against
Sarah Goudge and Alice Brimblecombe.

S3/13/7 (entry ii)
16 May 1685. Before Ric. Ridge., esq., Mayor, and Sam. Williams, gent.
Recognisance
        Prudence Pogson in £20.
For appearance at the next Sessions to prosecute Sarah, wife of Tho. Goudge,
and the wife of John Brickleton.[58]
See also no. 388 (9), (10).

---

[58] Brickleton is Brimblecombe above.

368
**THREATENED
ASSAULT**

S3/13/5 (entry ii). *Calendar number on document:* 11.

No date [15 May 1685]. No name of Justice (*probably before Ric. Ridge and Sam. Williams*).

Information

Sarah, wife of Tho. Goudge, said that Peter Pogson of Portsmouth, soldier, came to her house about 5 p.m. today with his naked sword in his hand and asked, Where is the bitch? and swore he would be the death of her, so that she went in fear of her life. *Signed.*

16 May 1685. Before Ric. Ridge, esq., Mayor.

Recognisances

    Peter Pogson in £20.

    Cha. Foxe, esq., in £10.

    Wil. Games in £10.

For appearance of Peter Pogson at the next Sessions to answer indictments and to keep the peace, especially towards Sarah Goudge.

Marginal note (Latin) against Games' name: He owes for his recognisance.

See also no. 388 (11).

369
**THREATENED
ARSON**

3/13/7 (entry i). *Calendar number on document:* 12.

16 May 1685. Before Ric. Ridge, esq., Mayor, and Sam. Williams, gent.

Information

Mary, wife of Tho. Wayman of Portsmouth, mariner, said that last Tuesday, the 12th, the day Mr Preist's money was lost, Prudence, wife of Peter Pogson, who lived in the house with her, said she hoped to see the town alight with fire and did not care if the burghers had no bed to lie on. *Signed by mark.*

Recognisances

    Peter Pogson in £40.

    Wil. Shread in £20.

For appearance of Prudence, wife of Peter Pogson, at the next Sessions.

Marginal note (Latin): They owe.

See also no. 388 (12).

370
**ABUSING
AUTHORITY**

S3/13/4

4 June 1685. Before Sam. Williams, gent.

Information

John Wilce of Wanstead [in Southwick], butcher, said that last Saturday, 30 May, being at the back of his standing in the open market he heard (*blank*) Bradley, Capt. Fox's man, say that the Mayor (meaning Mr Ridge) was a rogue and had abused his master, but now that the colonel had come to town, he had not a word to say for himself. *Signed.*

Recognisance

    John Wilce in £20.

For appearance at the next Sessions to prosecute and give evidence against Bradley.

371
TREASON

S3/13/13. *Calendar number on document:* 13.

29 May 1685. Before Ric. Ridge, esq., Mayor, and Sam. Williams, gent.

Informations

(a) Rob. Froud of Portsmouth, yeoman, said that yesterday, the 28th, about 7 p.m. he was at the house of John Geary at the sign of the Garter in Portsmouth, drinking with Nic. Mellersh, Miles Porter, John Geary and Step. Smith. Smith was talking with Porter about £50 he had borrowed from Porter's wife, for which one Booker since dead stood bound. Smith said that if it had not been for the man that was dead and his children he would have gone to Argyll rather than pay the money.

Signed by mark.

(b) Nic. Mellersh said that the first three above-mentioned were drinking between 5 and 7 p.m. and Smith asked to be admitted to their company. They asked him to come in and when he had been there some small time the discourse about £50 above-mentioned began. Porter had had Smith arrested and Smith had paid the £50 on arrest. *He then repeated the concluding part of Froud's evidence*, adding for the sake of Booker's wife (who had been bound with him) as well as of the children. *Signed.*

(c) Miles Porter of Portsmouth *repeated the foregoing evidence.* He put the time at 6 p.m. and added that the arrest and payment were about the latter part of April last. He said that Smith also declared that, if it had not been for Booker's wife and children, he would have gone to Argyll and made James Boyes who married Booker's widow pay it. *Signed by mark.*

Recognisances

> Nic. Mellersh in £20.
> Rob. Froud in £20.
> Miles Porter in £20.

For appearance of all three at the next Assizes and General Gaol Delivery for Hampshire to prosecute and give evidence against Step. Smith for speaking treasonable words and not to depart [the jurisdiction of] the Court without licence.

Examination

Step. Smith of the parish of St Pancras ('Pankridge') near Chichester,[59] Suss., wheelwright, said he did not know whether any such words were spoken by him as were sworn against him. He had been crossed by his wife before he came from home and was in drink and did not remember what he had said. *Signed.*

6 June 1685. Before Ric. Ridge, Mayor.

Recognisances

> Step. Smith of St Pancras ('Pankeridge'), in the City of Chichester, Suss., wheelwright, in £50.
> John Fugar of Arundel, Suss., shipwright ('nafrangius'), in £25.
> Henry Roill of St Pancras ('Pankeridge') aforesaid, lime-burner, in £25.
> John Roill of the same, lime-burner, in £25.

For appearance of Smith at the next Sessions.

See also no. 388 (13).

372
ASSAULT

S3B/27. *Calendar number on document:* 14.

12 June 1685. Before Ric. Ridge, esq., Mayor.

Informations

(a) John Eastwood of Portsmouth, cordwainer, said that last Wednesday about 4 p.m. he was at the inn called Neptune's Court without Portsmouth and went into a room where Mr John Blose and Ric. Hunt were to drink with him. Margaret, wife of Chr. Mitchell, came in with a tankard of beer in her hand. She sat down and said 'I will set down in my owne house in despite of anyone'. Wil. English, who had had some hot words with her previously, now came in with a glass of wine in his hand and threw it in the woman's face. Her maid came to help, but English threw her down and kicked and struck the maid. *Signed.*

(b) John Wheeler of Portsmouth, shoemaker, *confirmed the above evidence.*

(c) John Blose of Portsmouth said that in their argument English told the woman that if she did not hold her peace he would throw in her face the tankard of beer which he held. Blose took the tankard from him. English then fetched a glass of wine and threw it in her face. She ran and took hold of him and her maid came to help. English kicked at the maid and threw the mistress down with such a fall that she lay as if she were dead. *Signed.*

(d) Ric. Burton of Portsmouth, soldier belonging to Capt. Cornwallis, *deposed the same.* *Signed by mark.*

Recognisances

> (a) John Eastwood of Portsmouth, cordwainer, in £20.
> John Wheeler of the same in £20.
> John Blose of the same in £20.
> Ric. Burton in £20.

---

[59] St Pancras is one of the parishes in present day Chichester.

To appear at the next Sessions to prosecute and give evidence against Wil. English for assaulting Margaret Mitchell.

(b) Wil. English of Portsmouth, barber, in £20.
Wil. Tanner of the same, victualler, in £10.
Henry Mills in £10.

For appearance of English at the next Sessions.

See also no. 388 (14).

373
SEDITION

S3/13/14. *Calendar number on document:* 15.

15 June 1685. Before Nic. Peirson, gent.
Information
Alice, wife of Tho. Crampton, said that about a month ago she was with Ann, wife of July Wood, and there was some talk of Argyll and the Duke of Monmouth. Ann said that for aught she knew the Duke of Monmouth was no more a bastard than she was.   *Signed.*
Recognisance
Alice Crampton in £20.

For appearance at the next Sessions to prosecute and give evidence against Ann Wood for speaking words of high misdemeanour.

No date. Before Nic. Peirson.
Recognisances
Henry Seager of Portsmouth, baker, in £20.
Peter Pecke of the same, shipwright ('nafrangius'), in £20.

For appearance of Ann, wife of July Wood, at the next Sessions to answer for speaking words of high misdemeanour.

See also no. 388 (15).

374
TREASON

S3/13/2. *Calendar numbers on document:* 16, 17.

15 June 1685. Before Ric. Ridge, esq., Mayor.
Examination
Joan, wife of Rob. Martin, Jane Roberton, spinster, and Rachel Gregge, spinster, examined on what they knew of words spoken by Jos. Gregg going to the west, all said that they never heard him say anything.

18 June 1685. Before Ric. Ridge, esq., Mayor.
Examination
Nat. Harwood examined said that he never heard Jos. Gregge say anything.
Recognisances
Jos. Gregge in £40.
Ben. Gregge in £40.
Rob. Martin in £20.
James Harris in £20.

For appearance of Jos. Gregge and Ben. Gregge at the next Sessions.

See also no. 388 (16), (17).

375
ASSAULT

S3/13/3. *Calendar number on document:* 18.

19 June 1685. Before Ric. Ridge, esq., Mayor.
Information
Ann Wortley, daughter of Wil. Wortley of Portsmouth, said that the same night that And., son of John Mills, was scalded she heard Mary, wife of Step. Olding, say that she would wash them all away and threw a dish of water amongst Goodwife Mills' other children.   *Signed by mark.*
Examination
Alice Cozens said she was coming from Mr Selden's with a saucepan of water in her hand in which she had boiled eggs. There were several children at play together by the stable wall and they thrust her against the wall and some water spilled and scalded John Mills' son, but it was against her will.   *Signed by mark.*

Recognisances

> (a) Alice Cozens, spinster, in £30.
>
> > Step. Olding of Portsmouth in £15.
> >
> > Nic. Mellersh in £15.

For appearance of Alice at the next Sessions to answer indictments for scalding And., son of John Mills.

> (b) John Mills in £10.

To appear to prosecute and give evidence against Alice Cozens.

20 June 1685. Before Ric. Ridge, esq., Mayor.

Informations

> (a) Elizabeth Wilkinson, daughter of Walt. Wilkinson, said that about 8 o'clock last night her father sent her to Mr Selden's for a pot of beer and when she came back Tho. Mills, one of the sons of John Mills, was in the street. Mrs Olding came out and bade her son go and beat that chuckle-headed boy (meaning Tho. Mills); then Alice Cozens, Mrs Olding's servant maid who was at the door, went and beat Tho. *Signed by mark.*

> (b) Mary, wife of Tho. Coxe, said that last night she saw Alice Cozens run after Tho. Mills, son of John Mills, in the street driving him before her and when she could not overtake him she threw a stone at him. This was done after she had been before the Mayor. *Signed by mark.*
>
> *Footnote:* Mary Coxe bound to prosecute.

> (c) Eleanor, wife of John Fiveash, said that last night she heard Wil. Bible call Mary, wife of John Mills, an old bitch. *Signed by mark.*

Recognisance

> Wil. Bible in £40.

For appearance at the next Sessions to answer indictments.

S3/13/15

19 June 1 James II [1685].

Presentment (Latin)

Presents Alice Cozens of Portsmouth, spinster, for causing an affray, beating, wounding and ill-treating And., son of John Mills of Portsmouth, joiner.

> *Endorsements:*
>
> (a) Witnesses, John Mills, Ann Wortley, Mary Coxe, sworn.
>
> (b) Ignoramus.

See also no. 388 (18).

376

SEDITION

S3/13/12. *Calendar number on document:* 19.

28 (or 23?) June 1685. Before Ric. Ridge, esq., Mayor, Isaac Betts, gent., and Sam. Williams, gent.

Information

John Page of Portsmouth, soldier in Capt. Foxe's Company, said that yesterday about 4 p.m. he was at the house of Mark Cullemore at the sign of the Crown drinking with Wil. Reynolds. He heard Reynolds say that the Duke of Monmouth had a great force and would have a bigger straight, and that he was a true Protestant. *Signed by mark.*

Recognisances

> (a) John Page in £10 for appearance at the next Sessions to prosecute and give evidence against Wil. Reynolds for speaking words of high misdemeanour.

> (b) Wil. Reynolds of Portsmouth in £20.
>
> > David Ridge of the same in £10.
> >
> > Mark Cullimore in £10.

For appearance of Reynolds at the next Sessions.

Marginal note (Latin): Discharged by the Mayor.

See also no. 388 (19).

377
ABUSE

S3B/29. *Calendar number on document:* 21.

9 July 1685. Before Ric. Ridge, esq., Mayor.

Information

Ann, wife of Hugh Ridley, esq., of Portsmouth, said that on that day Jean Mills, widow, in the middle of the market accused her of going to others to buy when she had money and of coming to her when she had none, saying that Ann was a cheat and an unworthy base woman.

Recognisances

    Jean Mills, widow, in £20.
      Wil. Fullham of Portsmouth, glover, in £10.
For appearance of Jean at the next Sessions.

See also no. 388 (21).

378
SEDITION

S3/13/11. *Calendar numbers on document:* 23, 24.

11 July 1685. Before Ric. Ridge, esq., Mayor.

Informations

(a) Ric. Marvell of Portsea, mason, said that about 9 a.m. that day he heard Chr. Pinchen say that he was told that the King, James II, had been dead about a fortnight.

(b) Chr. Pinchen said that about 8 a.m. that day, being at work with John Winter on the wall, Winter told him that he heard a couple of soldiers in the street say that the King was dead and he told Ric. Marvell.   *Signed by mark.*

Examination

John Winter said that about 8 or 9 a.m. that day he told Chr. Pinchen that last night he heard two soldiers in the street say that the King was dead.   *Signed.*

Recognisances

    John Winter in £40.
      Ric. Hunt of Portsmouth, mason, in £20.
    John Blose of the same, baker, in £20.
For appearance of Winter at the next Sessions.

13 July 1685. Before Sam. Williams, gent.

Recognisances

    Chr. Pinchin in £40.
    John Fiveash, mason, in £20.
    Mat. Gibbins, labourer, in £20.
For appearance of Pinchin at the next Sessions.

11 July 1685. Before Ric. Ridge, esq.

Recognisances

    Rob. Waters of Portsmouth, mason, in £40.
    Ric. Marvell of the same in £40.
For appearance of both at the next Assizes and General Gaol Delivery for Hampshire to prosecute and give evidence against Chr. Pinchen and John Winter for reporting false and scandalous words concerning the death of the King.

See also no. 388 (23), (24).

379
SEDITION

S3B/30. *Calendar number on document:* 25.

15 July 1685. Before Ric. Ridge, Mayor.

Examinations

(a) Alice, wife of Sam. Soane of Fratton, said that John Gover one day last week told her that Mrs Emet said she would feed her dogs with Protestant hearts.
    Signed by mark.

(b) John Gover said he heard his wife say Mrs Emett said she would have Protestant hearts enough to feed her dogs all this winter. Joan his wife acknowledged the same.
    Signed by mark.

Recognisances
  John Gover in £20.
  Rob. Olding of Portsmouth in £10.
For appearance of Joan, wife of John Gover, at the next Sessions to answer indictments by Mrs Winifred Yeomett.
See also no. 388 (25).

380
ABUSING
AUTHORITY

S3B/31. *Calendar number on document:* 26.

24 July 1685. Before Ric. Ridge, esq., Mayor.
Recognisances
  Cuthbert Benbridge of Gosport in £40.
  Wil. Edwards of Gosport, rope maker, in £20.
  Wil. Tanner of Portsmouth in £20.
For appearance of Benbridge at the next Sessions.
 Bound over at the request of the Earl of Gainsborough, Lord Lieutenant, for abusing the officers of the trained bands and after next Sessions to continue bound over for one year.
See also no. 388 (26).

381
SUSPECTED
TREASON

S3/13/9. *Calendar number on document:* 27.

21 July 1685. Before Ric. Ridge, esq., Isaac Betts, gent., Sam. Williams, gent., and Rob. Shales, gent.
Examination
John Chapman of Portsmouth, glover, said (*blank*).

28 July 1685. No name of Justice.
Recognisances
  John Chapman of Portsmouth, glover, in £100.
  Edw. Chapman sen. of the same, glover, in £50.
  Ric. Preist of the same in £50.
  John Lewen of the same in £50.
  Tho. Inwod of Portchester in £50.
For appearance of John Chapman at the next Sessions.

S3B/28
July 1685.
Affidavits with summary[60]
John Chapman is certified to have been at the following places on the dates stated:
 (i) House of Tho. Inwod at Portchester, 12–15 June.

 (ii) House of Moses Holloway, clothier, in Romsey on 19 June. Affidavit of 23 July 1685 to this effect sworn and signed by Holloway before Wil. Kent, esq., Mayor of Romsey, who signed.

 (iii) House of Tho. Inwod at Portchester, 21–24 June. Affidavit of 25 July 1685 confirming the two visits sworn and signed by Tho. Inwod before Sam. Williams, who signed.

 (iv) Affidavit signed by Dan. Baker of Hambledon that Chapman lodged in his house on 24 June. Sworn on 24 July 1685 before Col. Ric. Norton, who signed.

 (v) Affidavit signed by John Goldsmith, keeper in East Bere Forest, that he saw Chapman cutting a holm stick in the forest on 25 June and spoke to him. Sworn on 24 July 1685 before Col. Ric. Norton, who signed.

 (vi) House of Edw. Warner at Owslebury on 25 or 26 June. Certified by John Jackson, Vicar, Dan. Clarke, Churchwarden, Tho. Spencer, Collector, and Ric. Paige, yeoman, who all sign.

 (vii) House of Sarah Gosling, widow, at Southwick, 26–29 June. Affidavit to this effect, signed by mark by Sarah, sworn 24 July 1685 before Col. Ric. Norton, who signed.

---

[60] There are five surviving affidavits together with a note summarising most of the details.

(viii) House of Wil. Simes of Belney ('Belony') at Southwick on 30 June and 1–2 July. Affidavit to this effect, signed by Simes by mark, sworn 24 July 1685 before Col. Ric. Norton, who signed.[61]

(ix) House of And. Hall, husbandman, at Deane, 3–6 July. Affidavit to this effect, sworn 24 July 1685 before Cha. Wither, esq., J.P.[62]

(x) House of Tho. Steele at Broughton, 6–18 July. Affidavit missing but said to have been sworn by Steele and Wil. Knight before John Pollen, esq.
See also no. 388 (27).

382
SLANDER

S3/13/10

28 July 1685. In full Court.
Information
Greg. Peachy of Gosport, in the parish of Alverstoke, gent., said that last Sunday as he came out of church she (*sic*) heard Elizabeth, wife of John Barnard, say Mr Grice preached blasphemy, false doctrine and cursed in the pulpit.

Recognisances
> Newton Newland of Gosport, mercer, in £20.
> Wil. Francklin of Portsmouth in £20.
For appearance of Elizabeth Barnard at the next Sessions.
Marginal note (Latin): Discharged by Mr Mayor.

383
ASSAULT

S3B/32. *Calendar number on document: 28.*

29 July 1685. Before Ric. Ridge, esq., Mayor.
Information
Wil. Avenell of Petersfield, locksmith, said that about 11 a.m. yesterday he was selling pears in the market when a boy belonging to Mr Wil. Terrell at the Red Lion came out and threw a surrevrance into his face and then ran back into the Red Lion. Avenell went in and told John the ostler what the boy had done and returned to the market. About half an hour later Mr Terrell was at the door and asked him what the boy had done and he told him. Terrell swore at him, took hold of his hair with one hand and struck him in the face with the other hand and then with both his hands threw him down and kicked him.   *Signed by mark.*

Recognisances
(a) Wil. Avenell in £10.
To appear at the next Sessions to prosecute and give evidence of assault against Mr Terrell.
(b) Wil. Terrell in £20.
> John Starkes in £10.
> Henry Belfeild in £10.
For appearance of Terrell at the next Sessions and to keep the peace, especially towards Wil. Avenell.
Marginal note (Latin): He owes 2s 6d.
See also no. 388 (28).

384
ASSAULT

S3B/42. *Calendar number on document: 29.*

4 August 1685. Before Ric. Ridge, esq., Mayor, and Sam. Williams, gent.
Information
Mary, wife of Tho. Beeswabber of Portsmouth, mariner, said that she went to the house of Ric. Butcher of Portsmouth about her quarter money. She asked him if he had been with Mr Stubbs about the quarter money. He said 'Yes'. She then asked him if he had the conscience to take all the quarter money of a soldier. He again said 'Yes' and bid her go about her business like the pitiful whore she was. At this, she took up a chair to throw at him (but did not throw) and then he came at her and kicked her. His wife Joan then came and scratched her face and struck her with a broom.   *Signed by mark.*

---

61 Statements iv, v, vii and viii are all made on the same document which Norton signs at the bottom.
62 i.e. Cha. Wither of Hall, Deane, near Basingstoke.

L

Recognisances

    (a) Ric. Butcher in £20.

        Wil. Undershershell in £10.

        Tho. Jackson in £10.

For appearance of Ric. Butcher and Joan his wife at the next Sessions and to keep the peace, especially towards Mary, wife of Tho. Beeswabber.

    (b) Mary Beeswabber in £10.

To appear at the next Sessions to prosecute Ric. Butcher.

See also no. 388 (29).

385

ABUSE

S3/13/8. *Calendar number on document:* 30.

12 August 1685. Before Ric. Ridge, esq., Mayor.

Informations

    (a) Amy, wife of Wil. Goater, (*signs* Amy Lifton) said that James, son of James Arnold, was going along when Peter Foy followed him and struck him several blows. She asked the child why he did not go and tell his father and Foy called her a quaking jade and a quaking whore and bid her mind her own business.   *Signed by mark.*

    (b) Grace, wife of James Beale, said that this morning she was in the garden weeding when she heard blows and looking out saw Goodwife Goater and Foy together.

Recognisances

    (a) Amy Goater in £10.

        Grace Beale in £10.

For appearance of both to prosecute and give evidence against Peter Foy.

    (b) Peter Foy in £10.

        Sam. Tailor in £10.

        Alex. Forebush, barber, in £10.

For appearance of Foy at the next Sessions and to keep the peace, especially towards James, son of James Arnold.

    Marginal note (*Latin*) *against Tailor's name:* He owes for his recognisance.

See also no. 388 (30).

386

ABUSING AUTHORITY

S3/13/1. *Calendar number on document:* 31.

14 September 1685. Before Sam. Williams, gent.

Recognisances

        Geo. Bolton of Portsmouth, miller, in £20.

        Ant. Binsted sen. in £10.

For appearance of Bolton at the next Sessions.

Bound over for abusing Mr Mayor in the open street.

See also no. 388 (31).

387

RIOT

S3/13/16

16 September 1 James II [1685].

Presentment (*Latin*)

Presents Step. Olding of Portsmouth, yeoman, Miles Porter of the same, yeoman, Tho. Bowes of Wymering, tailor, Tho. Baker of Portsea, yeoman, Ric. Thomas of the same, yeoman, Dan. Mihill of the same, yeoman, James Aylward of the same, yeoman, Jos. Aylward of the same, yeoman, Tho. Goldfinch of the same, house-carpenter, Jos. Cunditt of the same, tailor, as rioters and disturbers of the peace in Portsea.

    Note over each name: Non cul.

    Endorsements:

    (a) Witnesses, Rob. Harford, Ric. Crocker, Rob. Hogben, Tho. Hayes, Henry Mills, sworn.

    (b) True bill.

S3B/35

23 September 1685. Before Ric. Ridge, esq., Mayor.

Recognisances

(a) Step. Olding in £20.
    Miles Porter in £20.
For appearance of Olding at the next Sessions to answer for riot committed by him and others.

(b) Miles Porter in £20.
    Step. Olding in £20.
For appearance of Porter.

(c) Dan. Mihell in £20.
    Ric. Thomas in £20.
For appearance of Mihell.

(d) Ric. Thomas in £20.
    Dan. Mihell in £20.
For appearance of Thomas.

(e) Jos. Cundit in £20.
    John Young of Milton in £20.
For appearance of Cundit.

(f) James Aylward in £20.
    Tho. Baker in £20.

(g) Tho. Baker in £20.
    James Aylward in £20.

(h) Jos. Aylward in £20.
    Tho. Goldfinch in £20.

(i) Tho. Goldfinch in £20.
    Jos. Aylward in £20.

Footnote (Latin) to (f)–(i) : On condition aforesaid.

28 September 1685. No name of Justice.

Recognisance

    Rob. Harford in £20.
To appear at the next Sessions to prosecute and give evidence against Step. Olding, Miles Porter, Dan. Mihell, Ric. Thomas and Jos. Cundit for riot on 16 Sept. last.
See also no. 388 (32)–(40).

388
CALENDAR[63]

S3B/36

[8 October] 1685. Michaelmas Sessions.

(1)	Rob. Matthewes	Bound anew for assaulting John Dove.	Tho. Damarum
(2)	Geo. Stuckey		Ric. Stoe

See no. 365.
Notes against both names : Discharged by the Court.

(3)	David Stephens. Suspicion of sheep stealing.		Ric. Talbot
			Geo. Compton
(4)	John Stephens		Ric. Stephens
			James Armoner
(5)	Tho. Guy	Riot in burning an effigy of the Pope on 1 May last, when there were 200–300 people met together.	John Taylour
			Rob. Martin
(6)	Tho. Wood		Geo. Reynolds
			John Santloe
(7)	John Abbott		Henry Tilden
			Tho. Tomes
(8)	Rob. Butt (*also* Batt)		John Eastwood
			Tho. Crewes

See no. 366.
Notes against nos 4, 6 *and* 8 *:* Discharged by the Court.

---

[63] All notes giving decision of the Court are in the margin and in Latin.

(9)	Sarah, wife of Tho. Goudge. Bound over to behaviour, [for abuse]. *See no.* 367.	Joanna Parnell, widow
(10)	Alice, wife of John Brumblecome. Bound over to behaviour, [for abuse]. *See no.* 367. *Note:* Discharged.	Nic. Mellersh Edm. Lowance
(11)	Peter Pogson. Assaulting Sarah, wife of Tho. Goudge. *See no.* 368.	Cha. Fox, esq. Wil. Games, gent.
(12)	Prudence, wife of Peter Pogson. Bound over to behaviour, [for threatened arson]. *See no.* 369.	Peter Pogson
(13)	Step. Smith. Speaking treasonable words at the time of the Rebellion, saying that if it had not been for the sake of the wife of one Booker deceased, who stood bound with him to Miles Porter for £50, he would have gone to Argyll rather than have paid the money. *See no.* 371. *Note:* Discharged by the Court.	Jos. Fugar[64] Henry Royle John Royle
(14)	Wil. English. Assaulting Margaret, wife of Chr. Mitchell. *See no.* 372. *Note:* Non cul.	Wil. Tanner Henry Mills
(15)	Ann, wife of July Wood. Speaking seditious words at the time of the Rebellion, saying that the late Duke of Monmouth was no more a bastard than she was. *See no.* 373. *Note:* Discharged by the Court.	Henry Seagar Peter Pecke
(16) (17)	Jos. Gregge Ben. Gregge } Suspected of intent to go into Monmouth's army. *See no.* 374. *Notes against both names:* Discharged by the Court.	Rob. Martin James Harris
(18)	Alice Cozens. Assaulting John, son of John Mills. *See no.* 375. *Note:* Discharged by the Court.	Step. Olding Nic. Mellersh
(19)	Wil. Reynolds. Speaking seditious words, saying the Duke of Monmouth had a great force and would have a bigger and that he was a true Protestant. *See no.* 376. *Note:* Discharged.	David Ridge Mark Cullimore
(20)	John Eames. Saying, God refuse the souls of them that refuse to drink the Duke of Monmouth's health.	Wil. Page Roger Smith
(21)	Jean Mills, widow. Abusing Ann, wife of Capt. Ridley. *See no.* 377. *Note:* Discharged by the Court.	Wil. Fullham

[64] The forename here is given as Joseph but in no. 371 it is said to be John.

(22) John Softley. Speaking seditious words, viz. that   James Bartle
whereas Wil. Right said he hoped Monmouth would   Jeffery Soane
be hanged, Softley replied, You dare not say so a
month hence.
Note: Discharged by the Court.

(23) John Winter   ⎤ Speaking seditious words   Ric. Hunt
                      ⎬ that the King was dead.   John Blose
(24) Chr. Pinchen   ⎦   John Fiveash
                                                    Mat. Gibbens

See no. 378.
Note against both names: Discharged by the Court.

(25) Joan, wife of John Gover. Speaking seditious words.   John Gover
                                                            Rob. Olding

See no. 379.
Note (Latin and English): [Case] heard and is sorry.
Discharged by the Court.

Sarah Austen.[65] *No offence stated.*   John Patten
                                          Geo. Deacon

Note: Discharged by the Court.

(26) Cuthbert Benbridge. Abusing the trained-band   Wil. Edwards
officers and soldiers, saying they were cowards.   Wil. Tanner
See no. 380.
Note: Discharged by the Court.

(27) John Chapman. Suspected of having been in   Edw. Chapman sen.
Monmouth's army.   Ric. Preist
See no. 381.   John Lewen
Note: Discharged by the Court.   Tho. Inwood

(28) Wil. Terrell. Assaulting Wil. Avenell.   John Starkes
                                               Henry Benfield

See no. 383.
Note: Discharged.

(29) Ric. Butcher and Joan his wife. Assaulting Mary   Wil. Undershell
Beeswabber.   Tho. Jackson
See no. 384.
Note: Discharged by the Court.

(30) Peter Foy. Assaulting James, infant son of James   Sam. Tayler
Arnold.   Alex. Firebush
See no. 385.
Note: Discharged.

(31) Geo. Boulton. Abusing Mr Ric. Ridge, Mayor.   Ant. Binsted
See no. 386.
Note: Discharged by the Court.

(32) Step. Olding   ⎤   Miles Porter
(33) Miles Porter   ⎮   Ric. Thomas[66]
(34) Dan. Mihell   ⎮ Riot in driving the   Ric. Thomas
(35) Ric. Thomas   ⎮ common fields without   Dan. Mihell
(36) Jos. Condict   ⎬ the Chamberlain, and   Tho. Baker
(37) James Aylward   ⎮ making several people   Tho. Baker
(38) Tho. Baker   ⎮ pay them money.   James Aylward
(39) Jos. Aylward   ⎮   Tho. Goldfinch
(40) Tho. Goldfinch   ⎦   Jos. Aylward
See no. 387.
Note by no. (32): Discharged.

---

[65] No number – an interlineation.
[66] Ric. Thomas is named as surety here; possibly a mistake for Step. Olding (cf. no. 387).

EASTER SESSIONS 15 April 1686

No papers survive except for entry in Sessions Books; see Appendix II, no. 98.

MICHAELMAS SESSIONS 7 October 1686

No papers survive.

EASTER SESSIONS 7 April and 10 May 1687[67]

No papers survive.

MICHAELMAS SESSIONS 6 and 25 October 1687 [68]

389
Subject unknown

S3/14/1 (entry i)[69]

No date [April] 1687. No name of Justice.
Recognisances
      Elizabeth Joanes renewal in £20.
      Tho. Hancocke in £10.
  For appearance [of Elizabeth] at the next Sessions.
See also no. 408 (1).

390
Subject unknown

S3/14/1 (entry ii)

No date [April 1687]. No name of Justice.
Recognisances
      Fra. Chidley in £20.
      John Levet in £10.
      Tho. Morgan in £10.
  For appearance [of Chidley] at the next Sessions to prosecute his traverse and pay costs if adjudged.
    Footnote (Latin): Sessions of the Peace adjourned until Tuesday month [10 May].
See also no. 408 (2).

391
THEFT

S3/14/3

7 April 1687. Before Ric. Ridge, gent.
Examination
Rob. Fleming, soldier under the command of Capt. Grimes, confessed that last Tuesday about 11 p.m. he broke the brick wall of the house of James Blowes, entered the shop and took a piece of cheese, about half a dozen halfpenny loaves and one shirt.
Signed by mark.

Information
  James Blowes (*signs* Blos) said that last Tuesday night his shop was broken into and there was taken a pound or two of cheese, four halfpenny loaves and a shirt which was left with him by Rob. Fleming. This morning he found one such loaf in the Barracks where Fleming lodged which had his mark on it and he believed it was one of the loaves he had lost.
Signed.
Recognisances
      Rob. Fleming in £20.
      Renald Graham in £10.
  For appearance [of Fleming] at the next Sessions.

---

[67] Date for adjournment of this Sessions only to be found in no. 390.
[68] Date for adjournment of this Sessions only to be found in no. 409.
[69] Headed 'Kalender since Lady Day 1687'.

S3/14/2

29 April 1687. Before Ric. Ridge, gent.

Information

Lucy King of Portsmouth, widow, said that six or seven weeks before last Christmas Jonathan Godard of Portsmouth, joiner, had twice carnal knowledge of her body at the Dun Cow on the Point and that he was the father of the child she went with now. Nobody else had ever had carnal knowledge of her body except Godard and John King her husband who had been dead over fifteen months.   *Signed by mark.*

Recognisances

    Jonathan Godard in £20.
    John Patten jun., gunsmith, in £10.
    Tho. Orpington, glazier, in £10.

For appearance [of Godard] at the next Sessions and 'to perform the order of Sessions etc.'

S3B/37

10 May 1687. By Isaac Betts, gent., Deputy Mayor, and John Grundy, gent.

Bastardy order

In the matter of a female bastard child born at Portsmouth of Lucy King, spinster, we adjudge Jonathan Godard of Portsmouth, joiner, the reputed father. He shall within six days of notice given to him pay to the Churchwardens and Overseers of the parish of Portsmouth the sum of 37s for the keeping of the child from birth to date of notice, and shall further pay 2s weekly on Fridays (so long as the child is chargeable to the parish until the age of eight). Within one month of the child attaining the age of eight he shall pay £5 towards putting out the child as an apprentice.

Lucy King for her punishment shall remain in the common gaol for six weeks and receive due correction.

Jonathan Godard shall be bound in £40 to perform so much of this order as concerns him.

    Signed and sealed by both Justices (both use the same seal: on a bend three escallops).

See also nos 408 (3), 409.

S3/14/27

1 May 3 James II [1687].

Presentment (Latin)

Presents Edw. Carter of Portsmouth, shipwright, for breaking into the house of Geo. Gray of the same and assaulting him.   *Signed by* [Edw.] Archer.

Footnote: He submitted under protest because he did not wish to oppose the King and paid a fine 6s 8d.

    Endorsements:
    (a) Witnesses, Geo. Gray, Rebecca Gray, sworn.
    (b) True bill.

S3/14/28.

21 May 3 James II [1687].

Presentment (Latin)

Presents Edw. Carter of Portsmouth, shipwright, for having Geo. Gray arrested and imprisoned for six hours or more without just cause.   *Signed by* [Edw.] Archer.

Footnote: He submitted under protest because he did not wish to oppose the King and paid a fine 6s 8d.

    Endorsements:
    (a) Witnesses Geo. Gray, Rebecca Gray, sworn.
    (b) True bill.

S3/14/4

26 May 1687. Before John Grundy, gent.

Recognisances

    Edw. Carter in £50.
    John Mudd, shipwright ('nafragius'), in £25.
    Ben. Upjohn, shipwright ('nafragius'), in £25.

For appearance [of Carter] at the next Sessions.

Bound over for imprisoning Geo. Gray and threatening him bodily harm.

S3/14/7

12 July 1687. Before John Grundy, gent.
Information
Ben. Upjohn of Portsmouth, shipwright, said that on Saturday 21 May last about 7 p.m. by the invitation of Edw. Carter he was at his house. Carter told him that he would be divorced from his wife and would go to Mr Archer to have it done. When he told him that it could not be, Carter swore that, if not, he would plague her some other way and presently fell on her and beat her, called her bitch and told her to go on her knees and ask forgiveness of him, which she did. Carter said if he could find a way to be revenged on the rogue Grey he would be satisfied. His wife said she would contrive a way and suggested that he should pretend to go away and be out of town that night but convey himself into a chamber closet and she would trepan Grey into the same chamber. When Upjohn left Carter's house he saw Carter's wife talking to Grey in his porch. This was the day before Grey was committed to the guard. Some time after this Carter asked him what day it was that he beat his wife, to which he answered the Saturday above mentioned. Carter replied that that would undo him and asked him to say it was the Monday following. He said he could not.
Signed; countersigned by the Justice.
See also no. 408 (4).

394
FRAUD

S3/14/18

1 June 1687. Before John Grundy, gent.
Information
Ric. Post of London, silk-weaver, said that about a month before Michaelmas he took a gilt sixpence of Jean White of Gosport for half a guinea. She refused to change it.
Signed by mark.

395
ASSAULT

S3B/38

31 May 1687. Before Isaac Betts, gent., Deputy Mayor.
Information
Bart. Stanesmore of Portsmouth, labourer, said that last night about 10 p.m. while drinking with one Ponter at Ric. Goodin's house on the Common, others there were James Martin, James Etherington jun., John Osborne, Tho. Richards, John Frith, Henry Richards, Wil. Waterman, John Roe, Wil. Symons, Ric. Goodin and others he did not know. Waterman and Henry Richards came to him and asked him to join their corporation, which they had there amongst themselves. He refused and asked Waterman to leave his room. Waterman and Roe threatened to do Stanesmore's business by the morrow morning, and afterwards they waylaid and beat and wounded him as he was going to the Dock.
Signed by mark.
Marginal note: £20.

S3/14/11

2 June 1687. No name of Justice.
Examination
John Osborne (*signs* Osburne) said that last Monday about 10 p.m. he was at Ric. Goodin's house on the Common with several men making merry, among whom were James Etherington calling himself mayor, James Martin, recorder, Wil. Symons, Henry Richards, Tho. Richards, John Trift[70], Wil. Waterman, Ric. Goodin, Rob. Padison, Israel Pownall, John Froud and others of their corporation. *Signed.*
Recognisances
> John Row jun. in £20.
> John Row sen. in £10.
> Jos. Grig in £10.
For appearance [of John Row jun.] at the next Sessions.

[70] The name is Frith in the above information but clearly Trift here.

396
ABUSE

S3/14/5
Information
14 June 1687. Before Rob. Shales, esq., Mayor.
Information
Jos. Gregg (*signs* Grigg) said that yesterday afternoon he was at Capt. Skelton's house on the Point and Nic. Roaker came to Madam Skelton to demand money for amending the highway. She said she had never paid any yet and would not. He answered that he would return her name to London and make her husband's commission shake and other provoking words. *Signed.*
Recognisances
  Cha. Skelton, esq., in £10.
  Jos. Gregg in £10.
For appearance at the next Sessions to prosecute and give evidence against Nic. Roaker.

17 June 1687. Before John Grundy, gent.
Recognisances
  Nic. Roaker of Portsmouth, yeoman, in £20.
  Ant. Binsted of the same, cooper, in £10.
  Wil. Tanner of the same, victualler, in £10.
For appearance of Roaker at the next Sessions to answer indictments preferred against him by Cha. Skelton, esq., and Ann his wife.
See also no. 408 (5).

397
ABUSE

S3/14/15
20 June 1687. In Court.
Information
Ann Bronne (*or* Broune) of Portsmouth, widow, said that last Saturday John Yatman came to Geo. Eker's wife and said this was his weight. After some talk Yatman said she was a cozening, cheating woman and would cheat anybody for 7½d. He then came into the shop and carried away the weight with more abuse. *Signed by mark.*
Recognisance
  John Yatman in £20.
For appearance at the next Sessions.
Marginal note (Latin): Discharged by Mr Grundy, one of the Justices.

398
VAGRANCY

S3/14/19
24 June 1687. Before John Grundy, gent.
Recognisances
  Ann Pearson, spinster, in £10.
  Mar. Fountaine in £5.
  John Harwood in £5.
For appearance of Ann at the next Sessions.
Bound over for being a person of ill repute and not being at service.
Marginal note (Latin): Discharged by Mr Grundy.

399
Subject unknown

S3/14/14
28 June 1687. No name of Justice.
Recognisances
  Geo. Gray in £20.
  Wil. Griffin, in £10.
  Nic. Mellersh, in £10.
For appearance [of Gray] at the next Sessions.
See also nos 408 (6), 409.

400

LIBEL

S3/14/17

28 June 1687. In full Court.

Informations

(a) Jean New said she heard Mary Blisset tax Sam. Henty with making libels on his mistress. He owned he made the libel now shown to her and said he would swear it to be true.

(b) Mary Blisset *said the same.*

Marginal note (Latin): Discharged by Mr Grundy, one of the Justices, by agreement of the parties.

Recognisances

      Sam. Henty in £20.

      Roger Carter in £10.

      John Taileur in £10.

For appearance [of Henty] at the next Sessions.

401

FORNICATION AND ADULTERY

S3/14/8

15 July 1687. No name of Justice.

Information

Wil. Cozens of Gosport said he heard Abraham Penfold say three weeks ago last Sunday that he had lain with Sarah, wife of Ben. Morris, before and after she was married.   *Signed by mark.*

Marginal note: £10.

Recognisances

(a) Abraham Penfold jun. in £20.

     Abraham Penfold sen. in £10.

For appearance [of Abraham Penfold jun.] at the next Sessions.

Marginal note (Latin): Discharged by Mr Grundy.

(b) Ben. Morris in £10.

     Wil. Cozens in £10.

For appearance at the next Sessions to prosecute against Abraham Penfold.

402

ABUSING AUTHORITY

S3/14/16

18 July 1687. Before John Grundy, gent.

Recognisances

      Tho. Wells in £20.

      Tho. Smith in £20.

For appearance of Tho. Wells and Joan his wife at the next Sessions.

Bound over for abusing Mr Ric. Ridge, Justice.

Footnote (Latin): He owes for his recognisance.

See also no. 408 (7).

403

NEGLECT OF DUTY

S3/14/29

1 August 3 James II [1687].

Presentment (Latin)

Presents John Rutter, a Constable of the Vill of Gosport, for neglect of duty for failing, when provided with a warrant, to arrest Step. Carver jun. and John Still and to bring them before Rob. Shales, gent., one of the Justices. *Signed by* [Edw.] Archer.

Endorsements:

(a) Witnesses, Edw. Furze, Cha. Bissell, sworn.

(*b*) Ignoramus.

404

THREATENED ASSAULT

S3/14/12

2 August 1687. No name of Justice.

Information

Frances Plumbridge said she believed Wil. Sumner will beat, wound or do her some bodily hurt.   *Signed by mark.*

Marginal note: £10.

Recognisances
> Wil. Sumner in £20.
> Edw. Brooker in £10.
> Bart. Kempster in £10.

For appearance [of Sumner] at the next Sessions and to keep the peace, especially towards Frances Plumbridge.

See also no. 408 (8).

405
ABUSING
AUTHORITY

S3/14/22

11 August 3 James II [1687].
Presentment (Latin)
Presents James Rice of the parish of St James in the Fields, [London], barber-surgeon, for maliciously abusing Rob. Shales, lately Mayor of the Borough.

Signed by [Edw.] Archer.

Endorsements:
(a) Witnesses, Lucy Upjohn, Sarah Upjohn, Mary Jackson, sworn.
(b) True bill.

S3/14/6

11 August 1687. No name of Justice.
Informations

(a) Lucy, wife of Tho. Upjohn, said that on that day when James Rice was at her house she told him she would make a complaint to the Mayor against him for abuses he had offered her. He answered with obscenity that he was a better man than any of them. *Signed.*

Marginal note (Latin): Examined by me Edw. Archer, Clerk of the Peace..

(b) Sarah Upjohn said that on that day when James Rice, collector of the hearth money, was at her father's house she told him that the Mayor should know what he did. He answered with obscenity that when he was out of office he was as good a man as Mr Mayor. *Signed*

(c) Mary Jackson *repeated the same evidence, referring to her master's house (so she was evidently a servant in the house).* *Signed.*

S3/14/10

No date. No name of Justice.
Recognisances
> James Rice of St James in the Fields ('St Jacobus in Campis'), barber-surgeon, in £20.
> Tho. Gayton, in £10.

For appearance [of Rice] at the next Sessions to answer all such contempts or misdemeanours as shall be objected against him.

See also nos 408 (9), 409.

406
SETTLEMENT

S3/14/9

13 August 1687. No name of Justice.
Information
Joan Nossiter, spinster, said she lived in service three-quarters of a year with Edm. Ward, then three-quarters of a year at the London in Portsmouth, then she went to Petersfield on the Saturday before Whitsun last and stayed three weeks, then to Tho. Newnam at Atherton, I.W., for a month or five weeks but kept under warning, then to Newchurch, [I.W.], from which she was sent here by the Justices. She was born in the parish of Newchurch.

407
DISTURBANCE

S3B/39

16 September 1687. Before Ric. Ridge, gent.
Examinations

(a) Henry Coward of Portsmouth, painter-stainer, said that last night Nat. Harwood came and knocked at his door, saying he would have his wife or pull down the house. He afterwards broke windows and disturbed Coward's wife very much. *Signed.*

(b) Margaret Roaker (*signs* Roocker) said that last Wednesday night, when she was at Henry Coward's house, Mrs Harwood who was there gave her a key to take to her husband. She delivered it to him but he said it was none of his. Mrs Harwood then gave her three keys to give him, but as he had left Coward's house she laid them in the window and yesterday Coward took them in. *Signed.*

Marginal note against both examinations: £20.

Recognisances

        Nat. Harwood in £20.
        Wil. Terrell in £10.
        Tho. Prude in £10.

For appearance of Harwood at the next Sessions.

See also no. 408 (10).

408

CALENDAR[71]

S3/14/21

[6 and 25 October] 1687. Michaelmas Sessions.

(1)	Elizabeth Jones. *See no.* 389. *Note* (*Latin*): Discharged by the Court.	Tho. Hancocke
(2)	Fra. Chidley. *See no.* 390. *Note* (*Latin*): Discharged by the Court.	John Levet Tho. Morgan
(3)	Jonathan Godard, [for bastardy]. *See nos* 392, 409.	Tho. Orpington
(4)	Edw. Carter, [for assault and wrongful imprisonment]. *See no.* 393.	John Mudd Ben. Upjohn
(5)	Nic. Roaker, [for abuse]. *See no.* 396. *Note* (*Latin*): Discharged by the Court.	Ant. Binsted Wil. Tanner
(6)	Geo. Gray. *See nos* 399, 409. *Note:* Bound anew.	Wil. Mellersh[72] Wil. Griffen
(7)	Tho. Wells, [for abusing authority]. *See no.* 402.	Tho. Smith
(8)	Wil. Sumner, [for threatened assault]. *See no.* 404. *Note:* Stands upon his recognisance.	Edw. Brooker Bart. Kempster
(9)	James Rice, [for abusing authority]. *See nos* 405, 409. *Note* (*Latin*): Writ of certiorari issued.	Tho. Gayton
(10)	Nat. Harwood, [for disturbance]. *See nos* 407, 412. *Note* (*Latin*): Discharged.	Wil. Terrell Tho. Prude

---

[71] The cases have no numbers on the original Calendar. All notes were written beside the name of the defendant as the nature of the case was not given.

[72] The forename here is given as William, probably a mistake for Nicholas (cf. no. 399).

409
COURT ORDERS

S3/14/13

No date [6 October 1687].

(a) The Court confirms the order that Jonathan Godard shall give security to keep the bastard.

See nos 392, 408 (3).

(b) The Court orders James Rice to pay back to Mr Brimblecome 14*s* 6*d* and to Step. Coombes 7*s*.

See nos 405, 408 (9).

6 October 1687. In full Court.

Recognisances

>   Geo. Gray in £20.
>   Wil. Griffin in £10
>   Geo. Gittins in £10.

See nos 399, 408 (6).

Court adjournments

Court adjourned from Tuesday next for a fortnight 9 o'clock.

Court Leet adjourned from Tuesday for a fortnight.

410
ASSAULT

S3/14/20

7 October 1687. In Court of Sessions.

Information

Geo. Steventon said that last Wednesday when he was at John Knapper's house in Gosport James Stares came into the room and assaulted him and his wife, striking his wife in the face.   *Signed.*

Marginal note: £20.

Footnote (Latin): Recognisance of Rutter discharged by the Court and recognisance of Stares shall stand as it is.

EASTER SESSIONS 26 April, 29 May and 13 June 1688

411
Subject unknown

S3/15/8

26 April 1688. At the Sessions.

Recognisances

>   Ric. Smith in £20.
>   Nic. Windover of Portsmouth, tailor, in £10.

For appearance of Smith at the next Sessions to prosecute his traverse with effect and pay costs if adjudged against him.

412
DISTURBANCE

S3/15/9

26 April 1688. In full Court.

Recognisances

>   Nat. Harwood of Portsmouth, butcher, in £20.
>   Tho. Prude of the same, tailor, in £10.

For appearance of Harwood at the next Sessions to prosecute his traverse with effect and pay costs if adjudged against him.

See also nos 407, 408 (10).

413
Subject unknown

S3/15/10

26 April 1688. At the Sessions.

Recognisances

>   Wil. Drapier of Gosport in £20.
>   Edm. Ward of Portsmouth in £10.

For appearance of Drapier at the next Sessions to prosecute his traverse with effect and pay costs if adjudged against him.

414
ABUSE

S3/15/11

26 April 1688. In Court.
Recognisance
    John Mills of Portsmouth, joiner, in £20.
For appearance of Jean his wife at the next Sessions.
Bound anew for abusing Elizabeth and Mary Carter.

415
THREATENED
ASSAULT

S3/15/12

26 April 1688. In Court.
Recognisances
    Wil. Brag of Portsmouth, house-carpenter, in £20.
    Wil. Coales of Fareham, yeoman, in £10.
For appearance of Brag at the next Sessions.
Bound over for threatening Nat. Harwood.

MICHAELMAS SESSIONS 2 October and 6 November 1688

416
ASSAULT

S3/12/26

3 May 4 James II [1688].
Presentment (Latin)
Presents John Stone of Portsmouth, sailor, for assault on Mary Gill.
                      Signed by [Cha.] Bissell for [Sam.] Ely.

S3/15/1

5 May 1688. Before Tho. Hancocke, gent.
Information
Mary, wife of John Gill, said that last Thursday, the 3rd, John Stone called her 'brended bitch' and asked if she had been to get him four soldiers more. Then he pulled down her clothes line so that the clothes fell on the ground and he stamped upon it. He then threw a bone which broke her window and came into the room. When she tried to save her clothes from falling to the ground, he drew his knife and cut her gown. She believed he would do her some bodily hurt for he had threatened her several times and swore he would sacrifice her, for her husband was going to sea. Eliza, Stone's wife, had several times threatened her.   *Signed by mark.*

S3/15/2

Recognisances
    John Stone of Portsmouth, mariner, in £20.
    John Hooper of the same, sailor, in £10.
For appearance of Stone and Eliza his wife at the next Sessions to answer indictments preferred by Mary, wife of John Gill.

417
THREATENED
MURDER

D11A/16/32

14 May 1688. By [Sir] R[ob.] Wright, [Lord Chief Justice].
Warrant for arrest
Addressed to all Mayors, Sheriffs, Bailiffs, Constables and all other officers and ministers whom these may concern.
    Complaint has been made by Ann, wife of John Garrett jun. of Portsmouth, that her husband and Elizabeth Garrett and John Garrett sen. have conspired to take her life. Her husband, at the instigation of Elizabeth, had several times in a barbarous manner abused her when she was with child and with a drawn knife threatened to murder her and rip the child out of her belly and burn it. Four or six days after she was delivered, her husband and John Garrett sen. violently forced the child from her before it was christened and she did not know where it had been taken. At the same time John Garrett the father said he would give a man £40 to swear against her to take away her life and threatened to throw her behind the fire. She has been turned out of her habitation and her husband and his sisters Hester and Elizabeth Garrett

and Elizabeth Stone have taken all her goods she had before marriage and her clothes, so that she is destitute.

Mandate to bring John Garrett jun., John Garrett sen., Elizabeth his wife, Hester and Elizabeth the sisters and Elizabeth Stone before one of the Justices near the place where they are taken to give security to keep the peace against Ann Garrett and be further dealt with. *Signed and sealed (wafer seal: a chevron between three fleur-de-lis and on a chief three spear-heads).*

S3/15/5
26 May 1688. Before John Grundy, esq., Mayor.

Recognisances

   (a)   John Blakely of Portsmouth, mercer, in £40.
         Tho. Harling in £40.
For appearance of John Garret sen. and Eliza his wife at the next Sessions and meanwhile to keep the peace towards Ann, wife of John Garret jun.

   (b)   John Blakely in £40.
         Tho. Harling in £40.
For appearance of Hester, daughter of John Garret sen., at the next Sessions.

   (c)   John Blakely in £40.
         Tho. Harling in £40.
For appearance of Elizabeth, daughter of John Garret sen., at the next Sessions.

   (d)   John Blakely in £40.
         Tho. Harling in £40.
For appearance of Eliza, wife of John Stone, at the next Sessions.

   (e)   Thomas Harling in £10.
         John Doe in £10.
For appearance of John Garret jun. at the next Sessions.

**418
THREATENED
ASSAULT**

S3/15/4
22 May 1688. Before John Grundy, esq., Mayor.
Information
Mary, wife of Nic. Salterly, said she believed that Rebecca, wife of Tho. Busbridge, would kill, wound or do her some bodily hurt.

Recognisances

   (a)   John Rutter of Gosport in £20.
For appearance of Rebecca, wife of Tho. Busbridge, at the next Sessions.

   (b)   Nic. Salterly in £10.
         Geo. Hews in £10.

**419
ASSAULT**

S3/15/7
23 June 1688. Before Tho. Hancocke, gent., Deputy Mayor.
Informations
   (a) John Baker of Portsmouth, mariner, said that yesterday about noon John King struck him with his fist on the side of his head when Baker was on board his own vessel and threatened to knock his brains out.   *Signed.*

   Footnote (Latin): Discharged by order of Mr Hancocke and by agreement of the parties.

   (b) Tho. Matthewes *confirmed the evidence of Baker.*   *Signed.*

Recognisances

         John King in £20.
         Wil. Arnold of Gosport, shipwright ('nafrangius'), in £10.
For appearance of King at the next Sessions.

420

DESERTING THE COLOURS

S3B/41

25 June 1688. Before Tho. Hancock, Deputy Mayor.

Examination

John Darrell, esq., Ensign to Capt. Edw. Saville in the Hon. Col. Cha. Trelawny's Regiment of Foot, said that about 16 June Ant. Nash, a soldier of Capt. Saville's Company, ran from his colours out of the Garrison at Portsmouth, having been listed and mustered in the said Company nearly three years ago. Darrell entered him into the Company and gave him 1*s* at the time of listing. *Signed.*

Recognisance

  John Darrill, esq., in £20.

To appear at the General Gaol Delivery for the county of Hampshire to prefer a bill of indictment against Ant. Nash for running away from his colours and to give evidence against him.

421

ABUSE

S3B/43

8 August 1688. Before John Grundy, Mayor.

Examinations

(a) Eleanor, wife of James Tompson of Portsmouth, said that, on the evening of the 7th, Frances, wife of Edw. Paine of Portsmouth, was talking with her on the Point and abused her saying she was a 'bastard bearing whore', and that Eleanor's mother (meaning Catherine Haswell long since dead) murdered Eleanor's bastard, breaking its neck, and she would go before the Mayor and swear to it. *Signed by mark.*

(b) Elizabeth, wife of Wil. Roper, said that the above was true.

        Signed by mark; countersigned by the Justice.

(c) Sarah, wife of Tho. Goodale, said that she heard Frances Paine say to Alice Goodfaith 'Goe unto the bastard bearing whore your mother (meaninge Ellenor Tompson) that tooke her bastard and hove it over the bedd against the wall'.

        Signed by mark; countersigned by the Justice.

Recognisances

  Frances Paine in £20.

  Ric. Page in £10.

  Wil. Langstone in £10.

For appearance of Frances at the next Sessions.

422

WIFE-BEATING

S3/15/6

11 August 1688. Before John Grundy, esq., Mayor.

Information

Ann, wife of John Becket of Portsmouth, mason, said that her husband had several times beaten her and yesterday turned her out of doors. This morning he beat her and she believed he would kill, wound or do her some bodily hurt. *Signed by mark.*

Recognisances

  John Becket of Portsmouth, mason, in £20.

  John Bye of the same, gent., in £10.

  John Doe of the same in (*blank*).

For appearance of Becket at the next Sessions to answer indictments preferred against him and meanwhile to keep the peace, especially towards Ann his wife.

10 August 1688. Before John Grundy, esq., Mayor.

Recognisance

  John Becket in £40.

On the same condition.

423

ASSAULT

S3/12/22

28 September 4 James II [1688].

Presentment (Latin)

Presents Eleanor, wife of James Thompson of Portsmouth, sailor, for assault on Eliza Skipper. *Signed by* [Cha.] Bissell for [Sam.] Ely.

Footnote : She submitted under protest because she did not wish to oppose the King and is fined by the Court 3*s* 4*d*.

Endorsements :

(a) Witnesses, Elizabeth Skipper, Martha Skipper.

(b) True bill.

S3B/44

2 October 1688. No name of Justice.

Information

Elizabeth Skipper of Portsmouth, widow, said that on Friday last she was told that Goody Thompson wanted to speak to her. When she got into the room the door was shut behind her and Goody Thompson told her she was bewitched and that Elizabeth had bewitched her. She gave her several blows and pinched her arm. *Signed by mark.*

Marginal notes :

(a) In £20.

(b) 'Doctor (*blank*), Elizabeth Dorrell and her selfe and man.'[73]

Recognisance

John Blakely in £20.

For appearance of Eleanor, wife of James Thompson, at the next Sessions.

424
DISLOYALTY

S3B/45

26 October 1688. Before Tho. Hancock, esq., Mayor, and Rob. Shales, gent.

Informations

(a) John Collins, soldier in Capt. Clud's Company, said that last night lodging at the house of Margaret Bee he had and paid for a flagon of beer and would have had another, but she refused and said the Duke[74] was a rogue and the King was a fool for sending such fellows thither. *Signed by mark.*

(b) Patrick Molonne, soldier in Capt. Barnald's Company, said he was present drinking beer with John Collins. Collins told him Margaret Bee said these words but he did not hear her say them. *Signed.*

Recognisances

Margaret Bee in £20.

Wil. Browne in £10.

James Bartlet in £10.

For appearance of Margaret at the next Sessions.

---

[73] These names could be the sureties in this case.
[74] Duke of Berwick (title erased). He was James Fitz-James, natural son of James II, 1670–1734, created Duke of Berwick 1687 and appointed Governor of Portsmouth 1688.

M

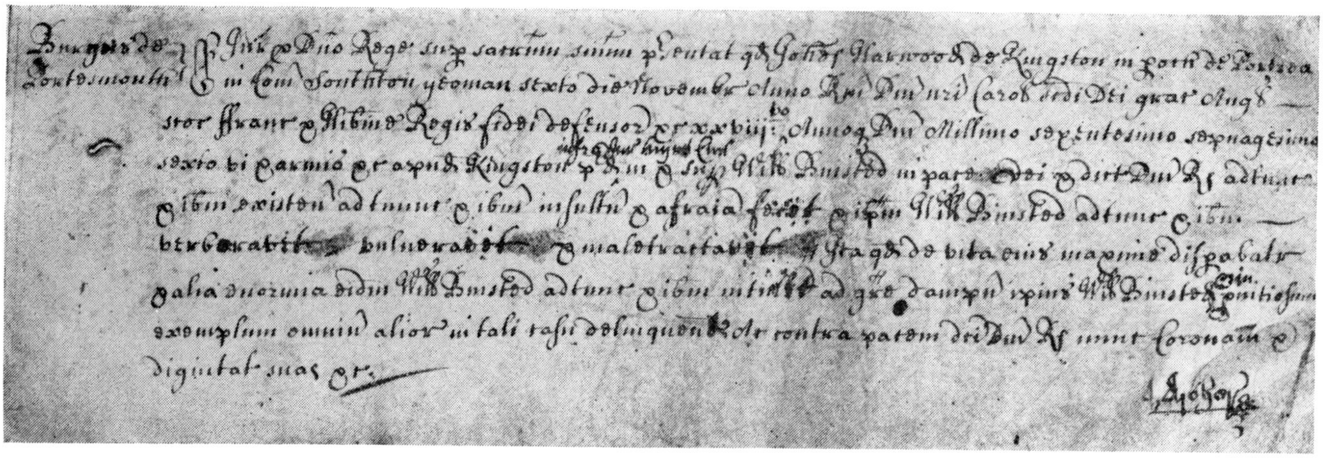

Fig. 2 PRESENTMENT IN A CASE OF ASSAULT, 1676 (no. 197). S3/5/21

Fig. 3 RECOGNISANCE TO KEEP THE PEACE, 1659 (no. 41). S3A/35

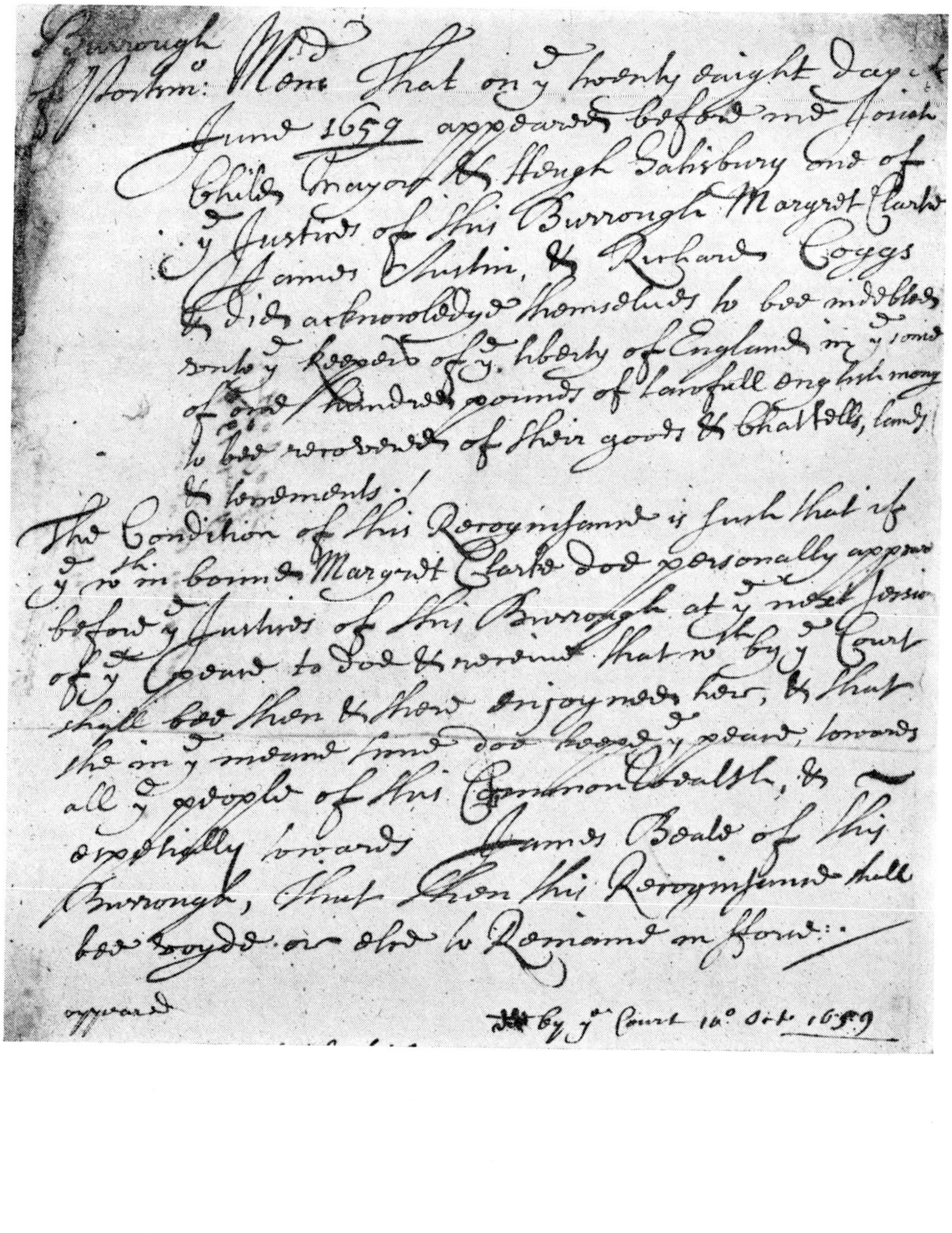

Appendix I
Full texts of specimen documents

1 Presentment

Burgus de
Portsmouth

S3/5/21 (see fig. 2 and no. 197: assault).

Juratio pro D*omi*no Rege sup*er* sacr*amen*tum suum presentat q*uod* Joh*ann*es Harwood de Kingston in paroch*ia* de Portsea in C*omitatu* South*amp*ton yeoman sexto die Novembr*is* Anno R*e*gni D*omi*ni n*ost*ri Caroli s*ecun*di Dei gra*cia* Angl*ie* Scoc*ie* Franc*ie* et Hib*er*nie Regis fidei defensor*is* etc*etera* xxviij*to* Annoque D*omi*ni Mill*e*simo s*e*xentesimo sepuagesimo s*e*xto vi et armis etc*etera* apud Kingston pred*ictam* infra jur*is*dictionem hujus Cur*ie* in et super Will*elmum* Binsted in pace Dei et dict*i* D*omi*ni R*egi*s adtunc et ib*ide*m existen*tem* adtunnc et ib*ide*m insultum et afraia*m* fecit et ip*su*m Will*elmum* Binsted adtunc et ib*ide*m verberavit vulneravit et maletractavit ita q*uo*d de vita eius maxime disperaba*tur* et alia enormia eidem Will*e*lmo Binsted adtunc et ib*ide*m intulit ad gr*ave* dampnum ip*s*ius Will*elmi* Binsted et in pernitiosum exemplum omniu*m* alioru*m* in tali casu delinquen*tium* ac contra pacem d*ic*ti D*omi*ni R*egi*s nunc Coronam et dignitat*es* suas etc*etera*.

Translation:

Borough of
Portsmouth

The jury on behalf of the Lord King on their oath present that John Harwood of Kingston in the parish of Portsea in the County of Southampton, yeoman, on the 6th day of November in the 28th year of the reign of our Lord Charles the Second by the Grace of God King of England, Scotland, France and Ireland, Defender of the Faith, etc., and in the year of Our Lord 1676, by force and arms etc. at Kingston aforesaid within the jurisdiction of this Court, made an assault and caused an affray on and upon William Binsted who was then and there in the peace of God and of our said Lord King and then and there beat, wounded and maltreated the person of William Binsted so that his life was despaired of and then and there committed other outrages on the same William Binsted causing serious injury to the said William Binsted, a pernicious example to all others committing such offences and against the peace of the said Lord and present King, his crown and dignity, etc.

2 Recognisances

Burrough of
Portsmo*uth*

1 The fullest form of entry, in English.
S3A/35 (see fig. 3 and no. 41: subject unknown).

Mem*orandum* That on ye twenty eaight day of June 1659 appeared before me Josiah Child Mayor & Heugh Salisbury one of ye Justices of this Burrough Margret Clarke James Austin & Richard Coggs & did acknowledge themselves to bee indebted unto ye keepers of ye liberty of England[75] in ye some of one hundred pounds of lawful english mony to bee recovered of their goods & Chattells, lands & tenements.

The Condition of this Recognisance is such that if ye within bound Margret Clarke doe personally appear before ye Justices of this Burrough at ye next Sessions of ye peace to doe & receive that w*hich* by ye Court shall bee then & there enjoyned her, & that she in ye meanetime doe keepe ye peace towards all ye people of this Commonwealth, & especially towards James Beale of this Burrough, that then this Recognisance shall be voyde or else to Remaine in Force.

Burgus de
Portsmouth

2 The fullest form of entry, in Latin.
S3/5/3 (see fig. 4 and no. 195: regrating).

iiij*to* die Novembr*is* Anno D*omi*ni 1676 coram Samuel*o* Williams Ar*migero* Majore ac S*t* Joh*ann*e Steventon gen*er*oso un*o* Justic*iariorum* ad pacem infra Burgum pred*ictum* conservand*am* assigna*torum* ven*it*

Thom*as* Heather de Havant in Com*itatu* South*amp*ton Lan*ius* et cogn*ovit* se debere D*omi*no Regi in x. l*ibris*.

---

[75] This example is, of course, in the period of the Commonwealth. Otherwise indebtedness would be acknowledged to the King.

Fig. 4 RECOGNISANCE IN A CASE OF REGRATING, 1676 (no. 195). S3/5/3

Sub condicione
    That if the said Thomas Heather shall and doe appeare at his Majesties next Sessions of the peace to be holden in and for this Burrough and the Libertye thereof & doe then and there prosecute and give in evidence against Nathaniell Harwood for regrateing the markett and shall not depart ye Court without lycence Then this Recognizance to be void or else to remaine in full force.

3 An extreme example of the abbreviated entries of recognisances often found in the Sessions Papers.
S3A/124 (see fig. 5 and no. 130: subject unknown).

<table>
<tr><td>Burgus de
Portsmouth</td><td colspan="2">x° Octobris 1665 coram Beniamin Johnson Armigero Majore</td></tr>
<tr><td></td><td>Robertus Reynolds cognovit etcetera</td><td>xx libris</td></tr>
<tr><td></td><td>Johannes Childs</td><td>x libris</td></tr>
<tr><td></td><td>Jacobus Austen</td><td>x libris</td></tr>
<tr><td colspan="2">sub condicione</td><td></td></tr>
</table>

    To appeare at opening of the Law day 24 of October next.

3 Information

Information is the term used for the evidence of witnesses. The evidence of the accused is in similar form but termed an 'examination'.
S3/2/8 (see fig. 6 and no. 162: abusing authority).

Burgus de
Portsmouth
Sessiones

The Information of John Greenaway taken upon oath ye 29th day of 9ber 1671 Before Hugh Salesbury, Samuel Williams & Grantham Wyan gentlemen Justices of ye peace of ye said Burrough.

    This Informant sayth that about a Fortnight since he being Churchwarden of Portsmouth and comeing to ye house of John Moody in Portsmouth to gather ye Rate charged upon him for ye repaire of ye Church the said John Moody complayned

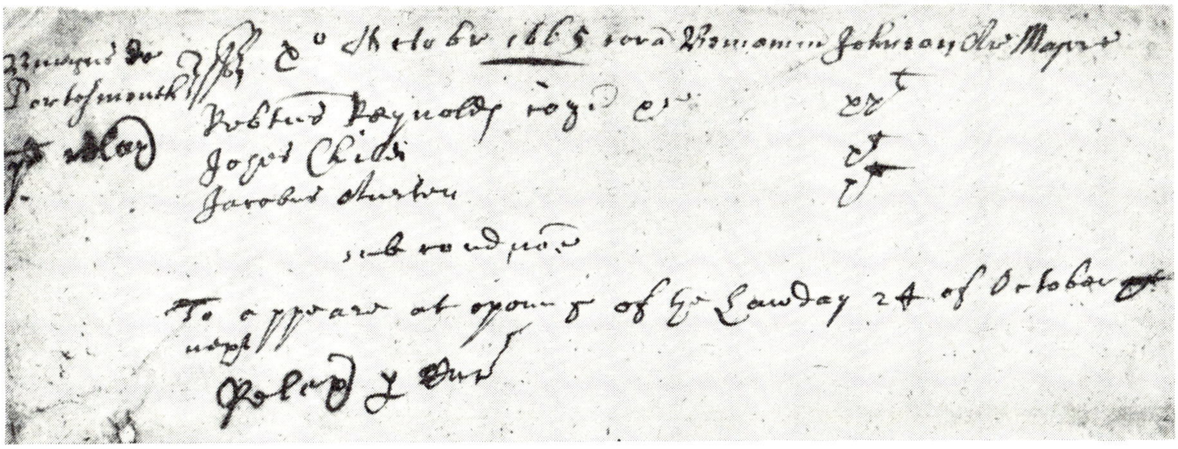

Fig. 5 RECOGNISANCE TO APPEAR IN COURT, 1665 (no. 130). S3A/124

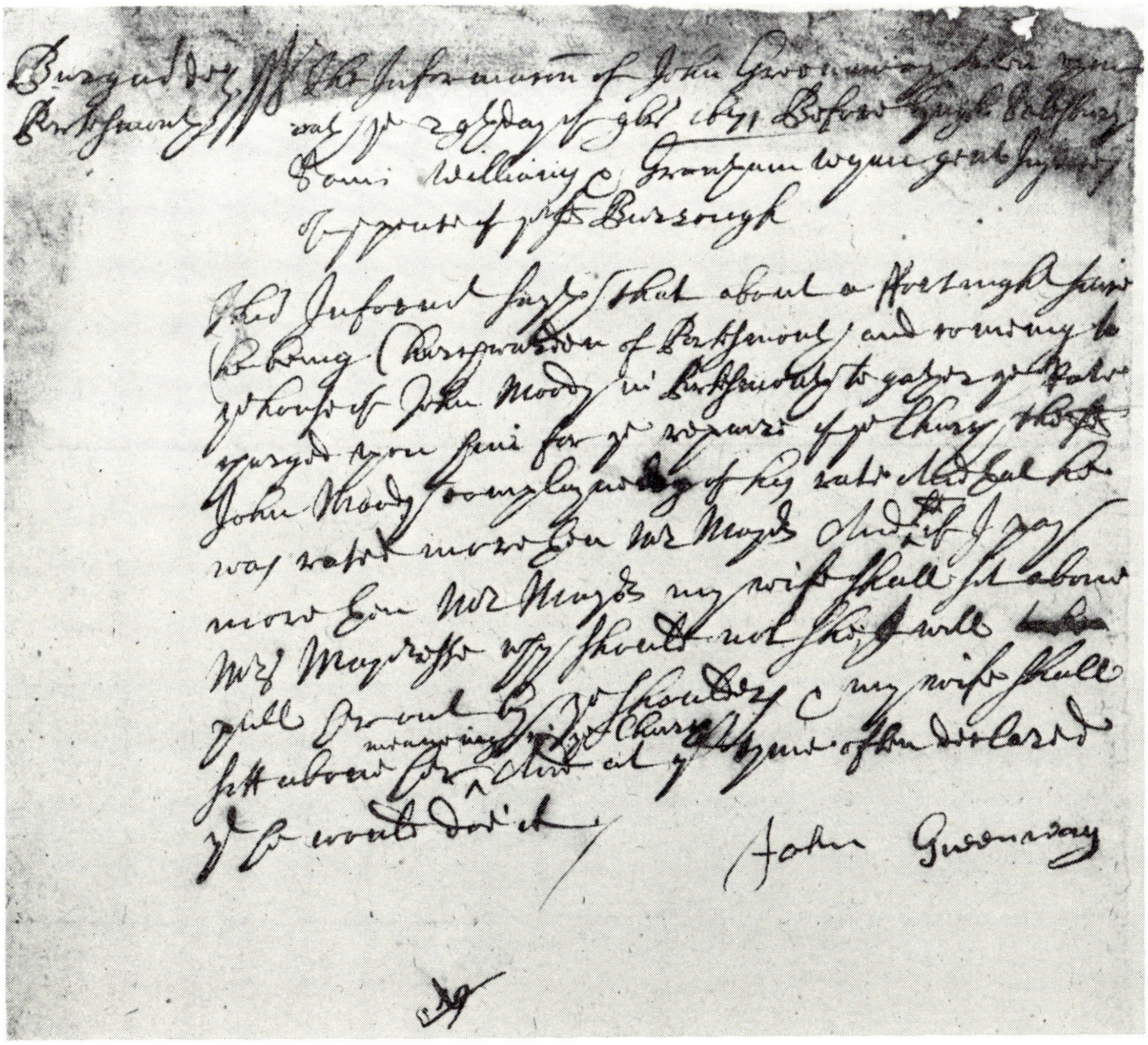

Fig. 6 INFORMATION IN A CASE OF ABUSING AUTHORITY, 1671 (no. 162). S3/2/8

of his rate And that he was rated more then Mr Mayor and said if I pay more then Mr Mayor my wife shall sit above Mrs Mayoresse why should not she, I will pull her out by ye shoulders & my wife shall sitt above her meaning in ye Church And at yᵗ tyme often declared yᵗ he would doe it.   [*Signed*] John Greenway.

4 Memorandum and Sentence, with Certificate of a Seditious Conventicle

D11A/16/20 (see fig. 7 and no. 206).

Burrough of
Portsmouth

Memorand*um* that upon Sunday ye one and Twentieth Octo*ber* instant 1677 Informacon was given unto us Henry Beverley Es*quier* Mayor Samuell Williams & Phillippe James gent*lemen* Justices of the peace of ye said Burrough upon the oathes of Thomas Henning & Thomas Nixon that Richard Drinkewater of Portesmouthe aforesaid yeoman was found by them about Eleaven of ye Clocke in ye forenoone of the same day preaching and teaching in a sedicious Conventicle or meeteing held at a certaine house belonging to William Cozens thelder within ye said Burrough where there were Assembled & met together above ye number of five *p*ersons over & besides them of ye same household every one of them being above ye Age of sixteene yeares & subjects of this Realme to heare ye said Drinkewater who were there Assembled & met together under pretence of Exercise of Religion in other manner then according to ye Liturgy & practice of ye Church of England And contrary to the late Act of Parliam*ent* in that case made & provided Intituled an Act to prevent & supresse sedicious Conventicles. Upon which Informa*ci*on ye said William Cozens being the Lawful owner & proprietor of ye said house wherein ye said Conventicle or meeteing was held is convict before us for that he wittingly and willingly suffered ye said Conventicle & unlawfull Assembley to be held in his said house contrary to ye said Act of Parliament. Wherefore we ye said Justices doe impose upon ye said William Cozens as a fine for ye *s*aid offence ye sume of Twenty pounds to be leavied on his goods & Chattles according to ye said Act. In witnes whereof We have hereunto set our Hands & Seales according to ye direccon of ye *s*aid Act ye day & yeare first above written Anno*que* R*e*g*ni* R*egi*s Car*o*li secu*n*di nunc Angl*ie* etc xxix*no*.

                         [*Signed*] H. Beverley Mayor
                                   Sa: Williams
                                   Phillip James
                    [*The seals once attached are missing.*]

[*The following is appended:*]
Wee the within named Henry Beverley Es*quier* Mayor Sammuell Williams and Phillip James gent*lemen* Justices of the peace of the said Burrough doe according to the direccion of the within mencon*e*d Act Intituled an Act to prevent Sedicious Conventicles Certifye the within men*ci*oned Recorde and Convic*ci*on into his M*aj*esties Sessions of the peace held in and for the said Burrough the eighteenth day of october in the Nine & Twentieth yeare of his M*aj*esties Reigne and from that day adjourned to ye Sixth day of November followeing. As witnes our Hands the Fower and Twentieth day of october Anno D*omi*ni 1677.

                         [*Signed*] H. Beverley Mayor
                                   Sa: Williams
                                   Phillip James.

Another document (D11A/16/21) in almost exactly the same wording names certain people who were present and fines them 5*s* each.

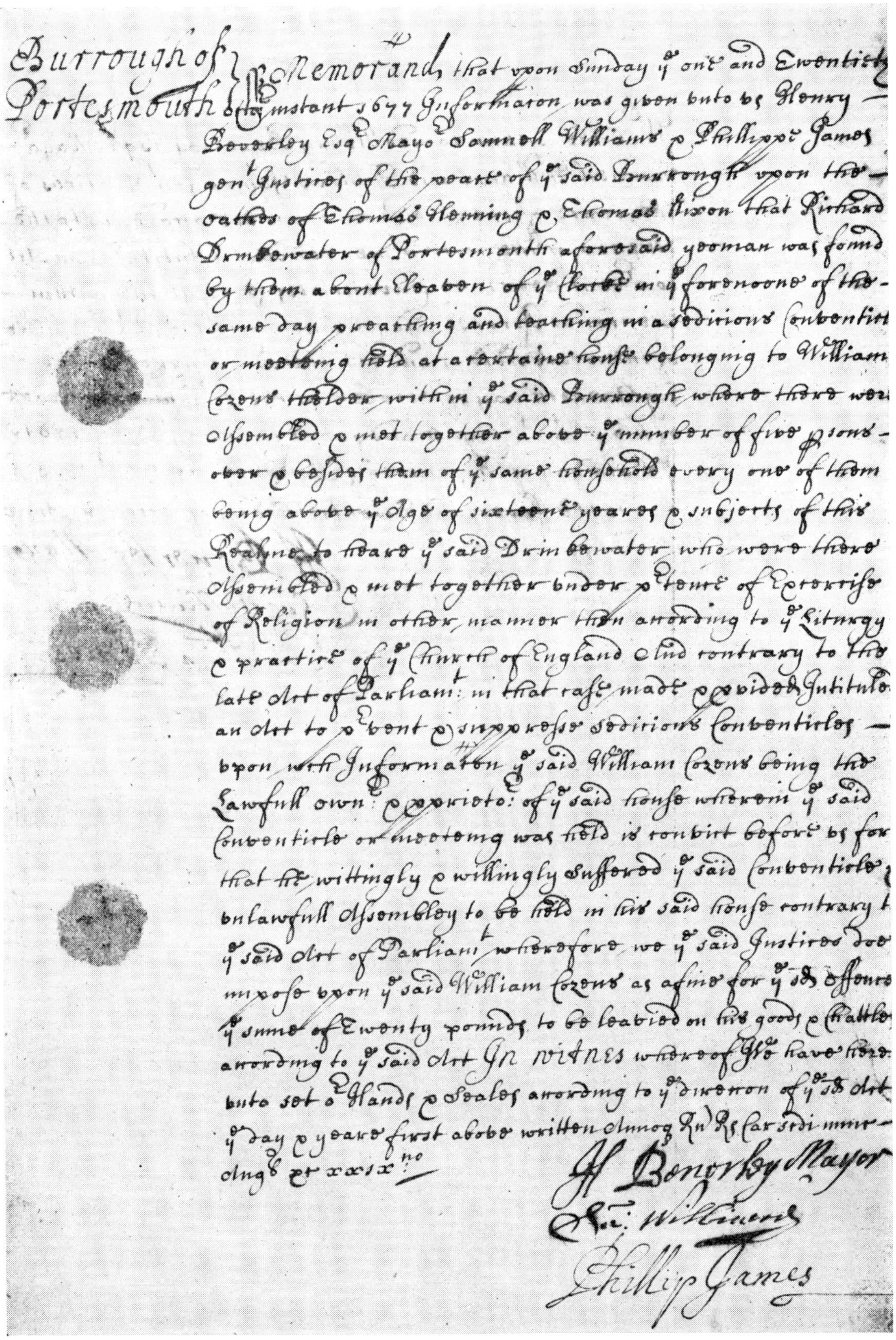

Fig. 7 MEMORANDUM AND SENTENCE CONCERNING A SEDITIOUS CONVENTICLE, 1677 (no. 206).
D11A/16/20

Appendix II

Sessions entries abstracted from Election and Sessions Books

1 Assault (?)

CE1/6, f.40v.
11 January 1652/3. Before Ant. Belbin, esq., and Wil. Wynter, gent.
Recognisances
>   John Hart of Rotherhithe ('Redriffe'), Hants. (*recte Surr.*), in £20.
>   Tho. Thorowgood of Limehouse, Mdx, mariner, in £10.
>   James Cadman of Rotherhithe ('Redriffe'), Surr., mariner, in £10.

For appearance of Hart at the next Sessions for the Borough of Portsmouth and in the mean time to keep the peace, especially towards James Austin of Portsmouth, baker.

2 Assault(?)

CE1/6, f.40v.
21 January 1652/3. Before Ant. Belbin, esq.
Recognisances
>   John Beale in £20.
>   Tho. Marshaw in £10.
>   Ric. Fawlkner in £10.

For appearance of Ann, wife of John Beale, at the next Sessions and in the mean time to keep the peace, especially towards Joan, wife of Ric. Granger.

3 Subject unknown

CE1/6, f.40v.
19 February 1652/3. Before John Holt, esq., Mayor.
Recognisances
>   Paul Richards in £40.
>   John Compton in £20.
>   Tho. Butteresse in £20.

For appearance of Richards at the next Sessions to answer such trespasses and offences as shall be objected against him.

4 Bastardy

CE1/7, f.1.
27 July 1653. Before Ant. Belbin, esq., Mayor, and Edw. Deane, gent.
Recognisances
>   Tho. Hill of Portsmouth, carpenter, in £20.
>   Peter Marden in £10.
>   Edw. Ansell in £10.

For appearance of Hill at the next Sessions. Hill said to be the father of a child Elizabeth Lawrence said she was expecting.

CE1/7, f.6v.
20 January 1653/4.
Memorandum
Tho. Hill now a prisoner for having a bastard child laid to him by Elizabeth Lawrence; see the examination.
See also no. 6 in the main Calendar.

5 Subject unknown

CE1/7, f.1.
28 July 1653. Before Ant. Belbin, esq., Mayor.
Recognisances
>   Geo. Langrish jun. of Portsmouth, blacksmith, in £20.
>   Geo. Langrish sen. of East Dean, blacksmith, in £10.
>   Wil. King of Portsmouth, mason, in £10.

For appearance of Geo. Langrish jun. at the next Sessions to answer trespasses against him.

Footnote: See the examination.

Marginal note: Released by the Court.

6 Theft

CE1/7, f.6v.

17 January 1653/4.

Recognisances

Of Tho. Chilton and Wil. Worthen *as in no. 8 in the main Calendar.*

Marginal notes:

(a) See examination.

(b) Released by the Court by the consent of the parties.

7 Trading irregularly

CE1/7, f.6v.

20 January 1653/4.

Recognisances

Of Lettice ('Letuce') Buck *as in no. 9 in the main Calendar.*

Marginal note: See examination.

8 Bastardy

CE1/7, f.6v.

7 March 1653/4. Before Roger Granger, esq., Mayor.

Recognisances

John Davis of Portsmouth in £20.

Simon Laurence 'of P.', labourer, in £10.

Nicholas Lawrence 'of P.', labourer, in £10.

For appearance of Davis and Elizabeth his wife at the next Sessions and to pay 12*d* a week towards the keeping of a bastard child born to Elizabeth.

Marginal notes:

(a) Elizabeth did appear and was committed.

(b) The said John did pay 12*d* per week.

9 Abusing authority

CE1/7, f.6v.

7 March 1653/4. No name of Justice.

Recognisances

Tho. Tomes in £10.

Ric. Card in £5.

Alex. Carter in £5.

For appearance of Tomes at the next Sessions.

Bound over for abusing the Constable.

Marginal notes:

(a) (*Against Tomes' name*) Sick.

(b) Discharged by the Court and the consent of the parties.

10 Subject unknown

CE1/7, f.8.

10 April 1654. Before Roger Granger, esq., Mayor, Wil. Michell and Edw. Deane.

Recognisances

Henry Crowcher in £20.

John Rockwell in £10.

Rob. Carver in £10.

For appearance of Crowcher at the next Sessions.

Marginal note: Discharged by the Court at the Sessions here 9 Apr. 1654 (*sic*).

11 Subject unknown

CE1/7, f.8.

22 April 1654. Before Roger Granger, esq., Mayor.

Recognisances

John Coke in £10.

James Mills in £10.

For appearance of Debora, wife of John Coke, at the next Sessions.

Marginal note: Discharged by the Court 9 Apr. 1654 (*sic*).

12 Assault(?)

CE1/7, f.8v.

12 May 1654. Before Roger Granger, esq., Mayor.

Recognisances

Geo. Graham of Portsmouth, yeoman, in £10.

Laur. Sannenough of Lewes, Suss., gent., in £5.

John Jones of Portsmouth in £5.

For appearance of Graham at the next Sessions and to keep the peace, especially towards Mary Pay.

Footnote: Mary swore the peace against him.

Marginal note: Discharged by the Court at Sessions held 9 Oct. 1654.

13 Forestalling

CE1/7, f.8v.

8 June 1654. Before Roger Granger, esq., Mayor.

Recognisances

John Ballard of Portsmouth, butcher, in £10.

Rob. Bishop of Portsmouth, yeoman, in £5.

Ric. Stone of Portsmouth, labourer, in £5.

For appearance of Ballard at the next Sessions and in the mean time he was not to 'sell any beer, ale, wine or order, nor in any wise forestall the market'.

Marginal note: Discharged at the same Sessions.

14 Threatened rape

CE1/7, f.8v.

21 June 1654. Before Roger Granger, esq., Mayor.

Recognisances

Wil. Bissell in £10.

Rob. Hawks in £5.

Wil. Walder in £5.

For appearance of Bissell at the next Sessions and in the mean time to keep the peace towards Henry Johnson and Winifred his wife, who had sworn the peace against him. Winifred said Bissell would have ravished her and forced her in the street.

Marginal notes:

(a) (*Latin*) They agreed.

(b) Exonerated by fee.

15 Abusing authority

CE1/7, f.8v.

27 June 1654. Before Roger Granger, esq., Mayor, and John Holt.

Recognisances

Wil. Saynt in £10.

Ric. Joyce in £5.

Rob. Grigge in £5.

For appearance of Saynt at the next Sessions.

Bound over for abusing Mr Peirson in his office; see the examination of Ransted and the Recorder's opinion.

See also no. 10 in the main Calendar.

16 Assault(?)

CE1/7, f.8v.

10 July 1654. Before Roger Granger, esq., Mayor.

Recognisances

John Gallant in £10.

John Coke in £5.

Wil. Lyon of Fareham in £5.

For appearance of Gallant at the next Sessions and in the mean time to keep the peace, especially towards John Cooke, soldier of the Garrison, who had sworn against him.

Marginal note: Discharged at the same Sessions.

17 Suspected felony	CE1/7, f.8v.
	No date.
	Sentence
	Joan Goard committed to prison for suspicion of felony upon the complaint of Ralph Betts. Discharged by the Court by proclamation.

18 Illegal marriage

CE1/7, f.9.

26 July 1654. Before Roger Granger, esq., Mayor.

Recognisances

    Mary Pay, widow, in £10.

    Elizens Godwyn in £5.

    Wil. Collins in £5.

For appearance of Mary at the next Sessions.

'Bound over for being married by a minister, Geo. Graham, and not married by the late Act of Parliament.'[76]

Marginal note : Discharged by same Sessions.

19 Assault(?)

CE1/7, f.9.

2 August 1654. Before Roger Granger, esq., Mayor.

Recognisances

    Dan. Crocker, carpenter, in £10.

    Tho. Dale of Portsmouth, blacksmith, in £5.

    Simon Coward of Portsmouth, weaver, in £5.

For appearance of Crocker at the next Sessions and in the mean time to keep the peace, especially towards Giles Dorman, who swore against him.

Marginal note (Latin) : They agreed.

20 Forestalling

CE1/7, f.9.

17 August 1654. Before Roger Granger, esq., Mayor.

Recognisances

    Ric. Preist of Salisbury, Wilts., chapman, in £10.

    Reynold Saywell of the same, joiner, in £5.

    John Damaree of Whiteparish, Wilts., cheesemonger, in £5.

For appearance of Preist at the next Sessions for Portsmouth.

'Bound over for that he confessed he sold prunes, incle and other haberdasharies on this markett day – vide S[t]at[ute] 1 and 2, P & M.c7'.

Marginal note : Discharged by the Court.

21 Drunken behaviour

CE1/7, f.9.

26 August 1654. Before Ant. Belbin, esq., Deputy Mayor.

Recognisances

    John Wyat, saddler, in £10.

    John Wyat sen. in £5.

    John Prentice of Milton in £5.

For appearance of John Wyat, saddler, at the next Sessions.

Bound over for being drunk and swearing that he would kill his wife, which Henry Lun his man and Margaret Sanders made oath of.

Marginal note : Discharged by the Court at the same Sessions.

22 Disturbance

CE1/7, f.9.

12 September 1654. Before Wil. Michell, gent., and Ant. Belbin, gent.

Recognisances

    Wil. Tayler of Portsmouth, victualler, in £20.

    Wil. Har[v]ey of Portsmouth, rope maker, in £10.

    John Chestle of Portsmouth, brazier, in £10.

---

[76] An Ordinance how marriages shall be solemnised and registered passed on 24 Aug. 1653 (c.6), by which all marriages were to be before a Justice of the Peace and registered by a Registrar appointed in each parish. (H. Scobell, *Collection of Acts and Ordinances made in Parliament* 1640–1657).

For appearance of Tayler at the next Sessions.

Bound over for riding through the town and Garrison at noonday with a trumpet sounding before him and other misdemeanours.

Marginal note: Discharged at the same Sessions.

23 Abusing authority

CE1/7, f.16v.

24 October 1654. Before Fra. Holt, esq., Mayor, Roger Granger, Wil. Michell and Ric. Lardner.

Recognisances
Jonas Goffe in £20.
Alex. Carter in £10.
Edw. Heberden in £10.

For appearance of Goffe at the next Sessions.

Bound over for abusing the jury etc.

Marginal notes:
(a) Continued.
(b) Discharged at the Sessions 8 Oct. 1655.

24 Threatened robbery

CE1/7, f.16v.

25 October 1654. Before Fra. Holt, esq., Mayor.

Recognisances
Tho. Coleman of Newchurch, I.W., yeoman, in £20.
John Carpenter of Portsmouth, labourer, in £10.
Tho. Yong of Portsmouth, labourer, in £10.

For appearance of Coleman at the next Sessions.

Bound over for threatening to rob Wil. Andrewes; see the examination.

See also no. 14 *in the main Calendar.*

25 Abusing authority

CE1/7, f.16v.

28 November [1654]. Before Fra. Holt, esq., Mayor, and Roger Granger.

Recognisances
Rob. Potter in £20.
John James in £10.
Wil. Bissell in £10.

For appearance of Potter at the next Sessions.

Bound over for calling the Constables robbers and thieves in the execution of their office by warrant from the Mayor.

Marginal note: Discharged by the Court.

26 Fornication

CE1/7, f.17.

10 January 1654/5. Before Fra. Holt, esq., Mayor.

Recognisances
Dorothy Hayter in £20.
John Patten in £10.
Wil. Evans in £10.

For appearance of Dorothy at the next Sessions.

Bound over for fornication; see the examination.

Marginal note: Discharged at the Sessions held 8 Oct. 1655.

See also no. 13 *in the main Calendar.*

27 Abusing authority

CE1/7, f.17.

16 January 1654/5. Before Fra. Holt, esq., John Holt, esq., Wil. Michell and Ric. Lardner.

Recognisances
James Mills in £20.
Henry Elzey in £10.
Wil. Walker(?) in £10.

For appearance of Mills at the next Sessions.
Bound over for abusing the Corporation; see the examination.
Marginal note: Discharged by the Court.
See also no. 15 in the main Calendar.

28 Abuse CE1/7, f.17.
26 February 1654/5. Before Fra. Holt, esq., and Ric. Lardner, gent.
Recognisances
  Griffin Jones in £20.
  John Sismore in £10.
  Henry Jenner in £10.
For appearance of Joan, wife of Griffin Jones, at the next Sessions; see the examination.
Marginal note: Discharged by the Court.
See also no. 18 in the main Calendar.

29 Drunkenness CE1/7, f.17.
1 March 1654/5. Before Fra. Holt, esq., Mayor.
Recognisances
  Wil. Worthen of Portsmouth, seaman, in £20.
  Tho. Woodman of Gosport, seaman, in £10.
  John Tege of Portsmouth, seaman, in £10.
For appearance of Worthen at the next Sessions.
Bound over for being taken upon the walls last night and being drunk.

30 Assault(?) CE1/7, f.17v.
3 March 1654/5. Before Fra. Holt, esq., Mayor.
Recognisances
(a) Wil. Boulter of Portsmouth, gent., in £20.
  Edw. Tuke in £10.
  John Hawes in £10.
For appearance of Boulter at the next Sessions and in the mean time to keep the peace towards James Austin, who swore against Boulter, Tuke, Whittington and Gunnet.
Marginal note: Continued.
(b) Peter Tuke in £20.
  Edw. Tuke in £10.
  John Hawes in £10.
On the same condition for Peter Tuke.
Marginal note: Continued.
(c) Edm. Whittington of Portsmouth in £20.
  Edw. Tuke in £10.
  John Hawes in £10.
On the same condition for Whittington.
Marginal note: Discharged by the Court.
(d) Fra. Gunnet of Stepney, [Mdx.], in £20.
  Edw. Tuke in £10.
  John Hawes in £10.
On the same condition for Gunnet.
Marginal note: Continued.

31 Abuse CE1/7, f.17v.
6 March 1654/5. Before Fra. Holt, esq., Mayor, and Roger Granger, gent.
Recognisances
  John Sheppard in £20.
  Tho. Plover in £10.
  John Bartholmew in £10.

For appearance of Dorothy, wife of Sheppard, at the next Sessions; see the examination.

Marginal note: Discharged by the Court.

See also no. 17 in the main Calendar.

32 Assault(?) CE1/7, f.19v.
16 July 1655. Before Fra. Holt, esq., Mayor.
Recognisances
> Fra. Chilton of Portsmouth in £10.
> Rob. Scot of Portsmouth in £5.
> Wil. Hancock of Portsmouth in £5.

For appearance of Chilton at the next Sessions and in the mean time to keep the peace, especially towards Joan, wife of Tho. Wilks.

Marginal note: Discharged by the Court.

33 Assault(?) CE1/7, f.19v.
17 July 1655. Before Fra. Holt, esq., Mayor, Roger Granger, gent., and Ric. Lardner, gent.
Recognisances
(a) John Oakeshot in £10.
> James Austin in £5.
> John Collins in £5.

For appearance of Rebecca, wife of Oakeshot, at the next Sessions and in the mean time to keep the peace towards Grace Whitman.
(b) James Beale in £10.
> James Austin in £5.
> John Collins in £5.

On the same condition for Beale.
(c) Margaret, wife of Ric. Clarke, in £10.
> James Austin in £5.
> John Collins in £5.

On the same condition for Margaret.

Marginal note: Discharged by the Court.

34 Assault CE1/7, f.20.
1 July 1655. Before Fra. Holt, esq., Mayor.
Recognisances
> John Voake in £20.
> Geo. Sargeant in £10.
> John Ballard in £10.

For appearance of Voake at the next Sessions.
Bound over for putting his hands under the stays of Ann, wife of Tho. Hunt.

Marginal note: Discharged by consent of the parties.

35 Assault CE1/7, f.20.
30 August 1655. Before Fra. Holt, esq., Mayor.
Examinations
(a) Swyn Swynson confessed that he beat Tho. Hurleston.
(b) John Slooter confessed that he broke his sword.
(c) Dan. Howe said he saw Swynson with a knife in his hand cut Hurleston's head and draw blood.

Footnote: Discharged the next day.

36 Receiving stolen goods and trading irregularly CE1/7, f.20.
19 September 1655. Before Fra. Holt, esq., Mayor.
Recognisances
> Charity Goddard of Portsmouth, widow, in £10.
> Tho. Goddard of the same, sawyer, in £5.
> Mat. Hacker of the same, cordwainer, in £5.

For appearance of Charity at the next Sessions.

Bound over on the complaint of Ric. Ridge sen. that she had several pipe-staves in her house which it was supposed belonged to the State. She confessed that she had them but did not know whose they were. Also for selling beer without licence she paid 20s and was discharged.

Marginal note: Discharged by the Court.

37 Abuse and disloyalty

CE1/7, f.20.

20 September 1655. Before Fra. Holt, Mayor.

Recognisances

Jos. Rickman in £10.

Wil. Swayne, miller, in £5.

Wil. Pope, miller, in £5.

For appearance of Rickman at the next Sessions; see the examination.

Marginal note: Discharged.

See also no. 22 in the main Calendar.

38 Assault(?)

CE1/7, f.26.

15 November 1655. Before John Tawke, esq., Mayor.

Recognisances

John Noseworthy of Plymouth, pewterer, in £10.

John Mason 'of P.', baker, in £5.

Phil. Rogers in £5.

For appearance of Noseworthy at the next Sessions for Portsmouth and in the mean time to keep the peace, especially towards Sam. Hintey.

Marginal note: Discharged by the Court.

39 Abusing authority

CE1/7, f.26.

19 February 1655/6. Before John Tawke, esq., Mayor, and Ric. Lardner, gent.

Recognisances

Henry Jenner of Portsmouth, cutler, in £10.

John Sismore in £5.

Wil. Yong, glazier, in £5.

For appearance of Jenner at the next Sessions; see the examination.

Marginal note: Discharged by the Court.

See also no. 23 in the main Calendar.

40 Assault(?)

CE1/7, f.26.

21 February 1655/6. Before John Tawke, esq., Mayor.

Recognisances

John Ballard in £10.

Rob. Hawks in £5.

Wil. Bissell in £5.

For appearance of Ballard at the next Sessions and in the mean time to keep the peace, especially towards Nic. Peirson.

Marginal note: Discharged by the Court.

41 Theft

CE1/7, f.26.

10 March 1655/6.

Recognisances

Enrolment of recognisance for appearance of Ric. Ascue.

Marginal note: Discharged by the Court.

See also no. 24 in the main Calendar.

42 Keeping a bawdy-house

CE1/7, f.26v.
19 March 1655/6. Before John Tawke, esq., Mayor.
Recognisances
    Charity Goddard, widow, in £10.
    Peter Harmewood 'of P.', husbandman, in £5.
    Mat. Hacker 'of P.', cordwainer, in £5.
For appearance of Charity at the next Sessions.
Bound over on the oath of Wil. Cozens, Constable, who said she kept a common bawdy-house.
    Marginal note: She is bound over again, see later.
See also App. II, no. 48.

43 Keeping a bawdy-house

CE1/7, f.26v.
29 March 1656. Before John Tawke, esq., Mayor.
Recognisances
    Joan, wife of Tho. Wilks 'of P.', seaman, in £20.
    Ant. Baker of Fareham, husbandman, in £10.
    Mat. Hacker 'of P.', cordwainer, in £10.
For appearance of Joan at the next Sessions.
Bound over for being reputed to keep a common bawdy-house. See certificate on file.
    Marginal note: Discharged by the Court.
See also no. 21 *in the main Calendar.*

44 Assault(?)

CE1/7, f.26v.
10 April 1656. Before John Tawke, esq., Mayor.
Recognisances
    John Venables 'of P.', tailor, in £10.
    Walt. Thurman 'of P.', grocer, in £5.
    Wil. King 'of P.', mason, in £5.
For appearance of Venables at the next Sessions and in the mean time to keep the peace, especially towards Wil. Walker who swore against him.
    Marginal note: Discharged by consent of the parties.

45 Bastardy

CE1/7, f.26v.
17 April 1656. Before John Tawke, esq., Mayor.
Recognisances
    Rob. Rescrowe of Portsmouth, brazier, in £20.
    Sam. Hintey of (*blank*), yeoman, in £10.
    Rob. Hintey 'of P.', brazier, in £10.
For appearance of Rescrowe at the next General Sessions for Hampshire concerning Elizabeth Broade of Brading, [I.W.], who swore before Sir Rob. Dillington that Rescrowe had got her with child.

46 Trading irregularly

CE1/7, f.28.
26 April 1656. Before John Tawke, esq., Mayor.
Recognisances
    Wil. Tayler in £20.
    Ric. Cogge in £10.
    Wil. Ransteed in £10.
For appearance of Tayler at the next Sessions; see the examination.
    Marginal note: Committed.
See also no. 25 *in the main Calendar.*

47 Assault(?)

CE1/7, f.28v.
27 April 1656. Before John Tawke, esq., Mayor.
Recognisances
> Tho. Later of Portsmouth, cordwainer, in £20.
> John Lewin 'of P.', baker, in £10.
> Henry Lun 'of P.', cordwainer, in £10.

For appearance of Later at the next Sessions and in the mean time to keep the peace, especially towards Ann Lymeburner.
> *Marginal notes:*
> (a) Discharged by the Court.
> (b) By [Edw.] Archer.

48 Keeping a bawdy-house and abusing authority

CE1/7, f.28v.
21 April 1656. Before John Tawke, esq., Mayor.
Recognisances
> Charity Goddard in £20.
> Nic. Laurence 'of P.', gardener, in £10.
> John Blender 'of P.', seaman, in £10.

For appearance of Charity at the next Sessions.
Bound over again for keeping a reputed bawdy-house and for abusing the Court at the last Sessions.
> *Marginal note:* Committed and discharged the next day by proclamation.

See also App II, no. 42.

49 Service

CE1/7, f.28v.
1 May 1656. Before John Tawke, esq., Mayor.
Recognisances
> Jos. Rickman in £20.
> Peter Marden in £10.
> Ric. Cogge in £10.

For appearance of Rickman at the next Sessions.
Bound over for living out of service and sent to prison by Mr Michell.
> *Marginal note:* Discharged by the Court, 13 Oct. 1656.

50 Trading irregularly

CE1/7, f.29.
3 May 1656. Before John Tawke, esq., Mayor.
Recognisances
> Wil. Norman of Bristol, seaman, in £20.
> Wil. Earle 'of P.', yeoman, in £10.
> Wil. Coleman of Great Yarmouth ('North Yarmouth'), Norf., mariner, in £10.

For appearance of Norman at the next Sessions in Portsmouth; see the examination.
> *Marginal note:* Committed.

See also no. 25 in the main Calendar.

51 Subject unknown

CE1/7, f.29.
8 May 1656. Before John Tawke, esq., Mayor.
Recognisances
> John Lymeburner in £20.
> Ric. Joyce in £10.
> John Eastman in £10.

For appearance of Lymeburner at the next Sessions. 'See the examinations upon ye Mayor's Book.'
> *Marginal note:* Discharged by the Court, 13 Oct. 1656.

52 Abusing authority

CE1/7, f.29.
19 May 1656. Before Ric. Lardner, gent.
Recognisances
 Rob. Hawks of Portsmouth, innholder, in £20.
 John Collens in £10.
 Peter Goosetree in £10.
For appearance of Elizabeth, wife of Rob. Hawks, at the next Sessions.
Bound over for saying scandalous words against the Mayor that he would hang Jane Goodchild if he could in order to get Rob. Hawk's money that was found on the beach.
Marginal note: Discharged by the Court, 13 Oct. 1656.

53 Assault(?)

CE1/7, f.29v.
27 May 1656. Before John Tawke, esq., Mayor.
Recognisances
 James Newnam of Portsmouth, carpenter, in £10.
 Rob. Newnam of Portsmouth, blacksmith, in £5.
 Mic. Tayler in £5.
For appearance of James Newnam at the next Sessions and in the mean time to keep the peace, especially towards Mary his wife.
Marginal note: Discharged by the Court, 13 Oct. 1656.

54 Fornication

CE1/7, f.29.
23 July 1656. Before John Tawke, esq., Mayor.
Recognisances
(a) Jasper Davis 'of P.', mariner, in £20.
 Ric. Mittins 'of P.', brewer, in £10.
 Wil. Sheppard 'of P.', husbandman, in £10.
For appearance of Davis at the next Sessions.
Bound over for fornication committed with Mary Mittins.
(b) Mary Mittins 'of P.', spinster, in £20.
 Ric. Mittins in £10.
 Wil. Sheppard in £10.
On the same condition for Mary.

55 Assault

CE1/7, f.30.
23 July 1656. Before John Tawke, esq., Mayor.
Recognisances
 John Lane 'of P.', blacksmith, in £20.
 Ambrose Lynn 'of P.', blacksmith, in £10.
 Peter Goosetree in £10.
For appearance of Lane at the next Sessions.
Bound over for striking and wounding Nic. Rich.
Marginal notes:
(a) He owes 6d.
(b) Discharged by the Court, 13 Oct. 1656.

56 Receiving stolen goods

CE1/7, f.30.
4 August 1656. Before John Tawke, esq., Mayor.
Recognisances
 Rob. Hintey of Portsmouth, brazier, in £20.
 Edw. Raye 'of P.', gent., in £10.
 Ric. Powell in £10.
For appearance of Hintey at the next Sessions.

Bound over on the complaint of Mr Ric. Ridge sen. and Mr Josiah Child for receiving iron hoops belonging to the State. Hintey confessed he had 150 iron hoops which might belong to the State but he bought them.

Marginal notes:
(a) Continued.
(b) Discharged by the Court, 6 Apr. 1657.

57 Drunken behaviour

CE1/7, f.30.
26 August 1656. Before John Tawke, esq., Mayor, Wil. Stephens, esq., Recorder, and John Holt, esq.
Recognisances
    Tho. Jones 'of P.', rope maker, in £20.
    John James, gent., in £10.
    John Sismore in £10.
For appearance of Jones at the next Sessions.
Bound over for being drunk in the presence of the Mayor and for striking Capt. Peacock in his presence.

58 Assault (?)

CE1/7, f. 30v.
19 August 1656. Before John Tawke, esq., Mayor.
Recognisances
    John Voake in £20.
    Ric. Voake in £10.
    Ric. Clare in £10.
John Voake to keep the peace towards his wife Phyllis.

59 Contempt

CE1/7, f.30v.
27 September 1656. Before Fra. Holt.
Recognisances
    Ric. Godden of Hambledon ('Hambleton'), butcher, in £20.
    Ric. Bensteed of Wickham, butcher, in £10.
    Tho. Godden of Hambledon ('Hambleton'), butcher, in £10.
For appearance of Ric. Godden at the next Sessions.
Bound over for contradicting the Mayor's order about his standing in the market. James Money to testify.

Marginal notes:
(a) Referred.
(b) Discharged by the Court.

60 Subject unknown

CE1/7, f.31v.
3 October 1656. Before John Comfort, esq., Mayor.
Recognisances
    Wil. Walker 'of P.', tailor, in £20.
    Ric. Joyce 'of P.', butcher, in £10.
    Fra. Lucas 'of P.', cloth-worker, in £10.
For appearance of Walker at the next Sessions to answer trespasses against him.

61 Subject unknown

CE1/7, f. 39.
6 April 1657.
Enrolment of recognisance for appearance of Ann Woodyer.
See also no. 31 in the main Calendar.

62 Keeping a bawdy-house

CE1/7, f.39.
9 May 1657. Before Roger Granger, Deputy Mayor, and Ric. Lardner.
Informations
    (a) Winifred Johnson confessed that last night she broke Wil. Erles' windows.

(b) Mr Newbury and Mr Lucas declared that Winifred was reputed to keep a common bawdy-house and that Mary Elliot was suspected of being a whore living with her.

(c) David Lucas swore that last night he heard Henry Johnson 'swear By God'.

63 Trading irregularly

CE1/7, f.39v.
9 May 1657. Before Roger Granger, gent., Deputy Mayor.
Recognisances
> John Voake in £10.
> James Mills in £5.
> Fra. Gardner in £5.

For appearance of Voake at the next Sessions; for the next three years he is not to sell or retail any beer or ale according to the form of the Statutes.
Marginal note: Discharged by the Court, 12 Oct. 1657.

64 Assault (?)

CE1/7, f.45v.
13 January 1657/8. Before Hugh Salesbury, esq., Mayor, and Roger Granger, gent.
Recognisances
> Step. Carver of Portsea, cordwainer, in £20.
> Rob. Carver of Portsea, cordwainer, in £20.
> Wil. Andrewes of the same, yeoman, in £10.
> John Betsworth of the same, yeoman, in £10.

For appearance of Step. Carver, Martha his wife, Rob. Carver and Sarah his wife at the next Sessions and in the mean time to keep the peace, especially towards Wil. Emes.
Marginal notes:
(a) Continued by the same security.
(b) Recognisance to enter.
(c) Discharged by the Court held 11 Apr. 1658.

65 Subject unknown

CE1/7, f.45v.
2 March 1657/8. Before Hugh Salesbury, esq., Mayor, and Ric. Lardner, gent.
Recognisances
> John Knight of West Cowes, I.W., gent., in £20.
> Tho. Gellet 'of P.', innholder, in £10.
> Tho. Barnard of the same, saddler, in £10.

For appearance of Knight at the next Sessions to answer trespasses against him.
Marginal note: Discharged by the Court, 19 Apr. 1658.

66 Subject unknown

CE1/7, f.47.
22 July 1658. Before Hugh Salesbury, esq., Mayor, Roger Granger and Ric. Lardner, gent.
Recognisances
> Wil. Hawley in £20.
> Paul Richards in £10.
> Geo. Sargeant in £10.

For appearance of Hawley at the next Sessions to answer trespasses against him.
Footnote: See the examination.
Marginal note: Discharged by the Court.

67 Assault (?)

CE1/7, f.47.
31 August 1658. Before Hugh Salesbury, esq., Mayor, John Comfort, Roger Granger and Ric. Lardner.
Recognisances
> Sebastian Watts in £20.
> Tho. Butteres in £10.
> 'Jo.' Nevelock in £10.

For appearance of Watts at the next Sessions and in the mean time to keep the peace, especially towards Millicent Lloyd who swore the peace against him.
Marginal note: Discharged by the Court at the Sessions held 11 Oct. 1658.

68 Assault

CE1/7, f.47.
10 August 1658. Before Roger Granger, esq., Deputy Mayor, and Ric. Lardner, gent.
Recognisances
    Peter Juning in £20.
    James Plover in £10.
    Tho. Balch in £10.
For appearance of Juning at the next Sessions.
Bound over for striking Elizabeth Moore and his dog biting her. See the examination.
Marginal note: Discharged by the Court at the Sessions held 11 Oct. 1658.

69 Disturbing the Sabbath

CE1/7, f.56.
15 April 1659. No name of Justice.
Sentence
'John Bristowe, a Quaker, being committed for disturbing Mr Jackson ye Minister in ye publique ordinance upon the Lords day was discharged by the Court.'

70 Poisoning a dog

CE1/7, f.68v.
8 November 1659. Before John Tippetts, esq., Mayor, and John Timbrell, gent.
Recognisances
    Tho. Rookeley of Portsmouth, apothecary, in £20.
    Cha. Chapman of Portsmouth, apothecary, in £10.
    Nic. Powson in £10.
For appearance of Rookeley at the next Sessions.
Bound over for poisoning Wil. Peck's dog as Peck said.
Marginal note: Discharged by the Court, 27 Apr. 1660.

71 Theft

CE1/7, f.68v.
11 February 1659/60. Before John Timbrell, esq., Deputy Mayor.
Recognisances
    John Tiddersell of Brighton ('Brighthelmiston'), [Suss.], seaman, in £20.
    Nic. Tiddersell of the same, mariner, in £10.
    Zachary Later 'of P.', mariner, in £10.
For appearance of John Tiddersell at the next Sessions in Portsmouth.
Bound over for stealing billet from Nic. Peirson.
Marginal note: Discharged by the Court, 26 Apr. 1660, by consent of Nic. Peirson.

72 Theft

CE1/7, f.69.
11 February 1659/60. Before John Timbrell, esq., Deputy Mayor.
Recognisances
    Tho. Goudge 'of P.', seaman, in £20.
    Tho. Dale 'of P.', blacksmith, in £10.
    Ant. Haswell 'of P.', seaman, in £10.
For appearance of Goudge at the next Sessions.
Bound over for 'being taken in the Roapehouse at ye Dockyard where there was a greate quantity of Cordage stolen away'.
Marginal note: Forfeited.

73 Abusing authority

CE1/7, f. 72.
12 April 1660. Before John Tippetts, esq., Mayor.
Recognisances
    Edw. Archer of Portsmouth, gent., in £20.
    Ant. Haberley of Portsmouth, gent., in £10.
    Tho. Butteres of Portsmouth, innholder, in £10.

For appearance of Archer at the next Sessions.

Bound over for using threatening language to the Mayor, Mr Child, and the Justices sitting 3 Apr. 1660. 'Entered upon ye Court Booke.'

Footnote: A certiorari to remove this recognisance out of the Upper Bench at Westminster dated 13 Feb. 1659/60 returnable fifteen days from Easter. Broughton. 'Endorsed Rec. Newdigate'.

74 Assize of bread CE1/7, f.74.
27 April 1660.
Assize of Bread at 48s per quarter besides the allowance.

75 Abusing authority CE1/7, f.92.
11 October 1661. In Court.
Sentence
Rob. Wilkins said to the Mayor and Justices in Court: 'Do your worst I care not for you!' Fined 20s for disturbing the Court.
See also no. 78 in the main Calendar.

76 Neglect of duty CE1/8, f.31v.
30 April 1666. At the Sessions.
Sentence
Ric. White, one of the Constables, was fined 20 marks for being absent and not providing a deputy to do his duty.

77 Neglect of duty CE1/8, f.38v.
No date [circa October 1666]. In Court.
Sentence
Wil. Clapslooe, Constable of Kingston and Buckland, fined 20s for not attending Court on Michaelmas day.

78 False weights CE1/8, f.41v.
15 October 1666. At the Sessions.
Sentence
Ric. Elcombe of Hambledon was fined £5 for having false weights and committed to prison till he paid his fine and found sureties for his good behaviour.

79 Libel CE1/8, f.52.
18 April 1668. Before Hugh Salesbury, esq., Mayor, Sam. Williams, Ant. Haberley, St John Steventon, Sam. Burningham and Grantham Wyan.
Sentence
Wil. Triggs, who was committed at the last Sessions after he was convicted by the Grand Jury for publishing a libel against the Corporation, was on his present submission fined £5. He was to remain committed till he paid his fine and found sureties for his appearance at the next Sessions.

80 Riot CE1/8, f.71.
12 April 1670. Before Sam. Burningham, esq., Mayor, Hugh Salesbury, Ant. Haberley, St John Steventon, gent., and Sam. Williams, gent.
Sentence
Wil. Yeamett, yeoman, John Farley, yeoman, Ric. Churcher, husbandman, Tho. Hackman, husbandman, and Onesepherus Stanley, husbandman, all of Portsea, confessed that they riotously met together on 24 Dec. last at the house of Wil. Smedmore in Portsmouth called the Fountain and attempted to pull down the inn sign, putting Smedmore and his family in fear. They also admitted that Smedmore paid them 5s on their demand to save his sign post. They were bound over on recognisances to appear at the next Sessions but on their submission they were now discharged from them on payment of a fine of 15 marks and their fees.

81 Assize of bread CE1/8, f.124v.
7 October 1673.
'Mr Mayor doth order the Assize of Bread to be made after the rate of £9 per load and noe more'.

82 Abusing authority CE1/8, f.131.
14 May 1674. At the Sessions.
Sentence
Paul Richards, one of the Burgesses, who was bound over for his appearance at this Sessions and for contemptuously saying that he would not wear his gown while Nic. Hedger was Mayor, appeared and repeated his statement before the Court. For this he was disenfranchised.

83 Abusing authority CE1/8, f.131.
14 May 1674. At the Sessions.
Sentence
Tho. Hancocke, one of the Burgesses, hearing the above (*see App. II, no.* 82) stood up and in a mutinous way began to question the authority of the Court, whether they had any power to disenfranchise any Burgess without the consent of all the Burgesses. For slighting the Court he too was disenfranchised.

84 Apprenticeship CE1/9, f.28v.
18 October 1677. At the Sessions.
Order
John Champion, grandfather of James Willson, who was apprenticed to Tho. Parker of Portsmouth, cordwainer, reported that Parker had left Portsmouth with his wife and family, that all his goods had been seized by his creditors and that no provision had been made for Willson. The Court therefore discharged Willson from his apprenticeship and left him free to place himself as apprentice with anyone else of the same trade.

85 Slander CE1/9, f.29.
13 November 1677. At the adjourned Sessions.
Confession
Nic. Selden of Portsmouth, victualler, said falsely on 22 Oct. last in his own house before Nic. Peirson, gent., Edw. Archer, gent., Rob. Shales, gent., John Pitt, gent., and Dan. Selden that Nic. Hedger, gent., when he was Mayor did more than the King could do without Parliament, in that Hedger levied a tax for building an almshouse. Selden had paid 13s towards it, and he added that some of the money was put to their own use while Mr Archer had £40 to carry out the work. Selden also said that in Mr Hedger's mayoralty he had bought a vessel laden with coal, which Hedger took from him and sold at 7s the calder more than he paid for them. Selden was called before Henry Beverley, Mayor, and examined. He admitted his statements were false and asked for pardon. *Signed.*

86 Trading irregularly CE1/9, f.29.
20 January 1677/8.
Confession
Rob. Shorter of Portsmouth, victualler, admitted that he had sold beer without licence and asked for pardon.

87 Dissenters' conventicle CE1/9, f.29v.
14 October 1677.
Copy of memorandum and sentence *similar to D11A/16/17.* Meeting held in the presence of Tho. Hunt, Ant. Stratton, Rob. Hall, James Arnold, John Chapman, Rob. Gyles and others.
John Hickes fined £20.
See no. 205 in the main Calendar.

88 Dissenters'
conventicle

CE1/9, f.29v.
14 October 1677.
Copy of memorandum and sentence *as in D11A/16/17.*
See no. 205 *in the main Calendar.*

89 Dissenters'
conventicle

CE1/9, f.30.
14 October 1677.
Copy of memorandum and sentence *as in D11A/16/18.*
See no. 205 *in the main Calendar.*

90 Dissenters'
conventicle

CE1/7, f.30v.
21 October 1677.
Copy of memorandum and sentence *similar to D11A/16/21.*
     Ric. Drinkwater is fined £20.
See no. 206 *in the main Calendar.*

91 Dissenters'
conventicle

CE1/9, f.31.
21 October 1677.
Copy of memorandum and sentence *as in D11A/16/20.*
See no. 206 *in the main Calendar.*

92 Dissenters'
conventicle

CE1/9, f.31v.
21 October 1677.
Copy of memorandum and sentence *as in D11A/16/21.*
See no. 206 *in the main Calendar.*

93 Dissenters'
conventicle

CE1/9, f.32.
21 October 1677. By Sam. Williams, gent., and Nic. Hedger, gent.
Memorandum and sentence
Wil. Farmer and James Clifford said that on Sunday 21 Oct. 1677 Ric. Drinkwater
of Portsmouth, yeoman, was found by them at 3 p.m. preaching in a seditious con-
venticle at the house of Wil. Cozens sen. when Rob. Smith, Step. Knowler, Tho.
Crocker, (*blank*) Drinkwater, Tho. Boulton, John Collier and (*blank*), wife of Mic.
Richardson, were present. Ric. Drinkwater was fined £40 for this second offence.
See no. 208 *in the main Calendar.*

94 Dissenters'
conventicle

CE1/9, f.32v.
21 October 1677.
Copy of memorandum and sentence *as in D3A/1/3.*
See no. 208 *in the main Calendar.*

95 Dissenters'
conventicle

CE/1/9, f.33.
21 October 1677.
Copy of memorandum and sentence *as in D11A/16/22.*
See no. 208 *in the main Calendar.*

96 Dissenters'
conventicle

CE1/9, f.33v.
21 October 1677.
Copy of memorandum and sentence *as in D3A/1/2.*
See no. 209 *in the main Calendar.*

97 Bastardy

CE1/10, f.22.

8 October 1685. At the Sessions.

Order

The Overseers of the Poor of Gosport complained that Ann Morlen, widow, had left her bastard child in Gosport without providing for it. Ann had a tenement and brewhouse in Gosport worth (*blank*) pounds yearly, occupied by Wil. Creed, her tenant. Under the Act of 13 and 14 Cha. II, revised by Parliament on 19 May last,[77] the Justices may order the payment of such of the profits of the lands or tenements of the putative father or mother of a bastard child as was needed to maintain it. Therefore the Court ordered Creed as tenant to pay to the Overseers of the Poor for Gosport the sum of (*blank*) shillings monthly towards the maintenance of the child.

98 Bastardy

CE1/10, f.24.

5 April 1686. At the Sessions.

Order

The above order recited. Creed was to pay £4.5*s* a year at the rate of 8*s* a month, but he refused to obey this order. At this Sessions Creed by his counsel asked that the order be annulled, as he said Morlen's tenement was mortgaged for £200 and that the premises were not worth £20 per annum, which would not pay the interest on the mortgage and the repairs to the premises. Counsel for the Overseers said the tenement was worth more than £20 a year and could pay the mortgage interest and the bastardy order. Therefore the Court confirmed the above order.

---

[77] 13 & 14 Cha. II, c.12, An Act for the better relief of the poor. Renewed for seven years by 1 James II, c.17.

Appendix III

Portsmouth Sessions Papers in the Public Record Office (State Papers Domestic)

1 Loss of ship

S.P. 18/68/62 vi[78]

8 February 1653/4. Before Roger Grainger, Mayor, and Tho. Mullins, notary public.
Deposition
Dan. Amcotts and Cha. Hasleton, two members of the company of the frigate Ruby, said that on 17 Jan. last, the frigate met the ship Report of London which was going out of the Channel quarter wind, about three leagues off the Isle of Wight. The Report came foul of the Ruby, so Amcotts and Hasleton went with two other seamen from the Ruby on board the Report to clear her from the Ruby and to put the helm to starboard, where it had been to port. These four seamen and the master of the Report cleared her from the Ruby. On being asked, the master of the Report said there was only 3 in. of water in the hold but he wanted their help to save the ship. They then made for the shore so fast that the Ruby's boat which was coming up could not overtake them. They and the crew of the Report did their best to save the ship but there were not enough men or materials aboard to stop the leaks between wind and water. As they could not save the ship, they took all the company except the master of the Report aboard the Ruby. The Report sank about an hour and a half after the two had been parted. The master, passengers and goods which they then saved from the Report in its boat, they put on board the John and Katherine of London bound for Virginia. The master offered the four seamen of the Ruby his ship's boat and 20s for their pains but they refused the money and only took the boat before going on board the frigate President.

2 Disposal of prize goods

S.P. 18/89/19

6 October 1654. Before Fra. Holt, Mayor.
Deposition
Dan. Bradley of Gosport, mariner, Sam. Williams and Tho. Butteresse of Portsmouth, merchants, said that on that day they had been on board two ships now riding in Portsmouth Camber to survey them. One was called the Magdalen of La Rochelle having in her salt and a small quantity of brandy, and the other was called the Small Nut of Oléron (?'Olonne') having in her salt and some bales of paper. They reported that both ships were leaky and the decks uncaulked as they had been in the harbour over nine months. Much of the cargo was perishing and unless it were landed very soon it would be greatly damaged. *Signed by all three* before Tho. Mullins, notary public.
   Footnote: True copy. *Signed by* K. Whittell, clerk to the Commissioners for prize goods.

3 Theft

S.P. 18/110/31

8 June 1655. Before Fra. Holt, esq., Mayor, and Tho. Mullins, notary public.
Deposition
Frans Jansen-Brower, master of the ship Sampson of Amsterdam, Derrick Reijerse and Jan Jacobsen, two of his company, said that their ship was lately taken by the frigate Tiger commanded by Capt. Gabriel Sanders. After the Sampson was taken, the crew of the Tiger took from her, before she came into Portsmouth Harbour, two small barrels of powder weighing 1 cwt, one pistol, one cutlass, one copper pot, one copper pan and one pewter pot. They also took from the boatswain two pairs of breeches in the pockets of which were 18 guilders, one waistcoat, a sea plait, six shirts and six handkerchiefs. From the boatswain's mate they took a redingote, four shirts, two

---

[78] Of several depositions on this subject, this is the only one taken before the Mayor of Portsmouth. The rest were taken in the Admiralty Court or before the Judge-Advocate.

'pillowbers' and a pillow, one cotton waistcoat, three pairs of stockings, four handker-chiefs and a paper book. From the cabin-boy they took three shirts, one pair of stockings and three handkerchiefs. *Signed; countersigned by the Justice and notary public.*

4 Disposal of prize goods

S.P. 18/112/29
6 August 1655. Before Fra. Holt, esq., Mayor, and Tho. Mullins, notary public.
Certificate of deposition
Dan. Bradley of Gosport, Jeffery Keck, Ant. Clarke and Sam. Williams said that on that day they went on board the ship called Hare-in-the-Field of Middelburg now riding in Portsmouth Harbour, and inspected several packs of linen cloth that were wet and would rot or be greatly damaged unless they were soon disposed of. There were other packs which they could not see but which they believed were very damp.
Signed.

Footnote: True copy. *Signed by* 'Jo.' Digbey.

5 Disposal of prize goods

S.P. 18/112/30
7 August 1655. Before Fra. Holt, esq., Mayor, and Tho. Mullins, notary public.
Certificate of deposition
Dan. Bradley of Gosport, Jeffery Kecke, Ant. Clarke, Paul Hutton and Sam. Williams of Portsmouth, said that on that day they had been in the State's warehouse of Portsmouth to inspect the vessels of oils, sugar and tobacco lately landed from the hoy called the Orange Tree of Enkhuizen and found them all perishing, especially the oils, as they were in leaky and unsound casks. Unless the goods were soon disposed of, there would be much damage and loss. *Signed.*
Footnote: True copy. *Signed by* J. Digbey.

6 Irregular behaviour and drunkenness

S.P. 18/142/32
9 July 1656. Before John Tawke, Mayor, in answer to a letter to the Admiralty Commissioners from Capt. Cowes, commander of the frigate Paradox dated 27 June 1656.
Deposition
Capt. Alex. Farly, commander of the frigate Basing, John Ray, master, John Luist, gunner, Step. Patch, boatswain, Abraham Wells, carpenter, Ric. Dynham, surgeon, John Newton, steward, John Willson, John Painter, Geo. Farly, midshipman, John Burrill, quartermaster, and Sam. Lell, quartermaster, stated as follows:

(1) They denied that on 14 May 1656 their ship the Basing foolishly got in the way of the frigate Paradox when it was chasing a Spanish frigate which they might have taken but for the Basing's intervention.

(2) They did not separate the two ships. At 11 at night on 14 May they saw two ships off Mount's Bay, [Cornw.], lying near together and thought them both enemies. On coming up, they fired a gun and a man on their boltsprit end hailed her. When they got no answer they fired two guns and volley of small shot.

(3) They agree that they saw the candle Capt. Cowes had put in the poop lantern of the Paradox to give notice that they were chasing the Spanish frigate, but when they lit a candle in answer to his, Capt. Cowes took his in, which made them all the more suspicious. They had expected Capt. Cowes to leave his light out till they could definitely identify him.

(4) After the Basing had fired its guns, as soon as they could get their ship about, they did make after the Paradox for about two hours contrary to what Capt. Cowes said, but in tacking they lost sight of him as it was so dark. They therefore steered back to their own convoy in case the Paradox should have come up with it.

(5) Contrary to Capt. Cowes' statement that he put a candle on the poop as he took them to be friends, Capt. Farly said that when he met the Paradox at sea the next day he called to Capt. Cowes who said that the night before a stranger had given him a broadside and a volley of small shot. *Signed by the Justice.*

S.P. 18/142/33

9 July 1656. Before John Tawke, esq., Mayor, Peter Murford, John Tippetts and Cha. Thorowgood.[79]

Examinations

The following seamen of the frigate Basing made these statements against its commander, Alex. Farly:

(a) Art. Day, Rob. Toope and Cha. Whiteing said that Capt. Farly lent their ship's boat to the master of a ship from La Rochelle to carry seven hogsheads of French wine ashore to the vintner who keeps the Three Tuns in Leith, Scotland, such wine being prohibited goods.

(b) James Parsons, seaman and one of the boat's crew, said that they carried this wine ashore to Leith in two lots amongst their empty water casks. The boat's crew received 40s for their reward but he did not know about the captain lending the boat.

(c) Wil. Whaly, another of the boat's crew, *confirmed the above* but said he received his share of only 20s. Ric. Kent, another of the boat's crew, *also confirmed the above statements*.

(d) Art. Day said that Capt. Farly was drunk at Milford, [Pembs.], on 23 Nov. 1655 and when he came aboard asked what ship he was on.

(e) Wil. Smith said that Capt. Farly was so drunk at a house at Popton in Milford (*recte in Rhoscrowther, Pembs.*) that he found him on a chest on his back vomiting. The master's mate, the coxswain and he had to lead the captain back to the boat.

(f) Wil. Simonds, James Parsons, and Cha. Whiteing, seamen and of the boat's crew, *confirmed what Day and Smith said*.

(g) Art. Day said that Capt. Farly drank so much at Kinsale, [Ireland], on 7 Dec. 1655 that he quarrelled with Capt. Bennett and Capt. Bowen.

(h) Day also said that the captain was drunk at Plymouth on 2 Jan. last. John Heydon *confirmed this* and said that the captain had to be led aft to his cabin.

(i) Day then said that on 3 Jan. the captain was so drunk at the Bunch of Grapes in Plymouth that he could not eat the dinner he had ordered, but had to be laid vomiting on a bed in his clothes with his boots and spurs on. Walt. Glenen *confirmed this*.

(j) Art. Day said that on 29 Jan. 1655/6 at Hoylake ('Hillack') in Chester Water there were mustered as men belonging to the ship five men who were really passengers going to Ireland. Some of them to deceive the Muster-Master of Chester at the time of muster put on seamen's caps, and one put on a seaman's coat to hide his linsey buttons.

(k) Art. Day said that Rob. Suttcleife, the captain's brother-in-law, was a midshipman on the frigate Basing. He left the ship at Leith, Scotland, in the middle of Apr. 1655 but nevertheless he was included in the ship's muster at Hoylake on 29 Jan. last. The captain said to the Muster-Master that Suttcleife had just gone ashore with his own son, when in fact this son was with the captain's wife at Milford. Walt. Glenen, James Parsons, Tho. Beeten, Rob. Toope, Cha. Whiteing, Wil. Symonds, Tho. Wilkinson, Ric. Kent, Wil. Blackwell, Wil. Smith, John Haydon, Wil. Whaly and Peter Norington *confirmed this*.

(l) Walt. Glenen said that the steward took from one of these five so-called mustered men a knife and sheath, a pair of scissors, a hawking bag and would have had Glenen, being armourer, take the man's sword as he had not enough money to pay for his food.

(m) Art. Day said that the captain was drunk at Caldy, [Pembs.].

(n) Tho. Beeten, one of the boat's crew, said that on this occasion the captain was so drunk coming from Tenby to the boat to go on board the ship in Caldy Road, he reeled on the sand and fell.

(o) John Heydon said that when the captain came aboard at night on this occasion he invited a merchant called Pepper to come too. Peter Norington *confirmed this*.

---

[79] Only Tawke was a Justice of the Peace. The others were Dockyard officers.

(p) Art. Day said that Capt. Farly was drunk at Pembroke on 29 May last, falling in the street. John Heydon, Wil. Simonds, Wil. Blackwell, Wil. Smith sen., Wil. Smith jun., James Parsons, Tho. Beeten, Cha. Whiteing, Rob. Toope, Tho. Wilkinson, Walt. Glenen, Peter Norington and Wil. Whaly *confirmed this*.

(q) Wil. Simonds and Cha. Whiteing said that at Hoylake Capt. Farly was ashore together with Capt. Blunt and the master of the Basing, John Ray, in a house when Capt. Farly said 'what will not a man doe for money'. He would kill his father for money. He had then only 10s in his pocket but whoever took away that, would take away his soul. Money was his soul. *Signed by the Mayor.*

Marginal note by each statement except (c) : Sworn.

7 Theft

S.P. 29/152/14 i
27 February 1665/6. Before Ant. Haberley, esq., Deputy Mayor, and Wil. Michell, gent.

Information

Godf. Morgan of Portsmouth, rope maker, said that on Friday 16 Feb. by the order of Commissioner Middleton and Mr Salesbury, Justice of the Peace, he was sent to the houses of Wil. Standen and Henry Tovey, rope makers living on the Point. He found in Standen's house seven pieces of 5-in. hawser, a piece of 7-in. hawser, a piece of 9-in. cable and two small 'ratline' coils. The next day he went again to Standen's house with a boat for these goods and took them to H.M. Dockyard but whether any of these goods belonged to the King's ships he did not know.

At Tovey's house he found three coils of new rope which he took to the Dockyard where it was searched and opened by the foreman of the rope yard there and found to be not the King's. They have since been told that this rope had been made by Tovey and his servants. He did not know the boatswain of H.M. Frigate Oxford nor did he know of any ropes or rigging taken from it. *Signed.*

Examination[80]

Wil. Standen of Portsmouth, rope maker, said that about three weeks ago he bought from the boatswain of the Oxford 16 cwt of pieces of old rope which were only fit for paper stuff. He did not know the boatswain's name, nor did he know anything about the coils, piece of cable and piece of hawser mentioned above, but if they were brought to his house or yard it was after he had been committed to prison. *Signed.*

Marginal note (*Latin*) : Discharged.

Footnote: After being examined, Standen who had been in prison was allowed bail and stands bound to answer the above matters at the next Sessions 'thence to be sent to the next assizes for this county if cause so requires'. *Signed by* Tho. Mullins, Clerk of the Peace.

8 Theft

S.P. 29/153/95 i
9 April 1666. Before Ben. Johnson, esq., Mayor.

Informations

(a) John Leverett of Portsmouth, rope maker, foreman of H.M. Rope-yard, said that when he came to work at the rope-house last Saturday morning, 7 Apr., he found the doors of that and the stores as usual locked up, but on entry into the workhouse he missed two bundles or winches of cable yarn, which he knew were there the night before. On searching for them he found they had been rolled out of the workhouse, down the full length of the rope-house and out of the door at the far end. He followed the tracks through the Common field to the workhouse door of Henry Tovey, rope maker, who has a place between the town and the dockyard. There he found the two winches of cable yarn which he seized as being the King's goods and with the help of Tovey's two servants he took them first to a barn and then back to the King's stores. *Signed.*

Footnote: Bound in £40 to prosecute at the next Assizes.

---

[80] This was the case which caused Edw. Archer to be appointed attorney on behalf of the Admiralty Commissioners and got the Mayor, Ben. Johnson, into trouble (see Introduction pp. xxix–xxx, xxxii).

(b) William Leveret, master rope maker of H.M. Dockyard at Portsmouth, said that he knew the two winches of yarn seized last Saturday at Tovey's workhouse were the King's goods because they were spun in the King's rope-house. He had since noticed that the munnion of one of the windows of the rope-house had been forced and a stake head set up on the inside of the window. There were various footmarks by it as if some men had entered that way, but who they were or how they got the goods out he did not know.

Footnote: Bound in £40 to prosecute at the next Assizes.

Examinations

(a) Henry Tovey of Portsmouth, rope maker, said that the foreman of rope makers in the Dockyard sent for him last Saturday to come to his workhouse in the Common field. There he saw two winches of cable yarn which he believed to be the King's goods but when or how they got there he did not know. His servants told him they were there when they came to work early that morning.

Signed by mark.

(b) Edward Feates of Portsmouth, rope maker, said that last Saturday when he came to work at his master's, Tovey's, workhouse, he found there two winches of cable yarn which did not belong to his master. It was an hour before the foreman of the King's rope-house came to seize them. *Signed.*

(c) Tho. Ponnt of Portsmouth, rope maker, said that he was journeyman to Tovey. Last Friday he and three others of Tovey's servants worked at Tovey's rope-ground. Next morning on arrival at work they found two winches of cable which were not there the night before and signs that the door had been forced. They did not report what they had found to anyone. *Signed.*

(d) John Barfoote of Portsmouth, rope maker, said that when he went to work with others of Tovey's servants last Saturday his brother-in-law, Edw. Feats, entered first as he had the key. On seeing the winches of yarn he said to the rest that it was best to say nothing of it until they heard from their master.

Signed by mark.

11 April 1666. No name of Justice.

Examinations

(a) Rob. Sely of Portsmouth, rope maker, said that last Friday night he was at his lodgings near the Mill in Portsmouth with Henry Arnold, house-carpenter. He worked at H.M. Rope-house last Monday but not since.

Marginal note in Middleton's hand: 'This fellow undoubtedly was one of them. His two consorts beinge run away & he was runinge but prevented.'

(b) Ric. Neather of Portsmouth, rope maker, *confirmed what Tovey's other servants said.* He said he was the first to find the yarn and told his Master's brother of it.

Signed by mark.

9 Theft

S.P. 29/232/95 i

9 January 1667/8. Before Hugh Salesbury, esq., Mayor, and Sam. Williams, gent.

Informations

(a) John Leverett of Portsmouth, rope maker, said he was foreman of the rope-yard in H.M. Dockyard. This rope-yard was broken open at night on 16 Dec. last when 3 cwt of tarred yarn was taken away. He had searched several places but could not find it. Last Monday when he was talking to Tho. Damerum, he told him that Tho. Handcocke had said he knew that it had been taken past Widow Roaker's pump in a cart and that it had broken the handle of the pump.

(b) Godf. Morgan of Portsmouth said that last night when he was with Tho. Jones of Portsmouth, rope maker, at the Sovereign, the house of Mrs Hasted, they were talking about the stolen yarn. Jones said that Tho. Hancocke knew where it was.

(c) Tho. Damerum of Portsmouth, rope maker, said that last Friday night he was with Tho. Hancocke when Hancocke asked him how the yarn could have come by Goodwife Roaker's pump in a cart and broken the pump handle.

(d) Tho. Hancocke of Portsmouth, gent., said that he was at dinner at the house of Tho. Jones last Innocents Day [28 Dec.] when John Ayleward of Portsmouth, Constable, came in to search. Hancocke asked Jones why the search and he answered that he thought the Constables had carried his boy to the gaol. Rob. Gyles, who was also there, said that something had been lost from the Dockyard. Hancocke, not liking his company in the room, went out to the kitchen to Mrs Jones. She told him that the thieves brought the yarn in the miller's cart by Goodwife Roaker's pump in the field and turned the cart two or three times round the Common so that no one should find which way the cart went.

Each information signed by Hugh Salesbury.

9 January 1667/8. Before Hugh Salesbury, esq., Mayor, and Ant. Haberley, gent.
Information
Mary, wife of Tho. Jones of Portsmouth, rope maker, said that when she came to her rope-house near the Common on Tuesday 17 Dec. last, about 10 a.m., it being the day after Commissioner Middleton went up to London from Portsmouth, her servant told her that 'the divell had bin at worke that night again' and that a cart had come by Roaker's pump and broken the handle. *Signed by* Hugh Salesbury.

10 Theft

S.P. 29/235/202 ii
2 March 1667/8. Before Sam. Williams, Deputy Mayor, and Ant. Haberley.
Informations
(a) Rob. Smith of Portsea, yeoman, said that last Thursday night when he came in a barge with Capt. Tinker and Mr Steventon to the Dockyard from Sir Tho. Alleen's ship that lay in Spithead, they met a boat in which were two men from the Galloon and the Ostrich hulks. They hailed the boat, seized both men and took them to the Dockyard. They found in the boat a small spliced and decayed old warp, six old lead scuppers, two old grapnels and a small coil of twice-laid stuff.

(b) Roger Sparke of Portchester, yeoman, *confirmed all the above.*

Examinations
(a) Sam. Lenny said that he came with Henry Sparke last Thursday night in a boat from the Ostrich hulk. They had in it a coil of twice-laid stuff which they got from the boatswain of the York, and an old spliced warp which the boatswain of the Revenge brought to them on the hulk and asked them to land at Point. The six old lead scuppers had been brought there from the Montague and the two old Flemish grapnels came from the Revenge, but those who brought them said they were their own property.

(b) Henry Sparke *confirmed what Lenny said.*

(c) Tho. Kirke, carpenter of the Montague, said that his servant delivered five or six old lead scuppers to two boatmen.

(d) Rob. Button, boatswain of the Revenge, said that he took an old spliced warp which he had from a Flemish prize at Calais and two old grapnels which he found adrift 'the first June fight' to the Ostrich hulk for the men to bring to Point where he now lived.

(e) Ric. Driver, boatswain of the York, said he gave to Lenny an old piece of lashing line to make a mooring for his boat.

11 Theft

S.P. 29/255/157 i
10 February 1668/9. Before Ant. Haberly, esq., Deputy Mayor, and Hugh Salesbury, gent.
Information
Tho. Inwood of Portchester, aged about 33 years, said that on the warrant of the Deputy Mayor he searched the house of Edw. Bunckly, seaman, on the Point in Portsmouth, as Bunckly was suspected of being an accessory with others of stealing the King's goods. He found the following:
Cabled (? 'cablott') hawser of 5 in.
Hawser of about 3 in.
Junk about 12 fathom.
1 cwt tallow.
4 boat oars.

When asked, Bunckly admitted that these goods were the King's. They had been put in his custody by the boatswain of H.M. Frigate Pearl because the weather was so bad that no boats could go to the ship. The boatswain would remove them as soon as the weather was fit. Inwood ordered Bunckly to have these goods available whenever the King's officers should demand them, but when he went the next day, 5 Feb., they had all gone. Bunckly said they had gone on board the Pearl.

S.P. 29/255/157 ii
10 February [1668/9]. Before Ant. Haberly, esq., Deputy Mayor, and Hugh Salesbury.
Examination
Edw. Bunckly, inhabitant of Point, Portsmouth, *confirmed the above* but said it was the boatswain, gunner and carpenter of the Pearl who had put the goods in his custody. *Signed.*

Recognisances
    Edw. Bunckly in £20.
    Nic. Person in £10.
    Tho. Grant in £10.
(*No condition stated*).

12 Disloyalty

S.P. 29/382/34
10 June 1676.
'True coppy' *of informations as in D11A/16/12 but signatures of Rainsteed and Brooker omitted. See no.* 190 *in the main Calendar.*

Cosham

HAVANT

Ports-
bridge

WYMERING PARISH

tcombe

Extra-

Parochial

Hayling

Island

on

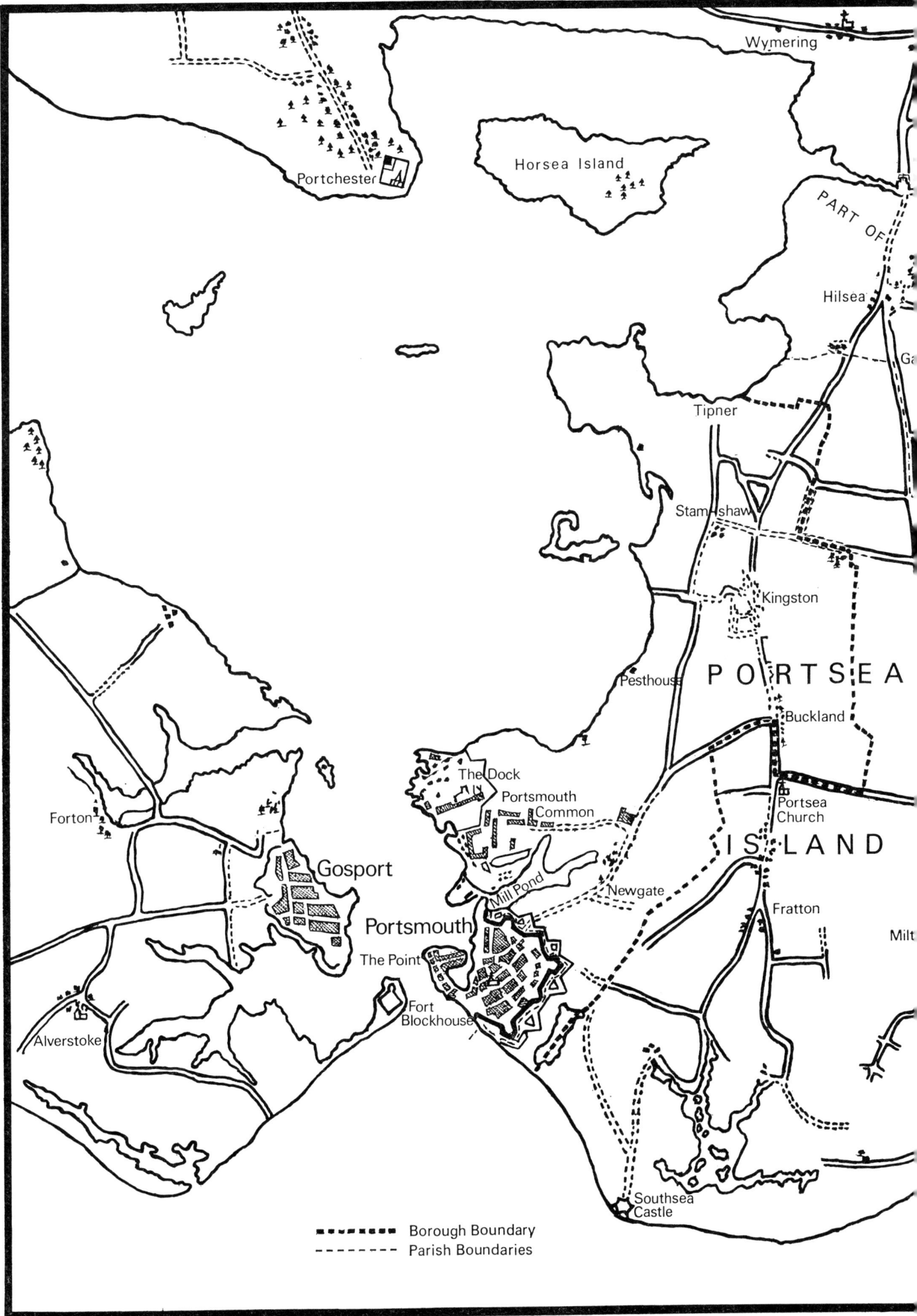

RECONSTRUCTED MAP OF PORTSMOUTH AND NEIGHBOURHOOD based on C. Lempriere's Survey of Portsea Island 1716

Appendix IV

Portsmouth Sessions Paper in the British Museum (Department of Manuscripts, Madden Collection)

Country of origin of ship

Add. MS. 33278, ff.35–36v.

4 January 1664/5. Before St John Steventon, esq., Mayor, and Hugh Salesbury, gent., Deputy to the Farmers of H.M. Customs, in the presence of Ben. Johnson, notary public.

Examinations

Taken under a Commission granted by the Court of Admiralty concerning the ship Hope, 'pretended of Hamburgh', which was taken as belonging to the United Provinces.

(a) Peter Harman Bauher of Hamburg, mariner, aged 33 years, 'speaking English', said that for the past eleven years he had been master and commander of the ship Hope of Hamburg, about 190 tons burden with eight guns. During all this time the ship had been owned jointly by himself, his father Harman Gertzen Bauher, Dan. Dorville, David de Berry, and John Dorville, all citizens of Hamburg. The present voyage began at Hamburg eighteen weeks ago when the ship was loaded by an English merchant with pipe staves and deals. This was delivered at Plymouth last October. On the owners' orders the ship then went in ballast to Nantes in Brittany where several French and Hamburg factors loaded her with 150 tuns of Nantes wine, 35 pipes of brandy wine, 20 pipes of prunes (?'prines'), and five or six small barrels of saffron and some walnuts, all of which were for the use of the owners and other Hamburg merchants as the bills of lading on the ship show and were to be delivered at Hamburg before the frost, but contrary winds made them put into Plymouth where because Dutch ships and goods were being seized, he was stopped on suspicion for some time but released after examination. He then sailed for the Isle of Wight, intending with the frost to winter off Cowes. Twelve days ago when under sail on the backside of the island he was met by a naval ketch and brought on board the Earl of Sandwich, which ordered his ship to be sent into Portsmouth Harbour where he is detained for some unknown reason.

Signed by: Hugh Salesbury, Peter Harman.

Marginal note:

1 Harman Gauetson Backer
2 Dan. Dorvile
3 David de Barry
4 John Dorville and
5 the deponent.

(b) Cornelius Lawrence of Hamburg, aged 39 years, said he was lately taken as steersman of the ship Hope of Hamburg, about 100 tons last burden, of which Peter Harman was master. He was entertained on this ship about nineteen weeks ago at Hamburg, to which city the rest of the ship's company belong. He confirmed the master's statement as to the owners of the ship and of the goods on board.

Signed by: St J. Steventon, Hugh Salisbury, Cornelius Lawrence, Wil. Franckelin.

Marginal note: The rest of the ship's company of the same place.

Endorsement: The Hope of Hamburg, Peter Harmanson Becker master.

1 Peter Harmonson Becker, master.
2 Cornelius Lawrence, steersman.

o

Appendix V

Table of Justices of the Peace in Portsmouth 1652–1688

The names are given in the order they are listed in the Election and Sessions Books. Whether this indicates an order of precedence is not known.

D.M. = appointed Deputy Mayor for part of the year.

* = known to be employed in the Dockyard.

Year	Mayor	Immediate Past Mayor	Other Justices
1652–3	Ant. Belbin	John Holt (Mayor 1651–2)	Ric. James (Mayor 1640–1: died Dec. 1652); Wil. Wynter (Mayor 1647–8: resigned because of age Apr. 1653); Wil. Michell (Mayor 1644–5); Edw. Deane (Mayor 1647–8: replaced James); Roger Granger (Mayor 1642–3: replaced Wynter).
1653–4	Roger Granger	Ant. Belbin (D.M.)	John Holt; Wil. Michell; Edw. Deane (died July 1654); Ric. Lardner (Mayor 1648–9: replaced Deane).
1654–5	Fra. Holt	Roger Granger	John Holt; Wil. Michell; Ric. Lardner.
1655–6	John Tawke, mercer	Fra. Holt	John Holt; Wil. Michell; Ric. Lardner.
1656–7	John Comfort	John Tawke	John Holt; Roger Granger (D.M.); Ric. Lardner.
1657–8	Hugh Salesbury*, Clerk of the Survey	John Comfort	John Holt; Roger Granger (D.M.); Ric. Lardner.
1658–9	Josiah Child, merchant	Hugh Salesbury* (D.M.)	Roger Granger; Ric. Lardner; John Comfort.
1659–60	John Tippetts*, Master Shipwright	Josiah Child	Roger Granger (D.M.); Ric. Lardner (D.M.); John Timbrell D.M.: Mayor 1650–1).
1660–1	Ric. Lardner	John Tippetts*	Wil. Michell; John Timbrell (D.M.); Josiah Child.
1661–2	John Timbrell*, Master Blacksmith	Ric. Lardner	Wil. Michell; Fra. Holt (D.M.); Hugh Salesbury*.
1662–3	Ant. Haberley, brewer	John Timbrell*	Wil. Michell; Fra. Holt; Hugh Salesbury*.
1663–4	Henry Perin	Ant. Haberley	Wil. Michell; Fra. Holt (D.M.: died Apr. 1664); Hugh Salesbury (D.M.).
1664–5	St John Steventon*, Clerk of the Check	Henry Perin	Ant. Haberley; Wil. Michell; Hugh Salesbury*.
1665–6	Ben. Johnson*, Storekeeper	St John Steventon*	Ant. Haberley (D.M.); Wil. Michell; Hugh Salesbury*.
1666–7	Sam. Williams, merchant	Ben. Johnson*	Ant. Haberley; Hugh Salesbury*; St John Steventon*.
1667–8	Hugh Salesbury*	Sam. Williams (D.M.)	Ant. Haberley; St John Steventon*; Ben. Johnson*.
1668–9	Grantham Wyan, surgeon	Hugh Salesbury*	Ant. Haberley; St John Steventon*; Ben. Johnson*.
1669–70	Cha. Chapman (died Oct. 1669) Sam. Burningham of Gosport	Grantham Wyan (D.M.)	Hugh Salesbury*; Ant. Haberley; St John Steventon*.
1670–1	Tho. Plover, butcher	Sam. Burningham	Hugh Salesbury*; Ant. Haberley; St John Steventon*.
1671–2	Phil. James	Tho. Plover	Hugh Salesbury*; Sam. Williams; Grantham Wyan.
1672–3	Nic. Peirson, shipowner	Phil. James	Hugh Salesbury*; St John Steventon*; Grantham Wyan (died Apr. 1673); Sam. Williams (replaced Wyan).
1673–4	Nic. Hedger, mercer	Nic. Peirson	Hugh Salesbury*; St John Steventon*; Sam. Williams.
1674–5	Edw. Archer, notary public	Nic. Hedger	Nic. Peirson (removed owing to disputed election, later re-appointed); St John Steventon*; Sam. Williams; Hugh Salesbury* (replaced Peirson).
1675–6	St John Steventon*	Edw. Archer	Hugh Salesbury*; Sam. Williams; Phil. James.
1676–7	Sam. Williams	St John Steventon*	Hugh Salesbury*; Phil. James; Nic. Hedger.

Year	Mayor	Immediate Past Mayor	Other Justices
1677–8	Henry Beverley	Sam. Williams (D.M.)	St John Steventon*; Phil. James; Nic. Hedger.
1678–9	John Moore*, Master Attendant (resigned on removal to Deptford Jan. 1679) Rob. Shales	Henry Beverley	St John Steventon* (died Feb. 1678); Sam. Williams (D.M.); Nic. Hedger; Phil. James (replaced Steventon).
1679–80	Theophilus Curtis*, Storekeeper	Rob. Shales	Sam. Williams (D.M.); Nic. Peirson (D.M.); Nic. Hedger.
1680–1	John Grundy, surgeon	Theophilus Curtis*	Sam. Williams; Nic. Peirson; Rob. Shales.
1681–2	Tho. Hancock	John Grundy	Sam. Williams; Nic. Peirson; Theophilus Curtis.
1682–3	Nic. Peirson	Tho. Hancock	Sam. Williams (D.M.); Sam. Burningham; Rob. Shales.
1683–4	Isaac Betts	Nic. Peirson	Sam. Williams; Theophilus Curtis; Rob. Shales.
1684–5	Wil. Legg (resigned as needed on King's business Feb. 1685) Ric. Ridge, brewer.	Isaac Betts (D.M.)	Nic. Peirson; Henry Beverley (died); Rob. Shales; Sam. Williams (replaced Beverley Apr. 1685).
1685–6	Theophilus Curtis*	Ric. Ridge	Sam. Williams; Nic. Peirson (died); Isaac Betts; John Grundy (replaced Peirson Apr. 1686).
1686–7	Rob. Shales	Theophilus Curtis*	John Grundy; Isaac Betts (D.M.); Ric. Ridge.
1687–8	John Grundy	Rob. Shales	Tho. Hancock (D.M.); Isaac Betts; Ric. Ridge.

Appendix VI
Table of Statutes referred to in the Introduction and Calendar

For individual references see the Index, under Acts of Parliament. The titles of the Acts are those given in *The Statutes of the Realm* (9v. and index, 1810–28).

13th cent.	Sometimes referred to as 51 Henry III, c.6	The Assize of Bread and Ale [known also as the Statute of Pillory and Tumbrel]; amended by An additional Act for ascertaining the measures of corn and salt (22 & 23 Cha. II, c.12).
1285	13 Edw. I	The Statute of Winchester.
1344	18 Edw. III, st.2, c.2	[Appointment and authority of Keepers of the Peace.]
1352	25 Edw. III, st.5, c.2	[Definition of treason.]
1360	34 Edw. III, c.1	[Appointment and authority of Justices of the Peace.]
1414	2 Henry V, st.1, c.4	[Powers and sessions of Justices of the Peace.]
1487	3 Henry VII, c.3	An Act that Justices of Peace may take bail.
1541	33 Henry VIII, c.9	An Act for maintenance of artillery and debarring of unlawful games.
1552	5 & 6 Edw. VI, c.14	An Act against regraters, forestallers and engrossers.
1554	1 & 2 Phil. & Mary, c.7	An Act that persons dwelling in the country shall not sell divers wares in cities and towns corporate by retail.
1554	1 & 2 Phil. & Mary, c.13	An Act appointing an order to Justices of Peace for the bailment of prisoners.
1555	2 & 3 Phil. & Mary, c.18	An Act touching commissions of the peace and gaol delivery in towns corporate, not being counties in themselves.
1563	5 Elizabeth I, c.4	An Act touching divers orders for artificers, labourers, servants of husbandry and apprentices.
1575	18 Elizabeth I, c.3	An Act for the setting of the poor on work and for the avoiding of idleness.
1576	18 Elizabeth I, c.7	An Act to take away clergy from the offenders in rape and burglary and an order for the delivery of clerks convict without purgation.
1601	43 Elizabeth I, c.2	An Act for the relief of the poor.
1603	1 James I, c.6	An Act made for the explanation of the Statute made in the 5th year of the late Queen Elizabeth's reign concerning labourers.
1609	7 James I, c.4	An Act for the due execution of divers laws and statutes heretofore made against rogues, vagabonds and sturdy beggars and other lewd and idle persons.

178

1623	21 James I, c.22	An Act concerning the traders of butter and cheese.
1653	c.6[81]	An Ordinance how marriages shall be solemnised, as also a register for births and burials.
1660	12 Cha. II, c.11	An Act of free and general pardon, indemnity and oblivion.
1661	13 Cha. II, st.2, c.1	An Act for the well governing and regulating of corporations.
1662	13 & 14 Cha. II, c.12	An Act for the better relief of the poor of this kingdom; renewed for seven years by An Act for reviving and continuance of several Acts of Parliament therein mentioned (1 James II, c.17).
1670	22 Cha. II, c.1	An Act to prevent and suppress seditious conventicles.
1677	29 Cha. II, c.7	An Act for the better observation of the Lord's Day, commonly called Sunday.

---

[81] All Acts passed in the Commonwealth period 1642–1660 were declared invalid by implication by the Act for the confirmation of judicial proceedings, 12 Cha. II, c.12.

Appendix VII
Concordance of Document Numbers

Over the centuries the original Sessions Papers have got scattered. This concordance is designed to show the position of each document in the text.

Office No.	Text No.	Office No.	Text No.	Office No.	Text No.
D3A/1/2	209	S3/1/6	154	S3/4/1	181
D3A/1/3	208	S3/1/7	153	S3/4/2 (entry i)	182
		S3/1/8	152	(entry ii)	183
D11A/16/1	13	S3/1/9	151	S3/4/3	180
D11A/16/2	21	S3/1/10	149	S3/4/4	180
D11A/16/3	32	S3/1/11	150	S3/4/5	184
D11A/16/4	80	S3/1/12	147	S3/4/6	186
D11A/16/5	97	S3/1/13	146		
D11A/16/6	167			S3/5/1	193
D11A/16/7	159	S3/2/1	155	S3/5/2	194
D11A/16/8	173	S3/2/2	160	S3/5/3	195
D11A/16/9	185	S3/2/3	160	S3/5/4	195
D11A/16/10	188	S3/2/4	159	S3/5/5	195
D11A/16/11	188	S3/2/5	169	S3/5/6	196
D11A/16/12	190	S3/2/6	163	S3/5/7	197
D11A/16/13	192	S3/2/7	164	S3/5/8	199
D11A/16/14	195	S3/2/8	162	S3/5/9	196
D11A/16/15	200	S3/2/9	162	S3/5/10	201
D11A/16/16	203	S3/2/10	157	S3/5/11	197
D11A/16/17	205	S3/2/11	165	S3/5/12	204
D11A/16/18	205	S3/2/12	156	S3/5/13	197
D11A/16/19 (entry i)	206	S3/2/13	166	S3/5/14	199
(entry ii)	207	S3/2/14	166	S3/5/15	198
D11A/16/20	206	S3/2/15	160	S3/5/16	201
D11A/16/21	206	S3/2/16	160	S3/5/17	202
D11A/16/22	208	S3/2/17	159	S3/5/18	202
D11A/16/23	210	S3/2/18	161	S3/5/19	202
D11A/16/24	210			S3/5/20	203
D11A/16/25	211	S3/3/1	168	S3/5/21	197
D11A/16/26	213	S3/3/2	178	S3/5/22	198
D11A/16/27	287	S3/3/3	177		
D11A/16/28	304	S3/3/4	179	S3/6/1	216
D11A/16/29	313	S3/3/5	179	S3/6/2	222
D11A/16/30	359	S3/3/6	179	S3/6/3	221
D11A/16/31 – No document with this number exists.		S3/3/7	179	S3/6/4	215
		S3/3/8	178	S3/6/5	223
D11A/16/32	417	S3/3/9	179	S3/6/6	224
		S3/3/10	177	S3/6/7	225
D22A/1/7	52	S3/3/11	177	S3/6/8	226
D22A/1/8a,b,c	60	S3/3/12	175	S3/6/9	227
D22A/1/9	94	S3/3/13	175	S3/6/10 (entry i)	228
		S3/3/14	176	(entry ii)	229
		S3/3/15	174	S3/6/11	228
S3/1/1	149	S3/3/16	174	S3/6/12	230
S3/1/2	149	S3/3/17	158	S3/6/13	231
S3/1/3	148	S3/3/18	172	S3/6/14	231
S3/1/4	145	S3/3/19	170	S3/6/15	232
S3/1/5	144	S3/3/20	171	S3/6/16	231

Office No.	Text No.	Office No.	Text No.	Office No.	Text No.
S3/6/17	221	S3/8/1	281	S3/11/5	332
S3/6/18	223	S3/8/2	279	S3/11/6	331
S3/6/19	228	S3/8/3	284	S3/11/7	333
S3/6/20	230	S3/8/4 (entry i)	282	S3/11/8	334
S3/6/21	233	(entry ii)	283	S3/11/9	335
S3/6/22	233	S3/8/5	278	S3/11/10	337
S3/6/23	236	S3/8/6	280	S3/11/11	337
S3/6/24 (entry i)	234	S3/8/7	277	S3/11/12	338
(entry ii)	235	S3/8/8	276	S3/11/13	338
S3/6/25	237	S3/8/9	275	S3/11/14	341
S3/6/26	238	S3/8/10	273	S3/11/15	339
S3/6/27	238	S3/8/11	274	S3/11/16	340
S3/6/28	239	S3/8/12	271	S3/11/17	342
S3/6/29	240	S3/8/13	272	S3/11/18 (entry i)	345
S3/6/30	241			(entry ii)	346
S3/6/31	242	S3/9/1	298	S3/11/19	336
S3/6/32	243	S3/9/2	297	S3/11/20	333
S3/6/33	244	S3/9/3	298	S3/11/21	343
S3/6/34	245	S3/9/4	295	S3/11/22	344
S3/6/35	246	S3/9/5	294		
S3/6/36	247	S3/9/6	296	S3/12/1	350
S3/6/37	249	S3/9/7	296	S3/12/2	348
S3/6/38	250	S3/9/8	292	S3/12/3	352
S3/6/39	251	S3/9/9	291	S3/12/4	351
S3/6/40	252	S3/9/10	290	S3/12/5	353
S3/6/41	253	S3/9/11	288	S3/12/6	353
S3/6/42	248	S3/9/12	289	S3/12/7	358
S3/6/43	245	S3/8/13	286	S3/12/8	355
S3/6/44	255	S3/9/14	285	S3/12/9	349
S3/6/45	256	S3/9/15	285	S3/12/10	357
S3/6/46	253			S3/12/11	356
S3/6/47	249	S3/10/1	319	S3/12/12	360
S3/6/48	254	S3/10/2 (entry i)	320	S3/12/13	363
S3/6/49	345	(entry ii)	322	S3/12/14	361
S3/6/50	236	(entry iii)	321	S3/12/15	362
S3/6/51	214	S3/10/3	323	S3/12/16	347
S3/6/52	215	S3/10/4	318	S3/12/17	364
S3/6/53	217	S3/10/5	326	S3/12/18	354
S3/6/54	219	S3/10/6	317	S3/12/19	365
S3/6/55	220	S3/10/7	312	S3/12/20	362
S3/6/56	218	S3/10/8	316	S3/12/21	353
		S3/10/9	314	S3/12/22	423
S3/7/1	269	S3/10/10	315	S3/12/23	360
S3/7/2	258	S3/10/11	311	S3/12/24	353
S3/7/3	267	S3/10/12 (entry i)	309	S3/12/25	352
S3/7/4	270	(entry ii)	310	S3/12/26	416
S3/7/5	264	S3/10/13	308		
S3/7/6	268	S3/10/14	308	S3/13/1	386
S3/7/7	267	S3/10/15	307	S3/13/2	374
S3/7/8	266	S3/10/16	306	S3/13/3	375
S3/7/9	266	S3/10/17	305	S3/13/4	370
S3/7/10	265	S3/10/18	302	S3/13/5 (entry i)	367
S3/7/11	265	S3/10/19	299	(entry ii)	368
S3/7/12	262	S3/10/20	300	S3/13/6	366
S3/7/13	269			S3/13/7 (entry i)	369
S3/7/14	263	S3/11/1	327	(entry ii)	367
S3/7/15	261	S3/11/2	329	S3/13/8	385
S3/7/16	260	S3/11/3	328	S3/13/9	381
S3/7/17	259	S3/11/4	330	S3/13/10	382

Office No.	Text No.	Office No.	Text No.	Office No.	Text No.
S3/13/11	378	S3A/4	5	S3A/59	68
S3/13/12	376	S3A/5	6	S3A/60	69
S3/13/13	371	S3A/6	7	S3A/61	70
S3/13/14	373	S3A/7	8	S3A/62	71
S3/13/15	375	S3A/8	9	S3A/63	72
S3/13/16	387	S3A/9	10	S3A/64	72
		S3A/10	11	S3A/65	73
		S3A/11	12	S3A/66	73
S3/14/1 (entry i)	389	S3A/12	15	S3A/67	74
(entry ii)	390	S3A/13	17	S3A/68	75
S3/14/2	392	S3A/14	19	S3A/69	76
S3/14/3	391	S3A/15	20	S3A/70	77
S3/14/4	393	S3A/16	22	S3A/71	79
S3/14/5	396	S3A/17	23	S3A/72	78
S3/14/6	405	S3A/18	24	S3A/73	81
S3/14/7	393	S3A/19	25	S3A/74	82
S3/14/8	401	S3A/20	26	S3A/75 – No document with
S3/14/9	406	S3A/21	27	this number exists.
S3/14/10	405	S3A/22	27	S3A/76	83
S3/14/11	395	S3A/23	28	S3A/77	84
S3/14/12	404	S3A/24	29	S3A/78	85
S3/14/13	409	S3A/25	30	S3A/79	85
S3/14/14	399	S3A/26	28	S3A/80	87
S3/14/15	397	S3A/27	31	S3A/81	87
S3/14/16	402	S3A/28	33	S3A/82	88
S3/14/17	400	S3A/29	34	S3A/83	89
S3/14/18	394	S3A/30	35	S3A/84	90
S3/14/19	398	S3A/31	36	S3A/85	90
S3/14/20	410	S3A/32	37	S3A/86	91
S3/14/21	408	S3A/33	38	S3A/87	92
S3/14/22	405	S3A/34 (entry i)	39	S3A/88	92
S3/14/23	301	(entry ii)	40	S3A/89	93
S3/14/24	303	S3A/35	41	S3A/90	94
S3/14/25	324	S3A/36 (entry i)	43	S3A/91	95
S3/14/26	325	(entry ii)	44	S3A/92	96
S3/14/27	393	S3A/37	42	S3A/93 (entry i)	98
S3/14/28	393	S3A/38	46	(entry ii)	99
S3/14/29	403	S3A/39	43	S3A/94	100
		S3A/40	45	S3A/95 (entry i)	101
		S3A/41	47	(entry ii)	109
S3/15/1	416	S3A/42	49	S3A/96	102
S3/15/2	416	S3A/43 (entry i)	53	S3A/97	103
S3/15/3	stub	(entry ii)	51	S3A/98	104
S3/15/4	418	S3A/44	54	S3A/99	105
S3/15/5	417	S3A/45	55	S3A/100	106
S3/15/6	422	S3A/46	56	S3A/101	107
S3/15/7	419	S3A/47	58	S3A/102	108
S3/15/8	411	S3A/48 (entry i)	56	S3A/103	110
S3/15/9	412	(entry ii)	57	S3A/104	113
S3/15/10	413	S3A/49	50	S3A/105	112
S3/15/11	414	S3A/50	59	S3A/106	112
S3/15/12	415	S3A/51	61	S3A/107	112
		S3A/52	62	S3A/108	114
		S3A/53	63	S3A/109	111
S3A/1	56	S3A/54	64	S3A/110	115
S3A/2 (entry i)	1	S3A/55	65	S3A/111	121
(entry ii)	2	S3A/56	66	S3A/112	116
(entry iii)	3	S3A/57	66	S3A/113 (entry i)	119
S3A/3	4	S3A/58	67	(entry ii)	120

Office No.	Text No.	Office No.	Text No.	Office No.	Text No.
S3A/114 (entry i)	117	S3A/137	142	S3B/22	292
(entry ii)	118	S3A/138	143	S3B/23	289
S3A/115	124			S3B/24	293
S3A/116	124	S3B/1	14	S3B/25	353
S3A/117	122	S3B/2	16	S3B/26	353
S3A/118	123	S3B/3	18	S3B/27	372
S3A/119	125	S3B/4	39	S3B/28	381
S3A/120	126	S3B/5	48	S3B/29	377
S3A/121	127	S3B/6	86	S3B/30	379
S3A/122	128	S3B/7	89	S3B/31	380
S3A/123	129	S3B/8	164	S3B/32	383
S3A/124	130	S3B/9	156	S3B/33 – back sheet to S3B/15	
S3A/125	131	S3B/10	187	S3B/34	366
S3A/126	133	S3B/11	189	S3B/35	387
S3A/127	132	S3B/12	189	S3B/36	388
S3A/128	132	S3B/13	191	S3B/37	392
S3A/129	134	S3B/14	203	S3B/38	395
S3A/130	135	S3B/15	212	S3B/39	407
S3A/131	138	S3B/16	216	S3B/40	94
S3A/132	136	S3B/17	266	S3B/41	420
S3A/133	139	S3B/18	257	S3B/42	384
S3A/134	140	S3B/19	258	S3B/43	421
S3A/135	137	S3B/20	263	S3B/44	423
S3A/136	141	S3B/21	266	S3B/45	424

Glossary

1 Obsolete English words found in the Sessions Papers

BARRATOR: fraudulent dealer

HILFE: handle

HOUSE OF OFFICE: privy

INCLE: tape

KEVER: kerchief

PILLOWBER: pillow case

PRUNES: (a) trimming (App. II 20)
       (b) prune plum as in modern usage (App. IV 1)

SKILLING: small addition to a cottage

SURREVRANCE: dung

TRUGG: harlot

2 Legal words and phrases

BIL: true bill, i.e. the presentment is proved true.

IGNORAMUS: we take no notice, i.e. the evidence is too weak to proceed further with the case.

NON CUL: plea of 'Not guilty'. 'Cul' or 'non cul' is frequently found written on presentments against the name of the accused. In a presentment of later date than this volume the note is 'placitat non cul' (he pleads not guilty) so 'cul' seems to stand for *culpabilis*, guilty. This seems preferable to *culprit* which has been defined as the prisoner at the bar after a plea of not guilty (*Dictionary of English Law*, ed. Earl Jowitt (1959)); *culpatus* would mean much the same. However, in no. 388 (14) 'non cul' could imply a verdict of 'Not guilty'.

PROSECUTE HIS TRAVERSE: make his defence to the accusation

WRIT OF CERTIORARI: order to transfer a case from a lower court to a court at Westminster

3 Unrecorded Latin words found in the Sessions Papers

The following words are to be found in neither R. E. Latham, Revised medieval Latin word-list (1965) nor C. T. Lewis and C. Short, Latin dictionary (1879). They are found in both Latin and English in presentments but have been translated in the text.

AGIGNATOR: petty chapman

ARCHITECTUS: house-carpenter

CULTRUS: knife

NAFRAGIUS, NAUFRANGIUS: shipwright. This can only be translated by deduction. It hardly seems that the classical meaning of *naufragus*, a shipwrecked person, can be applied, nor that it could be stretched to mean a ship-breaker. Tho. Crews, called *nafragius* in no. 366, is called *shipwright* in no. 355. Ben. Upjohn, also called *nafragius* in no. 393, is similarly *shipwright* later in the same case. The word seems to be the equivalent of *naupegus*, a shipwright, and has been so translated with the Latin form in brackets.

PASTRION: ornament

QUADRIFIDUM: fork

SALSAMENTUM: salt fish

STENQUILINEA: laystall, dung heap

Index

1 References to the Introduction are by pages, in roman numerals; all other references are to entry numbers.

2 No attempt is made to differentiate between persons bearing the same name, except where a person is identified by a description in italics. Persons named by forename only are listed at the end of the Index.

3 Outside the vicinity of Portsmouth, place-names are normally entered under the parishes existing at the time of the record. Cross-references to these are given from the name of the county (for England and Wales) or country.

4 The following subject headings are used in the Index, as well as others to which cross-references are given: administration, local; administration, national; aliens; antiquities; Army; articles of utility; arts; buildings and grounds; Church, clergy and religion; documents and diplomatic; drainage; education; fauna; flora; folklore and customs; food and drink; games and entertainments; industry and production; languages; law and justice; medicine; Navy; newspapers; political activity; trade and commerce; transport and communications; war and rebellion.

392; Recorder, pp. xxvii, xxx–xxxi, 73, App. II 15, *see also* Biggs, Sir John; Stevens, Wil.; mock recorder, 395; Sergeant-at-Mace, 53n, 164, 173, 190, 216, App. III 12; Surveyor of Highways, 10.

— local officers, Hampshire: Lord Lieutenant, 380; Sheriff, 360n; Sheriff's officers, 189.

— other local officers: Exeter, Mayor, 46; Gosport, Constable, p. xxxiii, nos 304, 403; Gosport, Overseers of the Poor, 326, App. II 97; Havant, Constable, 16; Kingston and Buckland, Constable, 197, App. II 77; Owslebury, Collector, 381; Portsea, parish officers, p. xxix; Romsey, Mayor, 381; Woolwich, Overseers of the Poor, 241.

— *see also* accounts; apprenticeship; Assize of Bread; Church, clergy and religion; Coroner's inquests; documents and diplomatic; fairs and markets; Hearth Tax; law and justice; poor-law; Quarter Sessions; rents; roads and road transport.

administration, national: government informer, 60; marking government property with broad arrow, 86, 90, 115; *see also* Acts of Parliament; Admiralty; Army; Assizes; Chancery, Common Pleas; Customs and Excise; documents and diplomatic; Hearth Tax; King's Bench; law and justice; Navy; newspapers; oaths; Parliament; Proclamations; Public Record Office; war and rebellion; writs.

Admiralty, Court of, App. III 1 n, App. IV.

Africa, *place indexed*, Guinea.

agriculture: common fields, 82; driving the common fields, 177, 388; other fields 97, 177, 197; green lane, 48; dung, 300, 325; haymaking, 192, 269; harvesting, 46, 60, 161; gleaning, 182, 185; other farm-work, 187; *see also* corn; occupations.

Alcocke, Tho., 50.

Alcorne (Alchorne), —, 97.
　Ric., 187.

Alden, *see* Aulden.

Aldridge (Aldred, Aldrige, Alldridge), David, 315.
　John, 96.
　Tho., 308.

ale, *see* beer and ale.

Aleme, *see* Allum.

Alford, Edw., 329.
　Elizabeth, 324.
　Henry, p. xxv, nos. 237, 256.
　John, 129.
　Tho., 240, 264, 280, 282.

aliens: Dutch, 175, App. III 3; French, 73, 112, 296; German, App. IV; Scottish, 238, 248, 256; unidentified, 135.

Alldridge, *see* Aldridge.

Alleen, *see* Allin.

Allen, John, 248.
　Tho., 196, 204.
　see also Allin.

Aller, *Som.*, 80.

Allin (Alleen), Sir Tho., *Controller of the Navy*, App. III 10.

Allum (Aleme, Allom), —, 83n.
　John, 50, 75, 84, 113n.

Alton, *Hants.*, 50.

Alverstoke, *Hants.*: Windmill Field, 325; *see also* Forton; Gosport.

Amcotts, Dan., App. III 1.

America, *places indexed*, Barbados; New England; Virginia.

Amsterdam, *Netherlands*, App. III 3.

Anabaptists, 60; *see also* noncomformists.

Anderson, James, 189.

Andover, *Hants.*, 46.

Andrewes, Wil., 14, App. II 24, 64.

Annett (Annet, Annott), Margaret, 60.
　Rob., 60.

Ansell, Edw., 6, 300, App. II 4.

antiquities, *see* heraldry; seals.

Apleford, Ric., 37.

apprenticeship, p. xvii, nos 62, 157, 250, 331, 392, App. II 84; apprentices to caulker, 351; to cordwainer, 358, App. II 84; to linen-draper, 238; to ship's master, 232; to unidentified trades, 5, 186, 302; apprenticeship indentures, 60; *see also* crimes (trading unapprenticed).

Archer, Edw., *Town Clerk of Portsmouth*, pp. xiii, xv, xx, xxxi–xxxii, nos 74, 155, 160, 171n, 177, 178, 197–199, 203, 216, 221, 223, 228, 230, 231, 233, 236, 245, 249, 253, 254, 258, 267, 279, 281, 284, 298, 301, 303, 310, 333, 344, 352, 353, 360, 362, 393, 403, 405, App. II 47, 73, 85, App. III 7n, App. V.
　James, 213.

architecture: evidence of plan or construction of houses, 4, 5, 7, 39, 77, 189, 294, 338; porch, 393; privies, 13, 285; stable, 51; *see also* occupations.

Argyll, Earl of, *see* Campbell, Archibald.

Armoner, James, 388.

Armorer, Edw., 366.

arms and armour: ordnance on land, 204; at sea, 46, App. III 6; gunpowder, 258, 270, App. III 3; pistol, App. III 3; swords, 247, 292, 368, App. II 35, App. III 6; knives, 316, 342, App. II 35, *see also* articles of utility (knives); cutlass, App. III 3; bill, 118; constable's staff, 187, 211.

Army: defensive works at Portsmouth, 221; sentries, 249; quartering soldiers, 110; soldier's Company coat, 277; desertion, 420; abuse to soldiers, 18, 22, 33, 201, 204, 380, 388; allegations of corruption in gaining commissions, 94; of false returns of numbers, 367; of concealment from Muster-Master, App. III 6.

— Governor of Portsmouth, pp. xxx, xxxii–xxxiii, 68, 94, 201, 292, 309, 424n; Deputy Governor of Portsmouth, 50, 94, 296; other officers, 18, 33, 36 (?), 50, 66, 94, 197 (?), 201, 221, 245, 247 (?), 273 (?), 277, 347 (?), 348, 355 (?), 367, 370, 372, 388 (?), 391, 396 (?), 420, 424, App. II 57 (?); Muster-Master of Chester, App. III 6.

— *see also* occupations.

Arnold, —, 119, 272.
   Henry, App. III 8.
   James, 159, 236, 385, 388, App. II 87.
   John, 94.
   Wil. 419.
Arthur, Jane, 7.
articles of utility:
   buckets, 231, 232.
   candles, 201, 259, 316, App. III 6.
   cane, 221.
   clothes-line, 416.
   coal, 169, App. II 85.
   combs, 160.
   dishes, pots, pans, etc., 68, 161, 318, 375, App.
      III 3.
   hat-case, 90n.
   hawking bag, App. III 6.
   iron, 149, 169, 316.
   keys, 64, 407, App. III 9.
   knives, 160, 337, 358, 416, 417, App. III 6, see
      also arms and armour.
   lanthorne, 161.
   lead, 67, 203, 204, 267, 270.
   leather, 232.
   looking-glass, 69.
   match, 182.
   paper, App. III 2, 3.
   paving-stone, 249, 256.
   pin, 362.
   purse, 39.
   screw, 247.
   sheath, App. III 6.
   snapsack, 277.
   spoons, 161.
   trunk, 350.
   tub, 352.
   wax, 8.
— see also arms and armour; books; clocks and
   watches; cloth; clothes; food and drink; furnishings; harness and riding equipment; jewels and
   plate; ships' stores; tobacco; tools and implements; woods and timber.
arts, see architecture, music, occupations, painting.
Arundel, Suss., 371.
Ascue, Ric., 24, App. II 41.
Ashley, Edw., 108.
Assize of Bread, pp. xiv, xviii, xxvii, nos 207,
   App. II 74, 81; weighing bread, 61; see also Acts
   of Parliament.
Assizes, p. xix; for Hants., 35, 49, 234, 350, 353,
   371, 378, 420, App. III 7; for Beds., 181.
Atherton, I.W., 406.
Atkins, Henry, 54.
Atkinson, Ant., 25.
Aulden (Alden, Houlden), Step., 112, 119, 124.
Austin (Austen), Edm., 43.
   James, 5, 11, 41, 97, 130, App. I 2, App. II 1,
      30, 33.
   Sarah, 388.
Avenell, Wil., 383, 388.
Avery, Edw., 49.

Ayerscough, see Ascue.
Ayliffe, —, 28.
Aylward (Ayleward), James, 387, 388.
   John, 151, App. III 9.
   Jos., 387, 388.

Backer (Bauher, Becker), Harman Gertzen or
      Gauetson, App. IV.
   Peter Harman or Harmanson, App. IV.
Backham, Geo., 348.
Badcocke, Mary, 221.
   Nic., 168, 172.
   Wil., 212, 221.
Badworth Park, in Lyminster, Suss., see Lyminster.
Bailiffs, see administration, local.
Baker, Ant., App. II 43.
   Dan., 56, 381.
   David, 60.
   Ellis, 177, 194n.
   John, 304, 419.
   Roger, 3.
   Tho., 156, 197, 387, 388.
Balch, John, 290, 338, 339, 345, 346.
   Tho., 106, App. II 68.
Ballard, John, App. II 13, 34, 40.
Barbados, West Indies, 94.
Barcombe, Geo., 154.
Barfoote, John, 60, App. III 8.
Barlow (Barlowe), —, 85.
   Sam, 222.
Barnald, —, 424.
Barnard (Bernard, Bernitt), Elizabeth, 382.
   John, 304, 382.
   Tho., 159, 164, App. II 65.
Barnes, Henry, 108, 204, 285.
   Ric., 202, 204, 214.
   Tho., 138.
Barnett (Barnat), Ann, 96.
   John, 336.
Barret, Tho., 355.
Barrow (Barrowe, Barrowes), Ric., 192.
   Tho., 156, 169, 192, 288.
Barry, de, see De Berry.
Bartholomew, John, App. II 31.
Bartle, James, 388.
Bartlett (Bartlet), James, 350, 356, 424.
Barton, James, 21.
   Lewis, 218, 345, 347.
   Tho., 332, 345.
Basingstoke, Hants., 132.
Bateman (Batman), John, 32, 35.
Batt, see Butt.
Batten, Wil., 29.
   Sir Wil., Surveyor of the Navy, p. xxx n.
Bauher, see Backer.
Baxter, Rob., 242.
Beach, Elizabeth, 360.
Beacham, And., 199, 204.
Beadle (Beedle), John, 231, 232.
Beadles, see administration, local.

Beale (Beell), Ann, App. II 2.
  Grace, 385.
  James, 19, 41, 385, App. II 33.
  John, 21, 105, App. II 2.
Beare (Beere), Henry, 293.
  Jane, 293.
  James, 152.
  John, 72.
Becker, *see* Backer.
Becket, Ann, 422.
  John, 422.
Bedford, *Beds.*: the Swan, 181.
Bedford, Edw., 109, 362.
  Elizabeth, 362.
Bedfordshire: Assizes, 181; *place indexed*, Bedford.
Bee, Margaret, 424.
Beecham, *see* Beacham.
Beedle, *see* Beadle.
Beell, *see* Beale.
beer and ale: ale, 173, 264, 290, App. II 13, 63;
  beer, 30, 70, 86, 132, 173, 180, 182, 201, 202,
  211, 224, 277, 285, 313, 338, 353, 361, 372, 375,
  424, App. II 13; brew-house in Gosport, App. II
  97; Assize of Ale, p. xviii; retailing beer, 16, 92,
  264, App. II 36, 63, 86; licensing beer-sellers,
  p. xiv; fine for short measure, 299; *see also*
  occupations.
Beere, *see* Beare.
Beeston, —, 197.
  Tho., 2.
Beeswabber, Mary, 384, 388.
  Tho., 384.
Beeten, Tho., App. III 6.
Belbin (Bellbin), Ant., 4, 5, 6, 7, 11, App. II 1, 2,
  4, 5, 21, 22, App. V.
Belfeild, *see* Benfield.
Bell, Isaac, 72.
Belney, *in Southwick, Hants.*, *see* Southwick.
Bembridge (Benbridge), Cuthbert, 303, 304, 325,
  380, 388.
Benet, *see* Bennett.
Benfield (Belfeild), Henry, 383, 388.
Benger, John, 71.
Bennett (Benet, Bennet), —, App. III 6.
  Elizabeth, 330.
  Sir Humf., 112, 119.
Bensted (Bensteed, Binsted), —, 180.
  Ant., 386, 388, 396, 408.
  Ric., App. II 59.
  Wil., 197, 204, 292, App. I 1.
Bentham, Cha., 33.
Bere Forest, *Hants.*: East Bere Forest, 381.
Berkeley, Sir Cha., 94.
Bernard, Bernitt, *see* Barnard.
Berry, —, 299.
Berry, de, *see* De Berry.
Berwick, Duke of, *see* Fitz-James, James.
Bessent (Bezzent), Hul., 351.
Beswell, —, 25.
Bettesworth (Betsworth, Betworth), John, 29, 215,
  App. II 64.

Betts, Isaac, 350, 351, 353, 354, 376, 381, 392, 395,
  App. V.
  Ralph, App. II 17.
Beverley (Beverly), —, 276.
  Henry, 205, 206, 210, 215, 218, 230, 264, 347,
  361, App. I 4, App. II 85, App. V.
Bevis, Wil., 320, 326.
Bezzent, *see* Bessent.
Bible, Wil., 375.
Biffin, John, 108.
Biggs, James, 79.
  Sir John, *Recorder of Portsmouth*, p. xxxi, nos 193,
  194, 234, 235, 350.
  Sam., 77.
Binsted, *see* Bensted.
Bird (Burd), Henry, 241.
Bishop (Bishopp, Bishoppe, Bushoppe, Byshopp),
  —, 83n, 240.
  Rob., 191, 222, 289, App. II 13.
Bissell (Byssell), Cha., *Town Clerk of Portsmouth*,
  pp. xxxii–xxxiii, nos 403, 416, 423.
  Elizabeth, 51, 86.
  Wil., App. II 14, 25, 40.
Blackstone, Sir Wil., *judge*, p. xxi.
Blackwell, Wil., App. III 6.
Blake, Fra., 186.
Blakely (Blackeley), John, 216, 218, 417, 423.
Blankley (Blankeley), Tho., 271, 282, 348.
Blender, John, App. II 48.
Blisset, Mary, 400.
Blowes (Blos, Blose), James, 391.
  John, 372, 378, 388.
  Sarah, 278.
Blunt, —, App. III 6.
Bocher, *see* Butcher.
Bolds, Roger, 318.
Bolley, Elizabeth, 260, 270.
  Wil., 260.
Bolton (Boulton), Geo., 386, 388.
  Tho. 206, 208, App. II 93.
Booker, —, 371, 388.
books: paper book, App. III 3; *see also* documents
  and diplomatic.
Boulter, Wil., App. II 30.
Boulton, *see* Bolton.
Bourres, *see* Burroughs.
Bowen, —, App. III 6.
Bowes, Tho., 210, 274, 387.
Boyes, James, 371.
Brading, *I.W.*, 365, App. II 45.
Bradley, —, 370.
  Dan., App. III 2, 4, 5.
Bragg (Brag), —, 36.
  Wil., 415.
Braintree, *Essex*, 7.
Bramble, Elizabeth, 362.
  Tho. 362.
Bramblecombe, *see* Brimblecombe.
Bramshaw, *Hants.*: Brook, 215.
Bramshott, *Hants.*: Liphook, 360n.
Branstone, Osmond, 221.

bread: bread with baker's mark, 391; *see also* Assize of Bread; occupations.
Brett, Ric., 348.
Brewer, Alex, 148.
   Elizabeth, 148.
Brewty, John, 181.
Brickleton, *see* Brimblecombe.
Bridger, Tho., 360n.
Brighton, *Suss.*, App. II 71.
Brignell, Geo., 348.
   Giles, 348.
Brigsdale, Tho., 269.
Brimblecombe (Bramblecombe, Brickleton, Brumblecome), —, 409.
   Alice, 367, 388.
   John, 353, 367, 388.
   Wil., 267, 270.
Brimson (Brimston), Mary, 333, 345.
Bristol, *Glos.*, 47, App. II 50.
Bristowe, John App. II 69.
British Museum: Dept of MSS., Madden Collection, p. xii, App. IV.
Broade, Elizabeth, App. II 45.
Brockenhurst, *Hants.*: the Unicorn, 80.
Brogden, Wil., 347.
Brome, Bart., 73.
Bromley, John, 6.
Bronncker, *see* Brouncker.
Bronne, Ann, 397.
Brook, *in Bramshaw, Hants.*, *see* Bramshaw.
Brooker, Edw., 143, 173, 190, 200, 204, 238, 256, 263, 270, 278, 282, 404, 408, App. III 12.
Brookes, Gardner, 336.
   John, 308.
Brooman, Mat., 182.
Broughton, *Hants.*, 381.
Broughton, —, App. II 73.
   Margaret, 253, 256.
Brouncker (Bronncker, Brunker), Henry, *3rd Viscount Brouncker*, 296.
   Tho., 193n, 203, 318, 345.
Brower, *see* Jansen-Brower.
Brown (Broune, Browne), —, 86.
   Ann, 397.
   John, 46.
   Tho., 46.
   Wil., 424.
Bruges, *Flanders*, 46.
Brumblecome, *see* Brimblecombe.
Brunker, *see* Brouncker.
Bryant, Wil., 1.
Buck, Lettice, 9, App. II 7.
Buckland, *on Portsea I., Hants.*, 197, 269, App. II 77.
Buckle, —, 6.
buildings and grounds, *see* architecture; furnishings; gardens; inns and public houses; mortgages; occupations; rents; trade and commerce.
Bull, —, 50.
Bunch, Nat., 327, 331, 345.
Bunckly, Edw., App. III 11.
Bunnell, —, 18.

Burges, *see* Burroughs.
Burgis, Ben., 148.
Burnet, James, 367.
Burningham, Sam., 77, 147, 149–152, 298, 300, 316, 320, 326, 336, App. II 79, 80, App. V.
Burrell (Burrill), John, 180, 223, 232, App. III 6.
Burridge, —, 94, 117.
Burroughs (Bourres, Burges, Burres, Burroughes), Sam., 73.
Burry, Tho., 350.
Burt, Ric., 196, 204.
   Sarah, 275.
   Tho., 275.
Burton, Ric., 372.
Busbridge, Rebecca, 418.
   Tho., 418.
Bushoppe, *see* Bishop.
Butcher (Bocher, Buttcher), Frances, 68.
   Joan, 384, 388.
   John, 68, 236, 256, 278, 282.
   Ric., 271, 282, 384, 388.
   Wil., 277, 285.
Butt (Batt), Rob., 366, 388.
Butteresse (Butteres), Tho., 23, App. II 3, 67, 73, App. III 2.
Button, Rob., App. III 10.
Bye, John, 193n, 422.
Byland, Edw., 87.
Byshopp, *see* Bishop.
Byssell, *see* Bissell.

C[. . .], H., 97.
Cadman, James, App. II 1.
Caen, *France*, 296.
Calais, *France*, App. III 10.
Caldy Road, *coast of Pembs.*, App. III 6.
Campbell, Arch., *9th Earl of Argyll*, 371, 373, 388.
Card (Carde), —, 287.
   Jos., 249, 256.
   Ric., App. II 9.
   Tho., 249, 256.
   Wil., 6.
Cardife, Jane, 287.
Carey (Carew, Cary), Wil., 244, 256, 271.
Carnell, Joan, 167.
   Tho., 167, 169.
Carpenter, John, App. II 24.
   Rob., 118.
Carricke, Elizabeth, 132.
   Henry, 132.
   Tho., 132.
Carter, —, 18.
   Alex, 7, App. II 9, 23.
   Edith, 26.
   Edw., 184, 344, 345, 393, 408.
   Elizabeth, 188, 192, 194, 204, 414.
   John, 238, 273, 282.
   Mary, 414.
   Ric., 188, 192.
   Roger, 400.
   Sarah, 344, 345.

Carver, Martha, App. II 64.
  Rob., App. II 10, 64.
  Sarah, App. II 64.
  Step., 301, 319, 322, 326, 403, App. II 64.
Cary, *see* Carey.
Cary, Castle, *Som.*, 80.
Casey, Elizabeth, 175.
  John, 175.
  Tho., 175.
Castle Cary, *Som.*, *see* Cary, Castle.
cattle, 177, 195, 198.
Cave, Ann, 117.
  Art., 117.
Chace, Wil., 71.
Chadborne, Tho., 228, 232.
Chagman, Ann, 357.
Challenge, Tho., 142.
Chambers, Margaret, 169.
Chamberlains, *see* administration, local.
Champion, John, App. II 84.
Chancery: enrolment of Commission of the Peace,
  p. xxvii.
Chandler, Fra., 304.
Chandles, John, 337.
  Mary, 337.
Chapman, —, 338n.
  Cha., 36, 313, App. II 70, App. V.
  Edw., 243, 256, 324, 381, 388.
  Jane, 357.
  John, 178, 236, 256, 270, 305, 381, 388, App. II
    87.
  Ric., 357.
charity: bequests to the poor, 12; building alms-
  house, App. II 85.
Charker, Dan., 381.
Charles I, *King*, pp. xxvii–xxviii, xxx.
Charles II, *King*, pp. xxviii, xxxi, xxxiii, nos 22, 50,
  52, 60, 66, 70, 71, 94, 113.
Charleton, Ant., 203, 204.
Charvell, Henry, 338.
  Mary, 338.
cheese: Cheshire, 316, 353; unspecified, 1, 311,
  326, 391; *see also* occupations.
Cheesman, Tho., 304.
Cheshire, *places indexed*, Chester; Hoylake.
Chester, *Ches.*, App. III 6.
Chestle, John, 131, App. II 22.
Chettle, Tho., 165.
Chichester, *Suss.*, 159, 238, 350; St. Pancras' parish,
  371; the Swan, 350.
Chideock, *Dors.*, 129.
Chidley, Fra., 390, 408.
Child (Childe, Childs), John, 130, 153, 204, 219,
  App. I 2.
  Josiah, p. xxxi, nos 41, 43–45, 47, 49, 50, 62,
    App. I 2, App. II 56, 73, App. V.
Chilton, Fra., App. II 32.
  Tho., 8, App. II 6.
Chivers, John, 153, 325.
Chubb, Wil., 21.
Church, clergy and religion: attendance at church,

27, 382; baptisms, 328, 417; marriages, 19,
App. II 18; burials, 83, 239; church-repairs rate,
162, App. I 3; clergy accused of blasphemy and
false doctrine, 382; of fornication, 188; failure of
Justice to take sacrament, 216; blasphemy, 81,
App. II 62; profaning a fast-day, 134; burning
Pope's effigy, 388; benefit of clergy, pp. xxiii–
xxiv.
— clergy: minister of Hound, 19; Vicar of Owsle-
bury, 381; minister of Portchester, 328; curate of
Wymering, 188; others, App. II 18, 69.
— Churchwardens: of Portsmouth, 162, 392, App.
I 3; of Alverstoke or Gosport, 303, 326; of
Owslebury, 381; of Woolwich, 241.
— *see also* Anabaptists; crimes (dissenters' con-
venticle, popery, religious assembly, Sabbath,
Sabbath breaking); nonconformists; Quakers;
Roman Catholics; witchcraft.
Churcher, Ric., App. II 80.
Churles, Ann, 165.
Civil Wars (1642–51), 60.
Clansy, John, 47.
Clapshaw (Clapshawe, Clapshowe), Ann, 179.
  Jane, 188, 192.
  John, 185.
  Ric., 76.
  Wil., 185.
Clapslooe, Wil., App. II 77.
Clare, Ric., 40, App. II 58.
Clarke, —, 33.
  Ant., App. III 4, 5.
  Elizabeth, 251, 260, 270.
  Geo., 222.
  Goodwins, 350.
  Joan, 268, 270.
  Laur., 260.
  Margaret, 41, 121, App. I 2, App. II 33.
  Ric., App. II 33.
  Sarah, 147.
  Tho., 147, 194n.
  Walt., 268.
  Wil., 193, 204.
Claston, Walt., 268.
Clay, Dan., 287.
Clayton, —, 161.
Cleaver, Alice, 148.
  John, 116.
Clement, Fra., 51.
Clements (Clemence), David, 79.
  Katherine, 317.
  Tho., p. xv, no. 317.
clergy, *see* Church, clergy and religion.
Clerk of the Peace, *see* administration local;
  Archer, Edw.; Bissell, Cha.; Ely, Sam.; Mullins,
  Tho.
Cleverley, John, 60.
  Wil. 275.
Clifford (Cliford, Clyfford), —, 246, 256.
  James, 208, App. II 93.
  John, 213.
  Tho., 246.

clocks and watches: watch, 296.

cloth: Holland, 246, 277, 350, 337; lace, 248; linen, 48, 238, 248, 360, App. III 4; linsey, App. III 6; muslin, 248, *see also* occupations.

clothes: boots and shoes, 266, 314, 350, App. III 6; hats and head-dresses, p. xxv, nos 59, 90n, 117, 202, 237, 246, 252, 256, App. III 6; other specified garments, 6, 9, 16, 39, 51, 59, 65, 94, 97, 117, 149, 160, 187, 202, 226, 228, 246, 247, 253, 265, 266, 269, 277, 314, 337, 350, 358, 391, 416, App. II 34, 82, App. III 3, 6; unspecified garments, 200, 216, 228, 257, 308, 315, 416, 417, App. III 6; washing clothes, 352; *see also* occupations.

Clud, —, 424.

Clyfford, *see* Clifford.

Coales, Wil., 415.

Coasier, Jane, 161.
  Jonathan, 161.

Cockes, *see* Coxe.

Cogge (Coggs), Ric., 41, App. I 2, App. II 46, 49.

coinage: specified English coins, 97, 117, 246, 296; gilt sixpence for half-guinea, 394; Dutch guilders, App. III 3.

Coke, *see* Cooke.

Coker, Tho., 117.

Colebrooke (Colbrooke), Ant., 300, 306, 326.
  Elizabeth, 294.
  John, 92.

Colecut, Tho., 220.

Coleman, Simon, 279.
  Tho., 14, App. II 24.
  Wil., App. II 50.

Coles, *see* Coales.

Collectors, *see* administration, local.

Collens, *see* Collins.

Collier, John, 206, 208–210, App. II 93.

Collingwood, Fra., 277.

Collins (Collens), —, 108, 188, 189.
  Dan., 211, 222, 353.
  John, 10, 21, 93, 95, 100, 103, 108, 115, 131, 336, 424, App. II 33, 52.
  Margaret, 4.
  Wil., 336, App. II 18.

Colmer, Wil., 175.

Comeings, *see* Cummings.

Comfort, John, 28, 31, 33–36, 39, 42, 77, App. II 60, 67, App. V.

Comings, *see* Cummings.

commerce, *see* trade and commerce.

Common Pleas, Court of, 189.

communications, *see* transport and communications.

Compton, Geo., 388.
  John, App. II 3.

Conduit (Condict, Condit, Cundit, Cunditt), Jos., 269, 270, 275, 292, 387, 388.

Constables, *see* administration, local.

conversation, quoted, 7, 17, 18, 22, 60, 78, 94, 113, 117, 201, 240, 245, 247, 274, 285, 291, 292, 294, 299, 300, 308, 309, 313, 332, 353, 368, 372, 421, App. I 3, App. II 75, App. III 6, 9.

Cooke (Coke), Sir And., 297.
  Debora, App. II 11.
  John, App. II 11, 16.
  Rob., 150, 167.
  Tho., 58, 260.

Coombes, John, 274.
  Step., 409.

Cooper, Wil., 56.

corn: barley, 185; wheat, 5, 76, 82, 97, 161, 225.

Cornelius, Tho., 189.

Cornish, Henry, 24.

Cornwall, *place indexed*, Mount's Bay.

Cornwallis, —, 372.

Coroners, *see* administration, local.

Coroner's Inquests, p. xix, no. 72.

Corps, Ant., 193, 204.
  Ric., 193.
  Wil., 204.

Cosham, *Hants.*, 75, 245, 292; marsh at, 292.

Costin, Grace, 169.

Cotton (Cotten), Edw., 99.
  John, 222.

Coulever, John, 27.

Courtney, John, 304.

Coventry, Sir Wil., *Commissioner of the Navy*, p. xxx.

Coward, Henry, 407.
  Simon, 197, 204, App. II 19.
  Wil., 275.

Cowes, *I.W.*, 260, 270, App. II 65, App. IV.

Cowes, —, App. III 6.

Coxe (Cockes), Elizabeth, 289.
  Mary, 289, 375, 388.
  Tho., 375.

Cozens, Alice, 375.
  John, 42.
  Margaret, 206.
  Tho., 71.
  Wil., 65, 98, 206, 208–210, 284, 401, App. I 4, App. II 42, 93.

Crampton, Alice, 373.
  Tho., 373.

Crawley, Jeremiah, 124.

Cray, Christian, 64, 85.

Creed, Mary, 362.
  Wil., 362, App. II 97.

Cresset, Ric., 201.

Crewes (Crews), Tho., 326, 355, 366, 388.

crimes, pp. xvi–xvii, xxi–xxiv.
— particular offences:
  abuse, p. xii, nos 17, 18, 28, 109, 146, 147, 169, 201, 204, 229, 232, 252, 273, 282, 289, 299, 302, 306, 326, 363, 367, 377, 385, 388, 396, 397, 408, 414, 421, App. II 28, 31, 37.
  abusing authority, pp. xii, xxv, nos 7, 10, 15, 20, 23, 33, 78, 88, 102, 110, 150, 162, 173, 191, 199, 204, 214, 272, 287, 313, 349, 370, 380, 386, 388, 402, 405, 408, 409, App. I 3, App. II 9, 15, 23, 25, 27, 39, 48, 52, 73, 75, 82, 83.
  abusing the Mayor, 61, 83–85, 103.

adultery, p. xii, nos 54, 401.

arson, 182; threatened, 53, 75, 271, 282, 369, 388.

assault, pp. xii, xix, nos 14, 34, 45, 49, 72, 74, 85, 89, 95, 101, 107, 108, 109, 116, 120, 122, 128, 135, 148, 153, 158, 163, 167–170, 172, 175, 185, 186, 196, 197, 202, 204, 211, 219, 221, 223, 224, 227, 232, 245, 247, 253, 256, 259, 262, 265, 266, 268–270, 275, 280, 282, 285, 286, 290–292, 298, 301, 308, 309, 311, 320, 326, 333, 342–345, 352, 354, 356, 358, 361, 362, 365, 372, 375, 383, 384, 388, 393, 395, 408, 410, 416, 419, 423, App. I 1, App. II 1, 2, 11, 16, 19, 30, 32–35, 38, 44, 47, 53, 55, 64, 67, 68; threatened, 36, 263, 270, 300, 326, 368, 404, 408, 415, 418.

assaulting authority, 93, 303, 326, 353.

assaulting a Justice, 144.

bastardy, pp. xii, xxvi, xxix, nos 6, 55, 80, 96, 164, 166, 169, 171, 176, 188, 192, 194, 200, 204, 212, 213, 241, 251, 274, 305, 307, 329, 330, 338, 392, 408, 409, App. II 4, 8, 45, 97.

bawdy-house, keeping a, 21, App. II 42, 43, 48, 62.

bigamy, 132.

blasphemy, 81.

bribery, 11, 97.

contempt, p. xii, nos 91, 110, 171n, 174, 178, 217, 236, 244, 256, 270, 278, 282, 319, 326, 332, 345, 357, App. II 59.

Customs evasion, 127.

deserting wife, 257.

deserting the colours, 420.

disloyalty, p. xxv, nos 22, 50, 52, 60, 70, 91, 100, 113, 190, 424, App. II 37, App. III 12.

dissenters' conventicle, 205, 206, 208–210, 297, 304, App. I 4, App. II 87, 93.

disturbance, 407, 408, 412, App. II 22.

driving irregularly, 204.

drunken behaviour, 69, App. II 21, 57.

drunkenness, 75, 113, 128, 141, 239, App. II 29, App. III 6.

failing to prosecute, 220.

false weights, p. xiv, App. II 78.

felony, suspected, 156, 169, App. II 17.

forestalling, pp. xiv, xxiv, nos 155, App. II 13, 20.

fornication, p. xii, nos 4, 7, 13, 32, 35, 97, 401, App. II 26, 54.

fraud, 394.

gaming, illicit, p. xv, nos 29, 279, 281.

housebreaking, 27, 169, 294.

irregular behaviour, App. III 6.

libel, 169, 347, 400, App. II 79.

marriage, illegal, 19, App. II 18.

misbehaviour in Court, 327, 345.

murder, p. xix; threatened, 169, 336, 417.

mutiny, inciting, 137.

neglect of duty, 243, 256, App. II 76, 77.

obstructing authority, 118, 187.

obstructing the highway, 325.

plague infection, 125, 142, 143.

poisoning a dog, App. II 70.

popery, 77, 215, 359.

poundbreach, 106, 151, 171n, 177.

profaning a holy day, 134.

rape, 169, 180; threatened, App. II, 14.

receiving stolen goods, 121, 246, 256, 277, 282, 283, App. II 36, 56.

refusing the watch, 136.

refusing to assist Constable, 37, 38, 129.

regrating, p. xxiv, nos 195, 198, 204, 230, 232, 324, App. I 2.

religious assembly, unlawful, 71.

riding, dangerous, 140.

riot, p. xii, nos 56, 179, 366, 387, 388, App. II 80; threatened, 28.

robbery, 296; threatened, App. II 24.

Sabbath, disturbing the, App. II 69.

Sabbath breaking, 30.

sedition, 355, 373, 376, 378, 379, 388.

service, 157, 169, 216, 226, 227, App. II 49.

slander, 94, 105, 117, 145, 152, 382, App. II 85.

theft, pp. xii, xiv, xix, xxii–xxiii, xxiv, xxix, nos 5, 8, 24, 26, 39, 43, 44, 48, 59, 63–65, 67, 68, 73, 76, 77, 82, 86, 87, 90, 92, 111, 112, 115, 119, 124, 138, 144n, 149, 161, 165, 169, 181, 203, 204, 225, 228, 231, 232, 249, 256, 258, 267, 270, 314–316, 318, 326, 331, 337, 345, 348, 350, 351, 353, 360, 388, 391, App. II 6, 41, 71, 72, App. III 3, 7–11.

trading irregularly, p. xii, nos 1, 3, 9, 25, 51, 126, 159, 160, 169, 183, 237, 238, 248, 256, 260, 264, 270, 276, App. II 7, 36, 46, 50, 63, 86.

trading unapprenticed, p. xv, nos 160, 233, 254, 256, 270, 284.

treason, 66, 371, 374, 388; suspected, 381, 388.

vagrancy, 398.

wife-beating, 75, 288, 422.

wrongful arrest, 16, 189.

wrongful imprisonment, 293, 393, 408.

Crispe, Elizabeth, 227.
    Thos., 314.
Critchell, Sam., 264.
Croberd, —, 148.
Crocker, Dan., App. II 19.
    Ric., 28, 387.
    Tho. 206, 208, App. II 93.
Crofts, Ric., 247.
Cromwell, Wil., 16.
Crooker, James, 156, 169.
    Ric., 156.
Crowcher, Ann, 352.
    Henry, 35, App. II 10.
Crow, Tho., 334.
Crutchfeild, Sam., 134.
Cullimore (Cullemore), Mark, 376, 388.
Cummings (Comeings, Comings, Cumings), Henry 277, 282, 283, 329, 340, 345, 352.
Cundit, Cunditt, see Conduit.
Curtis, Derek, 65.
    John, 185.

Phil., 76.
Theophilus, 245, 246, 257, 259, 260, 266, 268, 271, 272, 289, App. V.
Customs and Excise: Customs office and officers at Portsmouth, 245; Deputy to Farmers of Customs, App. IV; agent of Excise Commissioners, 173; Customs evasion, 127.

Dale, John, 263, 317, 326.
Tho., App. II 19, 72.
Dallerose, —, 345.
Damaree, John, 17, App. II 20.
Damarum (Damerum), Tho., 201, 204, 230, 232, 388, App. III 9.
Dane, John, 266, 270.
Darrell (Darrill, Dorrell), Elizabeth, 423.
John, 420.
Dartmouth, Lord, see Legge, Geo.
Davis (Davies, Davys), —, 59, 211.
Dan., 46.
Elizabeth, App. II 8.
Jasper, App. II 54.
John, 46, App. II 8.
Phil., 152.
Silvian, 194n.
Tho., 46.
Dawes (Dawe), John, 361.
Day, —, 239.
Art., App. III 6.
John, 301.
Deacon (Deacons), Edw., 113n, 132.
Elizabeth, 132.
Geo., 388.
Ric., 171.
Wil., 318, 326.
Dean, East, Hants., App. II 4.
Deane, Hants., 381.
Deane, Edw., 4, 9, App. II 4, 10, App. V.
John, 127.
Deaniye, Ric., 21.
De Berry (De Barry), David, App. IV.
De Gomme, Sir Bern., p. xxviii.
De Lannce, John, 165.
Delling, Tho., 88.
De Murcedo, Ferdinando, 135.
Dennis, Ben., 160, 169.
Deptford, Kent and Surr., 266, 330, App. V.
De Silvo, Verissimo, 135.
Devonshire, places indexed, Exeter; Plymouth.
Digbey, Jo[. . .], App. III 4, 5.
Dillington, Sir Rob., App. II 45.
Dinham, see Dynham.
Dismore, Henry, 157, 169.
Tho., 157.
dissenters, see nonconformists.
Dobbins (Dobins), Tho., 353.
documents and diplomatic: Sessions papers described, pp. xi–xii, xv–xvi; formation of Sessions files, pp. xiii–xvi; signatures on Sessions papers, pp. xiv, xv; stamped signatures, p. xv, nos 297, 309.

— particular types of document:
affidavits, 310, 381.
bills of lading, App. IV.
Book of Constitutions, pp. xvi, xxxi n.
Calendars of Sessions, p. xiii, nos 169, 204, 232, 256, 270, 282, 326, 345, 388, 408, fig. 1.
case for opinion, 216.
certificates, of depositions, App. III 4, 5; of dissenters' conventicles, 205, 206, 208, 209, 210, App. I 4, fig. 7; of naval service, 72.
Charters to Borough, pp. xiv, xxvii, xxviii, xxix, xxx, xxxiii, no. 313.
Commission of the Peace, p. xxvii; its enrolment, p. xxvii.
confessions, App. II 85, 86.
Court Book, App. II 73.
depositions, App. III 1–3, 6.
Election and Sessions Books, pp. xii, xv, xxvii, xxix, xxx, xxxi, xxxii, xxxiii n, App. II, App. V.
examinations, pp. xiii–xiv, xx, nos 4–420 passim, App. I 3, App. III 7, 8, 10, 11, App. IV.
indentures, apprenticeship, 60.
informations, pp. xiii–xiv, xx, nos 1–424 passim, App. II 62, App. III 7, 8, 9, 10, 12, fig. 6.
letters, 132, 181, 216, 245, 296, 347, App. III 6.
licence, innkeeper's, 240.
Mayor's Book, App. II 51.
opinion, counsel's, 216.
orders, apprenticeship, App. II 84; bastardy, 392, App. II 97.
passes, settlement, 20, 46, 240, 323, 332.
Poor Book, 199.
presentments, pp. xiii, xiv, xx, nos 149–423 passim, App. I 1, fig. 3.
recognisances, pp. xx–xxii, nos 8–424 passim, App. I 2, App. II passim, App. III 11, figs 3–5; list of, 169.
sentences, 3–210 passim, App. I 4, App. II passim, plate 8.
State Papers, Domestic, pp. xii, xxix–xxx, xxxii, App. III.
warrants, of Lord Chief Justice, 243, 256; of others, p. xx, nos 10, 89, 91, 187, 216, 257, 266, 304, 403, 417, App. II 25, App. III 11.
— see also accounts; seals; wills; writs.
Doe, John, p. xiv, nos 290, 345, 417, 422.
dogs, 379, App. II 68, 70.
Domineeke (Dominecke), Elizabeth, 191.
Wil., 144, 145, 147.
Dorman, Giles, App. II 19.
Dorrell, see Darrell.
Dorset, 226; place indexed, Chideock.
Dorville (Dorvile), Dan., App. IV.
John, App. IV.
Dove, John, 365, 388.
Dover, Kent, 323; St Mary's parish, 323; the Ship, 323.
Downer, —, 114n.
drainage: deep ditch of water, 185; watercourse bricked and boarded over, 275.

Drapier, Edm., 413.
Drinkwater (Drinkewater), —, 206, 208, App. II
    93.
    Ric., 206, 208, App. I 4, App. II 90, 93.
Driver, Ric., App. III 10.
Du Maine (Du Mane), Adam François, 296.
Dumfries, *Scotland*, 238.
Dunkinson, James, 149.
Dunmore, John, 321, 326.
Dunton, John, 18.
Dyer, John, 129.
Dymock, Wil., 51.
Dynham, Ric., App. III 6.

Eames (Emes), John, 388.
    Wil., App. II 64.
Earle (Erle, Erles), Susan, 92.
    Wil., 9, App. II 50, 62.
East, Elizabeth, 4.
    Rob., 4.
East Bere Forest, *Hants.*, *see* Bere Forest.
East Dean, *Hants.*, *see* Dean, East.
Eastman, John, 1, 39, App. II 51.
    Margery, 39.
Easton, Margaret, 337.
    Wil., 225, 232.
Eastwood (Eastwoort, Estwood), Alex., 50, 139.
    John, 366, 372, 388.
    Tho., 56.
Eddin, Step., 4.
education, *see* apprenticeship.
Edwards, Edw., 253.
    James, 79.
    John, 182.
    Walsingham, 253, 256.
    Wil., 380, 388.
Eeling, Ric., 312, 326.
Eker, Geo., 397.
Elcombe, Ric., App. II 78.
Eling, *Hants.*: Wigley, 161.
Eling, *see* Eeling.
Elizabeth I, *Queen*, p. xxvii.
Elliott (Elliate), —, 169.
    James, 304.
Ellis, Edw., 28.
    John, 73.
    Katherine, 28.
Elmes, Phil., 67, 69, 136, 147, 160, 179.
Elsey (Elzey), Henry, 34, App. II 27.
    Nic., 90n.
Ely, Sam., *Town Clerk of Portsmouth*, pp. xxxii–xxxiii,
    nos 416, 423.
Emes, *see* Eames.
Emett (Emet, Yeamett, Yeomet, Yeomett), —,
    187, 215, 269.
    Wil., App. II 80.
    Winifred, 215, 379.
England, *see* Ingland.
English, —, 175.
    Susan, 338.
    Wil., 139, 372, 388.

Enkhuizen, *Netherlands*, App. III 5.
entertainments, *see* games and entertainments.
Erle, Erles, *see* Earle.
Ernee, John, 304.
Essex, *places indexed*, Braintree; Maldon.
Estwood, *see* Eastwood.
Etherington (Etherrington), Bridget, 246.
    Dorothy, 313.
    Henry, 246.
    James, 191, 265, 270, 299, 313, 395.
    Wil., 251.
Evans, Henry, 182.
    Walt., 43, 101.
    Wil., App. II 26.
Excise, *see* Customs and Excise.
Exeter, *Devon*, 46.

Fairhill (Fairehill, Farehill), Alex., 109, 128, 159.
    Mary, 265, 270.
fairs and markets, 311, 377; market days, 198;
    stalls, etc., in market, 195, 370, App. II 59;
    sales in market, 155, 230, 324, 383; market dues,
    230; Court of Clerk of Markets, 150, 299n;
    proposed marriage announced in market, 19; *see
    also* crimes (forestalling, regrating, trading ir-
    regularly); Portsmouth (market).
Fareham, *Hants.*, p. xxvi, nos 90n, 164, 315, 415,
    App. II 16, 43.
Farehill, *see* Fairhill.
Farley (Farly), —, 197.
    Alex., App. III 6.
    Geo., App. III 6.
    John, 35, App. II 80.
Farmer, Wil., 208.
Farrant, John, 61.
fauna, *see* cattle; dogs; fish; horses; pigs; poultry;
    sheep.
Fawlkner, Ric., App. II 2.
Feats (Feates), Edw., App. III 8.
Feild (Feld), John, 46.
Fetherstonhaugh, Phil., 250.
Fettiplace, *see* Phetiplace.
Fewter, Rob., 203, 204.
Field, *see* Feild.
Fincher, —, 66.
Firebush, *see* Forebush.
fish: royal fish, p. xix; mackerel, 126; salt fish, 230;
    see also occupations.
Fishbourne (Fishborne), S.(?), 206.
Fisher, Elias, 50.
    Elizabeth, 277.
    Wil., 263.
Fitch, John, 249.
    Tho., 249.
Fitz-James, James, *Duke of Berwick*, 424n.
Fiveash, Eleanor, 375.
    John, 375, 378, 388.
    Tho., 95.
Flanders, *place indexed*, Bruges.
Fleet, Tho., 298.
Fleming, Rob., 391.

194

shaw; Bramshott; Brockenhurst; Broughton; Cosham; Dean, East; Deane; Eling; Fareham; Forton; Gosport; Hambledon; Havant; Hayling I.; Horsea I.; Hound; Langstone; Millbrook; Minstead; New Forest; Odiham; Owslebury; Penton Grafton; Petersfield; Portchester; Portsea I.; Portsmouth; Portsmouth Harbour; Romsey; Soberton; Southampton; Southwick; Spithead; Stoneham, South; Wickham; Winchester; Wymering.

Hampton, John, 73, 77.

Hancock (Hancocke, Hancoke, Handcocke), Isaac, 230.
  Tho., p. xv, nos 172, 285–297, 300, 302, 304, 305, 308, 309, 312–316, 318, 319, 323, 324, 328–332, 334, 337–340, 389, 408, 416, 419, 420, 424, App. II 83, App. III 9, App. V.
  Wil., App. II 32.

Hanny, Adam, 277.

Haore, see Hoare.

Harding, Tho., 113, 173.

Harford, Rob., 272, 387.
  Walt., 94.

Hargood, John, 231, 232.

Harling (Harlen), Tho., 359, 417.

Harman, Peter, see Backer, Peter Harman.

Harmesworth, John, 269, 270.

Harmewood, Peter, App. II 42.

harness and riding equipment: spurs, App. III 6; see also occupations.

Harper, Ric., 308.

Harris, —, 277.
  Bart., 16.
  Elizabeth, 54, 58.
  Henry, 242.
  James, 195, 204, 374, 388.
  John, 284.
  Ric., 54.
  Tho., 66.

Harrison, James, 302, 326.

Harrwood, see Harwood.

Hart, John, App. II 1.
  Tho., 74.

Harvey (Harvy), Alice, 148.
  Wil., App. II 22.

Harwood (Harrwood), —, 353, 407.
  Emm, 257.
  Geo., 204, 257.
  Jane, 298.
  John, 197, 204, 290, 398, App. I 1.
  Nat., 195, 198, 204, 254, 374, 407, 408, 412, 415, App. I 2.
  Tho., 297.

Hasham, Eleanor, 305.

Hasleton, Cha., App. III 1.

Hasted, —, App. III 9.

Hastings, Suss., 361.

Haswell, Ant., App. II 72.
  Catherine, 421.

Hatch, Tho., 56.

Hateley, see Heatly.

Hatton, Paul, 56.

Havant, Hants., 16, 195, 198, 290, 292, App. I 2; the Black Dog, 350; see also Langstone.

Haward, see Hayward.

Hawes, John, App. II 30.

Hawkes (Hawks), —, 95.
  Elizabeth, 274, App. II 52.
  Rob., p. xxv, nos 21, 34, 45, 92, 104, 136, 137, 142, 179, 188, 192, 194, 204, App. II 14, 40, 52.

Hawkins, Joan, 246, 256.

Hawkesworth, Nic., 326.

Hawley, Barbara, 77.
  Wil., 6, 77, App. II 66.

Hawtrey, Art., 91, 170.

Haydon (Heydon), John, App. III 6.

Hayer, Tho., 222.

Hayes, Tho., 213, 387.

Hayling I., Hants., 295.

Haynes, Phineas, 163, 169, 179.

Hayter, Dorothy, 13, 55, App. II 26.

Hayward (Haward), Ant., 127.
  Art., 128.
  Peter, 52, 94.

Hazelrig, Sir Art., 52.

Head, John, 134.

Hearth Tax, 287, 405.

Heather, John, 204.
  Ralph, 224.
  Tho., 195, 198, App. I 2.

Heatly (Hateley), James, 49, 110.

Heberden, Edw., 52, App. II 23.

Heddy, John, 226.

Hedger, —, 37, 236.
  Nic., 33, 186, 195, 197, 198, 202, 204, 208, 209, 212–219, 221, 226–229, 234, 235, 237–243, 245–252, 256, 258–265, 268, 273, App. II 81, 82, 85, 93, App. V.

Henning, Tho., 206, 209, App. I 4.

Henslow, Tho., 231.

Henty (Hentie), —, 83n.
  Rob., 240, 248, 264.
  Sam., 400.

heraldry: Sidney pheon as government mark, 86n; armorial seals, 89, 266, 392, 417.

Hewes, Hews, see Hughes.

Heydon, see Haydon.

Heyham (Hamie), Tho., 6.

Heyshott, Suss., 248.

Hicks (Hickes), Fra., 131.
  John, 205, App. II 87.

Higgin (Higgen), John, 250, 254.

Hill (Hills), Henry, 50.
  Joan, 269, 270.
  John, 366.
  Tho., 6, App. II 4.

Hillman, John, 267, 270.

Hilsea, on Portsea I., Hants., 187; Hilsea Common, 187.

Hintey, Rob., App. II 45, 56.
  Sam., App. II 38, 45.

Hoare (Haore, Whore), Ann, 295, 314, 338.
Hobbs, Dorothy, 293.
    James, 149, 293.
Hockley, Henry, 112, 124.
Hodely, Geo., 168.
Hodges (Hodgies), Geo., 334, 345.
    John, 334.
Hodgkin, see Hoskins.
Hogben, Rob., 387.
Holloway (Holawaye, Hollaway, Hollawaye),
    James, 78, 98, 138.
    John, 82.
    Moses, 381.
    Rob., p. xxxii, nos 219, 266, 270.
Holmes, Wil., 76, 82.
Holt, —, 11.
    Fra., 13-16, 18-20, 22, 80-82, 84, 85, 94, 101,
        App. II 23-37, 59, App. III 2-5, App. V.
    Henry, 252.
    John, 4, 5, 7, 8, 15, 23, App. II 3, 15, 27, 57,
        App. V.
    Mat., 225, 232.
Honywood, Sir Phil., 94.
Hoocker, Rob., 210.
Hooper (Hoopper), John, 416.
    Tho., 304.
    Wil., 306, 326.
Hopegood, —, 36.
Hopkins, Margery, 166, 169.
Horne, John, 292.
Horsea I., Hants., 156.
horses, 151, 160, 245, 292; see also harness and
    riding equipment.
Horsleydown, in Southwark, Surr., see Southwark.
Hoskins (Hodgkin), Hannibal, 46.
    John, 272.
Hotkins, James, 141.
Houlden, see Alden.
Hound, Hants., 19.
Hovell, Ric., 242.
Howard, Mary, 276.
Howe (How, Howes), Dan., App. II 35.
    Henry, 350.
Howell, John, 69.
Hoylake, Ches., App. III 6.
Hubbard, Alex., 231.
    Elias, 235.
Hughes (Hewes, Hews), Eleanor, 7.
    Geo., 418.
    Tho., 277, 282.
Hull, Yorks., E.R., see Kingston upon Hull.
Hull, —, 239.
    Bazell, 313.
    John, 304.
Hullum, Raleigh, 172.
Humfry, James, 96.
Hunt, Ann, App. II 34.
    John, 72.
    Ric., 116, 284, 372, 378, 388.
    Tho., 169, 199, 204, 245, 256, App. II 34, 87.
Hurleston, Tho., App. II 35.

Hurrall, John, 50.
Hutt, James, Portsmouth City Librarian, p. xi.
Hutton, Paul, App. III 5.

implements, see tools and implements.
industry and production: bread with baker's
    mark, 391; brew-house in Gosport, App. II 97;
    butchers' work, 195; see also agriculture;
    apprenticeship; occupations; Portsmouth (Dock-
    yard, Mill); shipbuilding; tools and implements;
    wages.
Ingland, Roger, 80.
Ingram, Sam., 222.
inns and public houses: innkeeper's licence, 240;
    for references to particular inns, see Bedford,
    Brockenhurst, Chichester, Dover, Gosport, Hav-
    ant, Kingston, Leith, London, Plymouth, Ports-
    mouth; see also beer and ale; occupations.
Inwood (Inwod), Tho., 381, 388, App. III 11.
Ipswich, Suff., 73.
Ireland, 6, 46; place indexed, Kinsale.
Ironmonger, John, 344, 345.
Isemonger, Ann, 311.
    Henry, 95.
Isger, John, 320, 326.
Isle of Wight, see Wight, I. of.

Jackman, Lydia, 4.
    Peter, 53.
Jackson, —, 167, 169, App. II 70.
    Eleanor, 82.
    John, 381.
    Mary, 405.
    Rob., 82, 167.
    Tho., 167, 384, 388.
Jacob, —, 246, 256.
    Tho., 196, 256.
Jacobsen, Jan, App. III 3.
James II, King, pp. xxxi, xxxiii, nos 378, 424; as
    Duke of York, 190, App. III 12.
James, John, App. II 25, 57.
    Phil., 156-167, 170-180, 188-191, 195, 197, 199,
        201, 206, 219, 220, 230, App. I 3, 4, App. III
        12, App. V.
    Ric., App. V.
Jansen-Brower, Frans., App. III 3.
Jefferyes, Amos, 88.
    Wil., 231, 232.
Jeffreys, Geo., 1st Baron Jeffreys, Lord Chief Justice,
    pp. xxxi, xxxiii, no. 205n.
Jellett, see Gellett.
Jelloffe, Margaret, 26.
Jenens (Jennance), Ric., 90n.
    Wil., 71.
Jenner, Henry, 23, 83, 102, App. II 28, 39.
Jennings, see Jenens.
Jent, see Gent.
jewels and plate: gold rings, 39; silver and jewelled
    buckles, 350; plate, 296; see also occupations.
Joanes, Johnes, see Jones.

Johnson, Ben., pp. xxviii, xxix, xxxii, nos 129–133, 135–143, App. I 2, App. III 7n, 8, App. IV, App. V.
  Henry, 16, 74, App. II 14, 62.
  John, 312, 326, 338n.
  Mary, 74.
  Winifred, App. II 14, 62.
Joiner, see Joyner.
Jones (Joanes, Johnes), —, 265.
  Ann, 58.
  Eliza or Elizabeth, 389, 408.
  Griffin, App. II 28.
  Humf., 71.
  Joan, 18, App. II 28.
  John, App. II 12.
  Jos., 181, 244, 256.
  Mary, App. III 9.
  Ric., 44.
  Tho., 24, 58, 73, 77, 111, 131, 266, 270, App. II 57, App. III 9.
Joslin (Josline, Jostlin), Margaret, 311, 318, 326.
  Wil., 311, 318, 326.
Joyce, Ric., 49, 64, 89, 101, 105, 110, App. II 15, 51, 60.
Joyner, Tho., 98.
Judson, Ann, 158, 169.
Juning, Peter, App. II 68.
justice, see law and justice.
Justices of the Peace: enrolment of Commission of the Peace, p. xxvii; see also Acts of Parliament; administration, local.

Keck (Kecke), Jeffery, App. III 4, 5.
Keden, Tho., 92, 121.
Kemp, —, 291.
Kempster, Bart., 404, 408.
Kempthorne, Sir John, Commissioner of the Navy, 203, 231.
Kent, places indexed, Deptford; Dover; Woolwich.
Kent, Jane, 88.
  John, 28, 29, 88.
  Ric., App. III 6.
  Wil., 381.
Kibe, Rob., 182.
Kill, Elizabeth, 275.
King, John, 392, 419.
  Lucy, 392.
  Wil., App. II 5, 44.
King's Bench, Court of, p. xix, no. 242.
Kingston, on Portsea I., Hants., 28, 30, 151, 156, 165, 170, 179, 180, 185, 187, 188, 192, 194, 197, 212, 215, 261, 269, 291, 292, 339, 348, App. I 1, App. II 77; the Blue Anchor, 156, 165.
Kingston upon Hull, Yorks., E.R., 47, 73.
Kinsale, Ireland, App. III 6.
Kippyn, Rob., 34.
Kirke, Tho., App. III 10.
Knapper, John, 410.
Knapton, Abbine or Albion, 319, 326.
  Jos., 321, 326.
  Ric., 362.

Kneller, Wil., 303, 326.
Knight, —, 119.
  John, 6, 66, 70, 122, 123, App. II 65.
  Sam., 141.
  Wil., 381.
Knowler, —, 221.
  Step., 206, 208.
Knowles (Knolles), Ben., 250.
  Elizabeth, 20.
  Tho., 20.
Kyte, —, 161.

Lambarde, Wil., historian of Kent, pp. xvii, xx.
Lambert, James, 200.
  John, 56.
Laming, Joan, 253.
Land or Laud, John, 268, 318.
  Sarah, 268, 270, 318.
Lane, —, 276.
  John, 266, 270, App. II 55.
Langerish, see Langridge.
Langford, Tho., 56.
Langley, Ric., 113.
Langridge (Langerish, Langrish), Frances, 360.
  Geo., 258, 270, App. II 5.
Langstone, in Havant, Hants., 198.
Langstone, Wil., 421.
languages: English, Latin, in Sessions papers, pp. xiv, xv; English spoken by German, App. IV; see also conversation.
Lannce, de, see De Lannce.
Lardner, Ric., 11, 14, 15, 18, 19, 23, 26, 27, 36, 39, 40, 46–49, 51, 54–56, 59, 62–75, 77, App. II 23, 27, 28, 39, 52, 62, 65–68, App. V.
La Rochelle, France, see Rochelle, La.
Laster, Elizabeth, 48.
  Tho., 48.
Later, Tho., App. II 47.
  Zachariah, Zacharias or Zachary, 93, App. II 71.
Laud, see Land or Laud.
Laurence, see Lawrence.
Lavis, Phil., 247.
law and justice: Lord Chief Justice, 243, 256, 266; Attorney-General, p. xix; notary public, 310, App. III 1–5, App. IV, App. V; searches for stolen goods, 86, 187, 231, 258, App. III 9, 11; economic laws, pp. xvi, xviii–xix, xxiv–xxv; pleas of debt and trespass, 90n; legal costs, 114n, 222; case for counsel's opinion, 216.
— Portsmouth courts: Court of Clerk of Markets, 150, 299n; Court of Record, p. xiii; View of Frankpledge and Court Leet, pp. xiv–xv, xx, xxvii–xxviii, xxx, nos 83n, 299n, 409.
— other courts: General Eyre, p. xvi; Grand Inquest, Grand Jury, pp. xix–xx, xxiii, nos 132, App. II 80; list of Grand Jurors, 222; see also Admiralty; Assizes; Common Pleas; King's Bench; Petty Sessions; Quarter Sessions.
— sentences: death, pp. xxii–xxiv; fines, p. xx, nos 205, 206, 208–210, 221, 223, 298, 299, 301, 303, 324–326, 333, 343, 344, 352, 362, 393, 423,

R

App. I 4, App. II 79, 80, 87, 90, 93; pauper excused fine, 253; stocks, 119; transportation, p. xxiv; whipping, pp. xx, xxvi, nos 4, 20, 26, 48, 59, 63, 68; imprisonment, see prisons.
— see also administration, local; Coroner's Inquests; crimes; mortgages; wills; writs.
Lawrence (Laurence), Christian, 6.
　Cornelius, App. IV.
　Dan., 353.
　Elizabeth, 6, App. II 4.
　Nic., 217, App. II 8, 48.
　Rolvo(?), 6.
　Simon, 217, 249, 256, App. II 8.
Lee, Nic., 54.
　Ric., 42.
Legg (Legge), Geo., *1st Baron Dartmouth*, pp. xxxi, xxxiii.
　Wil., 349, App. V.
Leith, *Scotland*, App. III 6; the Three Tuns, App. III 6.
Lell, Sam., App. III 6.
Lenny, Sam., App. III 10.
Leverett (Leveret), —, 299.
　John, 343, 345, App. III 8, 9.
　Wil., App. III 8.
Levesley, Rob., 62.
Levet, John, 390, 408.
Lewes, *Suss.*, App. II 12.
Lewin (Lewen), John, 52, 222, 381, 388, App. II 47.
Lewis (Lues), Abraham, 308.
Libett (Lybett), Wil., 319, 326.
Lifton, Amy, 385.
Light, Geo., 185.
Lightfoot, Tho., 169.
Limeburner (Lymeburner), Ann, App. II 47.
　John, App. II 51.
　Tho., 64.
Limehouse, *in Stepney, Mdx*, see Stepney.
Linton, Henry, 352.
Linvell (Lynfeild), Moses, 318, 326.
Liphook, *in Bramshott, Hants.*, see Bramshott.
Lisle, Lady Alice, *wife of John Lisle, regicide*, 205n.
Little, Leon., 357.
　Wil., 63.
Lloyd, —, 304.
　Godf., 5.
　Millicent, App. II 67.
　Theophilus, 297.
　Wil., 273.
Locke, Step., 297.
Lockeridge, *in West Overton, Wilts.*, see Overton, West.
Lockier, Ric., 87.
Loe, Dan., 354.
London, p. xxv, nos 46, 47, 90n, 132, 143, 181, 266, 296, 394, 396, App. III 1; Leadenhall parish, 263; St James in the Fields parish, 405; St Magnus' parish, 72; Newgate Market 238; Newgate St, 238; St Margaret's Hill, 166; the Hand in Hand, 238; see also British Museum; Public Record Office.

Long (Longe), —, 227.
　Ann, 200.
　Rob., 47.
　Sarah, 212.
　Tho., 47.
　Wil., 149, 169.
Lord, James, 281, 286.
Lovegrove, Elizabeth, 90.
Lowance, Edm., 367, 388.
Lowe, see Loe.
Lucas, —, App. II 62.
　David, 21, 63, App. II 62.
　Fra., 144, 145, 191, App. II 60.
　Simon, 169, 171.
Luckham, Avice, 342.
Lues, see Lewis.
Luist, John, App. III 6.
Lumpson, And., 114.
Lunn (Lun), Elizabeth, 71.
　Henry, 199, 204, App. II 21, 47.
　Mary, 71.
　Wil., 71.
Lutman, Tho., 268, 270.
Lybett, see Libett.
Lyme, Henry, 21.
Lymeburner, see Limeburner.
Lyminster, *Suss.*: Badworth Park, 350.
Lynfeild, see Linvell.
Lynn, Ambrose, App. II 55.
Lyon, Wil., 278, 282, 283, App. II 16.
Lysten, Amy, 153.
　Hendricke, 153.
Lyttleton, —, 277.

Mahón, *Minorca*, 266.
Maine, du, see Du Maine.
Maldon, *Essex*, 135.
Male, Wil., 363.
Mane, du, see Du Mane.
Manley, Sir Roger, *cavalier and author*, 201.
Mansbridge, Phil., 5, 21.
March, see Marsh.
Marchant, Ann, 161.
　John, 161.
Marden, Peter, App. II 4, 49.
markets, see fairs and markets.
Marlborough, *Wilts.*, 350.
Marsh (March, Mersh), Ant., 353.
　Fra., 262.
Marsham, John, 242.
Marshaw (Marshawe), —, 13.
　Tho., App. II 2.
Martin (Marten), Jane, 5.
　James, 395.
　Joan, 374.
　John, 290.
　Rob., 366, 374, 388.
Marvell, Ric., 378.
Mason, Ann, 197.
　John, 150, App. II 38.
Massingham, Dan., 40.

Matthews (Mathewes, Mathews, Matthewes),
  Henry, 196, 204, 209.
  Ric., 234.
  Rob., 361, 365, 388.
  Tho., 419.
May, Rob., 231.
Mayors, *see* administration, local.
Mazarin, Jules, *Cardinal and French statesman*, 77.
Meader, John, 3n, 97.
measures, *see* weights and measures.
medicine: injuries described, 74, 116; illness, 227,
  295, 308; death in childbirth, 328; *see also*
  occupations; plague.
Meers, And., 196, 204.
Mellish (Mellersh), Nic., 357, 367, 371, 375, 388,
  399, 408n.
  Ric., 175.
  Wil., 293, 408.
Merehen, Tho., 122.
Meriweather, *see* Merriweather.
Merricke, John, 66.
Merritt (Merriot, Merriott, Merrit), John, 200,
  204.
  Ric., 12
Merriweather (Meriweather, Meryweather),
  David, 141.
  Elizabeth, 169.
  Mary, 141.
Mersh, *see* Marsh.
Michell, *see* Mitchell.
Middelburg, *Netherlands*, App. III 4.
Middlesex, *places indexed*, Stepney; Westminster;
  Whitechapel.
Middleton, Ric., 300.
  Tho., *Commissioner of the Navy*, pp. xxix–xxx, xxxii,
  nos 119, App. III 7, 8, 9.
Mihell (Mihill), Dan., 387, 388.
  Tho., 290.
Mijer, Chr., 27.
Milford, *Pembs.*, App. III 6.
Mill, Sir John, *Bart.*, 360n.
Millbrook, *Hants.*: Redbridge, 263.
Mills, And., 375.
  Eleanor, 362.
  Geo., 366.
  Henry, 372, 387, 388.
  James, 15, 32, 34, App. II 11, 27, 63.
  Janura *or* Jonura, 154.
  Jean, 377, 388, 414.
  John, 300, 375, 388, 414.
  Nic., 362.
  Tho., 21, 90, 375.
mills and milling: *see* occupations; Portsmouth.
Milton, *on Portsea I.*, *Hants.*, 60, 215, 387, App. II
  21.
Minorca, *place indexed*, Mahón.
Minstead, *Hants.*, 360n.
Mishman, Jane, 360n.
Mitchell (Michell), Ant., 335.
  Chr., 372, 388.
  Margaret, 372, 388.

Wil., 22, 76, 83, 87, 88, 90, 91, 96, 118, 132,
  App. II 10, 22, 23, 27, 49, App. III 7, App. V.
Mittins (Mittens), Mary, App. II 54.
  Ric., 177, 192, App. II 54.
Mollomes, *see* Mullins.
Molonne, Pat., 424.
Money, James, App. II 59.
  Tho., 112.
Monmouth, Duke of, *see* Scott, James.
Monmouth's Rebellion (1685), p. xiv, nos 205n,
  373, 374, 376, 388.
Monsey, J., 3n.
Montagu, Edw., *1st Earl of Sandwich*, 110.
Montgomery, *see* Mountgomery.
Moody, John, 92, 162, App. I 3.
Moone, John, 53.
  Sam., 190, App. III 12.
Moore, —, 169.
  Elizabeth, App. II 68.
  James, 361.
  John, *Recorder of Portsmouth*, p. xxx.
  John, 203, 214, 216, 218, App. V.
Mooren, Ann, 155.
  John, 155.
Mordlin, Tho., 91.
Moreing, Tho., 134.
Morey, *see* Murrey.
Morfeld, Mic., 34.
Morgan (Morgin), Dorothy, 122.
  Elizabeth, 123.
  Godf., 86, 107, 111, 123, App. III 7, 9.
  Henry, 263, 270.
  John, 123.
  Tho., 353, 390, 408.
Morley, Elizabeth, 246, 256.
Morlin (Morlen), Ann, 334, 345, App. II 97.
  Jarvis, 194n.
Morris, Ben., 401.
  Mary, 307.
  Sarah, 401.
mortgages, App. II 99.
Mosier, Joan, 28.
Mosse (Mose), Rebecca, 241.
  Tho., 330.
  Wil., 84, 108, 113, 114, 132.
Mounsier, Abraham, 361.
Mountgomery, John, 277.
Mount's Bay, *coast of Cornw.*, App. III 6.
Mudd, John, 393, 408.
Mullins (Mollomes, Mullinns), —, 355.
  Tho., *Town Clerk of Portsmouth*, pp. xv, xxxi,
  xxxiin, nos 31, 50, 62, 82, App. III 1–5, 7.
Munday Elizabeth 245, 274.
  John, 74.
  Wil., 298.
Murcedo, de, *see* De Murcedo.
Murford, Peter, 43.
Murrey (Morey), —, 183.
  John, 178.
Musgrave, Simon, 83.
music: drummers, 189; trumpet, App. II 22.

Nantes, *France*, App. IV.

Nash, Ant., 420.

Navy: Navy Board, Commissioners for the Navy, pp. xii, xxix–xxx, nos 43, 112, 144n, 203, App. III passim; principal officers of the Navy, 86; Clerk to Commissioners for Prize Goods, App. III 2; Judge-Advocate, App. III 1n; Foreman of Portsmouth Ropeyard, App. III 7; Dockyard officials as Justices, pp. xxix–xxx, App. V; Navy victuallers, 225; the fleet at Portsmouth, 22; inciting mutiny in the fleet, 137; ship with twelve guns, 46; chase of Spanish frigate, App. III 6; loss of ship, App. III 1; disposal of prize goods, App. III 2, 4, 5.

— naval officers, 16, 25, 36(?), 72, 197(?), 203, 247(?), 273(?), 347(?), 355(?), 388(?), 396(?), App. II 57(?), App. III 3.

— *see also* Admiralty; occupations; Portsmouth (Dockyard); shipbuilding; ships and shipping; ships' stores.

Naxton, Wil., 16.

Nealer, Tho., 159.

Neather, Ric., App. III 8.

Neave (Neve), Ric., 102, 222.

Netherlands, App. IV; *places indexed*, Amsterdam; Enkhuizen; Middelburg.

Nevelock, Jo[. . .], App. II 67.

New (Newe), Edw., 67.
    Jean, 400.
    Ric., 304.

Newberry, —, App. II 62.

Newchurch, *I.W.*, 406, App. II 24.

Newdigate, Sir Ric., *1st Bart.*, App. II 73.

Newe, *see* New.

New England, *America*, 132.

New Forest, *Hants.*, 215, 360n.

Newland, Newton, 382.

Newnam, James, App. II 53.
    Mary, App. II 53.
    Rob., App. II 53.
    Tho., 406.

Newport, *I.W.*, 139.

newspapers: *London Gazette*, 181.

Newton, John, App. III 6.

Nicholls, Wil., 156.

Nicholson (Nichoalson), John, 231, 277.

Nixon, Tho., 206, App. I 4.

Noel, Edw., *1st Earl of Gainsborough*, 380.

nonconformists, Protestant, p. xiv, nos 71, 205, 206, 208, 209, 210, 297, 304, App. I 4, App. II 87, 90, 93; *see also* Anabaptists; Quakers.

Norfolk, *place indexed*, Yarmouth, Great.

Norington, Peter, App. III 6.

Norman, Wil., 25, App. II 50.

Northcotte, Geo., 74.
    Mary, 74.

North Warnborough, *in Odiham, Hants.*, *see* Odiham.

Norton, —, 245.
    John, 104, 142.
    Ric., 381.

Noseworthy, John, App. II 38.

Nosse, Nic., 189.

Nossiter, Joan, 406.

Oakeshot (Okeshott), John, 21, App. II 33.
    Rebecca, App. II 33.

oaths: of allegiance and supremacy, 71, 91, 100, 190, 215, App. III 12; Justice's failure to take oaths, 216; swearing the peace, p. xxi.

occupations:
    apothecary, App. II 70.
    armourer, App. III 6.
    baker, 7, 11, 52, 97, 116, 191, 205, 229, 258, 353, 373, App. II 38, 47; baker's boy, 4.
    barber, 94, 113, 211, 221, 340, 348, 349, 352, 359, 372, 385.
    barber surgeon, 405.
    blacksmith, 35, 51, 67, 356, App. II 5, 19, 53, 55, 72, App. V.
    block maker, 66, 87, 97, 200, 247.
    boatswain, 25, 73, 317, App. III 3, 6, 7, 10, 11; boatswain's mate, App. III 3; boatswain's boy, 25.
    box maker, 60.
    brazier, 193n, 350, App. II 22, 45, 56.
    brewer, App. II 54, App. V.
    bricklayer, 68, 263, 284, 290.
    butcher, 13, 26, 42, 49, 108, 195, 198, 254, 256, 270, 276, 301, 327, 366, 370, 412, App. I 2, App. II 13, 59, 60, App. V.
    cabin-boy, App. III 3.
    carpenter, 6, 27, 76, 112, 124, 132, 153, 249, 366, App. II 4, 19, 53, App. III 6, 10, 11.
    carrier, 50, 139, 181.
    caster maker, 202.
    caulker, 203, 351.
    chandler, 96, 349.
    chapman, App. II 20.
    cheesemonger, 39, App. II 20.
    clerk, 350n.
    clothier, 54, 381.
    cloth-worker, 157, App. II 60.
    comb maker, 160.
    cook, 58, 132, 244, 298.
    cooper, 265, 298, 363, 396.
    cordwainer, 50, 155, 159, 235, 244, 250, 255, 264, 292, 358, 372, App. II 36, 42, 43, 47, 64, 84.
    corporal, 201, 211, 338.
    coxswain, 307, App. III 6.
    currier, 132.
    cutler, 67, 132, App. II 39.
    draper, 157.
    fishmonger, 9.
    gardener, 217, 268, App. II 48.
    gingerbread-baker, 354.
    glazier, 392, App. II 39.
    glover, 58, 268, 324, 377, 381.
    goldsmith, 124, 149, 347.
    grocer, App. II 44.
    gunner, 228, 249, 258, 267, 305, 338n, 359, App. III 6, 11.

gunsmith, 51, 392.
house-carpenter, 219, 261, 284, 332, 387, 415, App. III 8.
husbandman, 38, 42, 187, 219, 225, 226, 245, 337, 381, App. II 42, 43, 54, 80.
innholder, 139, 140, 295, 338, 347, 350, 366, App. II 52, 65, 73.
joiner, 113, 239, 275, 300, 354, 375, 392, 414, App. II 20.
keeper, 381.
labourer, 5, 10, 38, 43, 54, 66, 84, 149, 153, 159, 160, 179, 180, 196, 202, 213, 228, 231, 261, 267, 274, 285, 306, 323, 337, 359, 378, 395, App. II 8, 13, 24.
lime-burner, 371.
linen-draper, 46, 238.
locksmith, 383.
maltster, 42, 74.
mariner, 8, 16, 34, 47, 49, 62, 72, 73, 129, 135, 167, 212, 221, 233, 266, 310, 312, 316, 330, 336, 352, 361, 369, 384, 416, 419, App. II 1, 50, 54, 71, App. III 2, App. IV.
mason, 6, 76, 223, 249, 339, 353, 366, 378, 422, App. II 5, 44.
master of ship, 47, 228, 230, App. III 6, App. IV.
mercer, 97, 216, 233, 382, 417, App. V.
merchant, 46, App. III 2, 6, App. V.
metal-man, 328.
midshipman, 72, App. III 6.
midwife, 338.
miller, 249, 386, App. II 37.
musketeer, 211.
nailer, 51.
ostler, 337, 383.
painter, 249.
painter stainer, 407.
pedlar, 256.
pedlar woman, 18.
petty chapman, 159, 160, 248.
pewterer, 291, App. II 38.
plug keeper, 149.
quartermaster, App. III 6.
rope maker, 70, 86, 111, 141, 148, 175, 202, 224, 230, 292, 315, 366, App. II 22, 57, App. III 7, 8, 9.
saddler, App. II 21, 65.
sailor, 327, 333, 343, 365, 366, 416, 423.
sawyer, 90n, App. II 36.
seaman, 16, 21, 27, 48, 49, 52, 60, 67, 73, 94, 109, 161, 165, 166, 196, 262, 308, 329, 338, 362, App. II 29, 43, 48, 50, 71, 72.
sempstress, 295.
sergeant, 271.
servant (including maid, man, servant maid, serving maid), 5, 6, 7, 22, 39, 46, 51, 59, 63, 128, 148, 164, 166, 169, 176, 180, 182, 188, 197, 198, 204, 212, 216, 226, 227, 228, 238, 246, 264, 277, 293, 297, 307, 309, 316, 343, 345, 352, 354, 358, 360, 372, 375, 405, App. III 8, 9.
servant of the King, 70, 201.

ship owner, App. V.
shipwright, 37, 56, 87, 119, 144, 145, 171, 185, 191, 223, 239, 241, 266, 298, 303, 323, 350, 355, 366, 371, 373, 393, 419, App. V.
shoemaker, 38, 263, 271, 372.
silk-weaver, 394.
smith, 63, 187.
soldier, 18, 39, 45, 50, 66, 68, 70, 71, 80, 92, 113, 184, 221, 258, 260, 268, 276, 277, 285, 292, 304, 306, 311, 353, 362, 367, 368, 372, 376, 378, 384, 391, 416, 420, 424, App. II 16.
spurrier, 344.
steersman, 310, App. IV.
steward, App. III 6.
stonemason, 284.
surgeon, 96, 355, App. III 6, App. V.
tailor, 9, 19, 48, 176, 193, 209, 258, 269, 294, 387, 411, 412, App. II 44, 60.
tallow-chandler, 268.
tanner, 50, 164.
tapster, 165, 189, 285.
tobacco-pipe maker, 260.
turner, 64.
victualler, 52, 70, 159, 164, 167, 180, 201, 202, 213, 217, 220, 225, 258, 271, 279, 281, 302, 325, 330, 332, 337, 348, 349, 354, 357, 362, 365, 372, 396, App. II 22, 85, 86.
vintner, 181.
wagoner, 360n.
waterman, 257.
weaver, 7, 80, 132, App. II 19.
wheelwright, 76, 371.
worsted comber, 51.
yeoman, 14, 35, 50, 54, 118, 139, 156, 161, 177, 184, 194, 196, 197, 206, 208, 215, 269, 274, 353, 371, 381, 387, 396, 415, App. I 4, App. II 12, 13, 24, 45, 50, 64, 80, 93, App. III 10.
— see also administration, local; apprenticeship; Army; Church, clergy and religion; Customs and Excise; industry and production; law and justice; Navy.
Odiham, *Hants.*: North Warnborough, 50.
Okeford, Ann, 59.
Okeshott, *see* Oakeshot.
Olding, Ann, 216.
    Mary, 375.
    Rob., 379, 388.
    Step., 226, 375, 387, 388.
Oléron, *France*, App. III 2.
Orpington, Tho., 392, 408.
Orrell, Jonathan, 73.
Osborne (Osburne), Alice, 152.
    John, 395.
Osmont, John, 56.
Outhwaite, *see* Uthwaite.
Overseers of the Poor, *see* administration, local.
Overton, Jerome, 189.
Overton, West, *Wilts.*: Lockeridge, 157.
Owslebury, *Hants.*, 381.
Oxford, *Oxon.*, 60.
Oxfordshire, *place indexed*, Oxford.

Padison, Rob., 395.
Page (Paige), John, 376.
   Ric., 337, 345, 381, 421.
   Wil., 388.
Paice (Payce), Alex., 50.
Paine, *see* Payne.
Painter, John, App. III 6.
painting: frescoes in the House of Commons, 205n;
   see also occupations.
Palmer, John, 185.
   Wil., 174.
Pansfard, *see* Penford.
Parbus (Porbus), Abraham, 53.
Parker, Elizabeth, 191.
   Jane, 49.
   Mary, 191.
   Rob., 49, 89.
   Tho., App. II 84.
Parkes (Parcks, Parks), Ric., 43.
   Tho., 43, 45, 51, 106.
Parliament: military service for Parliament, p. xxv,
   nos 22, 70; writ for election, 360n; disfranchise-
   ment of burgesses, App. II 82, 83; frescoes in the
   House of Commons, 205n; *see also* Acts of
   Parliament.
Parnell (Purnell), Hezekiah, 56.
   Joanna, 367, 388.
Parsons, James, App. III 6.
Pascoe (Paschoe), Mary, 183, 291.
   Roger, 183, 291.
Passenger, James, 258, 270.
Patch, Step., App. III 6.
Paterson, *see* Padison.
Patten, John, 3n, 15, 388, 392, App. II 26.
Paul, Elizabeth, 149.
Pay (Paye), Mary, App. II 12, 18.
   Tho., 56, 171.
   Wil., 326.
Payce, *see* Paice.
Payne (Paine), —, 191.
   Edw., 421
   Frances, 421.
   Rob., 127, 129.
   Wil., 295.
Peachy, Greg., 382.
   James, 216.
Peacock, —, 72, App. II 57.
Peagan, *see* Pegan.
Pearson (Peerson, Peirson, Person), Ann, 398.
   John, 215.
   Mary, 269.
   Nic., 8, 10, 24, 116, 129, 179, 180, 184, 185, 230,
      234–238, 257–260, 268, 269, 271, 272, 274,
      287, 289, 297, 299, 300, 302, 304–309, 311,
      313, 315–319, 323, 326, 327, 330, 333–335,
      338, 341, 342, 348, 349, 352–355, 359, 361,
      363, 365, 373, App. II 15, 40, 71, 85, App.
      III 11, App. V.
   Phil., 186.
Peck (Pecke), Chr., 31, 53n.
   Peter, 373, 388.

Wil., App. II 70.
Peerman (Perman), Jos., 179, 180.
Pegan (Peagan), Wil., 238, 256.
Peirson, *see* Pearson.
Pembrokeshire, *places indexed*, Caldy Road; Milford;
   Rhoscrowther; Tenby.
Pen, *see* Penn.
Penfold, Abraham, 401.
Penford (Pansfard), Henry, 16.
   Wil., 132.
Penn (Pen), —, 292.
   Henry, 156, 169, 223, 232.
   Mary, 180.
Penticost, Ric., 69.
Penton Grafton, *Hants.*: Weyhill, 46.
Pepper, —, App. III 6.
Pepys, Sam., *Secretary of the Admiralty*, pp. xxixn,
   xxxn, xxxii.
Percivall, Fra., 29, 96, 146.
Perkins, Cha., 348.
   Fra., 215.
   Geo., 348.
Perman, *see* Peerman.
Perrin (Perin, Perryn), Henry, 36, 95–98, 100, 102–
   109, 111–113, 118–120, App. V.
   John, 293, 315.
Perry, Walt., 102.
Person, *see* Pearson.
Pescod, Ric., 164.
Petersfield, *Hants.*, p. xxxi, nos 3, 383, 406.
Petherton, South, *Som.*, 244.
Petty Sessions, pp. xx–xxii.
Phetiplace, Hannah, 108.
Philip, Mary, 295.
Phillips (Phillipps), Dinah, 60.
   Mary, p. xxvi, nos 164, 169.
   Rob., 60.
Phillpott, Jos., 173.
Pickering, Edw., 359.
pigs, 84, 197.
Pigget, Roger, 316.
Pike, Spicer and Co., *brewers*, p. xi.
Pinchen (Pinchin), Chr., 378, 388.
Pitt, Edw., 272.
   John, App. II 85.
Pitter (Peter), Rob., 60, 83n.
   Sarah, 60.
plague: of 1665–6, pp. xiv, xxv, xxix, nos 125, 142,
   143.
plate, *see* jewels and plate.
Pledgen, John, 119.
Plover, —, 276.
   James, 83n, App. II 68.
   Tho., 157, 165, 172, 177, 198, 204, 276, App. II
      31, App. V.
Plumbridge, Frances, 404.
Plymouth, *Devon*, App. II 38, App. III 6, App. IV;
   the Bunch of Grapes, App. III 6.
Poate (Poat, Poett), John, 275, 291, 300, 326.
   Mary, 275.
   Ric., 106, 118.

Tho., 146.
Pocock (Pococke), Joan, 182.
 Mary, 117.
Poett, *see* Poate.
Pogson, Peter, 367, 368, 369, 388.
 Prudence, 367, 369, 388.
political activity: opposition to the Commonwealth, 18; the Restoration of 1660, p. xiv; abuse
 of the royal court, 94; the Revolution of 1688,
 p. xiv; political rumours, 60, 355, 378, 379, 388;
 see also Civil Wars; crimes (disloyalty, sedition,
 treason); Monmouth's Rebellion; war and
 rebellion.
Pollen, John, 381.
Ponnt, Tho., App. III 8.
Ponter, —, 395.
Poore, John, 48.
 Mary, 48.
poor-law, pp. xvi, xviii, xxiv, xxvi; cases concern-
 ing settlement, pp. xviii, xxvi, nos 20, 46, 164,
 215, 240, 248, 295, 323, 328, 406; case con-
 cerning parish-child, 250; *see also* administration,
 local; crimes (bastardy, vagrancy); documents
 and diplomatic.
Pope, Ellen, 22.
 Jo[...], 45.
 Margaret, 22.
 Wil., App. II 37.
Popejoy, Nat., 157, 169.
Popton, *in Rhoscrowther, Pembs.*, *see* Rhoscrowther.
Porbus, *see* Parbus.
Portbury, Wil., 35.
Portchester, *Hants.*, 37, 152, 156, 231, 238, 381,
 App. III 10, 11.
Porter, Miles, 371, 387, 388.
Portland, Margery, 147.
 Rob., 147.
Port Mahon, *Minorca*, *see* Mahón.
Portsbridge, *on Portsea I., Hants.*, 48, 258, 270, 292.
Portsea, *on Portsea I., Hants.*, pp. xxviii, xxix, nos
 14, 22, 32, 35, 71, 76, 118, 166, 258, 269, 274,
 275, 292, 339, 366, 378, 387, App. II 64, 80,
 App. III 10; church, churchyard, 90, 197; *see
 also* Portsmouth.
Portsea I., *Hants.*, p. xxviii, nos 48, 97; *places
 indexed*, Buckland; Fratton; Gatcombe; Hilsea;
 Kingston; Milton; Portsbridge; Portsea; Ports-
 mouth; Southsea; Stamshaw; Tipner.
Portsmouth, *Hants.*: City Library, p. xi; City
 Record Office, pp. xi–xii; Penny St. Chapel,
 p. xi; St Thomas' Church, pp. xi, xii.
— Portsmouth town, minor names and buildings:
 Almshouse, 196.
 barracks, 391.
 Camber, App. III 2.
 common gaol, 392.
 court-house, 272.
 Customs office, 245.
 Garrison, 12, 68, 92, 355, 420, App. II 16, 22.
 God's House, 249.
 God's House Yard, 13.

 Guildhall, 32.
 High St., 245.
 Horne Court, 295.
 Main Guard, 71, 277.
 market, 155, 178, 195, 198.
 Market Cross, 94.
 Pennyless Bench, 265.
 Platform, 265.
 Point, the, p. xxv, nos 21, 24, 25, 86, 94, 119, 201,
 221, 237, 245, 249, 264, 265, 266, 273, 329,
 338, 353, 392, 396, 421, App. III 7, 10, 11.
 Pointgate, 94, 265.
 Square Tower, 249.
 Stoes' quay, 361.
 Town Hall, 77, 132.
 Town Prison, 173, 190, App. III 12.
 Town Quay, 230.
 walls, 378, App. II 29.
 Warblington St., 367.
 water house, 249.
 Whitehouse, 190, App. III 12.
— Portsmouth liberties (Portsea parish), minor
 names and buildings:
 Coldharbour, 177.
 Common, the, 111, 151, 360, 395, App. III 9.
 common fields, 82, 185, 388, App. III 8.
 Dockfield, 185.
 Dockyard: pp. xxix–xxx, xxxii, nos 87, 111, 119,
 141, 144n, 149, 169, 203, 230, 267, 293, 308,
 395, App. III 7–10, App. V; Dockgate, 308;
 rope-yard, App. III 7–9; rope-house, 224,
 App. II 72, App. III 8.
 Havencroft, 177.
 lane beyond the Fountain, 177.
 Mill, 148, 338, 353, App. III 8.
 Newgate, 14.
 Pesthouse, 185.
 pound, 177.
 powder houses, 360.
 Pudshole, 166.
 State's warehouse, App. III 5.
— Portsmouth town and liberties, inns and public
 houses:
 Anchor, 29.
 Crown, 376.
 Dolphin, 348.
 Dun Cow, 392.
 Five Bells, 277.
 Fountain, 177(?), App. II 80.
 Golden Ball, 205.
 Garter, 371.
 London, 25, 119, 305, 406.
 Neptune's Court, 189, 372.
 Queen's Head, 13.
 Rainbow, 127.
 Red Lion, 285, 383.
 Rose and Crown, 290.
 Scotch Cross, 353.
 Sovereign, App. III 9.
 Unicorn, 175(?).
 White Dog, 148.

through marsh, 292; levy for highway repair, 396;
riding on highway, 292; carts, 258, 300, App. III
9; packhorses, 160; *see also* crimes (driving
irregularly, obstructing the highway, riding);
occupations.

Roaker (Rooker), —, App. III 9.
  John, 182, 202, 275, 291, 300, 326.
  Margaret, 407.
  Mary, 275, 291.
  Nic., 219, 225, 232, 275, 396, 408.
Roberts, Tho., 204.
Robertson, Jane, 374.
Robinson, Bridget, 101.
  Elizabeth, 323.
  John, 202, 323.
Roche, —, 135.
Rochelle, La, *France*, App. III 2, 6.
Rockwell, John, 35, 67, App. II 10.
Roe, *see* Row.
Rogers, Elizabeth, 185.
  Geo., 185.
  Joan, 185.
  Phil., App. II 38.
Roill, *see* Royle.
Rolfe, Wil., 164.
Roman Catholics: suspected, 215; the Pope's health
  drunk, 77, 359; the Duke of York a papist, 190,
  App. III 12.
Romsey, *Hants.*, 381.
Rooke, —, 347.
Rookeley, Tho., App. II 70.
Rooker, *see* Roaker.
Roper, Elizabeth, 421.
  Wil., 421.
Rotherhithe, *Surr.*, App. II 1.
Row (Roe), John, 395.
Rowter, Tho., 8.
Royle (Roill), Henry, 371, 388.
  John, 371, 388.
Rudge, Katherine, 220.
  Tho., 220.
Rumble (Rumball), Alice, 189.
Russell, Jos., 116.
  Mic., 223, 232.
Rutter, —, 410.
  Dorothy, 71.
  John, 403, 418.
  Ric., 51.
  Wil., 71.

Sachell, —, 13.
Sacheverell, Theophilus, 56.
Saint, *see* Saynt.
Salisbury, *Wilts.*, 9, 263, App. II 20.
Salisbury (Salesbury, Salisburie), —, 245.
  Hugh, pp. xxviii, xxix, xxx, nos 5, 35–43, 77, 80,
    83–86, 88, 94, 102, 109, 113, 114, 126, 144,
    145, 149, 162, 173, 179, 192, App. I 2, 3,
    App. II 64–67, 79, 80, App. III 7, 9, 11,
    App. IV, App. V.

Salterly, Mary, 418.
  Nic., 418.
Sampson, John, 68.
  Rebecca, 68.
Sanders, *see* Saunders.
Sandwich, Earl of, *see* Montagu, Edw.
Sannenough, Laur., App. II 12.
Santloe, John, 366, 388.
Sargeant, Geo., App. II 34, 66.
Saunders (Sanders), Cha., 308.
  Gabriel, App. III 3.
  John, 13.
  Margaret, App. II 21.
  Ric., 134.
  Susanna, 182.
  Wil., 154.
Savile, Edw., 420.
Saynt, Wil., 10, App. II 15.
Saywell, Reynold, App. II 20.
Scotland, *places indexed*, Dumfries; Leith.
Scott (Scot, Stot), Henry, 21.
  Humf., 303, 304.
  James, *Duke of Monmouth*, 205n, 373, 376, 388.
  Rob., App. II 32.
Scrace, John, 12.
Scroggs, Sir Wil., *Lord Chief Justice*, 266.
Seager (Seagar), Henry, 259, 353, 373, 388.
seals, p. xv, nos 89, 266, 392, 417, missing from
  documents, 205, 206, 208, 209, 297, App. I 4.
Seamar, Seamer, *see* Seymor.
Selden, —, 375.
  Dan., App. II 85.
  Nic., 151, 230, 359, App. II 85.
Selman, —, 94.
Sely, Rob., App. III 8.
Sergeants-at-Mace, *see* administration, local.
Seymor (Seamar, Seamer), —, 221, 338.
  Tho., p. xxxi, nos 21, 334, 345.
Shackelwell, John, 279.
Shafte, Rob., 31, 35.
Shales, —, 357.
  Rob., 214, 215, 223, 224, 225, 230, 231, 234,
    246, 264, 267, 300, 302, 304, 381, 396, 403,
    405, 424, App. II 85, App. V.
Shaw (Shawe), John, 337, 345.
sheep, 388.
Shenke, John, 79.
Sheppard, Dorothy, App. II 31.
  John, 17, App. II 31.
  Rob., 284.
  Wil., 62, App. II 54.
Sheriffs, *see* administration, local.
Shilling, John, 266, 270.
shipbuilding, 149, 203, 351; *see also* occupations.
Shipley, *Suss.*, 20.
ships and shipping: fly-boat, 73; ketch, App. IV;
  hoys, 315, 316; guard-boat, 316; hulks, App. III
  10; barge from ship at Spithead, App. III 10;
  ship seized as enemy (cargo specified), App. IV;
  prize ships (cargoes specified), App. III 2, 4, 5;
  capture of prize, App. III 3; passengers to Ireland,

App. III 6; cargo of coal, App. II 85; ballasting, 361; death on voyage to America, 132; assault on board ship, 266, 419; ship's master drunk at sea, App. III 6; loss of ship described, App. III 1; entertaining seamen, 110; bills of lading, App. IV.
— parts of ships: boltsprit, App. III 6; gallery, 203; poop lantern, App. III 6.
— ships named:
  America, 329.
  Basing, App. III 6.
  Bristol, 338.
  Cygnet, 72.
  Dartmouth, 305, 338n.
  Earl of Sandwich, App. IV.
  Edgar, 228.
  Galloon, App. III 10.
  Gloucester, 47.
  Golden Buss, 112.
  Hare-in-the-Field, App. III 4.
  Harwich, 203, 308, 359.
  Henrietta Maria, 68.
  Hope, App. IV.
  John and Katherine, App. III 1.
  John of London, 46.
  Kingfisher, 307, 308, 338, 351.
  Little Charity, 16.
  Magdalen, App. III 2.
  Marmaduke, 72.
  Matthias, 73.
  Montague, App. III 10.
  Orange Tree, App. III 5.
  Ostrich, App. III 10.
  Oxford, App. III 7.
  Paradox, App. III 6.
  Pearl, App. III 11.
  Phoenix, 52, 132.
  President, App. III 1.
  Report, App. III 1.
  Resolution, 166.
  Revenge, App. III 10.
  Ruby, App. III 1.
  Rupert, 203.
  Sampson, App. III 3.
  Small Nut, App. III 2.
  Tiger, 52, App. III 3.
  Unicorn, 175(?).
  Wexford, 27.
  Wildman, 25.
  Willing Wind, 73.
  York, 165, App. III 10.
— seaways: see Caldy Road; Mount's Bay; Portsmouth Harbour; Spithead.
— see also Navy, occupations, shipbuilding; ships' stores.
ships' stores, 86n; mast, 156; mizzen-yard, 361; ropes, etc., 25, 73, 111, 112, 185, 351, App. II 72, App. III 7–11; tackle, 112; oars, App. III 11; anchor, 73; buoy, 73; other items, 25, 43, 51, 63, 86, 87, 90, 115, 149, 204, 338, 351, App. II 56, App. III 10, 11.

Shore, John, 52.
Short, —, 25.
Shorter, Rob., 258, 270, 292, 299, App. II 86.
Shread, Wil., 369.
Sidney, Sir Phil., statesman and poet, 86n.
Silver, Tho., 301, 320, 326, 327, 345.
Silvo, de, see De Silvo.
Simonds (Symonds, Symons), Mat., 70, 167.
  Wil., 395., App. III 6.
Sims (Symes, Symms), John, 312, 326.
  Ric., p. xxv, no. 125.
  Wil., 381.
Sismore, John, App. II 28, 39, 57.
Sistence (Sistense, Sistons), Elizabeth, 353.
Skarvill, Ric., 21.
Skelton, —, 273, 347, 396.
  Ann, 396.
  Cha., 340, 396.
Skilton, Wil., 90n.
Skinner, John, 269.
Skipper, Eliza or Elizabeth, 287, 423.
  Martha, 423.
Slingsby (Slingsbye), —, 201, 348.
  Henry, p. xxxiii.
Slooter, John, App. II 35.
Smaledridge, Edw., 140.
Small, John, 231, 232, 234.
  Tho., 294.
Smart, Rob., 29, 30.
Smedmore, Wil., App. II 80.
Smith (Smyth), Henry, 281.
  James, 336.
  John, 5, 26, 284, 306.
  Ric., 165, 354, 357, 411.
  Rob., 38, 71, 206, 208, 209, App. II 93, App. III 10.
  Roger, 326, 337, 345, 388.
  Sam., 112, 113, 122.
  Step., 371, 388.
  Tho., 47, 265, 270, 402, 408.
  Wil., 106, App. III 6.
Snelling, John, 281.
Soames, Geo., 254, 256, 270.
Soane, —, 258.
  Alice, 379.
  Jeffery, 388.
  Sam., 379.
Soberton, Hants., 42.
Softly (Softley), John, 301, 320, 326, 388.
  Jos., 179.
Somerhill, Wil., 73.
Somerset, places indexed, Aller; Cary, Castle; Petherton, South.
Southam, Sam., 25.
Southampton, Hants., p. xxv, nos 113, 125, 142, 263, 291, 296, 361.
South Petherton, Som., see Petherton, South.
Southsea, on Portsea I., Hants.: Castle, 12, 249.
South Stoneham, Hants., see Stoneham, South.
Southwark, Surr., 46, 157; Horsleydown, 176.

Southwick, *Hants.*, 381; Belney, 381; Wanstead, 370.
Sowill, John, 280.
Sparke, Henry, App. III 10.
    Roger, App. III 10.
Sparkes (Sparcks), Ric., 51.
    Rob., 231.
Spashot, Ann, 352.
Speed, Frampton, 163.
Spelman, Sir Henry, *historian and antiquary*, p. xxiii.
Spencer, Tho., 381.
Spereing, John, 202.
Spithead, *coast of Hants.*, App. III 10.
Squier, Tho., 356.
Staines, *see* Stean.
Staire, *see* Stare.
Stallerd, Chr., 112.
Stamshaw, *on Portsea I.*, *Hants.*, 118.
Standen, Wil., 201, 202, 204, 211, App. III 7.
Stanesmore, Bart., 395.
Staning (Stoneing), Peter, 316, 326.
Stanley, Onesepherus, App. II 80.
Stare (Staire, Stayre), Rob., 197.
    Tho., 27.
Stares, James, 410.
Starke (Starkes, Starks), John, 348, 383, 388.
    Rob., 112.
Stayner, John, 305.
    Walt., 245.
    Wil., 255.
Stayre, *see* Stare.
Stean (Staines, Steane), Tho., 48, 216.
Stebbens (Stebbins, Stebens), Geo., 337.
Steele, Ric., 308.
    Tho., 381.
Stephenson, *see* Steventon.
Stepney, *Mdx*, App. II 30; Limehouse, App. II 1; Ratcliff, 72; *see also* Whitechapel.
Stevens (Stephens), David, 388.
    John, 135, 366, 388.
    Ric., 366, 388.
    Wil., *Recorder of Portsmouth*, 5, 10, 22, App. II 57.
Steventon (Stephenson, Stephenton), —, App. III 10.
    Elizabeth, 216.
    Geo., 410.
    St John, pp. xxviii, xxix, nos 110, 111, 113, 114, 116–124, 126–128, 145, 149, 150, 152, 188–191, 195, 199–205, 210, 216, App. I 2, App. II 79, 80, App. III 12, App. IV, App V.
Still, John, 403.
Stockman, Wil., p. xv.
Stockwell (Stockell), Tho., 139.
Stoe (Stoes), Ric., 289, 361, 365, 388.
Stone, Eliza *or* Elizabeth, 416, 417.
    John, 416.
    Ric., App. II 13.
Stoneing, *see* Staning.
Stoner, Tho., 323.
Stoneham, South, *Hants.*, 164.
Stot, *see* Scott.

Stow, *see* Stoe.
Stratton, Ant., 158, 169, App. II 87.
Streaper, Frances, 191.
    Wil., 191.
Street, John, 148.
Stripe, Edm., 288.
    Rob., 288.
Strong (Stronge), Nat., 56.
Stubber, Averne, 32, 35.
    Bart., 269, 270.
Stubberfeild (Stuberfeild), John, 202.
Stubbs (Stubs), —, 384.
    John, 302, 326, 349.
Stuckey, Geo., 361, 365, 388.
Sturt, Elizabeth, 343, 345.
Sturton, Elizabeth, 182.
    Geo., 182.
Suffolk, *place indexed*, Ipswich.
Sumner, Wil., 404, 408.
Supple, James, 70.
Surrey, *places indexed*, Deptford; Godalming; Guildford; Rotherhithe; Southwark.
Surveyors of Highways, *see* administration, local.
Sussex, *places indexed*, Arundel; Brighton; Chichester; Hastings; Heyshott; Lewes; Lyminster; Shipley; Westbourne.
Suttcleife, Rob., App. III 6.
Sutton, Henry, 328.
    Mary, 328.
Swaine, James, 141, 146.
    John, 174.
    Wil., App. II 37.
Sweete, Ric., 6, 62.
    Wil., 62.
Sweetingham (Swettingham), Hugh, 316, 322, 326, 327, 345.
    Jane, 322, 326.
Swetland, Mary, 17.
Swynson, Swyn, App. II 35.
Symes, Symms, *see* Sims.
Symonds, Symons, *see* Simonds.

T[. . .], A., 97.
Tailer, Taileur, Tailor, *see* Taylor.
Talbot, Ric., 388.
Tanner, Henry, 201.
    Joan, 286.
Tarrant, Henry, 115, 120.
    John, 50.
Tawke (Tawk), —, 97.
    John, 23, 24, 26, 27, 33, 77, App. II 38–40, 42–58, App. III 6, App. V.
taxes, *see* administration, local; Customs and Excise; Hearth Tax.
Taylor (Tailer, Taileur, Tailor, Taylear, Tayler, Tayleur, Taylour), —, 25.
    David, 350.
    John, 250, 256, 273, 282, 292, 341, 351, 366, 388, 400.
    Mic., 138, App. II 53.
    Sam., 56, 385, 388.

Wil., 11, 39, App. II 22, 46.
Tege, John, App. II 29.
Tenby, *Pembs.*, App. III 6.
Terrell (Terrill), Elizabeth, 252, 364.
    Wil., 222, 245, 252, 256, 285, 295, 309, 337, 338,
        364, 383, 388, 407, 408.
Thatcher, Wil., 40.
Thirman, *see* Thurman.
Thomas, Edw., 123.
    John, 194n.
    Ric., 9, 84, 159, 387, 388.
    Step., 304, 355.
Thompson (Thomson, Tompson, Tomson), Elean-
    or, 287, 421, 423.
    Elizabeth, 184.
    Henry, 266.
    Humf., 335.
    James, 287, 333, 345, 421, 423.
    John, 338, 353.
    Jos., 259.
    Margaret, 335.
    Wil., 181, 184.
Thorne, John, 94, 105, 201, 204, 222, 272, 281, 347.
Thorowgood, Cha., App. III 6.
    Tho., App. II 1.
Thurman (Thirman), Walt., 99, App. II 44.
Tiddersell, John, App. II 71.
    Nic., App. II 71.
Tiddiman, —, 299.
    John, 365.
Tilden, Henry, 366, 388.
timber, *see* woods and timber.
Timbrell (Tymbrell), John, 50, 53, 54, 60, 62, 63,
    69, 71, 78, 79, 81, 82, 84–88, 92, 140, App. II 70,
    71, 72, 75, App. V.
Tinker, —, App. III 10.
Tipner, *on Portsea I., Hants.*, p. xxviii.
Tippetts, John, p. xxix, nos 46–49, 51, 52, 57,
    59–61, 73, App. II 70, 73, App. III 6, App. V.
Tither, Fra., 63.
tobacco, 258, 260, 270, App. III 5; pipe, 201.
Todd, Eleanor, 107.
Tomes (Tommes, Toomes), Tho., 56, 66, 192,
    249, 366, 388, App. II 9.
tools and implements:
    axe, 266.
    bellows, 161.
    bill, 187.
    broom, 23, 384.
    cleaver, 108.
    crow, iron, 51.
    dung-fork, 301.
    fire-fork, 108, 189.
    hammer, 187.
    hatchet, 9, 266.
    pickaxe, 275.
    prong, 163, 300.
    pump, 202, App. III 9.
    pump hook, 247.
    rake, 269.
    scissors, 160, App. III 6.

    scythe, 187.
    shovel, 275.
    spit, 290.
    wheelbarrow, 275.
    windlass, 316.
— *see also* arms and armour.
Toomes, *see* Tomes.
Toope, Rob., App. III 6.
Tooth, Wil., 357.
Tovey, Henry, 107, App. III 7, 8.
Town Clerks, *see* administration, local.
trade and commerce: economic laws, pp. xvi,
    xviii–xix, xxiv–xxv; shops, 174, 309, 397; trader
    with France, 46; Barbados planter, 94; *see also*
    apprenticeship; Assize of Bread; beer and ale;
    coinage; crimes (Customs evasion, false weights,
    forestalling, regrating, trading irregularly, trad-
    ing unapprenticed); Customs and Excise; fairs
    and markets; inns and public houses; occupa-
    tions; prices; roads and road transport; ships
    and shipping; weights and measures.
transport and communications, *see* crimes (driving
    irregularly, obstructing the highway, riding);
    occupations; roads and road transport; ships
    and shipping.
Treblecocke (Trebelcocke), Fra., 358.
Trelawny, Cha., *Major-General*, 420.
Trift, John, 395.
Trigg, —, 97.
Triggs, Tho., 126, 169, 222, 228, 232, 349.
    Wil., App. II 79.
Tuke, Edw., App. II 30.
    Peter, App. II 30.
Turnepenny (Turnepeny), Wil., 280, 282.
Turner, —, 197.
Tyler, Tho., 209.
Tyley, Tho., 332, 345.
Tymbrell, *see* Timbrell.

Undershell (Undershershell), Wil., 384, 388.
Uphman, James, 21.
    Rob., 81, 89, 90n, 134, 140.
Upjohn, Ben., 393, 408.
    Lucy, 405.
    Sarah, 405.
Upsdale (Upsdall), Ann, 338.
    John, 133.
    Roger, 260, 270.
    Tho., 197, 204.
Urline (Urlene), Elizabeth, 342.
    Wil., 342, 358.
Uthwaite (Uthwait, Uthwatt), Ric., 133, 134,
    136, 137, 291.

Venables, John, App. II 44.
Vibeard, Dan., 174.
Vining, *see* Vyneing.
Virginia, *America*, App. III 1.
Voake (Voakes), John, 8, 53, 69, 75, App. II 34,
    58, 63.

A SURVEY of
PORTSEA ISLAND
Shewing the Towns and Fortifications
of PORTSMOUTH and GOSPORT the DOCK
BLOCKHOUSE FORT, Portsmouth and
Langston HARBOURS, with ŷ Castles
Islands, Channels, Sands, &c. in and
about the same done in the Year 1716.
by C.Lempriere

N.B. The Figures are the Soundings at Low Water
in Feet and the Ground coloured Yellow shews
the Kings Land, that mark'd A being purchas'd
in the Year 1710.

Port Cæsar

Port Cæsar Castle

Horsey Island.

Marshy

Ouze

Tipner Island

Ouze

Stampsey Point

Brick kiln

Port Cæsar Lake

Ouze

Whale Island

P

Ouze

Stubbington Farm

Brick kiln

Kingston

Ouze

PORTSMOUTH
HARBOUR

S

Ouze

Fresh water

Kingston Church

Salt Marsh

A

M A I N

Forton Lake

Burrough Fort

THE DOCK

Lake Lane

Mill

Ridges Brewery

A

L A N D

Ouze

Brewer

THE COMMON

Spring Garden

A

Spring Garden

GOSPORT

Charles Fort

New Wharf

Mill Pond

A

Stoke

Drake Lake

Ouze

The Canal

PORTS
MOUTH

Kickergill

Blockhouse Grounds

Blockhouse Fort

STOKES
BAY

Royal Hospital

Stoke Morrass

Gilkicker

Inward Spit

THE CHANNEL

Swatch

Great Morrass

Lumps

South-Sea Castle

Outward Spit.

A Scale of one Mile or 5280 Feet.

SPITHEAD